Paddle to the Amazon

PADDLE TO THE AMAZON

by Don Starkell   edited by Charles Wilkins

The Ultimate 12,000-Mile Canoe Adventure

McCLELLAND & STEWART

Cloth edition published 1987
Mass-market edition printed 1988
Trade paperback edition printed 1994

Library and Archives Canada Cataloguing in Publication

Starkell, Don, 1932–
Paddle to the Amazon: the ultimate 12,000-mile canoe adventure

"A Douglas Gibson book."
ISBN13: 978-0-7710-8256-6
ISBN10: 0-7710-8240-1 (bound)   ISBN10: 0-7710-8256-8 (pbk.)

1. Starkell, Don, 1932–   . 2. Starkell, Dana.   3. Canoes and canoeing –
America.   4. America – Description and travel.   I. Wilkins, Charles.   II. Title

E27.5.S73 1987   910.4   C87-094518-1

Interior design by Richard Miller
Maps by James Loates *Illustrating*

We acknowledge the financial support of the Government of Canada through the Book Publishing Industry Development Program and that of the Government of Ontario through the Ontario Media Development Corporation's Ontario Book Initiative. We further acknowledge the support of the Canada Council for the Arts and the Ontario Arts Council for our publishing program.

Printed and bound in the United States of America

A Douglas Gibson Book

McClelland & Stewart,
a division of Penguin Random House Canada Limited,
a Penguin Random House Company

www.penguinrandomhouse.ca

11   18

This book is dedicated to all those who helped us on our way –
and to our detractors, too. Without them our determination
would not have been the same.

Contents

Contents

Editor's Preface

I FIRST CROSSED PATHS with Don Starkell in 1983, when he was working for the Winnipeg YMCA. Our initial encounter was little more than a handshake, but a week or so later, as I walked by his office, he called me in and said, "I understand you're a writer." He told me that he had a manuscript – a diary – written between 1980 and 1982, while he was canoeing from Winnipeg to South America with his son Dana. He said, "I wonder if you'd take a look at the thing. I'd like to make a book of it; I need some advice."

A few days later he handed me a foot-high stack of pages, each page blanketed in a tiny illegible scrawl. I flipped through the pile and handed it back. "I can't read it," I apologized, "you'll have to type it out." Given the immensity of the task (and given that no typist would be able to make any better sense of it than I could), I was sure I'd never see the manuscript again.

I have since learned not to underestimate a man who can guide a canoe halfway around the world. Three months later, the typing was done – by Don himself; eight pounds of paper, 1,400 pages, densely typed. A million words in all.

Understandably, a diary written on windswept beaches, on tidal flats in a canoe, and in jungle and desert heat – often in extreme weariness and under heavy stress – is not written with primary regard for English usage. Don made no bones about this; the diary was full of rough spots and repetitions. Nevertheless, those million words were the most gripping and astonishing adventure story I had ever read. I immediately agreed to help turn them into a book.

The sifting and condensing that followed took me the better part of ten months, and saw the diaries reduced to about an eighth of their original length – a million words would have produced a book of some 2,000 pages. My intention throughout the editing was to eliminate repetition, to compress and clarify where necessary, and, above all, to keep the events and continuity of the story intact. Along the way I got valuable advice – from my wife Betty Carpick, from my father Hume Wilkins, from the publisher, Doug Gibson, and, of course, from Don and Dana Starkell.

What pleases me as I read the current version of the manuscript is that, after ten months of work on it, I still find it every bit as fresh and captivating as it was the first time I read it in full diary form. It is an incredible story – both inspired and inspiring – and I am proud to be connected with it.

CHARLES WILKINS

And now nothing will be restrained from them,
which they have imagined to do.

GENESIS 11:6

Leaving Home

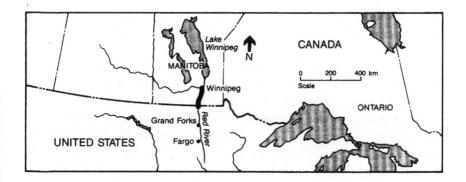

If we'd known we were going to make it, the challenge would not have been the same – we might not have gone. If we'd known what lay ahead, we *certainly* would not have gone.

On reaching Belém, Brazil, nearly two years after our departure, I would write in my diary: "We have taken some 20 million paddle strokes to get here and have travelled every variety of waterway. We have slept on beaches, in jungles, in fields – sometimes in the canoe, on the open water. We have shared simple food and lodgings with the Cuna Indians, the Guajiras, and the Miskitos; we have dined aboard million-dollar yachts. We have eaten shark, turtle, paca, tapir, wild pig, manioca, palm hearts, cactus. In Cartagena, we ate heaps of roasted ants. We have encountered hundreds of species of creatures: snakes, crocodiles, piranhas, morays, sharks, whales, bees, and scorpions. Strangely enough, the only animal that has given us any trouble was man; we have been arrested, shot at, robbed, jailed, and set upon by pirates. At one point we were led off at gunpoint to be executed. We have been taken for spies and saboteurs, have capsized 15 times at sea and spent terrifying nights in pitch blackness riding the ocean breakers without navigation. We have had brushes with the drug trade, suffered food poisoning, blood poisoning, and dehydration. Forty-five times our canoe has been broken on rocks or reefs. Our skin has been baked to scab by the sun. We have been close to starvation.

"In spite of all we've endured, our arrival here in Belém was anything but triumphal. No banners, no champagne, no tears or kisses. Nobody at all. . . . Perhaps we deserve such a fate. We have come too far."

Our departure date was set for June 1, 1980, and early in May we sent a duplicated letter to 70 or 80 friends. We gave them a final sketch of our plans and described our hopes and fears for the next couple of years. We also let them know that we intended to spend the eve of our departure camped on the bank of the Red River, a few blocks from our home. "We hope some of you will visit us there late Saturday afternoon or Saturday evening," I wrote. "Please try to drop down and say goodbye."

On the appointed day, during the early afternoon, we moved our canoe and supplies from our home in north Winnipeg to the river bank in Bronx Park. We erected our tent, and, by 4 p.m., friends had begun to arrive – at first just a trickle but, within a couple of hours, by the dozen.

Our intention had been to say our goodbyes during the evening and settle to a refreshing night's sleep around 11 p.m. We would be up and away without fanfare at dawn. But by 11 p.m. on this rather chilly night the party was just beginning to warm up. One of the last things I remember before tucking myself in at 4 a.m. was seeing a family friend doing a dance on the roof of a parked car. My feelings throughout the evening had swung between those of a child on Christmas Eve and those of a condemned man on the eve of his execution.

Dawn arrived clear and cool, and we soon saw that our discreet departure was not to be. My ex-wife Ann arrived with breakfast, and it wasn't long before 25 or 30 friends had returned to see us off. As cameras clicked, and a Canadian Broadcasting Corporation TV camera whirred, we carried our equipment and supplies to the waterfront and began packing the canoe. The largest part of our load was in four aluminum boxes that I'd built myself and of which I was particularly proud. Two of them contained food, one was full of clothes, and one held assorted gear. They were (almost) watertight and sat neatly on a set of aluminum tracks I'd had built into the base of our fibreglass canoe. When in place, they allowed seven feet of sleeping space at either end of the canoe, while the top of the boxes made a third sleeping spot. We were well aware that, faced with an emergency or a difficult shoreline, we might have to sleep on the water or on a marsh or tidal flat some night.

Although we'd loaded the canoe as a test in the back yard, we'd never loaded it under paddling conditions, and as I saw it inching lower into the water I began to fidget. But it eventually levelled out with a good eight inches of freeboard.

We exchanged our final kisses and hugs, and climbed into the canoe. To a chorus of whistles and cheers, we pushed away from the big storm-sewer pipe that had served as our wharf, and headed upstream. About ten yards from shore, I turned and waved, bound for South America. I was proud, I was hopeful, I was scared.

I was also immediately aware that we were somewhat overloaded. We had *everything* in that canoe: tent, tarps, two spare paddles, three gas stoves, fuel, water containers, my home-made mosquito-netting "bug house", saws, axe, knives, machetes, medicines, first-aid kit, canoe-repair kit, radio, batteries, cameras, film, tape recorder, binoculars, snorkelling equipment, maps, documents, survival rifle, handgun, ammunition, sleeping shells, ropes, food, clothing. We had books on electronics so that Jeff could continue the electronics studies he'd begun in high school. We had Dana's music books and, riding on top of the load, his classical guitar, well waterproofed in a vinyl case. Our overall weight was a numbing 1,030 pounds.

In the excitement of the moment, however, we forged into the current as if paddling a 50-pound racing shell.

At the Redwood Bridge, my daughter Sherri and a girlfriend of Dana's hailed us to shore for more kisses and tearful goodbyes. At subsequent bridges, we were met by our canoe-builder, Bill Brigden, who bicycled from one bridge to the next, waving and calling encouragements as we passed beneath. Bill, a former Olympic paddler, was thrilled at our venture and lifted our spirits immeasurably through that first couple of hours. Between his appearances, all I could think was: What on *earth* have we gotten ourselves into?

Our first strokes that morning were the culmination of 10 years of planning – planning that had been precipitated by the break-up of my marriage in the summer of 1970. My wife's departure had been swift and painful – and thoroughly unexpected. One evening in late June I arrived home from a meeting, and she handed me a letter saying that she was leaving, immediately. Our three children were going with her. In fact, she had already taken the trouble to spirit them out of the house. After 12 years of marriage, I was on my own.

In the weeks that followed, I sank into a deep depression. I felt isolated, hostile, guilty – guilty that I'd been unable to keep my marriage together, especially for the sake of my children. I myself had suffered badly because of a broken home, and had vowed never to put my kids through the same grinder. I remember sitting alone in my living room one hot July night and having to admit to myself that my life had lost its meaning.

Fortunately for my sanity, it wasn't more than a month before my oldest son, Dana, who was nine at the time, decided to come back and live with me. Within a year, Jeff, who was eight, followed. Sherri, our youngest, stayed with her mother.

Over the years, my survival skills had been pretty well honed, and, as the shock waves of the separation subsided, I resolved that I wasn't going to be consumed by the break-up of my home. Nor would I allow the boys to be consumed by it. What we needed, I realized, was a new focus, a long-range plan of some sort that would carry the three of us purposefully into the future. Night after night I lay awake considering the possibilities, and, as the weeks passed, my mind turned increasingly to my long-time love of canoeing.

A plan emerged – at first a kind of fantasy plan, very unclear in its specifics. Somewhere down the line, when the boys were old enough, we would take a monumental canoe trip – not just of a few hundred miles or a few weeks but of many thousand miles and many months – possibly even years. In my keenest moments, I even imagined a trip that would take us further than anyone had ever gone by canoe. As my thoughts unfolded, I promised myself that, for the next ten years, till the boys were old enough, I would pour the best of my energies, the best of my imagination, into planning such a trip. My aim was to give the boys not only a challenge and an education but a sense of discipline and self-confidence that they would never lose. I needed the same things for myself.

By autumn of that year, a new seed had planted itself in my head: would it be possible, I wondered, to paddle all the way from Canada to South America? It had never been done, and the more I studied the maps the more the idea gripped me. I had always been fascinated by the great travels of Columbus and Cortés, of Orellana and von Humboldt, and, in more recent years, of Papillon. I had read about them since boyhood, and had never been more intrigued by their achievements than I was now.

By late 1970, I had made up my mind – or, more accurately, had made up my imagination. We would travel south from Winnipeg via the Red

River and the Mississippi to New Orleans; through the bayous and coastal canals of Louisiana and Texas to the Mexican border; along the entire east coast of Mexico; past the Caribbean coasts of Belize, Guatemala, Honduras, Nicaragua, Costa Rica, and Panamá; eastward past Colombia and Venezuela to Trinidad; a thousand miles up the Orinoco River to Tama Tama; 200-odd miles along the remote Casiquiare Canal; 800 miles down the Rio Negro to the legendary jungle city of Manaus, and a thousand miles down the Amazon to the port city of Belém, where the Amazon meets the Atlantic. The route would cover 12,000 miles – nearly 20,000 kilometres – and would take us two years to complete. If we made it, it would be the longest canoe trip ever, as well as the longest sea voyage by canoe – 6,000 miles of our route would be on the open seas. Could we do it? I had no idea. Frankly, I doubted it – which made me all the more determined to give it a try.

At this point in my life, I was working for the Winnipeg YMCA, and I believed that if I saved fanatically for 10 years I would be able not only to finance the trip but to take an early retirement in 1980, our projected year of departure. By that time, Dana would be 19, Jeff 18. I would be 47.

The commitment was great, and during the years that followed hundreds of winter evenings were spent mapping and deliberating and researching. I wanted every bit of information I could get about our projected route, and filled half a dozen notebooks with jottings and diagrams. Summer vacations were spent canoeing and testing equipment. One stint in northern Canada proved that we could easily carry a month's supply of food. Other trips told us that a standard 16-foot canoe would be far too small.

On request in 1975, my long-time friend and canoeing partner, Bill Brigden, built us a fine 20-foot fibreglass canoe with a 30-inch beam. But one day in 1978, in a heavy storm on Lake Winnipeg, it proved disastrously unseaworthy.

The following summer, we ordered a 21-footer with a 34-inch beam that would be deeper than its predecessor in the bow and stern. When we tested it, we knew we had our vessel. It was bright orange in colour and just over a hundred pounds in weight. We decided to name it after the first white man to navigate the Amazon River in 1541, Francisco de Orellana. So *Orellana* it was.

During the late 1970s, I primed my sons constantly for our great adventure, doing everything I could to erase their occasional doubts. I also took every opportunity to tell friends and acquaintances about our odyssey – the more people I told, I felt, the harder it would be for me to give up the idea.

"Twelve thousand miles?" they'd say, and they'd look at me as if I were crazy. But the more doubters I encountered, the deeper my commitment grew.

To burn our bridges once and for all, a few months before we left I rented our house, promising my tenant that he could have it for two years from our departure date. If the trip was over in a matter of months, we were out of a home.

In the years since, hundreds of people have asked me, *Why did you go? What drove you to do it?* In reply, I usually talk about the break-up of my marriage, and my subsequent need for redirection. I seldom go further. I am aware, however, that beyond the difficulties of 1970 lie motives that developed not from a single event but from a lifetime of experience and conditioning. To begin to explain those motives, and to explain the eccentric fellow who would undertake such a trip, I must briefly jump back to the year 1939.

I was six years old, and was living with my father, sister, and stepmother in a tiny frame house in the north end of Winnipeg. One of my clearest recollections of that house is the kitchen wood stove, where my sister and I huddled on winter mornings as we cooked up a pot of oatmeal for ourselves before going to school. A harsher memory is that of shivering for hours at night by the outside door, sometimes in 30-below temperatures, as I waited for my father or stepmother to come home and let me in. Where they were, I never knew – I have only the dimmest memories of their comings and goings. I do remember being beaten by my father, and once being kicked down the basement stairs and ending up in hospital.

In 1939, our household dissolved. My father's negligence had been brought to the attention of the Children's Aid Society, and a few weeks later my sister and I were paraded into a downtown courtroom. There, my father watched tearfully as a judge offered us the choice of returning home or going to live in the Children's Home, an enormous yellow-brick institution on Academy Road. We chose the Children's Home.

There must have been 200 of us in that awful place, and we did everything en masse, including lining up regularly for a hateful dose of cod-liver oil, which we all took from the same tarnished spoon. We ate together and slept together. We played together in a prison-like compound whose chain-link fence was a good seven feet high. One of the few treats of our week came on Saturdays when we were marched to the Uptown Theatre for movies. In order to get our charity admission, we had to say "Children's Home" as we passed the ticket taker.

Sunday was visitors' day, and, after lunch, I'd gather with the others at the windows, hoping for a glimpse of a father or grandfather or aunt coming up the walk. But in my five years at the Home I remember only four or five visits from relatives, none from my mother or father. Once I ran away, returning hungry and defeated. My penalty was confinement to bed and a meal of hot milk, bread squares, and sugar.

In June of 1944, after I had been there for four and a half years, the head matron at the Home called me into her office and said, "I want you to get your things together, Donny. You're going to be leaving us to live with a family." It was as if a stick of dynamite had exploded in the room. I was stunned, frightened, confused.

The next day, I was driven to meet my new foster mother, a strict little grey-haired widow named Mrs. Bale. I adapted quickly to my new existence and had just begun to feel comfortable in my new home when Mrs. Bale died suddenly of a stroke, and again my world was in chaos. For the second time in a year, I was on the move.

By this point in my life, most of the poisons that would affect me over the next thirty years had been injected. I was painfully insecure, and, from years of lining up for meals and baths and cod-liver oil, I had developed a profound distaste for regimentation and restriction. I had no love that mattered, no real friends or family, no home. As far as I could see, the world thought that I was a thoroughly insignificant human being.

Looking back, I can see that, even by the age of 8 or 9, I had developed a consuming need to overcome that insignificance, to be somebody. In the absence of any strong scholastic bent or encouragement, my ambitions were invariably physical: to be the fastest runner, the best climber, the strongest swimmer. Even as an adult, I would participate regularly in long-distance races of one sort or another – always with an eye to being first and strongest to the finish. One day, for no other reason than to test my endurance, I jumped into the Red River in Winnipeg and swam 13 miles to Lockport. On another occasion I swam 16 miles across Lake Winnipeg. The bigger the challenge overcome, the bigger my sense of worth.

The Roberts family took me in next, and a wonderful thing happened: I discovered the canoe, the most reliable antidote I have ever known for the above-mentioned poisons. My new family lived on a creek in North Kildonan, and, especially in spring when the waters were flooding, I could get into Eric Roberts's canoe and paddle miles in any direction. I felt free, independent, self-sufficient. When I was paddling that canoe, I was in control.

In the spring of 1950, Winnipeg, a city of nearly half a million people, was inundated by a disastrous flood, and for a couple of weeks I spent a good deal of time paddling up and down our street, delivering bread and milk to stranded neighbours. Later that summer, I joined the Kildonan Canoe Club and began competing in canoe and kayak races. By that time I had grown into a muscular youngster at five-foot-ten and 160 pounds; I was a strong paddler and a frequent winner.

Over the next couple of decades, I would compete in hundreds of races, including 12 professional races, of which I won 10. But none of these victories compared to the thrill I got from being selected to compete for Manitoba in the Centennial trans-Canada canoe race in 1967. My problem at the time was that the race in the path of the old voyageurs was to last nearly four months, and I had a full-time job as a sales representative with Canadian Pacific Railway. I asked for a leave of absence, and it was flatly denied.

"Why?" I remember asking my supervisor.

"We just can't do that," he said, and that was that.

In the course of my adult life, I had seldom broken form. I had done what was expected of me, and been what I was expected to be. In this case it was expected that, as a responsible 34-year old, I would abandon my personal ambitions and stay with my career of 17 years – just 31 years more of toeing the line, and I could take a responsible retirement, with all the time in the world for canoeing.

A month before the race, I walked into my supervisor's office and quit my job. For the first time in my life, I had made a major decision that was not subject to someone else's expectations or control. I had done as I pleased – I would do so from that point on.

In May of that year, ten teams of six paddlers, each team representing a Canadian province or territory, set out from Rocky Mountain House in Alberta. A hundred and four days later, our Manitoba team reached the Expo 67 site at Montreal, victorious.

Now it was 1980, and we were preparing for a trip which, by comparison, made the 3,300-mile Centennial race look like a recreational jaunt.

As the days were counted down, dozens of anxieties swam constantly in the back of my brain. But I had two main worries. One was the state of Dana's health. For 12 years, Dana had been severely asthmatic and heavily addicted to medications. At times I'd seen him blue with wheezing. In fact, in the weeks before our departure, he was strongly advised by his doctor not to make the trip, since the heavy exertion could do him serious harm. I believed in my heart, however, that the greatest drag on his condition was not exertion but the drugs themselves. Often I'd seen his weekly allergy shot bring on such a heavy asthma attack that he had gone into shock and had to be injected with adrenalin to balance the initial medication. The months of steady exercise, I was convinced, would not destroy but would improve his lungs – possibly to the point where he could free himself of the drugs. In all the years he'd been afflicted, his body had never been given a proper chance to heal. Now was that chance, and I could only hope I was right in my beliefs. If the plan backfired, I'd have a lot to answer for. Although we would carry emergency medications, Dana was happy to go without them for as long as he could.

My other major concern was that, off and on throughout the spring, Jeff's commitment to the trip had been something less than total. Over the past couple of years, he had become a serious student of electronics, and now that he was graduating from high school he feared the effect of a two-year break in his studies. What's more, he didn't like the idea of abandoning his circle of friends – he has always placed a higher value on an energetic social life than Dana or I.

At no time could I allow myself to think that Jeff would pull out on us, but I didn't want to have to beg for his participation either. The truth was, we needed him badly. He is a skilled athlete – a tenacious soccer player and distance runner – and his physical strength was going to be necessary to make up for any problems that Dana might suffer. Jeff is also an electronics wizard and a talented mechanic; I've seen him fix everything from stoves to radios to V-8 engines. We needed his skills as a handyman. More than anything, of course, we needed him as a son and brother. It bothered me that his relatives on his mother's side had encouraged him to do what *he* wanted to do, without obligation to the trip. An aunt and uncle had told him that if he decided to leave the trip at any time, he was welcome to come and stay with them. I knew that if the trip was going to work we needed singleness of mind, not options. We'd even agreed to give up all but the most casual involvement with women for the duration of the venture. To do otherwise, I felt, would compromise our sense of purpose, and would also risk alienating communities in 13 countries, each with different ideas of proper romantic behaviour. This trip was going to need total dedication if we were going to succeed.

By mid-afternoon on that first day, our heavy load and our lack of conditioning had begun to tell. It didn't help that we'd only had a couple of hours' sleep. Jeff, in fact, had had almost no sleep, having spent the entire night partying with his friends. We were as crotchety as chickens.

By the time we'd gone 25 miles upstream, we could barely pull another

stroke. We'd expected to be weary our first day out, but this was ridiculous. Our goal for the day, however, was 32 miles to the park at St. Adolphe,
and I wasn't about to start compromising this early in the trip. Besides,
we were to meet friends at the park for supper. So we kept going until, at
about 5:30, we dragged ourselves ashore.

We ate wearily, and by 9:30 p.m. Jeff and Dana were zonked out in the
tent. I was literally aching to join them, but not before I'd opened my
notebook and recorded my impressions of our first day on the water. One
of my firmest intentions during the years of our planning had been to
keep detailed diaries – a log if you like – of our travels and adventures. At
some point, I fantasized, they might be the basis for a book.

Into the U.S.A.

JUNE 5: *on the Red River, south of the American border*

Five days out of Winnipeg, and my concerns have shifted rather drastically from the trip at large to the battles of the moment. Dana is not himself; he is pale, his face thin, his expression blank. His asthma has caught up with him, and for much of the day I could hear his heavy wheezing from the bow seat. Most of the time he just sat, occasionally trying a stroke or two. In the mid-morning Jeff moved into the bow, and Dana took the #2 seat. Even now, Dana is sitting listlessly on the ground, unable to practise his guitar, which has put him in a foul mood. He couldn't help us unload the canoe this afternoon, and has barely been able to eat, as he's constantly sucking for air. He's going to try to get through the night without medication, and has decided to sleep in the open air, while Jeff and I occupy the tent.

With the river narrowing and the current increasing against us as we move upstream, our reduced power is all the more costly. On the afternoon of the 3rd, at the Roseau River Indian bridge, the water was so fast and boulder-strewn it brought us to a halt in a small set of rapids. We were forced to swing the canoe around and retreat through the boulders. We fluked the retreat without damage and took another run at the current. It was futile. In the 90-degree heat, our weary arms and backs wouldn't propel us, and we were obliged to portage. We decided to camp for the night. Had we swamped, *Orellana* would have been broken on the rocks; our canoe is of sturdy fibreglass construction but it's only a sixteenth of an inch thick and no match for rocks.

We've been further slowed by 20-25 m.p.h. headwinds. Yesterday it took us a full five hours to travel the 14 miles between our starting point and the American border, which we reached at 1 o'clock. Just across the boundary, we made camp and climbed up the steep bank at Pembina, North Dakota, to phone u.s. Customs. We soon had a Customs officer at riverside, but, as we expected, he chose not to wade down through the shore mud to check our canoe and equipment. He cleared us anyway, and our well-hidden survival rifle and handgun went undisturbed. I should mention that we have the guns along strictly for emergencies – either last-chance self-defence or situations in which we might have to shoot an animal for food.

Already we've encountered a profusion of wildlife: snapping turtles, owls, hawks, white-tail deer, enormous catfish and suckers spawning in the shallows. A bit of the area's natural history revealed itself today. At various points along the river bank, ancient buffalo bones (mostly skulls and horns) protruded from the clay. Some were buried under 5 to 10 feet of soil. Paddling up this Red River, with its heavily treed banks, can't be much different from what it was 200 years ago when the buffalo grazed by the numberless thousands in these parts.

At 3:30 p.m. we crawled ashore exhausted at Highway Bridge #175 close to Hallock, Minnesota. With only two paddlers, today's advance was a mere 25 miles, for over eight hours of labour – a sad 3 m.p.h. We're sharing tonight's campsite with a fisherman and his family from Iowa. The father was ecstatic with his catch of two big catfish, 12 and 13 pounds, and tells us Iowa people go crazy over catfish. We were our usual hungry selves, snapping up canned tuna, potatoes, green beans, apple sauce, tea, and peanuts, plus our daily vitamin pill. Our canoe-load of 1,000 pounds has to be lightened, and one way of doing it is to eat up the 150 pounds of canned food we're carrying.

Our plan is to get to Minneapolis, 850 miles to the south, by July 1st. But before thinking seriously about Minneapolis, we have nearly 400 miles of upstream paddling on the Red. From the source of the Red, we'll travel the Bois de Sioux River, then a series of lakes and reservoirs will take us into the Minnesota River. At Browns Valley, Minnesota, we'll portage the height of land that forms the Continental Divide. The Divide separates two great water systems: the north-flowing waters that lead to Hudson Bay and the Canadian Arctic, and the fabled Mississippi and its tributaries, which flow south to the Gulf of Mexico.

It is now 9:30 p.m., and as Dana and Jeff sleep, I lie waiting for the 10 o'clock news on our all-weather Sony radio. Weather reports have never been more important.

JUNE 6: *on the Red River south of Hallock, Minnesota*
During the night, all I could hear was Dana's laboured breathing from the canoe nearby. He got little or no sleep. Today he sat amidships like a tourist, while Jeff and I worked like galley slaves. Jeff didn't complain, putting his full heart into the additional challenge. But I know now that we can't go on this way. We're wearing down badly, and have come only 170 miles. I'm so drained, emotionally and physically, I'm afraid I won't be able to sleep.

Our goal for the day was Drayton, North Dakota, and in mid-afternoon, after hours of paddling, we passed a couple of bearded yokels on shore who told us the Drayton dam was only a couple of miles ahead. Our hearts lifted – we could look forward to an early day. A couple of miles gradually turned into 10, and our optimism into despair, as we snaked around bend after bend into the stiff current. At 7 o'clock, after eleven hours on the water, we landed and pitched our tent outside town. Our long day's labour had gained us 30 miles.

JUNE 9: *on the Red River south of Big Woods, Minnesota*
What a difference a few days make. Dana has more or less returned to health and is again taking his share of the paddling. The river is no kinder to us, however, and our days are as exhausting as ever. We are now two days behind schedule and are dismayed by our slow progress. Even the pleasures of stopping to camp have been spoiled by the slimy clay of the river banks. To make things worse, we are sunburnt – particularly our faces. Our lips are parched, and we've all been peeling large chunks of cremated skin from our noses. We haven't bathed properly in nine days.

Nevertheless, our spirits are high. The weather was near-perfect today, and as I sit on one of our equipment boxes writing, a warm sun is peeking over the treetops from the other side of the river in North Dakota. Against the challenge of the current, we are rounding into shape. Jeff and Dana are showing new muscles daily, and we're paddling at a better clip.

Several times today great blue herons swooped away from us as we approached them on the wooded shores. Some of them emit terrible squawks as they rise, which somehow belies their grace. We've been playing the Indian game, paddling close to shore, trying to stay out of the main currents, and today Dana shovelled several spawning carp out of the shallows with his paddle. We've seen beaver, muskrat, snapping turtles, cranes, and dozens of wild ducks. Mother ducks frequently fake a broken wing to lure us away from their young. We must be in a prime hatching area, as young coots and mallards are everywhere. Yesterday, a skinny red fox swam across the river in front of us.

Our spirits are such tonight that we really believe we can do what we set out to do – come hell, high water, whatever.

JUNE 11: *on the Red River south of Grand Forks, North Dakota*
Reached Grand Forks yesterday morning, and Jeff and Dana raced to the YMCA for showers. For the rest of the day, they chased around like sailors in a new port. The town bylaws don't permit camping in the park where we're stationed, so we waited till dark to pitch our tent. Even so, at about midnight, we were wakened by a pair of local cops who wanted to see our identification. "Where's your car?" they demanded.

"Right there," I said, pointing to the canoe. When we explained our situation, they politely let us stay the night.

This morning I awoke to the music of Bach, as Dana practised his guitar outside the tent. He'd been in bed by 11 or so and was well rested. Jeff had been out nighthawking till 1 a.m. and was still sound asleep. As we were about to pull out around 9 o'clock, we were surrounded by media – television, newspaper, radio – all wanting interviews. There was no clear indication of how they knew we were here – perhaps through the police. By 10:30 we were away, trailed to the river bank by a string of reporters.

Fifteen miles out of Grand Forks we passed our first canoeists since Winnipeg – two burly Grand Forks men who were sitting on shore drinking beer. They claimed they'd come from Grand Forks in an hour and a half, which would have meant 10 m.p.h. into the stiff current. Our own speed is 3 or 4 m.p.h. I wheedled a beer from them and told them they should race professionally; 7 or 8 m.p.h. would be more than enough to beat the best pros.

We were bothered throughout the day by numerous biting insects. The heat and sun dehydrate us, and we've each been consuming a gallon or so of water a day.

JUNE 14: *on the Red River south of Shelly, Minnesota*
Just before 5 p.m. yesterday we saw a canoe coming towards us around a bend. We pulled alongside and met our first serious paddler, a young Ver-

mont man named Jim Mullen. He is paddling from St. Paul, Minnesota, to Hudson Bay via the Hay River in Canada's north, a distance of some 2,000 miles. We floored him when we told him of our destination 12,000 miles away. He was ready to call it a day, and we camped together, staying up till 10 o'clock, swapping stories and route information. It was great to have some fresh company, a fellow adventurer. Jim tells us he's been very sick with heat prostration and had to stop and rest for a couple of days at a riverside house. He also says we have two big portages ahead, about 7 miles each. These will get us, first, over the Divide, and then into the Minnesota River.

Our night was disturbed by a powerful windstorm which flattened our tent on top of us. We lay in it for an hour, then put it up at dawn for a couple more hours of valuable sleep. The morning quiet was shattered by cries of "Help! There's a bull behind my tent! Help!" Jim had unwittingly pitched his tent on a cattle trail, where he was blocking the route of ten thirsty cows that wanted to get to the river. I was soon out of the tent yelling "Toro! Toro!" which stampeded the cows in all directions. Anything for a fellow canoeist.

After breakfast we said our farewells and headed off to opposite ends of the world.

Under the bridge at Halstead we met five men who appeared to be local Indians but turned out to be Mexican migrants working the local sugar beet fields. They asked where we were going, and we astounded them by saying, "Tampico! Veracruz! Cancún!" They laughed and didn't believe us. "Hasta la vista!" they yelled as we paddled away.

Again today we had trouble finding a decent camping spot and had to be satisfied with a deserted farmsite. The place has obviously been hit by floods over the years. Broken dishes, antique bottles, rusted cans, old leather boots and shoes are strewn everywhere around the rotting house and shed. Jeff went to bed early, worn out, while Dana practised his guitar, and I explored this once proud homestead.

In bed tonight, I noticed a minor infection from a bad wood-tick bite on my side. Every night we have to clear a few ticks from our grimy bodies.

JUNE 17: *Fargo, North Dakota*

Our hard days of paddling in the heat have begun to catch up to us – mentally as well as physically. During the first hour of paddling yesterday morning I could feel our speed lagging. I boosted my stroke, but couldn't convince the boys to match me. The current was strong, the water shallow and smelly. In many places, fallen trees and debris blocked the flow.

The clutter grew worse, and we began to see the bloated bodies of cows and pigs and dogs among the filth along shore. The smell was atrocious. It was hard to believe we were in affluent North America. Everything started getting to me. I pulled even harder and again called for more steam up front. When I didn't get it I blew up and threw my paddle into the canoe. "Why should I kill myself while you guys loaf?" I shouted.

"Why should we kill ourselves?" said Jeff.

The boys shut down, and we sat in the shallows for half an hour doing nothing.

I gradually cooled out and apologized, and for the rest of the day Jeff and Dana paddled like giants – all the way to Fargo, where we pitched camp in Lindenwood Park at about 10 p.m. We had paddled nearly 15 hours and had advanced only 27 miles. We sat at a picnic table in the dark and stuffed ourselves with macaroni, canned peaches, and fruit cocktail. Later, as I lay in the tent, I could think only of the Mississippi, whose southbound current will give us a free ride all the way to New Orleans.

No paddling today, our well-earned sabbath after 17 days of exertion. We started the day with showers at the YMCA, then shopped for groceries and reorganized our load. A friendly local lawyer, Gene Johnson, has been by several times to visit, bringing us state decals for the canoe and a gift of bananas and ice cream. He's thrilled about our adventure – I'm sure he'd love to jump in the canoe with us and take off for the south.

Around noon, a local park official showed up and told us we couldn't camp overnight. He went so far as to send a truck around this afternoon to move us. Fortunately the driver was more sensitive than his boss, and we talked him into letting us stay. We promised we'd be gone first thing tomorrow morning.

Our last visit of the day came from a reporter for the local newspaper. He'd interviewed us earlier and wanted to drop off a photo and a copy of his article on us. Dana and Jeff were suitably impressed.

I continue to lose weight and am having trouble gaining muscle tone. Too much daily work, and my age won't allow me to develop as in years gone by. I sit behind the boys and watch their shoulders and backs develop almost by the hour.

JUNE 22: *on the Bois de Sioux River*

Three weeks out of Winnipeg, and this morning at 8 a.m. we came to the end of our battle with the Red River. The past few days have been anything but easy. The current has been fierce, the insects have been vicious, and Dana has been sick again. On Wednesday and Thursday he sat stiff as a wooden Indian in the middle of the canoe, wheezing and sucking for air.

Our worst battle with the river occurred just north of Wahpeton, North Dakota, where the shallow flow was obstructed with everything from dead trees to rusting automobile bodies and farm implements. Garbage cluttered the banks. I've taught my children faithfully about the pleasures of a clean natural environment, and this disgusting negligence made us boil. We can't understand how the states of North Dakota and Minnesota could allow it to happen. I suppose most stretches of the river are hidden from the casual eye, and the abuses aren't widely known.

Yesterday, Dana put in half a day, and today he's been pretty well normal. But if it weren't for Jeff's heavy effort we wouldn't be where we are. He has compensated mightily for Dana, and I'm more than pleased with his performance.

As we reached the headwaters of the Red, the Ottertail River appeared from the east, the pretty Bois de Sioux from the south. I got out on a bridge at the junction and sent Jeff and Dana up the Ottertail, so that I could film them coming back into the Red. It was a sweet moment for us, 500 miles into our trip. A few minutes later, we spotted a golden eagle on a branch high above the river. Nearby was a family of mallards, whose mother was nearly done in by a swooping brown owl as we glided past.

Ten miles up the Bois de Sioux, the river changed into a narrow steep-banked ditch with few trees alongshore. We moved easily, and by the time we camped this afternoon had covered 35 miles, one of our best days yet. We climbed the high banks and, to our surprise, could see the river stretching for miles to the south, straight as a poker. It was no real river at all but a man-made channel. Thousands of acres of wheat fields lay to the west. Our waterway is only two or three feet deep, quite clean, and moves with only a gentle current... An hour ago, Jeff and I gave in to the 90-degree heat and took a dip, while Dana practised guitar in the steamy tent.

JUNE 26: *on the Minnesota River, south of Ortonville, Minnesota*
Our route over the past few days has taken us from the Bois de Sioux into Mud Lake and Lake Traverse, and across the Continental Divide.

The day before yesterday, a Minnesota State Conservation officer advised us to visit Labs' Tourist Resort about two miles from Browns Valley at the south end of Lake Traverse. The Labses, he said, owned a big boat trailer which he thought we'd be able to borrow for our portage across the Divide.

The Labses were hospitable, and yesterday morning Fred Labs hauled his trailer a mile to the south end of the lake, where we met him after a short paddle. We packed the canoe and equipment on the trailer, hitched it up with a cross pole for pulling, and Jeff and I harnessed ourselves in like horses. We could have saved ourselves a lot of time, trouble, and sweat simply by putting the canoe on the back of Fred's pick-up truck, as he suggested. But we promised ourselves months ago that every mile of our journey would be achieved under our own power. No lifts, no tows. No temptation to cut corners.

The portage was tough, as Dana was sick again and unable to help much. Our load was poorly balanced, with too much weight up front, and for 5 miles we sweated and strained, our padded rope harness cutting into our shoulders. Dana wheezed along behind, but by the time we reached the Little Minnesota River, he was breathing easier, having apparently benefited from the walk. We launched the canoe, paddled a mile downriver, then managed 17 sweltering miles down Big Stone Lake. Dana by now was able to pull his share.

We camped in Hartford Beach Park, where Dana and Jeff, with their tans and muscles and good looks, made quite a hit. They love the attention, and really have a story to tell. After supper they went off chasing girls, while I was driven into the tent by mosquitoes chasing me.

We began strongly this morning, with 20 breezy miles on Big Stone Lake. But within minutes of finding our way through the reeds onto the Minnesota River at Ortonville, we were in the worst mess of our trip. The water was shallow, dirty, and so heavily blocked with deadfall trees and boulders that it was unnavigable. Jeff got out and walked alongshore for a mile, reporting that the route was blocked for as far as he could see. The two of us walked to a nearby farm belonging to a couple named Gayle and Colleen Hedge. Gayle told us that the obstructions extended for 6 miles. He suggested we portage around them.

The Hedges had no boat trailer, but we noticed an old farm wagon in the yard. It had car tires and a pulling bar out front for horses.

"Would you mind if we used it?" I asked.

"Be my guest," said Gayle, "but it weighs 1,300 pounds, and I don't think you're gonna get far with it."

We placed our canoe upside down on the wagon, the bow sitting 6 feet in the air, supported by the front gate. We then loaded in our equipment and hitched steering reins to the pull bar. Dana climbed onto the canoe, as if straddling a horse, and took the reins. Jeff and I got behind the wagon and began to push. Our load, which now weighed over 2,000 pounds, groaned across the yard. Our incredulous friends told us they'd follow later by car and pick us up; they were sure they'd find us defeated along the roadside.

We twisted through and around part of Ortonville, and came to a gully that led beneath an overpass. It was easy enough to get to the bottom of the 15-foot decline, but murderous to get back up. We thought for a minute and hit on the idea of pushing 10 inches or so at a time and blocking the wheels. Dana climbed down to do the blocking – *grunt, groan, 10 inches, block – grunt, groan, 10 inches, block.* Our legs ached. Sweat poured.

We made the summit and struggled on through town and out onto the highway that would lead us back to water. Cars and trucks passed us from ahead, blasting their horns in disbelief at seeing Dana coming down the highway on top of this monstrous wagon, driving a team of non-existent horses (Jeff and I were out of sight behind the wagon). The whole scene was an agonizing comedy, and we laughed and sweated and complained. Several drivers passed us cold beer.

In all we pushed six miles, finally reaching the river at a game refuge south of Ortonville. The wagon nearly got away from us on the downhill grade to the water, and only by digging our heels hard into the gravel for a hundred yards were we able to prevent it from crashing. Dana sat high on his perch, apparently in shock.

Tonight we are happy beyond belief, almost giddy with pride over our big achievement. We cannot be stopped and are now on our downhill route to Minneapolis and the Mississippi.

JUNE 27: *on the Minnesota River*

Although our route today was shown as a "canoe route" on the map, it might as easily have been designated a Marine Obstacle Training Course. The first 7 or 8 miles took us through water that bore a powerful resemblance to lumpy pea soup. The surface was covered by six inches of duckweed, and the flow was clogged by hundreds of flooded trees, some living, some dead. We passed the town of Odessa, and spent the next seven hours battling the two miles of river below town. I have *never* encountered worse paddling conditions – stagnant water, endless barricades of deadfall trees, swarms of hungry mosquitoes. At times I had to get out of the canoe into waist- or chest-deep water and hack through the branches and trunks with my axe. Tiny black leeches feasted on my legs, making open, painless wounds that bled freely – until I felt like Humphrey Bogart in *The African Queen.* Dana wasn't feeling well, and for the most part he and Jeff watched me from the canoe. Infuriating. At one point the deadfall made a six-foot wall, and we had to unpack and portage over the top, lodging our gear precariously among the tangled trunks and branches. The heat and humidity were monstrous.

As we resumed paddling, the mosquitoes had become unbearable, swarming beneath the canopy of trees that overhung the narrow waterway. Our faces and arms were smeared with blood from swatting at the things. They bit through our T-shirts, infested our hair, flew into our mouths and ears. We yelled our torment, as the canoe zigzagged across the water.

At 9:30 p.m., having come a measly 17 miles in 15 hours, we pitched camp and crawled into the tent, our energy and desire at a new low. We ate supper in the tent, and Dana and Jeff fell quickly asleep. I was too hyper to relax. I lay silently cursing the Minnesota Department of Natural Resources for showing the miles we'd paddled as a canoe route. Had their mapmakers never been here? At the same time, I felt that no conditions could possibly be worse and that, having persevered, we were probably the tougher for it.

JUNE 29: *Granite Falls, Minnesota, on the Minnesota River*
Another wild day yesterday, as we paddled Lac Qui Parle, 40 miles north of here. The lake is really nothing more than a long, mile-wide broadening of the Minnesota River, but it is subject to treacherous crosswinds. We tried to paddle down the west shore, the protected shore, but were blown across to the east shore by winds of 30-40 m.p.h. The relentless onslaught of broadside waves threatened continually to crash us against the rocky bank. Waves, some up to 5 feet high, washed over our bow, dumping gallons of water into the canoe. We bailed constantly and would happily have gone ashore, but couldn't find a safe place to land.

When eventually we got back onto the safer waters of the river, Dana and Jeff broke their frightened silence and tore a terrific strip off me for risking their lives. "We should have been on the other shore," growled Jeff, and he was right. If I'd had any choice we'd have been there. It was the first major test for the canoe and makes me wonder how we'll fare when we reach the sea, 2,000 miles ahead.

Today, just before pitching camp here at Granite Falls, we made our 18th portage of the trip, around the town dam and power plant. It is now 8:30 p.m. and Jeff and I are sitting in a laundromat washing clothes while Dana guards the canoe and practises his music. Granite Falls is the perfect model of the small American town – everything neat and well-kept (pop. 4,000). The people are friendly, the setting so serene that wild ducks feel free to walk around the front lawns of the houses. One old gent we met phoned the mayor to get approval for our camping in the park. Three middle-aged men gave us lucky pennies and wished us well.

Each night, before climbing into the tent, I fill our three army canteens from the nearest drinking-water source and prepare the canoe for the next day. I insist on an orderly camp, with everything properly stowed, and with the canoe pulled up well beyond the waterline.

JUNE 30: *on the Minnesota River*

By late this afternoon, we had knocked off a fantastic 44 miles, for our best day yet. We had also had our biggest thrill, as we shot Patterson's Rapids during the mid-morning. As we approached the rapids, we cut through some large standing waves and roared downhill into the v of the flow. *Orellana* shot through the water like an orange missile, and Jeff let out an excited whoop. As our ride ended, Jeff turned to me with a big grin and said, "Let's go again."

"We're not going again!" blurted Dana.

The reactions were so typical of the boys' personalities. Jeff has always been the more daring and aggressive of the two. He loves sport and speed and competition – he undoubtedly gets some of this from me. As a kid, he used to ride his bike as if he were a circus performer, racing up to walls, or parked cars, or other bicycles, taking great delight in narrowly avoiding accidents – or in the accidents themselves if they occurred. Sometimes it's hard to believe he's from the same stock as Dana, whose main interests have always been art and nature. As a youngster, Dana kept pets, and often spoke of going to the jungle where he could live with the animals. "How are you going to get there?" I'd ask him, and he'd say confidently, "I'm going to walk." Now here he is on his way to the jungle – we'll hope there's not too much walking involved.

This area is heavily populated with turtles – plenty of the common painted variety and today a new kind with a flat, saucer-shaped shell. A local man, John Reinhart, who visited us at our river campsite, gave us three names for the unusual turtle – soft-shelled, pan, and leatherback. I asked John what he did for a living, and he said proudly, "cow milker and pig worker."

We have been on the water a month and have covered 750 miles.

JULY 6: *Minneapolis, Minnesota*

Conditions have improved steadily, and early this afternoon, we reached the first major milestone of our trip – the twin cities of Minneapolis and

St. Paul. Our first taste of the cities came yesterday morning, when the tranquillity of the river was shattered by an unfamiliar roar. A helicopter came bearing down on us from ahead, following the curves of the shoreline. Jeff yelled, "It's wcco from Minneapolis," as the chopper circled above, its crew shouting to us and making incomprehensible gestures. They flew on and disappeared, but we could still hear the thwacking of the blades up ahead. Rounding the bend we found our friends perched on top of a steep bank to our right. They wanted to interview us but didn't want to come down to the water through the dirty clay of the shore. We told them we'd meet them downstream at the first decent sandbar.

We found them around the next bend, and began a half-hour interview in front of the television camera. They had heard about our trip from the press in Minneapolis. As we paddled off, they chased us downriver, camera rolling, the cameraman strapped to the outside of the helicopter. They dropped to within 20 feet of us, and the canoe shook as the big propeller blades lifted the water into peaks. We put on an impressive display of river paddling, keeping our stroke in perfect time. The attention did us good, and our paddling remained strong for hours. We ended our day at Shakopee, Minnesota, just 27 miles from Minneapolis.

I might mention that, of the three of us, Jeff has the toughest paddling assignment. His #2 seat is located where the canoe is widest, which forces him to reach out in a sweep or sidestroke motion to get his paddle properly into the water. It's wearing on his arms, and he tends to shift his weight toward the side he's paddling on, so that he doesn't have to reach so far. Dana and I badger him to sit in the middle, to keep the canoe balanced.

We were up and away early this morning, anxious to see the Mississippi, not knowing what to expect. A few miles out of camp we sighted a canoe travelling well ahead of us. We picked up our pace, looking for a bit of company, or perhaps even the challenge of a race. Eventually, we caught up to a young couple, Paul and Suzanne Lehmberg, from Marquette, Michigan. We stuck with them and enjoyed the company as we all headed for Minneapolis.

In the early afternoon, we passed what appeared to be a large island on our left and carried on downstream. We knew we were close to Minneapolis, as powerboats were everywhere, including three paddlewheelers carrying Sunday tourists. A speedboat skidded by, and the driver hollered, "We saw you guys on television last night!" We asked how far we were from the Mississippi and were surprised to find we'd been on it for three miles. The island we'd passed a while back had apparently been the forks. We had reached the Mississippi without knowing it!

We and our Michigan partners climbed a steep concrete bank and made camp in Harriet Island Park, which was full of people celebrating the July 4th holiday weekend. As we stretched our legs, we discovered that the celebrants were Laotian and Vietnamese Americans who had gathered from across the u.s. for an Asian-American soccer tournament. One of them told me that January 1st is the big sports holiday in their homelands, but that here in their new country they've chosen to celebrate on the July 4th weekend.

Unfortunately not everyone has been as sociable as the soccer crowd. Dana spotted a man eating Kentucky Fried Chicken and approached him to ask where he'd bought it. The man snarled and told him to keep walking and find out for himself. Dana was upset and came and told me. I walked over and laid a good tongue-lashing on the guy. In the condition I was in – hungry, bone-weary, somewhat tense – he's lucky I didn't go further. Later, when Jeff and Dana went to the YMCA for a shower, they were taken for street bums and told to go jump in a fountain, or in the river – and this after they'd presented their membership cards.

Give us a small town any time.

JULY 7: *Minneapolis*
Today is our rest day, and we were awakened early by a noise at our tent door – someone poking around outside. I opened up and found a note stuck in the door zipper: "Don, Dana, and Jeff – Good-bye. Have a safe trip. It was great to paddle with you! The Lehmbergs."

Last night I phoned my friend Ed Allman in Winnipeg and got the name of Gary Meier, a Canadian now living in Minneapolis. This morning I phoned Gary and found him more than willing to give us a hand. He picked us up at one o'clock and chauffeured us around as we got traveller's cheques, groceries, books for Jeff's electronics studies, guitar strings for Dana, and so on. We were buoyed by the assistance, though by midafternoon the heat had withered us. The air is so bad that Dana's asthma is acting up. The city's noise and crowding and pollution, combined with our inactivity, are harder on us than the strain of paddling. The heat, of course, compounds everything.

This evening I sat and talked with three local men in the park. I mentioned our trip, and one of them looked at me blankly and said, "Have you got a motor for when you get to the ocean?"

"We've got three good human motors," I smiled.

"Oh, you've *got* motors," he said.

Back at the tent, the boys and I decided that from now on we'll try to stop in smaller cities and towns.

Down the Mississippi

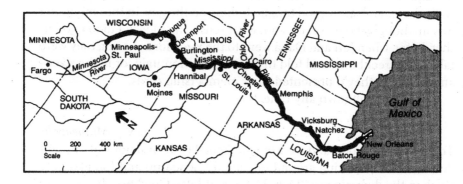

JULY 10, *Winona, Minnesota, on the Mississippi River*

Three days out on the Mississippi, and the scenery has been grand: limestone cliffs, rolling hills, fine sand beaches – plenty of willows and other hardwoods alongshore. The river moves in a slow, powerful sweep, and is travelled by hundreds of pleasure craft and industrial barges. We'd been warned that the barge traffic would swallow us up, but so far only the smaller boats have given us problems, with their wakes and carelessness. The barges are shunted along in lines of six or eight, or sometimes double rows of three or four.

While our progress has been good (115 miles in three days), it's not as rapid as we had hoped. The main reason is that the river is regularly slowed by lift locks and dams. Already we've come through six locks, which have dropped us anywhere from 7 to 12 feet each. The locks are maintained by the U.S. Army Corps of Engineers – everything very efficient. The stretches of water between locks are called pools. We enter a lock either by ourselves or with other boats, the big gates close behind us, the water pours out, and we're dropped to the level of the pool ahead. At Lock #5, at

Minneiska, Minnesota, we were pleasantly surprised to find an enormous white paddlewheeler, the *Mississippi Queen,* locking through. We filmed it reverently as it emerged from the lock toward us.

For the most part we follow the channel buoys, although yesterday morning we ignored them, using a distant bridge as our navigational guide and goal. Dana and Jeff picked the route, aided by a totally insufficient road map. We were soon lost in a maze of islands and backwaters, and wasted an hour finding our way back to the main channel. This morning heavy fog thwarted us. With visibility at no more than 20 or 30 feet, and with the buoys invisible, I suggested we follow the foggy shoreline south. We did so, and for the next three hours were thoroughly lost in a forested swamp. At about 10 o'clock the fog lifted, and we rediscovered the channel, but not before I'd suffered the wrath of my sons for wasting their time and energy.

The heat wave continues, with today's temperatures again around 100 degrees. Boaters frequently flag us down and give us beer or pop, or whatever they have to drink. Jeff and Dana don't care for beer but take it anyway. Dana puts the icy cans under his T-shirt, or against his forehead or neck. When the cans have lost their cooling power he passes them to me.

We are camped tonight in peaceful Levee Park in Winona, Minnesota. Shortly after supper, we were visited by Mike Cichanowski, a local canoe-racing pro, who also builds canoes. He paddled up in a narrow fibreglass single racing canoe, weighing only 20 pounds. I tried it out and was astounded at its speed – it almost leapt out of the water with each of my hard strokes. Mike gave us decals and three T-shirts bearing his We-No-Nah company logo. A local policeman named Carl brought us decals reading "Winona the All-American City."

JULY 12: *Lynxville, Wisconsin, on the Mississippi River*
We are warped and brutalized and drained by the ferocious heat. Even the water has become so warm it is barely refreshing. I walk into it up to my neck, and can still feel the sweat pouring off my face. At supper last night, I heated our canned goods by sticking them in the sand, which gave Jeff and Dana a good laugh. The sand radiated heat all night, so that we lay in our own sweat, getting little sleep in the tent.

We were up at 6:30 this morning, but our poor sleep had done its mischief. Jeff and Dana were in no mood to work, so that most of the preparations for the day were left to me. I began harassing them, until they got so angry they jumped into the canoe and paddled off without me, tucking themselves out of view behind a houseboat a hundred yards down-shore. By this time I was boiling, but had to let on I didn't care; their mutiny wasn't going to get the better of me. An hour passed, and they returned to pick me up.

Afterwards, Jeff and I put our hearts into paddling, but for 13 miles Dana refused to take a stroke – all the way to Lock #8 at Genoa, Wisconsin. Here we were locked through by ourselves, feeling microscopic in the enormous 600-by-110-foot locking enclosure. As we came out, Dana resumed paddling, and with the help of a strong tailwind we finished the day with a remarkable 41 miles under our belts.

Tonight we're camped near Lynxville, Wisconsin, on the east shore of the river. Nearby is a small patch of cleared ground occupied by a 22-year-old squatter named Donny. He has a small wooden wharf and an outdoor fireplace. Three feet out from shore he has rammed a timber into the river bottom and crowned it with a red mailbox bearing the words "Donny – My Home – Pink Teddy Bear Lounge". He apparently sleeps under the stars, and gets around in an old duck boat, half filled with empty beer cans.

Shortly after we arrived, Donny told us he was going to get his supper, frog legs, and he walked off down the shore, looking for frogs. Later, during the evening, he had five callers, two of whom brought beer and stayed to drink it. All night I could hear the soft clinking of beer cans being tossed into the duck boat – this and the regular passing of freight trains as they rumbled through on a railway line a hundred feet behind our tent. The ground shook, the beer cans rattled, and I stewed. Dana and Jeff slept soundly.

JULY 14: *Dubuque, Iowa, on the Mississippi River*
We are now six weeks into our trip and have come 1,200 miles. It's easy to calculate distance on the Mississippi, because the milage is regularly marked by signs on shore. Right now we are at Mile 582, which represents the distance to Cairo, Illinois (Mile 0), where the Ohio River meets the Mississippi. Minneapolis was Mile 844.

Around noon today we pulled onto a sand bar that was occupied by a motorboat crowd from Iowa. They told us the next lock, at Dubuque, 29 miles away, would be closed tomorrow. Unless we got there tonight we'd be held up an entire day, or would have to make an exhausting portage. I quickly told my crew that Kentucky Fried Chicken was waiting for them in Dubuque on the other side of the locks. They opened up their diesels, and we locked through at 6:45 p.m.

The many locks have been a blessing, as each one obliges us to take a break – anywhere from 5 to 15 minutes. We can relax our muscles, and Jeff usually has time to scamper up the metal ladders in the lock walls and buy soft drinks from the lockmaster. As the water drops beneath us, we hold onto the mooring ropes dangled over the high concrete walls to us, and do our best to avoid scraping the gunwales of the canoe on the concrete. The big gates open ahead of us, a horn sounds, and we charge out, generally ahead of our fellow travellers.

Each locking takes us into a new world. We normally leave a large lake-like pool and emerge into a narrow, shallower channel. If a wind is blowing, we find that the drop in altitude cuts off the blow, leaving the new waters calm and inviting. By the time we reach the next lock we're again travelling wide, breezy waters.

As we left the locks this evening, we encountered two local men who advised us to camp at Riverview Park, ahead on our right. They met us there and chauffeured us in a rusty blue Gremlin to the Kentucky Fried Chicken outlet, then to a store for some grocery shopping. They're real Dan Tucker types; they start their car by sticking a screwdriver into the steering column – they don't have keys. They tie the doors shut with heavy rubber straps.

The mosquitoes are out tonight in force; yet, because of the heat, we're playing nudist. We lie on our blue foam pads, and the sweat runs off us into uncomfortable pools. A while ago we were visited by three local drunks. One looked in through our tent door and yelled, "Hey, man! What are you dudes doing?" In the pale light, I could see that one of them had lost or discarded his clothes. They had beer and wanted to trade it for whisky. "*Please*, man," they begged, "just a little bit." We humoured them, and after 15 minutes they staggered off into the darkness, leaving us to our solitude – and a chorus of bloodthirsty mosquitoes.

On a sand bar today we saw 20 big turkey vultures, with their red heads, big beaks, and tiny black eyes. They were about the only thing today that gave me anything approaching a chill.

JULY 20: *Burlington, Iowa, Mile 400 on the Mississippi River*
Today is Sunday, invariably a good day for us. The river is gorged with boaters, and the shoreline with picnickers, many of them more than willing to share their soft drinks, beer, and food. During the week we get less hospitality. This morning before we broke camp, two friendly local couples brought us fresh tomatoes and corn. A few hours later, a Canadian from Cardston, Alberta, came up to us in a powerboat and gave us Pepsis and chocolate cookies. He said he'd seen our Canadian flag from miles away. The sweet foods, while not substantial, provide a welcome infusion of energy.

We have paddled into the Mississippi Flyway, the famous migratory bird route, and find the river marshes scattered with duck blinds, new and old, some very large. The blinds seem to be used year after year, and many are marked with signs reserving them for the upcoming hunting season.

Sad incident Thursday: we were beating against a strong headwind as we came into Davenport, Iowa, and so were sticking within a few feet of a high rock and concrete wall that forms the river bank through part of the city. Numerous fishing lines were hanging over the wall, hitting the water 30 or 40 feet out from the bank. We passed beneath the lines, unable to see the fishermen 20 feet above. Suddenly I noticed a man leaning over the wall signalling frantically to us, his big black face alive with frustration. His gestures were half mad, but he wasn't saying anything, and we had no idea what he wanted.

Another black man appeared and shouted that his friend was deaf and dumb and was upset because his fishing line and rod had been caught by our flagpole and dragged out of his hands into the windy river. The flagpole rises ten feet behind us, and we often forget about it. We called out our lame apologies, but they did nothing to still the fury of the fishing-rod owner. Meanwhile we were being thrown around by the high wind, and had absolutely no way of getting up the wall to set things right. We were upset and embarrassed, but really couldn't do anything except keep paddling and swallow our guilt. As we moved away, my frustration was compounded by the scolding I took from Dana and Jeff for being so insensitive – yet they didn't have any constructive suggestions as to what we might have done to make amends.

JULY 23: *Hannibal, Missouri, Mile 309 on the Mississippi River*
Just past noon today, we made camp on the Illinois side of the river, across from Hannibal, Missouri, the home of Mark Twain. While Dana watched the canoe, Jeff and I crossed the bridge into town, nervous about our safety as the bridge traffic screamed by us, showing little regard for pedestrians.

Hannibal is the ultimate tourist town, complete with a Mark Twain paddlewheeler, statues of the characters from *Tom Sawyer* and *Huckleberry Finn*, rides, caves, food carts, and dozens of souvenir stores. We stopped a number of people to get information, and they all told us the same thing – "We're just visiting."

We bought a canoe decal at the Becky Thatcher bookstore, then returned to the quieter side of the river and enjoyed a swim. It has really been one of our better afternoons, with everyone in good spirits. Jeff and Dana are busy entertaining the local girls, attractive young Southerners with heavy drawls. We seem suddenly to have crossed an invisible line between the North and the South, and have heard a thousand "you-alls" today.

The river is slowly changing character. In the past couple of days we've hit a number of stretches where the banks and trees are overgrown with an unbroken canopy of lush vines and foliage. From a distance, the entire landscape looks like a range of velvety green hills.

JULY 26, *at Alton, Illinois, Mile* 203 *on the Mississippi River* During our long days on the Mississippi we've settled into a number of routines and rituals. We rise well before sunrise, and, while Jeff strikes the tent and packs the equipment boxes, I boil up water on our little army stove, and Dana and I prepare a simple breakfast. When we're ready to go, Dana is invariably first into the canoe, followed by Jeff, leaving me to shove off and get into my stern seat on the move. Dana sets the stroke – anywhere up to 40 long, deep working strokes a minute. He and Jeff paddle in unison, switching sides as they please. I switch sides frequently, as a means of steering the canoe. To steer in a more conventional way, by dragging my paddle or J-stroking (hooking the paddle outward at the end of each stroke) would only slow us down.

Late in the morning, the boys, especially Jeff, start clamouring for lunch. I give the okay, and Dana and I keep paddling while Jeff turns at his centre position and pries open our two food boxes. He rapidly prepares whatever we're having, and we eat it as we drift – or as I do a little easy paddling. What's the menu? Today, each of us downed two peanut-butter and jam sandwiches, a banana, a few Fig Newtons, and a Snickers bar. And cup after cup of water. The cooling effect of the river on the bottom of the canoe, and the protection afforded by our white vinyl tarp, have kept our food surprisingly cool. Even our margarine usually stays solid, if a bit soft. Yesterday I took a few minutes to supplement our food supply by raiding a riverside corn field. I felt like a kid, running through the rows grabbing cobs – 24 of them. But when I got them to the canoe we discovered they were pale cattle corn, undoubtedly nourishing but underripe and none too tasty, which serves me right.

On landing, we unload together, and I generally make supper, while Jeff puts up the tent, and Dana goes off to practise his guitar. Having eaten, Jeff turns to his electronics books, or to the radio, or both. Dana does the dishes and packs up.

Every evening when the sun is almost down I boil up a big pot of tea. I pour Dana and Jeff a mugful each, then pour myself a 34-ounce peach tin of the stuff. I add three large spoons of sugar and two spoons of powdered milk. I then wrap a thick cloth around the hot tin and carry it into the Mississippi till I'm up to my neck in water. The sand bottom is gentle, and as I stand immersed, I slowly drink the precious fluid.

Tonight, we're camped on a grubby stretch of shore at Alton, Illinois. As I was about to go for a swim a couple of hours ago, two young black men, Ed Hightower and Cascadora Havis, walked up the beach, and we struck up a conversation. They told me they'd like to go swimming but were frightened of the fast water that was being funnelled through Alton Lock and Dam. "Can you swim?" one of them asked me.

"I can swim the Mississippi," I told him, which made them laugh. They started needling me, telling me I couldn't even make it out and around a couple of mooring platforms a few hundred yards up river. I dived in and swam the distance – though I had difficulty doing the upstream part.

Unusual occurrence last night when we were camped on a sand bar a few miles south of the Cap au Gris Locks. We were awakened around midnight by a persistent howling. I left the tent with my flashlight and, across the water on another sand bar, could see a pair of golden eyes. A good-sized brown and white female dog swam across to me using my flashlight beam as a guide. It scratched out a sleeping pad in the brush and debris near our tent door and settled for the night. This morning we had to abandon our sad-faced friend, feeling guilty about leaving her stranded on a sand bar. Later we talked to some local hunters who told us the dog was a coon dog, and that these dogs will often chase a raccoon off into the bush and not return to their owners. They get stranded when the owners go off without them to teach them a lesson. Apparently most of them find their way home.

We're told that Abraham Lincoln conducted some important business here in Alton, but no one is quite sure what it was. Maybe he slept here, as we're going to do.

JULY 28: *Chester, Illinois, Mile 109 on the Mississippi River*
We have seen the last of the lift locks, and are now riding the stronger natural current of the Mississippi. Yesterday morning, we passed the mouth of the Missouri River and, just south of it, entered a narrow canal which we travelled for 10 miles to Lock #27 at Granite City. We emerged at a river level that will carry us to New Orleans.

During the early afternoon we passed through St. Louis and got a good view of its famous 650-foot Gateway arch. The waterfront activity was stupendous – parks, stores, and restaurants of all kinds, including a river-boat McDonald's. In one spot a German beerfest was going full tilt. We were tempted to stop, but the urge to keep moving was stronger, and we paddled on through a heavy traffic of paddlewheelers, sailboats, and run-abouts. It occurs to me that the force drawing us south must be every bit as strong as the force that drives migrating birds.

The real adventure of the day was passing a massive float made up of 50 barges, 5 abreast, 10 deep, being pushed upstream towards us by a pow-erful single tug. We shot by the barges at a terrific speed, within 6 feet of them, our hearts pounding at the risk of being so close.

Outside St. Louis a few latterday hippies called out to us from shore – "Come and get high!"

Often as we travel these days, I find myself thinking about Huckle-berry Finn and Jim, as they rafted south along this stretch of the Missis-sippi. One difference between Huck's and Jim's journey and our own is that we have the luxury of travelling by daylight, while they had to travel at night to avoid their pursuers.

Late this afternoon, we made camp on a big sand bar on the Illinois side of the river. Our chief complaint about these light-brown sand bars is – what else? – the sand. Mississippi sand is fine and clean, even down-stream from the pollution from St. Louis, but it has an almost magnetic quality that glues it to everything it touches. You can barely wipe it off your equipment or skin – it's in our hair, ears, clothes, even our equip-ment boxes. You'd think we'd been travelling in a desert.

With the increased current, our advance today was a record 49 miles. We called it quits at Chester, Illinois, and climbed the steep river bank to walk into town for food. We met a hospitable newspaperman named Joe Akers, whose wife, it turned out, is from Winnipeg. Joe picked us up in his car and drove us around town, pointing out the sights, including a small statue. "Do you know who that is?" he said, pointing. "Popeye!" smiled Jeff and Dana. Chester is the birthplace of Popeye – or, more accu-rately, of his creator, E.C. Segar.

We never did meet Joe's wife, but he insisted on taking us out for an excellent restaurant dinner. Like so many people we've met, Joe clearly got caught up in the romance of what we're doing and wanted to be a part of it, to give something to it and take what he could, however mar-ginal or brief.

Back at our campsite, we were joined by a u.s. Coast Guard tugboat and barge, which moored a few hundred feet downriver. Early in the evening, the Coast Guard crew headed up the river bank into town. We went to bed, but were wakened around midnight by the sound of breaking glass crashing down the bank around us. The 15 or so Coast Guard sailors had returned drunk and were hurling beer bottles down onto the rocks. "What are you idiots doing?" I yelled into the darkness. They cursed me from above, and another rain of bottles fell around us. When they ran out of ammunition they crawled and stumbled down the bank onto a gangplank that led back onto their barge. I could see the outline of one pathetic slob who crawled down the heights on all fours, like an over-grown river crab. He was dragged aboard by his staggering mates. In spite of my anger, I was relieved that these guys made no move to come after us – probably because they were too drunk to locate us in the dark; I'm sure they'd have thrashed us. Dana and Jeff were pretty quiet throughout the incident.

JULY 31: *Hickman, Kentucky, Mile 921 on the Mississippi River*
The Mississippi has been good to us, and we feel none of the resentment toward it that we felt toward the Red. We do have our little hardships: warm drinking water, Mississippi sand in everything, and of course the heat. Again today, the temperature was over 100 degrees. We kept filling our hats with water and slopping them back onto our heads. The water itself is so warm that it's barely refreshing, but as it evaporates it draws a little heat from our bodies.

The constant effort has knocked 15 to 20 pounds off my starting weight, and I now feel I'm about 175, which is prime for me. We are wiry and strong and can paddle hour after hour without much strain. Our only bug problems of late have come from horseflies, which follow us as we paddle and like to take chunks out of our hides when they get the chance.

This afternoon, we discovered a novel southern method of fishing, called "jugging" or "blocking". A crew of fishermen throws out anywhere up to a hundred plastic bottles or blocks of wood, each with its own line and baited hook. These drift downstream, spreading out as they go. The boat drifts among them, and when the fishermen see action at a float they retrieve it, with the caught fish. They gather everything up when the floats get too far apart to watch easily. It's a lazy but efficient method of fishing – perfect for the heat.

We continue to pass dozens of tugboats, or pushboats as they might better be called, since they push the barges instead of pulling them. We enjoy the names: *Co-operative Spirit, National Energy, Mary Weathers, Mr. Joey.* The boats have tremendous power and throw up good-sized waves, some up to six feet high. Yesterday, we were caught off guard when a couple of tugs came booting upriver, pushing a big tow of barges. Their enormous wake forced us towards a steep shoreline of rough concrete blocks. With nowhere to land, we were bounced around pretty severely and felt fortunate to escape with no more than a few gallons of wash in the canoe.

At the moment we're camped on a sand bar a mile south of Hickman, Kentucky. When we stopped in Hickman during the mid-afternoon for groceries, the streets were deadly hot, and everyone was moving in ultra-slow motion. The town is among the oldest on the Mississippi, and looks the part, with its narrow streets and variety of aging buildings. We got a kick out of the county jail, a small house-like frame building, with bars on the windows. Two inmates, one black, one white, were in the back yard lazily raking leaves and litter.

Even in the heat, our progress has been tremendous, and has us bubbling with success. Early this morning, we passed Mile Zero at Cairo, Illinois, where the Ohio River flows into the Mississippi. We're now on our new milage countdown – Mile 954 to Mile 98 in New Orleans.

We've been on the water two full months and have logged over 1,800 miles. This evening it occurred to me that we've come this far without using even a single Band-Aid or aspirin. Lots of sleep, good food and good water are doing the trick for us.

AUGUST 3: *on a sand bar in Arkansas, Mile 814 on the Mississippi River* Our friendly river turned ugly on us today, tossed into a frenzy by howling headwinds that gusted in the 40-to-50-m.p.h. range. Without the help of the strong current, progress would have been impossible. After a certain amount of frustration, we moved out into the main channel where the current is at its fastest. The wind was so strong it was picking up sand from the sand bars and driving it against our skin like needles, so that, despite the heat, we had to keep well covered with clothing. For miles downstream we could see Sahara-like sand clouds swirling above the river and banks, and twice we were driven off the water for an hour or so. At every bend we were hit hard by the high wind and waves.

Understandably, a day like this leaves us acutely conscious of our vulnerability – not just to weather but to other river hazards, such as wing dams and the whirlpools they create. There are hundreds of wing dams on the Mississippi, long dikes of crushed rock which project far out into the water, narrowing the flow, increasing the strength of the current. The increased current sweeps up debris and sediment that would otherwise settle in the channel. Thus the shipping lane is kept clear and deep. The problem is that most of the wing dams are just beneath the surface of the

murky water, where they are hazardous to small craft. Yesterday at
Caruthersville we heard of a recent drowning when a rowboat came around
a wing dam and got caught in its whirlpool.

We paddled today until 7 p.m., and are camped tonight on a sand bar in
Arkansas – I never *dreamed* we'd see so much sand. Across the river we
can see Mile Marker 814.5 in Tennessee. The milage markers are on
trees, on poles, on anything solid enough to hold them: red markers on
the east shore, green ones on the west.

AUGUST 5: *Memphis, Tennessee, Mile 735 on the Mississippi River*
Even if I never looked at our maps, I'd have no trouble calculating when
we're approaching a city. The evening before we arrive, Dana and Jeff
invariably have good baths and shampoo their hair, as they did last night,
getting ready to impress the girls. Jeff pays more attention to the radio –
Dana has less interest; he has his guitar.

Early this afternoon we paddled into Memphis. The harbour was full
of big white paddlewheelers, among them the impressive *Memphis Queen*.
We landed at the Memphis Yacht Club, and got the manager's permission to pitch our tent. We relaxed, ate our supper, then climbed the banks
behind the yacht club to visit Memphis, which is set high above the river.
We flagged a passing car to get information, and the considerate driver
took us several miles into the city to buy groceries. It was already 6 p.m.,
and the streets were ghostly quiet. Having looked around a bit, and not
having seen a great deal, we returned to our campsite where we could
keep an eye on our belongings.

I regret that we're not able to see a little more of the cities and towns
we pass. The main reason, of course, is that we're concerned above all
about guarding *Orellana* and our belongings. We can never really relax
and wander off in a strange city and forget about them. At any rate, we're
usually pretty tired when we pull in after a day's paddling. For the most
part, unfortunately, the high river banks cut us off from even the sight of
the towns and cities as we paddle by. Where the banks are not naturally
high they've been raised as a protection against flooding.

As we ate supper, Dana heard on the radio that the rock group Queen
is in Memphis. He has decided to attend the concert they're to give tonight.
He has no money, but is determined to see them, and says he'll get in
somehow. Off he went a while ago. Jeff is a bit under the weather, and
has chosen to stay in camp.

For my part, I sit contemplating the Mississippi. It is a romantic and
seductive river, far more beautiful and powerful than I'd imagined: I love

the wide sweep of the water; the beaches and sand bars and dunes; the landscapes and foliage. Much of the greenery is new to us, and is now in summer flower. The sun has made the whole experience almost tropical – it has been moving south since June 21 and, like us, is on its way to the equator.

It is now after midnight, and Dana has returned, thrilled by the concert. He succeeded in finding the promoter, explained his situation, his love of the guitar, and, presto, he was given a stage pass. He also managed a half-hour conversation with the group's lead guitarist, Brian May.

AUGUST 8: *south of Helena, Arkansas, Mile 601 on the Mississippi River* Tugboats everywhere: *Port of Brownsville, America, Leviticus, Captain Briscoe, Navigator, Three River Lady.* Each has its own character – some are brightly painted and well cared for, some less so. Some are like pretty street girls and really know how to show off. They toot their horns, and the crews wave, making us feel like an integral part of the river scene. How they've brightened our days! Yesterday one of them slowed down, and the captain called through a loudspeaker, "The last time we saw you, you were 450 miles upstream!"

Here we are on another torrid sand bar, half desperate for a breath of cool air. Today's temperature was a new high – 105 degrees! For the past couple of days, as soon as we land, we've been making a lean-to of our orange tarp to give us a bit of shelter from the sun. Today, I didn't have to prompt Jeff and Dana to get busy and set the thing up.

Jeff hasn't had a good day. The sun is baking the top of his head, giving him headaches, perhaps even a touch of heatstroke. A while ago, he took a white sailor's hat out of our clothes box, cut out the crown, and sewed it into his peaked visor, which has no crown of its own and has been giving him very little protection. He then tore apart one of my white shirts for a piece of material to sew onto the back of his hat, making a desert képi of it. He's now parading around in it, with a twinkle in his eye, having outsmarted nature. A few minutes ago he told me, "It makes all the difference in the world!"

Shortly after getting here I went wandering and found a strange dead fish about three feet long with an alligator-like head and mouth. In the shallow water I caught a much smaller silver-coloured fish which swam into a large peach can I had put into the water. I enjoyed this fellow traveller's company and soon returned him to his home.

Because of the heat, we haven't been closing the tent door, and tonight as we're ready to sleep we're being savaged by the hundreds of mosquitoes that have flown into the tent. The alternative to being bitten is to crawl into our sleeping shells, which are unbearably hot on a night of 90 degrees. We've been saving our mosquito netting "bug house" for the swamps and jungles, but will have to pull it out tomorrow, for more room and ventilation. South America can't be any worse than this.

Our route from here to Baton Rouge, Louisiana, is not fully along the original river. Many of the loops and bends of the early Mississippi have been eliminated by stupendous feats of engineering. One short cut is said to save 16.9 miles. The river has been diked and dammed and dredged – in spite of which it maintains its beauty. Still, I'd love to have seen it through the eyes of De Soto or La Salle.

AUGUST 14: *Natchez, Mississippi, Mile 364 on the Mississippi River* Passed Lake Providence, Louisiana, on the 11th, and now have Louisiana on our right and the State of Mississippi on our left. This is our 75th day out, and the terrible heat keeps us wondering how long it will be till we get some moderate temperatures. Each of us is now drinking a gallon and a half of water a day, and still we feel parched. We had a bit of a treat yesterday when the crew of an Army Corps of Engineers barge gave us 25 pounds of crushed ice in a plastic bag. We spent the afternoon eating it, and I took numerous handfuls and put them under my hat so that the runoff would come down over my face and neck.

This morning we saw our first signs of the Louisiana oil industry. We passed two drilling derricks on the west shore of the river, and further down a couple of pumping wells. By 11:30 we were camped on the waterfront of one of America's oldest cities, Natchez, Mississippi. Dana watched the canoe while Jeff and I headed up into the city for groceries. The streets were baking hot, and as we headed back down Silver Street towards our campsite a big front-end loader and tractor came rumbling up behind us as if to knock us into oblivion. The dinosauric contraption was being driven by a smiling black man who stopped the thing just behind us and called, "Wanna ride, m'friends?"

"Where are we gonna sit?" said Jeff.

"Sit ri' there in the bucket!"

We climbed aboard with our heavy load of groceries and were lovingly delivered to the waterfront.

Later we returned to the city, where many of the historic buildings are being restored. The staggering heat was doing its best to keep people off the streets. We went into a few buildings but found the air conditioning uncomfortable – possibly even harmful to our respiration, now finely conditioned to the heat and humidity. We bought three pints of ice cream and could hardly eat the stuff before it melted.

The river banks along here are covered with a thick blanket of vines that ranges over ground, trees, refuse, whatever stands in its path. Some locals told us the prolific vine was brought here from Asia many years ago to help prevent erosion. It may be doing its job too well, as it seems on the verge of swallowing up the entire landscape.

Shortly after sunset Jeff and Dana headed up into Natchez, leaving me alone with my thoughts. I'm always glad to be on my own for a while, and have no doubt the boys feel the same way. Yesterday I took off through the woods, and ended up playing hide-and-seek with a couple of deer that kept walking away from me, just within sight. In my quiet moments, I invariably start thinking about the trip, often gloating on our success thus far. At other times my thoughts grow dark, and I begin to wonder if we've been too ambitious, and whether or not we can maintain our health. Occasionally I spook myself and have to get back to the concerns of the moment.

Today we're back on our original schedule. We'd fallen behind with our delays on the Red and Minnesota Rivers. However, the advantages of the Mississippi and our relentless paddling (most days now we do between 40 and 50 miles) have put us where we'd hoped to be by mid-August. We now feel we can be in New Orleans by the 20th or 21st, which tickles us.

AUGUST 15: *Mile 318 on the Mississippi River*
I had two listless paddlers this morning. They went to some Natchez club last night and didn't get back until 2 a.m., which hasn't helped our progress. We were also pushing into headwinds for most of the day and are now getting less help from the current, which is slowing down as we move toward the wide mouth of the river.

Early this afternoon a storm came up in the north, and a bank of thunderheads rolled in behind us. We paddled till they were nearly on top of us, then made a beeline for the protection of a sandy point, where we secured our canoe and tarp. As we finished, a Coast Guard vessel came racing down the river with its loudspeaker blaring, "Can you people on the beach hear us?" We signalled that we could. "There's a big storm on the way behind us. Big winds. You'd better get tied down!"

The storm wasn't as severe as we'd expected, but it did drop the temperature dramatically, so that for the first time in months we felt uncomfortably cool – we were actually shivering. I was the storm's only casualty when I dropped our #4 equipment box on my toe. Blood oozed from beneath my toenail and quickly congealed with the help of Mississippi sand. The #4 box is our heaviest, and we've taken to calling it "the Howie box" because I, "Howie", am the only one who will carry it. Howie is Jeff and Dana's nickname for me – I have no idea why; it's a secret little joke they have on me. "Howie the Buffalo", they sometimes call me.

As I lie here tonight on the beach, I calculate that we've come 2,440 miles, and are about a fifth of the way into our trip. The miles from Winnipeg to New Orleans were to be our shakedown cruise, and they have taught us much.

We survive. We learn. We paddle.

AUGUST 16: *Mile 270 on the Mississippi River*
When I got up this morning before six, I placed the canoe parallel to the river's edge, partly in, partly out of the water, where it could conveniently be loaded. I began making hot chocolate as Jeff took down the bug house and Dana went off down the beach trying to walk off an asthma attack. Suddenly Dana came staggering toward us gasping, "The canoe! The canoe!" I scanned the water and began sprinting along the shoreline, shedding my clothes. The canoe was about 50 yards offshore and 100 yards down-current, drifting rapidly. I dived into the water in a panic swim, aware of what would happen if the canoe reached the main current – it was already riding a breeze, sitting high and light on the water. It took an exhausting swim to catch it, and I had some embarrassing explaining to do when I got back. The old canoeman had gotten careless, and his sons weren't about to let him off the hook. The best excuse I could raise was, "I can't do everything." Even to me it didn't sound very convincing.

We paddled well in the heat, but by 3 p.m. were running low on water. So when we spotted a house trailer we pulled up to the bank, which was covered with heavy concrete chunks. A large tug happened to be passing, and within seconds I realized its wake was going to hit us broadside, sending us hard onto the rough concrete. I jumped into the water between the bank and the canoe to cushion the impact. The first wave picked up the canoe and drove it against my legs, while Dana's guitar was tossed overboard and began to float downstream. Three more waves hit, and each time my poor legs took a pounding. I yelled at Dana to go after his guitar. He dived into the water, returning with it to give me a good strafing for what had happened to his beloved instrument. Anything that goes wrong is automatically my fault – I'm the captain, am I not? Unfortunately the crash enlarged a crack in the canoe, which will soon need attention. My legs are bruised and sore, and, as it turned out, we didn't get our water – no one was home at the trailer.

In all, not a banner day. Dana was unable to give us much help because of his asthma, and at this point we're in no mood for anything but sleep.

AUGUST 17: *south of Baton Rouge, Mile 224 on the Mississippi River*
Dana was paddling again today, and a good thing too, as for most of the day we were pushed by ferocious tailwinds that sometimes threatened to put us out of control. Our flagpole, made of a heavy green branch, was deeply bent by the wind, and our flag stood straight out to the fore, snapping like a whip. For a while during the late morning we couldn't even turn the canoe to shore, for fear the huge following waves would catch us broadside. Dana and Jeff kept calling to me for direction, and all I could do was yell at them to paddle and keep the canoe straight.

At mile 235 the wind eased, and we rounded a bend into Baton Rouge, the capital of Louisiana. At the docks we saw our first ocean-going vessel, the *Río Narapa* of Buenos Aires. We were called to shore by a Cajun named Duffy St. Pierre who had seen our flag and wanted to tell us that his family had come from Canada many years ago. He told us to stop off at his red tug which was downstream and to help ourselves to a meal. Before getting there, however, we were called aboard the *Captain Ed*, a tug from Pensacola, Florida, and treated to a big chicken dinner.

During the early evening, on the outskirts of Baton Rouge, we began looking for a place to buy the groceries we'd need to get to New Orleans, 130 miles away. At one point we tried to climb the banks for a better look, but couldn't penetrate the heavy shore growth. By this time the sun was sinking, and we couldn't find a suitable campsite on this industrial part of the river. We approached two tugs and tried to buy food – no luck. We were worried now that we wouldn't find a place to camp. Then we saw an Army Corps dredging barge, the *Jadwin*, and paddled up to it. Captain Bill Sutherland, a veteran of 29 years in the Corps, understood our plight and welcomed us aboard. We pulled the canoe onto the barge and settled to another enormous meal. How happy we are to be here, though sleeping conditions are far from ideal – the dredging seems to go on all night, shaking the barge and creating a constant racket. I lie here thinking about how much we've benefited from the Army Corps of Engineers and their river work – all the way from Minnesota to Louisiana. Here's to them!

AUGUST 18: *Mile 178 on the Mississippi River*
The marine traffic gets heavier, and today we are sharing our waters with great ocean-going vessels from China, Norway, Germany, Greece, India,

Liberia, Italy. They fly their national flags, and we fly ours, though we tend to feel like trespassers in such lofty company. The tugs are far less intimidating.

At Mile 209 we left the main channel for a short cut behind a large wooded island. In the sheltered water, we saw a flock of large birds feeding about 200 yards to our right. At that distance we couldn't identify them as we passed, but thought they might be geese. A few minutes later, having forgotten about them, we were startled by a flurry of splashing and wing-flapping, approaching us from behind. To our surprise a dozen large Canada geese dropped onto the water around us. They showed no fear, swimming up and pecking at our white canoe tarp, even allowing us to pat their heads and backs. We fed them wheat flakes and bread. We must have spent 15 minutes with our "Canadian" friends, and could barely get them to leave us alone. As they pursued us down the channel, I couldn't help thinking that one of them would go nicely in a cooking pot, or grilled slowly on a spit. I made the mistake of mentioning this to Dana who, for the next couple of hours, treated me like a bloodthirsty heathen. He holds all wildlife sacred – much too important to kill for mere food.

Before we land these days, I often remind the boys that our blood sugar is low, that we're tired and irritable, and that we must try to go easy on one another until we've eaten. Today Dana took my urgings as a personal affront, and we got into a spat, which ended on shore when he took a swing at me and then bolted down the beach, where he knew I wouldn't be able to catch him, although I tried. He laughed as I fumed. Jeff and I then got shoving (I can't even recall why), and he ended up with a bloody nose, though not from any direct hit by me. Dana by this time had returned and was watching, bug-eyed. I've been trying so hard not to be bossy that we've now got three captains in the boat, each with a mind of his own. It's a problem, and I'm going to have to be a little less democratic. If I go too far, however, I'll have a mutiny on my hands. I need my crew – need everything they can give me.

At dusk we stretched out in the bug house and watched as the sky darkened, and the stars appeared. The bug house, which I designed, is made almost entirely of mosquito netting and affords a 360-degree view of sky and surroundings. Slowly the moon rose, casting a silvery glow on the river. Tugs and barges and pleasure boats sparkled as they passed – the whole Mississippi looked like a festival. In spite of our afternoon quarrels, a wonderful peace overtook me. Even in my weariness I hardly wanted to sleep, much preferring the carnival of lights and the heady calm around me.

AUGUST 20: *New Orleans, Louisiana, Mile 102 on the Mississippi River*
Red-Letter Day. In the early afternoon, after 31 miles of exhausting work,
we paddled into New Orleans, the world's third largest port. Prosperity
was visible everywhere: petroleum, grain, chemicals, coal, manufacturing.
At 3 p.m. we climbed the river bank through bottles, cans, wrecked cars,
old mattresses, and dead rats, to the city's famous Audubon Park. The
park honours one of the world's great naturalists and nature painters,
and we were perplexed that its river boundary was in such bad shape. We
picked an open area not far from the park zoo and established camp.

It wasn't long before curious strollers had begun to approach us, and
we were warned to watch out for thieves and muggers in this part of the
park. One man told us not to be surprised if we were robbed at gunpoint!
At about 9 p.m. we met a fine young black couple who gave Jeff and me a
lift downtown to see the French Quarter. Dana baby-sat the canoe.

We were dropped at Bourbon and Canal Streets, where we were soon
adrift in a strange new dimension. The narrow streets were gorged with
tourists, hookers, dope pushers, street musicians, hucksters selling anything and everything. Most of the old French buildings were well pre-
served, looking just as they do in the tourist advertisements, with their
wrought-iron balconies and ornate trim. Rock music and jazz poured out
of the bars. Doormen tried to lure us into their buildings with promises
of lovely girls, the best food, the best music. Policemen walked the streets in
squads of four. At one point a clean-cut young man came roller-skating
along the street, bothering no one, enjoying his freedom. Suddenly, amid
the chaos, he was being manhandled by four cops, who took it as their
duty to knock him down and give him a ticket – *they actually gave him a
ticket!* For what, I have no idea. Drink or drug or eat yourself to death,
but don't try anything as wholesome as roller-skating.

In no time I'd seen enough and, while Jeff stayed for more, I caught an
electric streetcar which jounced and wobbled back to the quiet of
Audubon Park. This time I entered the park through its impressive front
gates. The darkness was broken by old-fashioned street lamps, and I realized that the main sections of the park were far more impressive than
what I'd seen this afternoon coming from the river. Wide lawns, palm
trees, hardwoods covered with Spanish moss. I walked some two miles
through a fine tribute to Mr. Audubon.

AUGUST 21: *New Orleans*
The heat wave continues, and on this our day off the temperature is a
humid 102 degrees. We were all up at 7 a.m., and no one had robbed us. I

wrote out a list of the things we had to accomplish, and we divided up the responsibilities. I made some minor canoe and paddle repairs, while Jeff tried to repair our army gas stoves. We phoned CBC Radio back in Winnipeg, then visited the local Army Corps of Engineers office to pick up maps. Later I phoned the Canadian Consulate and requested a new Canadian flag. Within an hour, a splashy consular car drove right up to our camp. A young official got out and presented us with the flag, as well as a pile of souvenir maple-leaf badges to hand out. He took a stack of our old maps and promised to mail them home, and away he went.

After supper, Jeff whisked Dana away for a guided tour of Bourbon Street. I stayed home and socialized with anyone who came along, and chased a couple of big river rats away from the campsite. At 10 o'clock, a couple of black policemen approached me and told me I'd have to move immediately, according to a city ordinance. I told them it was impossible; I wasn't going to be separated from my sons, and had no intention of paddling the Mississippi at night among ships and barges. When they persisted, I asked them if they'd like to help me move my equipment down the rat-infested river bank. This broke the impasse. They looked at one another and walked away muttering.

Our bug house has no floor, and during the night we were invaded by red fire ants, whose lingering bites kept us squirming and whining till dawn.

Southwest from New Orleans

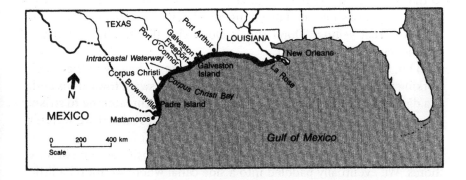

AUGUST 23: *on the Intracoastal Waterway*

Early yesterday morning, we charged away from Audubon Park, determined to conquer the world. Four more miles of the Mississippi, and we'd be off to the west into the canals and bayous of Cajun country. The Harvey Locks, just outside New Orleans, are the gateway to the Intracoastal Waterway, which follows the Gulf west all the way to Brownsville, Texas, at the Mexican border, 670 miles away. We entered the locks, and after a drop of a mere foot and a half dashed out into a very different scene from the Mississippi. The canal was barely over 100 feet wide, with no discernible current. The shores were lined with shrimp boats, trawlers, tugs, pushboats, every species of craft, all of them painted white – they seemed to form an honour guard for us. The landscape was overrun with oil-related industries. We knew from the attention we got from both water and land that we were far from a typical sight on these waters.

A few miles to the west we found ourselves in jungle-like surroundings. Spanish moss hung from the trees. Low plants with rhubarb-sized leaves blanketed the earth. Dana was delighted by a lovely palm tree.

At 7 p.m. we paddled into LaRose, Louisiana, and got permission to camp about two feet above water level in the small backyard of a retired Cajun fisherman and his wife. They watched us suspiciously, not sure whether we were being honest with them about our trip; they weren't going to be conned. Most of the canal dwellers are Cajuns who have grown up by water and call our canoe a "pirogue". They shake their heads as we glide by on our "pirogue trip".

This morning Dana told me that out for a walk after dark last night he met a young man coming the opposite way. They stopped and chatted, and the young man decided to walk Dana to our campsite. As they approached the canal, they stopped under a streetlight in front of a house, so that Dana could write out our address. A woman emerged from the house carrying a shotgun. The young man knew the woman and ran out into the street yelling "Don't shoot! Don't shoot!" She didn't, but the experience left Dana shaken.

So far, we've seen three water-moccasin snakes. They swim the canal, working the fertile banks for frogs and toads. One swam towards us and, at a distance of about two feet, drew its head back, threatening to strike. It wasn't one bit intimidated by our size. When it realized we weren't intimidated either, it swallowed its bluff and swam off.

By 4 this afternoon, we still hadn't found a campsite on the swampy shores. We eventually paddled into a side canal where we found a little rise, just solid enough to support us. I used my machete to cut some large-leafed plants for a floor, and we erected the bug house over them and ate supper inside. The world darkened around us, and we lit candles which gave off a cozy, eerie glow.

I am writing with the help of my small army signal flashlight. Jeff is lying on his foam pad, nearly naked, while Dana sits with a candle on one of the equipment boxes. Our net walls are swarming with mosquitoes, and now a couple of giant beetles are climbing the netting. In the bush, small animals make their rounds – a twig snaps, an animal squeals. We can't help thinking about snakes and gators; they're out there somewhere. We look at each other in the flickering light, as if waiting for something to happen. We have good imaginations.

AUGUST 26: *Intracoastal City, Louisiana*
Our fifth day on the waterway, and it seems many boats have been using their radios to pass along information about us. Daily we get cheers and greetings from all sorts of craft. For the most part we're travelling narrow canals, but occasionally these open into lake-like areas whose shallows

support cypress trees, thickly hung with Spanish moss. On Sunday we found ourselves running against our first inland tide – as if we were dragging an anchor. Under the tidal influence of the Gulf, the canal flows like a river, sometimes with us, sometimes against us.

This evening as I wandered the canal bank I met Junius Lombas, the middle-aged captain of the pushboat *Mike and Ann*. With him was his one crew member, 18-year-old Don Eves. They invited me aboard their beat-up old tug and told me that they were trying to put it back in shape. Junius has spent time at sea and was once shipwrecked off the Georgia coast; he spent a week on the ocean with no drinking water. Don told me he caught a 10-foot gator last week and that it tasted just fine. We spent a few hours drinking coffee and swapping tales, and before I left they gave me a battery-powered light with a leather headband, as well as navigation maps that will see us through to Brownsville, Texas. They didn't want me to go, and I had a hard time breaking away to return to camp.

AUGUST 28: *on the Intracoastal Waterway*
As we came ashore late this afternoon, a 4-foot water moccasin slithered out of the high marsh grass. I held my paddle out to it, and, quick as a flash, it struck the blade, then struck it again. We were determined to stay, as we wanted to make use of a vacant duck-hunting cabin a few yards back from shore. So I picked up the snake on my paddle and flung it 20 feet out into the water, where for the past half hour it has been swimming around watching us. I keep hoping it won't return, as if it does I'll have to kill it – we can't risk stepping on it in the long grass. The other morning when Dana flipped the canoe, a moccasin or cottonmouth crawled from beneath it into the brush. The thought of it in the canoe made me shudder. We no longer break camp without checking our gear for snakes.

Yesterday we survived a violent storm. The wind came up first into our faces, drenching us with cold rain. The shoreline was overgrown with trees, and we couldn't find a landing spot. What scared us was that two tugboats with barges had pulled to shore on the other side of the canal. These rigs seldom stop for anything – obviously, they'd heard something on their radios that we didn't know. At this point we couldn't join them as we couldn't turn our flank to the wind to cross the canal. Just as we expected the worst, everything went calm, and we thought we'd ridden out the gale. But within seconds the wind hit harder, having reversed itself 180 degrees. It drove us down the canal at a frightening speed, our flag whipping and cracking above us, while the rain hit us like bullets in the back. We passed a moving tug coming toward us and could see the crew looking at us in amazement through its flooded windows. We covered 3 miles of waterway in what seemed like a matter of seconds, and then the wind suddenly died. We got to shore and sheltered for two hours while the rain poured around us. About all we could do when we got the tent up at suppertime was huddle in it, trying to restore some of the body heat the storm had drained from us.

AUGUST 31: *in Texas, on the Intracoastal Waterway*
Texas at last! And as we crossed the border yesterday, we looked around for some sign that we were finally in the Lone Star State. Nothing presented itself, and I burst into song, "The stars at night are big and bright – deep in the heart of Texas." My sons, so often disdainful of my exuberance, turned and told me to shut up.

Thus we entered the last state on our journey to the sea. We also saw our first live gator (we'd seen a dead one a few days back). It was about 100 feet away, with only its snout and eyes visible above the water. As we approached it, it dived and disappeared.

Our whole route from New Orleans has been one great engineering marvel – long well-dredged canals, some cut perfectly straight through the coastal flatlands. Today we paddled one stretch of 16 miles without a bend. Since the Texas border yesterday, the high banks have been mostly clay and stubble – anything but scenic. However, when we climbed them this afternoon, we could look out over miles of glowing pasture land. Half a mile away was the first true sign that we were indeed in Texas — a big herd of longhorn cattle. I walked toward them, and as I drew close could see dozens of powerful bulls staring at me. I hope they have as much respect for us as we have for them – we're going to be tenting on their land tonight. In fact, the terrain beneath me in the bug house as I write is a baked-clay embossment of hundreds of lumpy hoofprints.

The heat has been as ferocious as ever, with temperatures rising daily to nearly 100 degrees.

SEPTEMBER 1: *in Texas, on the Intracoastal Waterway*
This afternoon, we passed through the Anahuac Wildlife Refuge and saw a black and white shore bird called a skimmer, whose red bill must be 10 inches long. Also saw some pinkish crane-like birds that we thought might be flamingos.

For the past couple of days we've been paying wary attention to passing barges. In the narrow canal they push so much water ahead of them that they leave a kind of vacuum behind. When they've gone by, this vacuum is filled by a rush of turbulent water, much of which is drawn from the shallows along the banks. On a couple of occasions this vacuum effect has swept a foot or more of water from beneath the canoe, leaving us sitting temporarily on bottom.

Late this afternoon when we were ready to quit, we saw a little canal leading off the main waterway and decided to explore it; we could see well-kept cottages on its banks. All we needed was one kind Texan to give us permission to camp on a cottage lawn for the night, and we'd be spared having to camp on the swampy shores of the waterway. We talked to four cottage owners, all of whom looked at us as if we were demented pirates and turned us down. Then we came across a man of perhaps 50 fishing from his dock. We called to him, apparently startling him, and he quickly retreated into the screened porch of his cottage. We landed at his dock, walked to the porch and peered in. "Move on," he said softly, "you can't stop here." Only as he spoke did I realize he was now wearing a holster and gun, and that his hand was resting nervously on the butt. We'd been warned in Louisiana to watch out for rednecks, but hadn't expected anything quite this straightforward.

As we paddled off we met another Texan who roared up to us in his big motorboat, looked down at our canoe, and told us with a proud sneer, "You won't get to Galveston in that!"

To get to Galveston Island we must cross a 2-mile stretch of water, more or less open to the Gulf of Mexico.

SEPTEMBER 2: *Galveston Island, Texas*
We pulled into Galveston late this morning, and landed on the small beach of an Army Corps of Engineers post. The only threat to our crossing came from the heavy traffic, which included two large ships and a trawler. The trawlers' flared hulls send up a dangerously steep wake that always gives us the jitters. We're much more comfortable on the rolling wake of the ocean vessels.

We were met on arrival by a Texas City couple, John and his wife Ronnie, who said they'd seen us from a ferry and were curious about what we were doing. They wanted to help, and when we'd got permission to camp, they drove us in their pick-up truck to the Galveston YMCA, where we cleaned up.

After dinner, they drove us across the island to see Galveston's fine beaches and to look out over the Gulf of Mexico. What I saw made me sick with fear. The waves were rolling in with tremendous force, and row on row, close together. The waters here are shallow, so that the waves break into surf a long way out. The gentler rolling seas are hundreds of yards offshore. I have a good eye for water conditions and knew there was no way we could launch our canoe in such heavy surf.

At no point in the trip had I felt so despondent. I had only one positive thought – that we still have 315 miles of protected waterway before we have to tackle the Gulf.

We've decided to take a few days off here to get our affairs and supplies in order. I lie here thinking about all that needs doing. We need water containers, food, a new tarp, rain jackets, new zippers in the tent. The canoe needs attention.

Beyond everything else now, a lurking fear of the Gulf is constantly in the back of my brain.

SEPTEMBER 5: *on the Intracoastal Waterway*
Yesterday was our last day in Galveston, and already we miss the place – "the city of verandas" I call it, as every house seemed to have a big veranda. The people were almost unbelievably friendly. We visited the Coast Guard ship *Valiant* yesterday afternoon and were given excellent maps of the Mexican and Central American coast. An Army Corps of Engineers general actually came to our tent to find out if there was anything he could do for us. And of course there are John and Ronnie. Yesterday morning, they picked us up and took us to a seaside restaurant, then drove us 45 miles inland to Houston to shop. We stopped at more than a dozen big stores looking for 5-gallon water containers but couldn't find any. Jeff bought himself a fishing rod and reel, and Dana bought guitar strings. We didn't have time to see much of Houston, and when we got back to Galveston John and Ronnie lent us their pick-up for grocery shopping. Late last evening, Captain Joe Braun, a bar proprietor whom we'd met through John and Ronnie, came along and presented us with a pair of 5-gallon plastic water containers.

The open waters west of Galveston gave us a hard time this morning. For a while I wasn't sure we were going to make it into the safer canals, since at one point the waves were flooding in over the bow of the canoe. Jeff bailed, and I screamed orders. To make matters worse, I made a navigational error which put us on the waters of a big bay called Jones Lake and cost us a couple of stormy miles. We're learning gradually how to handle the tougher waters, but will have to build our confidence and skill if we're to succeed further on.

During our struggles this morning, Jeff pointed out six big dolphins swimming along about a hundred feet from us. The other day when he first saw dolphins he yelled, "Sharks!" and neither Dana nor I knew enough to correct him. We realized they were dolphins only when they went into their jumping routines. They're so carefree and graceful it's great to have them near, but in these waters we really haven't been able to slow down and enjoy them.

This afternoon, shortly after we made camp at Oyster Lake, a tug went by and blared out that a major storm was coming. Jeff quickly tuned our radio to the weather band, which told us that Tropical Storm Danielle would be coming in off the Gulf tonight. We anchored the tent with our two biggest equipment boxes, loaded the canoe, and pointed it in the direction from which we expect the blow. We're only 4 miles from the open Gulf, and the only thing separating us is a very low tidal flat. It is 7:15, and we sit waiting. Dana is reading a book on the guitarist Andrés Segovia, and Jeff is sewing a new zipper into the tent. He has also been working on a design for a covering tarp for the canoe, so that we can enter the Gulf with at least a chance of staying afloat. We'll need a full cover with three cockpits and very secure fasteners at the gunwales. Otherwise every high wave will wash right in on top of us.

SEPTEMBER 6: *Freeport, Texas, on the Intracoastal Waterway* Danielle came in as expected, but didn't hit us particularly hard – the winds were about 30 m.p.h. However, our 10-year-old tent leaked badly. Two of its three door zippers are gone, and we spent the night soaked and fighting off mosquitoes. Jeff was in a terrible mood this morning, grousing away at me, criticizing me for everything from the condition of our tent up to and including the weather. I'm sorry to report that we got into another of our push-and-shove matches before breaking camp. I'm not quite sure what to make of these spats, but have to accept them as some sort of necessary release of tension – our stress levels, day after day, have been stupefying. I also have to accept that my sons have inherited their defiant attitudes at least partly from me. Nothing serious developed, except that I got no help in loading the canoe and, for several hours of paddling, felt dismally alienated from my sons. Finally, just outside Freeport, we negotiated a tentative truce.

We told our friends from Galveston that we'd meet them at the Coast Guard base at Freeport, and at 2 p.m. there they were, ready for a cold beer. They brought a pint bottle of waterproofing liquid for our tent and took Jeff downtown to try to buy some zippers. I applied the waterproofing, which covered only a small portion of the tent, so I finished the job by rubbing wax into the Egyptian cotton. A couple of hours later it poured

rain, and the liquid worked, but the wax failed miserably, apparently preventing the fibres from swelling. Another lesson.

Jeff and I walked a mile over the sands to the open waters of the Gulf
where 7-foot breakers were smashing the beach. Jeff body-surfed for a
while, and I swam a bit to test the strength of the waves. Then I just
stood there, looking out to sea, worrying.

SEPTEMBER 11: *Port Aransas, Texas, on the Intracoastal Waterway*
The weather has been nothing but beneficial to us as our days on the
Waterway wind down. The temperatures have dropped into the low 90s,
and the breezes have been gentle. Nonetheless, our endless obsession
with milage and progress leaves me wondering whether we can possibly
maintain the incredible desire that has brought us this far. Few people
have any idea what it is, what a toll it takes, to average over 30 miles a day
in a canoe, regardless of weather, weariness, or sickness. Will Jeff and
Dana fade? Will I fade? I grudgingly admit that I'm the true motor behind
the trip, and that the boys don't necessarily share my conviction.

It's clear to me that we're going to have to start watching our health a
little more closely. For the past few nights we've been invaded by red fire
ants which get into everything and seem to attack more voraciously the
harder we try to repel them. Their bite burns for several minutes, and
tonight my legs are a mess of tiny festering wounds. An hour ago I waded
into the salt water, which is painful to the bites – I can only hope it will
cleanse them. In the meantime, my palms, which are pocked with shallow black craters from the chemicals in the Mississippi, have begun to
heal. But Dana's asthma has not troubled him in some weeks.

From his bow seat, Dana has the best opportunity to see things in the
water, and today he spotted three 7-foot fish which swam beneath the
canoe. He continually reports his sightings, which at times are shadowy,
making me wonder if he's imagining things.

As I lie here listening to the weather band, I find myself thinking about
the many seismic blasts we've heard recently from the oil and gas outfits
as they blow up the sea floor in their search for offshore deposits. The
shocks must come as something on the level of nuclear explosions to our
dolphin friends, not to mention the more delicate marine organisms.
Makes me wonder if the searchers have any way of warning them, or
whether they care.

I phoned Winnipeg this afternoon and reported our progress to Richie
Gage who has been covering our trip in the *Winnipeg Free Press*. He
reported in turn that our hometown football team, the Blue Bombers,

are in first place in the Canadian Football League and that the Montreal Expos, my baseball team, are leading their National League division – tidbits from afar, trivial and yet exhilarating.

SEPTEMBER 12: *on the Intracoastal Waterway*
We are now down to a mere 112 miles to the Río Grande and Mexico, and I find myself more nervous than ever about what lies ahead. Our physical danger is only a part of it; I am equally daunted by the thought of being stopped, of failing. I have never before allowed myself to fail. Then again, I have never paddled the open seas.

If we were lulled into thinking the weather was on our side during the past few days, we got a powerful reminder this morning that wind and water are no respecters of wishful canoeists. In an attempt to cut off some miles, we abandoned the highway of buoys that guides sensible boaters across the 12-mile-wide Corpus Christi Bay and headed off south in our own direction. Our safety seemed assured by Mustang Island, which shelters the bay and which we would pass on our left, at 2 or 3 miles' distance. To our right was an expanse of bay whose shoreline was all but invisible. We were barely out on our own when heavy wind met us head-on, forcing us to dig in hard. Normally we can tough these situations out, but about 4 miles out from land we met an unexpected tide coming hard into our teeth. We might as well have been paddling a barge, and Dana and Jeff started giving it to me both barrels – again, I was an unthinking fool toying with their safety. Two hours of brutal paddling took us ashore at Mustang Island, where we collapsed on the beach, our muscles cramped and quivering. What next? We knew we'd eventually have to deal with our adversary, and cross the rest of the bay. When we'd recovered to the point of mobility, we took a compass reading and headed out again in the direction of the J.F.K. Causeway Bridge, connecting Padre Island to the mainland. We could see its faint superstructure 10 miles away on the horizon. To get to it, however, we still had to paddle 5 miles of wild Corpus Christi Bay and 5 miles of canal.

Two hours later, half desperate with fatigue, we sighted a buoy on the main channel. Half an hour later we were back in the protection of the canal system. We stopped at a marina a few hundred yards south of the bridge and took on 17 gallons of water. When we asked the locals about a camping spot they pointed across the waterway to a dismally barren island. We paddled up to it, dragging the canoe through a final hundred yards of muddy shallows and up onto a mucky shoreline. Here we camped, beaten and drained and aching.

Days like this dampen our spirits severely, and it is only in the after-math, in the slow reawakening to our incredible progress and spirit, that we can look back on the pleasures as well as the pains of our journey. Today, for instance, amid the turmoil, we saw dozens of elegant dolphins out on Corpus Christi Bay. When we spot them, we bang our hands on the sides of the canoe, or our paddles against the gunwales. The sounds reach them and they race towards us like torpedoes, appearing and disap-pearing in the waves. At the last moment they dive beneath the canoe, as if in greeting.

Even Ugly Island here has its pleasures; in the shallows there are numer-ous wading birds: blue herons, sandhill cranes, cattle egrets, all strutting around on their cartoon legs.

At the moment, Dana is alone with his Bach and Jeff is sitting in the tent mending his hat. The setting sun is a glorious red ball, something of a reward for our labours. We pass our days in the immensity of nature, and at times like these I feel terribly small in the face of it. In spite of that immensity, or perhaps because of it, we grab daily at tiny confirmations that we are advancing, that our endeavour is meaningful. We plot our course on bits of paper; we think in times, miles, latitudes, all of which are really nothing more than numerical hedges against the larger un-knowns. Those poor guys who travelled without maps – they were the real heroes.

In the cross-Canada Centennial canoe race in 1967, the six men in our Manitoba canoe, *Radisson*, covered 3,283 miles in 104 days to win the race. Jeff, Dana, and I have now been paddling 104 days and have come 3,220 miles. And back then I was with some of the strongest paddlers in the world. I am truly proud of my sons.

SEPTEMBER 14: *on Laguna Madre, Texas*
The last stretch of our route to the border is Laguna Madre, a 100-mile-long mixture of tidal flats and open water, protected from the Gulf by the equally long Padre Island. The lagoon varies from 2 to 3 miles in width and is dangerously shallow except for a dredged channel, well marked with buoys. This being the weekend, the lagoon is a regular highway for pleasure boats and speed jockeys. They scream up to us and pass at full throttle, showing none of the sensitivity of the Louisiana Cajuns. But some of them are good-hearted, and we've had the usual handouts of pop and beer.

Yesterday afternoon a tug warned us over its loudspeaker, *"Don't camp on the west shore. That's the King Ranch. You'll be run off or branded!"*

The ranch is said to be the biggest in Texas (it's surely the least scenic), and we laboured past it, looking for cowboys – anything for a diversion. Late in the afternoon we heard faint yelling from our right and spotted a handful of people standing on a dock in front of a cottage. We imagined they were friendly and interrupted our paddling for a family discussion: should we keep going under excellent conditions, or quit for the day and go ashore?

A few minutes later we pulled up at the dock and were greeted by a fetching brunette, a former Canadian from Sault Ste Marie, who had seen our Canadian flag and had been doing most of the yelling. Her name was Pat Smith, and she and her husband Bob invited us to join their party of 15 for a fresh shrimp dinner. We've never had a feed quite like it: jumbo shrimp not long out of the Gulf, barbecued steak, salad, corn on the cob, mushrooms, wine.

During the evening, Bob introduced us to "net casting", a type of fishing common in Mexico and South America but seldom seen up north. The trick is to cast a circular net, 6 feet or more in diameter, flat onto the water. The outer edges of the net are weighted so that they drag the net down, trapping fish on the bottom. A drawstring around the edges closes the net into a neat sack and brings it in. Bob's demonstration netted 15 tiny silver mullet which he saved for bait, telling us with a wink they'd bring some tasty "redfish".

Today's route has shown us an intriguing mix of humanity and wildlife. At one point this afternoon, on an open stretch of water, a tiny bird fluttered up to the canoe, obviously looking for a place to rest. We stopped dead still, and after a few seconds the little thing landed on Dana's paddle, which was lying across his knees. It then hopped into his lap. A few minutes later, having regained its strength, it took off. Within minutes we had an equally surprising visitor; a man pulled alongside us in a powerboat and gave us Cokes and, insistently, a $10 bill. "Git yerselves some steaks in Brownsville!" he hollered, as he roared off down the lagoon.

Our impressions of Texans have been varied, but are not without a stereotypical cast: almost everyone we encounter or hear about seems larger than life – the hospitable Smiths, the Kings and their ranch, the ten-dollar man. Today, as we came down the lagoon, we were assaulted by a shrill, amplified voice which at first seemed to be coming out of the heavens, but which we soon realized was coming from a loudspeaker on a waterside shack: "You long-haired hippies going around smoking pot and sinning – Repent!" came the voice. The preaching continued, apparently for our exclusive benefit, until we were hundreds of yards down the lagoon.

We've since learned that the voice belonged to Brother Lester Roloff, a well-known character in these parts.

Just now, I'm reminded of a motorboat that cruised by us yesterday as we were tied to a channel buoy eating lunch. The driver was a loud-talking type who, within earshot of us, informed his passengers that we were a u.s. Army Corps of Engineers "buoy canoe". "They're checking the boo-ees," he said loudly, which gave us a good laugh. This afternoon we met the same boat, same driver, who this time told his passengers we were connected with the Coast Guard – our authority is escalating.

We're now three days from Port Isabel and the crossing into our third country. I knew we could get at least to Mexico and have told many people that I'd bet my life on it. What happens beyond the Río Grande is another matter.

SEPTEMBER 17: *South Padre Island, Texas*
We have come to the end of our u.s. travels, though not without a few last impediments. Yesterday by 3:30 we were whipped, but couldn't locate a suitable camping spot on the ever-widening lagoon. We decided to carry on 10 miles to the Coast Guard base at Port Isabel, where we hoped we'd find hospitality, as we generally have at Coast Guard stations. No luck – they didn't want us. So, with weary strokes, we paddled another half mile to Isla Blanca Park on the tip of Padre Island. We cooked in the dark and flaked out on the beach, too tired to set up our tent.

As I lay trying to sleep, I started fretting about all the preparations we had to make for our assault on the Gulf. We had to get a canoe cover made, reorganize our equipment, lay in food and water, and get to a bank for cash. It became clear to me that we needed a safe place to store the canoe while we worked, and that the Coast Guard station was the only logical base for us. Before I went to sleep, I resolved that we'd return at daybreak, and would not take no for an answer.

At 8 a.m., Dana and I walked to the base and found Station Chief Bauer – "Cue Ball" his men call him. We hectored and whined, and eventually got permission to pitch our tent on a patch of dagger-like cane stubble a few hundred feet from the main buildings. Having checked out this horrible site, we pitched the tent on a nearby lawn, hoping Cue Ball would ignore our recalcitrance. A while later, he actually gave us some help, assigning two of his men to help us design and construct our canoe tarp. Cue Ball himself made a few phone calls to help us find materials.

At about 11 o'clock, we borrowed a jeep and crossed the long Queen Isabel Causeway to Port Isabel, then drove on through the desert to the big city of Brownsville. There we picked up varnish for our paddles, 24 feet of white, nylon-reinforced vinyl for our canoe cover, and $400 U.S. which we converted to pesos. We spent $90 to bring our food supply up to scratch.

I must say that Cue Ball and his men are not encouraging about our chances of making it on the Gulf. "It just ain't *possible*," they keep telling us, shaking their heads. This evening, to reinforce the point, Cue Ball brought out photos of Coast Guard rescue boats at work – "unsinkable Molly Browns" the boats are called, because they right themselves when capsized. The photos depicted such heavy seas on the Gulf that our confidence has pretty well bottomed out – it has nowhere to go but up.

SEPTEMBER 18: *U.S. Coast Guard Base, Port Isabel, Texas*
Jeff and I spent a good chunk of this morning and afternoon in Brownsville at the Port City Tent and Awning factory, watching a chubby young Mexican cut and sew our canoe cover. I kept urging him *"Pronto, pronto,"* and before lunch gave him a $5 tip to coax him on. He kindly gave up his lunch hour to the cause (though he did take a dozen or more Pepsi breaks) and by 4 o'clock we had our cover – a steal at $32, plus tip. We gloated over our creation as we returned to the base. The thing has three cockpits, each with a drawstring at the waist and a bronze zipper in front to permit access to the interior of the canoe. Chrome-plated clips and a stretched nylon rope hold the cover to the gunwales.

Cue Ball is getting restless, and late this afternoon sent a courier to ask us when we'd be getting off the base. He worries about everything and nothing. We fired back an honest reply: "As soon as possible."

Beaten by the Gulf

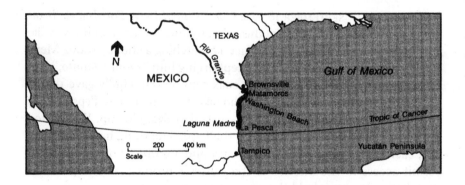

SEPTEMBER 20: *Washington Beach, Mexico*

D-day at last, and after a Coast Guard breakfast we walked the canoe nervously to the waterfront. Our load is at absolute maximum, with over 20 gallons of drinking water, enough we hope to last us for seven to ten days. We expect no water taps between here and Tampico, several hundred miles down the coast.

Having said goodbye to our friends and delayed as long as possible, we shoved off at about 9 a.m., paddling slowly and silently. "Keep cool," I told the boys, "and listen to my instructions."

In no time, we'd rounded the tip of South Padre Island and were approaching the open sea through the channel of a walled jetty. The swells began to build. We passed a couple of trawlers, one of which sent up a wake that greatly compounded the swells, sending us into a panic. We'd never been in anything like it, and somehow water was pouring in over our gunwales beneath the tarp.

We persevered and stabilized, and were soon on the open sea heading for Mexico.

68

We paddled for three hours – perhaps 10 miles – but by this time the wind was up, and the swells were getting trickier. Jeff and Dana were clearly frightened. "We've gotta go in!" Dana called. "We're not going to make it out here!"

I angled to within a quarter-mile of land only to realize that the carrying waves in the shallower water were too dangerous for navigation. Each of them pasted us broadside from the left. With no place in sight to land and despite the boys' protests, I again headed into deeper water. But not for long. The wind gained strength, and increasing volumes of water poured into the canoe along the gunwales. We now realized that the clips fastening the tarp beneath the gunwales had fallen off, and that the best we could do was bail and paddle hard until we got to a decent landing spot. Somewhere, to our right, hidden by the breakers, was the shallow mouth of the Río Grande.

We struggled for another couple of miles, until I knew we had to get off the sea, or we would capsize. "We're going in!" I shouted, swinging toward land. The waves picked us up from behind and threw us forward. As hard as we dug in to slow our momentum, we were no match for the power of the breakers, which drove us hard aground in the shoreline surf 30 or 40 feet from shore. There we sat, momentarily stunned, the canoe half full of water. "Get out and save the canoe and equipment!" I yelled.

Within seconds, we had dragged the swamped canoe ashore – no small task with a ton or more of water aboard – and had stripped off the cover and dragged our equipment above the water line. As we gathered our wits, we counted ourselves lucky to get in safely, but our morale was severely shaken. Looking at our maps, we placed ourselves some two miles into Mexico on Washington Beach.

The wind continued to gain strength during the late afternoon, and the waves and surf mounted. Our beach here is shallow and flat and extends back landward into a mile or more of tidal flats – no trees, no plants to speak of. Sand to the west, water to the east. A shallow tide-fed lagoon runs parallel to the Gulf 50 or 60 feet from the water's edge. It is on the sand between the surf and this lagoon that we've decided to make our camp. We prepared a simple supper and were surprised in the late evening when a number of Mexican vehicles, apparently those of weekend vacationers, came down the hard-packed sand behind us. The drivers and passengers stared out at us; "Who *are* those idiots?" we imagined them saying. We're not sure whether to be pleased or nervous about our proximity to the makeshift highway.

SEPTEMBER 21: *Washington Beach, Mexico*
One look at the water at dawn told me there would be no paddling today. If anything, the breakers are getting higher.

About mid-morning a vehicle pulled up on the beach behind us, and we had our first visit from the Mexican Policía. Two officers in light-brown uniforms approached us politely, and we pulled out the Mexican visas we've carried all the way from Winnipeg. The officers were anything but fastidious, failing to notice that our visas had not been stamped at point of entry. They didn't ask for our passports or check the canoe, where we have our survival rifle and handgun.

When they'd gone, I headed down the beach to walk off some of my frustration at being weatherbound. Not far from camp, I found dozens of thick pads of tar a foot or so in diameter. They're undoubtedly vestiges of the Campeche oil spill, which not long ago flooded beaches around here with millions of gallons of crude. It's not difficult to see what irreparable damage such a spill could do. Yet numerous blue crabs, whose 6-inch shells give them the appearance of armoured vehicles, wandered unconcerned among the tar pads.

Late in the morning, desperate to be moving, we tied guide ropes to the copper support brackets in the bow and stern of the canoe and pushed it out into the surf, hoping to drag it through the shallows for a few miles. But the breakers smashed into it broadside, and in no time it was half full of water, in spite of the tarp. An hour's tough effort gained us all of a quarter-mile.

We'd barely quit when a military truck appeared behind us. The passengers sat watching us for a few minutes, then an officer jumped out and ordered five rifle-toting soldiers out of the back. At the officer's command, they fanned out and began marching toward us, rifles at the ready. When they got to the shallow lagoon, however, they stopped dead, unwilling to get their boots wet. The officer screamed, and they entered the water, dipping their feet like reluctant puppies, then emerging and surrounding us in a broad semicircle. The moment I spotted the truck I'd hidden my handgun and pulled out our various documents, which we now presented to them, along with a written explanation of our trip, typed neatly in Spanish. Initially they seemed satisfied, but after a brief conference, they again began questioning us, apparently puzzled by all our military and quasi-military equipment. Half an hour of intense interrogation convinced them we were indeed innocent Canadians, and they decided to leave us alone. But not without impressing upon us the absolute importance of dealing shrewdly and convincingly with Latin American police and military personnel. We expect to see plenty more of them.

SEPTEMBER 22: *Washington Beach, Mexico*

Excitement first thing in the morning: the night's high tide had filled our lagoon to a width of a hundred feet or more, and deepened it to ten or twelve inches in parts. It now seemed to extend indefinitely to the south. Too excited to eat, we packed the canoe and attached 50-foot guide ropes to its bow and stern. We put it on the lagoon and began towing it southward – I hauled from one side of the lagoon, Jeff and Dana from the other. In places the water was little more than an inch deep, and we had to walk out to the canoe and drag it into deeper water. We laughed and cele- brated our progress, daring to imagine we could go up to 20 miles a day at our current pace – assuming conditions held. In no time, however, we were obliged to shorten our ropes and move closer to the canoe. For half an hour, we slogged along through an inch or less of muddy water and gravel. But the effort became too exhausting to endure. I did a little recon- naissance and realized there was no deeper water ahead. Our folly was over.

Disappointed and tired, we again made camp. We figured we'd gained a meagre 3 miles, and had probably sweated out more precious body fluids than we could afford to lose.

For a couple of hours we lay beneath the low sun shelter we'd made from our tarp, doing our best to conserve energy. By noon, our original 22 gallons of water were down to 14. Later, however, we flagged down three passing vehicles, each of which was able to add a gallon to our supply. "*Agua dulce*" the Mexicans call their drinking water – "sweet water". Coincidentally, what we were given was scented with a faint perfume. We added a few drops of Chlorox bleach to make sure it was pure.

As we sit here tonight, we are disguising our feelings well. But I for one am severely disheartened – the Gulf may have us licked. We do have one hope, however: if we can get to Laguna Madre, 50 miles south of here, we will have a hundred miles of protected travel, similar to what we had in the Texas lagoons. Right now, this is about all we have to cling to.

SEPTEMBER 23: *Washington Beach, Mexico*

How quickly our fortunes change. This morning the wind was down, and we saw a chance to get on the sea. We launched at 8:30 and established a steady course a half-mile offshore. We made reasonable progress through- out the morning, though a tidal current was running against us from the south. On large waters, it's difficult to know exactly how fast we're mov- ing. Dana, our navigator, has to take a good look at the shore, figure out roughly how far we are from it, then fix his eye on some stationary landmark. Using a rough geometry of distances and changing angles, he can figure out approximately what progress we're making.

By 2 o'clock, the seas had begun to build, and we suspected we were getting our first taste of Tropical Storm Hermine. We'd heard it was on its way north from the Yucatán Peninsula and would probably develop into a hurricane. With the seas mounting and our control over the canoe slipping, we headed for shore.

About 100 yards out a giant breaker pitched us forward at a frightful speed. In seconds our bow had plunged into the wave trough in front, and our stern was high in the air, sliding sideways. Suddenly we were upside down in the water, thrashing to free ourselves from the drawstrings of our canoe cover. I was the last to surface, powerfully relieved to see two heads bobbing near the overturned canoe. We were still a good way from shore, but fortunately the canoe cover had stayed in place, keeping our equipment in the canoe. We could tow it in as a unit. The only item that escaped was Dana's guitar, which he quickly retrieved, though not without a good deal of yattering.

Ashore, we tore open our equipment boxes, and were dismayed to find everything awash in seawater: passports, maps, guns, radio, clothes, food. My Minolta Super 8 movie camera was full of water, as were my German 35-mm. and binoculars. We spent hours wiping and wringing and setting things out to dry. The problem is that no matter how dry we get the articles, we won't be able to rid them of salt, which means they'll continue to attract any moisture around them. Before our eyes, rust began to form on our machetes and guns.

Despondently, we plotted our day's progress, the boys insistent that we had paddled 15 miles, though my own guess would be more like 10 or 12. Any advance is welcome, although in a way we're worse off than we were, as we no longer have the makeshift beach road behind us. Now the endless stretches of sand to our west are broken only by a range of dunes perhaps a mile and a half inland. There is no visible plant or animal life. The sun is brilliant, the sky is a maniac blue. The wind is ceaseless. Our canoe is sitting in the middle of the tidal lagoon, apparently floating but actually resting on bottom.

As I sit here listening to Dana's guitar, it occurs to me that the northernmost stretch of Laguna Madre extends about 15 miles north of the sea entrance that we'll be using to gain access to the lagoon. If we could somehow get to that northern part of the lagoon without having to paddle all the way south to its entrance, we could cut off 15 miles of sea paddling. We may be within 20 miles of the top of the lagoon, a mere day's paddle. We're 30 or 40 miles from the entrance proper. The question is, will we be able to portage overland from the coast to the northern end of the protected water? Only a good day's paddling will tell.

In the meantime, the surf is driving us crazy with its roar – all day, all night. Any time we're more than a few yards apart we have to shout to one another to be heard.

SEPTEMBER 29: *Washington Beach, Mexico*
Nearly a week has passed since I wrote last, and Laguna Madre is as far away as ever. Day after day we sit here, sheltering from the wind and sun, hoping desperately for a sea change. The incredible thing about our enforced stay here is not so much the length of it, but that, in spite of our anxiety and discomfort – in spite of our *thirst* – we haven't panicked or retreated.

Last Friday, with the wind and waves as high as ever, we were obliged to shift our priorities from any notion of progress to plans for mere survival. Our water was down to nine gallons, and our strict rationing left us perpetually parched in the heat and wind. To preserve body fluids I took to wearing a T-shirt tied to my head, two shirts, and my green nylon jacket. I was hot, but didn't want my sweat evaporating in the wind.

On Friday afternoon, Dana and I walked a mile or more back across the sand flats to the higher dunes inland. From there, in the distance, we could see a stretch of new water that seemed to go on forever. Could it be fresh? Could it be the north end of Laguna Madre? If so, could we portage the canoe across the dunes to get to it? As we walked toward it I fantasized being able to stick my entire head in it and drink until my belly ached.

As we drew close, however, we realized we'd been fooled. The water was only a few inches deep, and when I sampled it, I had to spit it out – it was brackish and useless.

In spite of our bad luck, both of us at a certain point felt a strange peace come over us. We spoke of it, gradually realizing what it was. The silence! Behind the dunes we were liberated from the awful din of the sea. The constant intimidation of the waves and water had been left behind.

Later that day, I walked a couple of miles up the beach, and was surprised to find ten coconuts that had washed ashore. Though they are a potential source of food, I wasn't particularly pleased to see them, as the current that carried them had almost certainly come from the south and will be running against us if we ever get back on the water. I whacked them open with my machete and found all but two of them rotten. I also saw dozens of crabs, and will keep them in mind if our food supply gets short. That night, I might have thought they had *us* in mind for *their* food supply: about two in the morning I was shocked from my sleep by a large blue crab crawling slowly across my face. Its claws felt like a dozen or so sharp pencils, and with a yell I knocked it flying. The incident didn't help my sleep.

By the following afternoon we were down to 8 gallons of water. With the sun well past its zenith, and the heat easing off, Dana and I again headed for the sand dunes. The day before, we'd seen some distant vegetation to the northeast and wondered if there might be a stream or ranch out there somewhere. But miles of walking showed us nothing but sand, a few brittle shrubs, and more salt water.

As we walked back, we came across two struggling tortoises, both very sluggish, near the bleached remains of one that hadn't made it. I considered taking the two live ones for food, but Dana wasn't impressed by the idea. "Live and let live," he told me. "We're not starving yet." I thought, if these tough characters couldn't make it, we hadn't much chance ourselves.

As we lay in the tent after dark, I gave a little pep talk, trying to focus on potential improvements, such as preventing the canoe from capsizing as we come through the surf on our way to shore. We have to keep the stern down and the bow up, and we figure if Jeff jumps into the water a couple of hundred yards out it will substantially lighten the bow. As a further measure, he will swim to the stern and hang on to it, acting as a kind of sea drag or anchor.

I must say that, at this point, the boys were taking our predicament better than I was. Jeff was going about his business, reading his electronics books, and Dana was practising guitar. What worried me at times was that they didn't seem to realize the seriousness of our situation, stranded in a desert miles from anywhere, with the giant waves preventing our escape. Although they don't always reveal it, they have great faith in my leadership, and seem to assume that somehow I, their father, will be able to save their necks, no matter what the circumstance. I myself am not always so sure, and several times in the past few days have felt my confidence crumbling.

Last night it rained for a while, but, fools that we are, we didn't think to try to collect any of it. We could at least have caught a half inch or so in the canoe.

At about 10 o'clock this morning, Jeff spotted a reflection from what appeared to be a vehicle away down the beach. I took off expectantly and, after a mile or so of brisk walking, came upon an old truck. The three male occupants, all obviously very poor, were collecting driftwood boards for a house they were building. None of them spoke English, so I showed them the Spanish letter explaining our trip. When the driver had read it, he reached into his pocket and pulled out a shabby wallet. He took out two American one-dollar bills and held them out to me.

"No necesito moneda," I explained emphatically. "Necesito agua."

"Ahh," he grinned and immediately went to the cab of the truck, returning with a pair of one-gallon milk containers full of water. He handed them to me, and I thanked him and raced back to camp with the treasure.

But, under current conditions, two gallons of water are not even a full day's supply, and early this afternoon, Dana and I set out to the north, carrying two 5-gallon jerry cans and a couple of smaller containers. Five miles of walking in the 90-degree heat brought us to a muddy little rivulet which we followed inland until, marvel of marvels, we found a tiny house hidden among the sand dunes. "Hola!" we yelled, "Hello!" and within seconds a tiny Indian woman appeared in the doorway. As it turned out her husband was away, but her four children were with her. We showed her the letter explaining our trip, and she handed it to her teen-age son, Raul, who could read. We explained to Raul that we needed water, and, when he had conferred with his mother, he grabbed our containers and left the house, apparently heading back into the dunes.

While we waited for Raul we had a chance to look around. What a strange little place it was – one large room and a veranda. The total furnishings were a couple of chairs and several plank beds, on one of which a pretty little girl of perhaps 13 lay reading a booklet. Outside were a dozen scrawny head of cattle and several chickens scratching among a few shrubs and tufts of grass. On a black sheet of plastic, dozens of shrimps were drying in the sun. The doorstep to the house was a chunk of tar, perhaps four feet wide and a foot thick – undoubtedly a remnant of the Campeche oil spill.

Raul returned with our water and proudly refused our offer of 50 pesos for his effort. After grateful goodbyes, we set off down the beach like a couple of Mexican mules. I carried the 5-gallon containers, Dana the smaller ones. We staggered along until our arms and shoulders could stand the strain no longer. To make matters worse, we were walking in our bare feet, so that every pebble stung under our increased weight. We were reduced to moving in 100-step stages, each of which left us panting and cursing the weight of our life-saving load.

A brutal two hours later, we spotted our tent, a welcome blue speck in the distance to the south. Jeff had been watching for us, and it wasn't long before we could see him, a tiny stick-figure, sprinting down the sand towards us. What a pretty sight he was! He reached us with whoops and welcomes, and I unloaded my containers on him, then took Dana's lighter ones, leaving Dana to walk unburdened.

The whole complexion of things has changed as we lie here this evening contemplating the sea and sky. Our thirst is quenched, and we can again turn our whole attention to advancing down the coast. For the first time in days, our confidence is high.

SEPTEMBER 30: *Washington Beach, Mexico*
Unfortunately, confidence cannot do for us what a few windless days might. The seas were slightly reduced this morning, so we packed the canoe and launched into 3-foot surf. After 3 miles of labour against strong currents and running shore tides, we found the wind rising, and a rainstorm mounting in the east. We headed for shore. But before we had a chance to implement our new landing technique, a powerful side current caught us and swung us round. In a sickening re-enactment of our previous attempts at sea landings, we were over and treading water in the foaming surf.

Again, everything we owned was soaked: radio, binoculars, flashlight, clothes, maps, documents – even my movie camera which I'd taken extra care to pack in plastic. *We simply cannot go on this way.*

As we limped through our clean-up, we discovered a 4-inch tear in the hull of the canoe. We raised the tent, and in no time the rain came in torrents, submerging the beach under two inches of fresh water. When the rain let up, we went out and dug holes in the sand to preserve what water we could. For a minute or more the three of us were on all fours with our heads in the holes, drinking like dogs. When we'd had our fill, we repaired the canoe with fibreglass patches.

Late this evening the sea began to mellow, and soon after dark, itching to get a little closer to Laguna Madre, we struck our tent, put the canoe in the shallow water, and began walking it along the coast. It wasn't easy, as we were continually hit broadside by waves that smashed the canoe against our legs and hips. We stopped every ten minutes to bail.

Sometime close to midnight, we staggered ashore, flung down our tarp and collapsed. We had gained another 2 miles, and have now come 6 miles in seven days.

OCTOBER 1: *at Mezquital, Mexico*
For the first time in ten days, I can happily report that we are not on Washington Beach. When we wakened this morning, the wind had shifted

to the north, giving us a tailwind down the coast. We started out as we'd finished last night, hauling the boat through the shallow water. But at a certain point, frustrated with our progress, and certain that we could paddle, I shouted to the boys, "Let's go!" A few minutes later we were into our cockpits and out on the open sea. Jeff was more or less himself as we paddled, but I couldn't help noticing a big change in Dana, who seemed to be in a sort of trance, desperate to get off the Gulf and into safer waters.

By mid-afternoon, after seven hours of ocean paddling, we were straining our eyes for any sign of an entrance to the lagoon. Then at about 4 o'clock we saw a double jetty in the distance, and my heart began thumping with hope. Could this be it?

We angled toward shore and saw a couple of anchored fishing boats, bouncing on the swells near the jetties. We paddled toward them calling, "Donde está Laguna Madre?" But we couldn't make out the muffled Spanish answers.

We were going in anyway, and in preparation for another dunking, Dana took off his dry pants, so that he was now naked beneath the canoe cover. We moved cautiously towards shore, then, true to form, were caught by a large wave. For all of 30 seconds, it drove us forward, totally at its mercy, then suddenly plunked us aground, safe on bottom 100 feet from land. In a fit of relief, Dana leapt from his bow seat and ran ashore, entirely oblivious of his nudity. It wasn't until a group of fisherman began laughing at him that he remembered he'd taken his pants off, and beat it back to the canoe.

We waded ashore and were told by the local fishermen that we were at Mezquital, a new northern entrance to Laguna Madre. I could have screamed for joy. We had made it. We were back in the game.

OCTOBER 3: *on Laguna Madre, Mexico*
This is our second full day on the lagoon, a massive, shallow body of water which teems with fish. Yesterday, in the murky water, we ran into a school of fish so thick that the impact literally shook our canoe. To our east is a narrow neck of land protecting us from the Gulf, to our west a ridge of barren clay hills. The lagoon reminds us of the Texas lagoons, except that here there are no marker buoys or dredged channel; it is really no place for boats. Several times yesterday and today, the water got so shallow we had to get out of the canoe and pull it to deeper water. Nonetheless we've come 50 miles, and are now about 50 miles out of La Pesca at the south end of the lagoon.

Late yesterday afternoon, we saw a tiny fishing village on the east bank and decided to stop for the day. We paddled toward a little tarpaper shack, from which two men emerged, signalling us to shore as if their lives depended on our arrival. As we reached land, they practically yanked us from the canoe and embraced us as if we were long-lost brothers.

Our appearance in their remote corner of the world was a kind of festival for them, and they were going to make the most of it, beginning with a whirlwind unloading of the canoe. It impressed me to see how tough these little guys were, hoisting even the biggest of our equipment boxes as if they were made of styrofoam. When they'd moved all our gear to higher ground, they let us know quite clearly that they'd appreciate a little booze – they undoubtedly felt our boxes were loaded with it. As it was, I did have some liquor, a 26-ounce bottle of 190-proof Everclear that had been with us from the start. I took it out, and one of the men, Modesto, ran to the shack for glasses – shots all around.

It soon became clear that the two were determined not to quit until the bottle was finished. Modesto's wife sat quietly in the background by the shack – no women's lib down here – and I eventually went over and offered her a round. This pleased her, but seemed to put her in a mild state of shock. I later wondered if I'd done the right thing, but didn't want to see her left out.

After dark, we went to visit a group of eight young fishermen who lived in a neighbouring one-room shack, lit by candles. They brought us cups of sweet, dark coffee, but no one really loosened up until I told Dana to go get his guitar. In no time, one of the young men disappeared and came back with another guitar with a cracked box. Dana and he were soon playing duets and singing. Then another of the men left, returning with a tape recorder, on which he recorded several of Dana's solos.

We had a fine, relaxed evening, and when we got up to go the young men insisted we stay, going so far as to offer us their beds. We thanked them, explaining that we'd rather sleep under the stars.

On our way back to the canoe, we saw Modesto's friend trying to get into one of our equipment boxes for the rest of the Everclear. Modesto was beside him beating him, attempting to run him off, which he succeeded in doing.

As we lay luxuriating in the calm night air, we could hear the tape of Dana's music being played over and over and over in the fishermen's shack. The background chatter seemed to suggest that the young men thought Dana was a major rock star.

Unlike last night's camp, tonight's is moody and quiet. We're sheltered in a decaying abandoned shack because we're expecting rain and can't stand the thought of another dousing.

After supper, Jeff went to work preparing pancakes for tomorrow's lunch. (He'd complained that the lunch I'd prepared today – soda crackers, peanuts, and water – was not up to his standards.) He tried one of the pancakes, then Dana wanted one. Jeff told him, "Only if there's enough for tomorrow," and they began to spat. I yelled "Cool it!" and suddenly Dana was in a rage. He picked up a 5-gallon water container and flung it 25 feet at the canoe, breaking it open. He then threw a gallon container, and I grabbed him to control him. After a heated exchange of words, he lashed out at me with his feet and fists, catching me a good one in the face. I threw him into a pile of brush, and the tussle was over. Both of us had some light bruises and nicks, but worst of all were the hurt feelings. For a few minutes, the three of us sat shaken and dismayed. I had a good talk with Dana, and we gradually cooled out. Everything has been so difficult, so stressful, and none of us has any room to breathe. Dana is naturally emotional, but tends to bottle things up until he can't hold them any longer. I sympathize deeply, but in our current circumstances don't always have the patience to show it.

OCTOBER 4: *on Laguna Madre, Mexico*
The maps we're using are pathetic – 50 or 60 miles to the inch – and we have no real idea where we are on this enormous water system. We ask information from the fishermen we meet, but none of them has any notion of distance. Three times today we asked how far it is to La Pesca, and all we got was *"Está lejos, está lejos,"* "It's far, it's far." We know it's far, but *how* far? We ask how many miles, and they don't know what we mean. "How many kilòmetres?" I ask, and they reply *"No sé,"* "I don't know." One old fisherman looked up at the sun and said *"Tres días,"* "Three days." We show them our maps, trying to pinpoint our location, and they become even more confused.
    At 3:30 p.m., after eight hours of tough paddling, we went ashore at a fine-looking island, with a beach of ground seashells. We landed by a fishing shack, disembarked, and began calling out blind greetings to the inhabitants. But no one appeared or answered, which surprised us, as the place had a look of habitation about it; there were six or seven hens strutting around. A sign out front said "Ignacio", presumably the owner's name.
    We cautiously entered the house, having to stoop to get through the door. The ceiling rafters were only 5 feet from the mud floor, and the bed and table were barely bigger than dollhouse furniture. In the cooking pit was a warm pot of rice and peppers that seemed to have been cooked

within the past hour. Had we frightened Ignacio off? Was he watching us from somewhere on the island?

We cooked our supper on the beach, and, as darkness settled, Ignacio had still not appeared. At 6:30, in the dark, Dana and I moved boldly inside and lit candles. Jeff was sleeping soundly on the beach by the canoe. Dana was soon at his music, I at my writing. Eventually, Dana left for the beach to sleep, and I crawled into Ignacio's bed, my feet extending a foot or more beyond the end of it. I leaned over, blew out the candle, and the darkness took over.

I awakened later feeling cold, and wrapped Ignacio's blanket tighter around me. But this time it wasn't as easy to get back to sleep. The bed was getting shorter and harder, and I was now beginning to feel bug bites – Ignacio's bedding was infested with fleas. But I was too cold to give up the blanket. As I lay there, I began thinking about this tiny man whose bed I occupied. I pictured him as a lonely old fellow with neither wife nor children to comfort him. I, too, was now alone, and, as I lay staring into the darkness, a most unusual feeling crept through me. I *am Ignacio*, I thought. For this fleeting moment, I am he.

OCTOBER 5: *on Laguna Madre, Mexico*
Just after lunch we met an old fisherman, and tried hard to get information from him about the way and distance to La Pesca. He pointed south, looked me squarely in the eye, and said emphatically, "*No camino! No camino! No camino!*" My translation for *camino* was "road", and we already knew there were no roads to La Pesca from anywhere around here. As we pulled away southward, into a brisk wind, he shrugged and looked at us with sad frustration.

Within half an hour, the water depth began to decrease dramatically. In no time the lagoon beneath us was a mere foot deep. We now realized what was happening. The strong south winds were pushing the waters of the entire lagoon north and out to sea. We zigzagged around, trying to find some kind of channel, but we were soon grounded in 3 inches of muddy brine. Our only alternative to sitting there was to get out our ropes and start hauling, which we did.

An hour of slugging through the shallows in our bare feet gained us another couple of miles. But by this time we were exhausted and had to stop and eat. Looking out behind, we could see an endless, snaking trail of little mounds of clay, each one sucked above the water surface by our footsteps. We sat there agonizing about what to do. None of us had any stomach for even attempting to go back on the Gulf – which was probably impossible anyway. We certainly knew now what the old fisherman had meant by "*no camino*".

After dinner we took to our ropes again, but the hauling grew even more difficult, until all we could manage were little bursts of 25 steps or so. At each pause, the canoe would bed down into the mud, creating an airtight seal that was next to impossible to break. A frantic hour of sweating and slogging netted us another mile, but we could go no further. "Let's go to shore," said Jeff.

"I'm not pulling another inch," Dana told him.

Jeff looked at me and said, "Can we leave the canoe here?"

"What if the water comes back?"

The only solution was for all of us to stay out here in the mud. With the sun sinking, we climbed back in the canoe and sat silently staring toward La Pesca, about 12 miles away.

At dusk, Dana stretched out below the bow seat on his foam pad. Jeff made his bed on top of our four equipment boxes, and I was left with the choice of sitting all night on the stern seat or hunching over in the 3-foot space in front of it. The 7-foot sleeping space that had been designed for me when the canoe was built was half full of cargo.

In the middle of a sleepless night, I heard sounds across the mud flats and could eventually make out the silhouette of a wandering coyote. Every so often I'd hear a frantic squeal, presumably that of a wading bird taken unawares. Above the horizon to the south I could see the soft glow of the lights of La Pesca.

OCTOBER 6: *on Laguna Madre, Mexico*

Yesterday, while we were hauling, Dana's feet were badly cut by bits of shell and debris in the mud, and first thing this morning he informed us he would not be leaving the canoe today. After breakfast, Jeff and I took to the ropes again and began hauling. Dana called out encouragement and poled with his paddle. Ten steps and rest – twelve steps and rest – nine steps and rest. On we went, until my feet, too, were severely torn and bleeding. The intense salt of the lagoon, which because of evaporation is far more concentrated than normal sea salt, gets into the wounds and stings mercilessly. After a mile of this bull labour we gave up, realizing that in the heat of the sun we were using up far too much energy and body fluid for what we were achieving.

Jeff and I decided to walk the couple of miles to the west shore of the lagoon to see if we could find any sign of life or water. But, having got there, we were unable to climb the steep clay bank which was overgrown with cacti and brambles that tore our hides as badly as the debris beneath the mud was tearing up our feet.

When we got back to the canoe, Dana was at his guitar, seemingly enjoying the leisurely practice time. Jeff and I now set out across a couple of miles of mud toward the Gulf. An hour of painful walking brought us to the top of a row of dunes, where we gazed out on a version of the Gulf we hadn't seen before – bright blue in colour and crashing onto a steep bank of shells and sand, not at all like the shallow sands of Washington Beach. Even the sight of those frightful breakers was enough to set my heart racing. We'd probably be able to paddle the softer rollers further out if we could get to them, but there's no way we'd survive launching in these fierce shore waves. We walked south along the beach for a couple of miles but found only a few coconuts, all but one of which turned out to be rotten.

To add to our miseries, as we headed back out across the baked-mud surface of the lagoon – or what had been a lagoon – our wasted feet began to break through into an oozy substratum that the sun had heated almost to cooking temperature. We hotfooted it back to shore and took another route to the canoe.

At 4 o'clock, I held an emergency council. Immediately after sunset, Jeff and I would walk south along the Gulf to find water, as we were now down to 2 gallons; we would probably have to go all the way to La Pesca. If things went well, we'd be back tomorrow by sundown. Dana would stay with the canoe.

And so at 7:30, in near-total darkness, we set out, leaving Dana with more than a gallon of water and our remaining food. If he kept himself covered and didn't move around too much, the rations would last him two days. It made me sick to leave him there on his own, but he didn't seem to mind.

When we got to the sea, we washed our feet, and I painfully pushed mine into my high leather boots. As we walked through the darkness, my feet grew increasingly painful, then finally numb.

After three hours, the lights of a number of fishing boats appeared in the distance, and we knew we were close. We could also see the ever-brightening glow from the lights of La Pesca. When we felt we were within a mile of town, we took off our boots, threw our sleeping shells on the beach, and climbed into them.

OCTOBER 7: on *Laguna Madre, Mexico*
By 7 a.m., we were standing at the south end of Laguna Madre, looking north over miles of baked clay. *No camino*, indeed. La Pesca was a tawdry

little place with one paved street and a wandering zoo of cattle, goats, burros, pigs, and chickens. We were directed to the Café Americano, where we stuffed ourselves with a massive Mexican breakfast. I felt guilty about Dana back at the canoe, eking out his meagre rations.

A few inquiries led us to a man named Israel, who, we were told, knew everything about La Pesca and its surroundings. We were happy to learn that he had a jeep and would drive us back to the canoe. He took us to a tiny store where we spent 750 pesos ($30 U.S.) on bread, canned goods, tortillas, cheese, almost anything they could sell us. The other customers looked at us as if we were decadent beyond redemption. Israel got us a couple of new 5-gallon water containers, which we filled at a barrel. He then told us something that buoyed our hopes: two days of north wind would fill the south end of the lagoon with water of navigable depth. What hope there was of a north wind, a *"norte"* he called it, we had no idea.

The jeep ride back to the patch of ground nearest the canoe cost us 150 pesos, and before Israel left us I had a difficult decision to make. I thought about things for a minute, then, while Jeff watched me, told Israel in Spanish that if we weren't in La Pesca in four days, he was to come out and get us.

With that, we began yet another agonizing walk through the slime. Although I hated to admit it, and hate to admit it now as I write, our odyssey may be over – at least the odyssey we planned, every inch of which was to be achieved under our own power. We can apparently go no further on either the lagoon or the Gulf. Unless the wind changes, in four days we'll have to quit.

Late this evening, I told Dana about the possibility of going to La Pesca by jeep. He immediately saw the implications and sat there like a wooden Indian, staring at me, saying nothing. Jeff spoke up, "I think it's the only thing to do."

"So do I," I said.

At least tonight we were a little more comfortable in the canoe. We hung things overboard or propped them across the gunwales so that each of us had six feet of sleeping space.

OCTOBER 9, 1980, *on Laguna Madre, Mexico*
Forty-eight hours have passed since I wrote last, and we have pretty well given up hope for a north wind. We did make a half-mile haul when the water rose marginally on the afternoon of the 7th, but we have not advanced since. We sit here in the mud stew, longing for even a few inches of water, to allow us to do some hauling. With so much time to brood, I'm

developing a near-psychosis about quitting the trip. I really have no adequate way of dealing with the possibility. It makes me sick even to think about going home to face the doubters and skeptics who thought we'd never make it in the first place. The thought of facing those who *did* think we'd make it is just as bad. I guess in reality I don't want to face myself, to allow that I've been defeated. Yet as we languish here, listening to the cannonade of the Gulf from across the mud flats, I'm constantly reminded of our shrinking chances of carrying on.

In the meantime, the area around the canoe has become an environmental disgrace: tin cans, food wrappers, trails leading off to our numerous makeshift latrines. I'm ashamed of it. But then I never could have imagined three adults living in a grounded canoe for four days under a blazing sun. Dana has not set foot on land since we left Ignacio's island. His feet are better than they were, though my own are still severely swollen and painful – so bad, in fact, that I was unable to leave the canoe yesterday. I'm beginning to believe that the swelling is not blood poisoning but acute infection from the intense salt of the mud and brine that surround us.

If there's anything even remotely positive about being here it's that we've had more than enough time for study – Dana his music, Jeff his electronics, and Spanish for me. I sit here in the awful heat, optimistically trying to perfect my Spanish pronunciation.

This evening as I write, the sun is low, and the cool night air is creeping in. And like the Old Man of the Sea, our thoughts have turned to baseball. This afternoon, Jeff fixed the radio, and as I sit huddled in my jacket in the twilight, I slowly scan the dial, hoping to pick up a major-league broadcast. No luck.

OCTOBER 10: *Laguna Madre, Mexico*
We have been forced to accept our fate. This morning we made the 2-mile haul from the centre of the lagoon to the shore of the Gulf. Dragging the canoe has never been harder, what with the drying mud flats and the condition of our feet. Before setting out, Dana wrapped his feet in bandages; Jeff and I went barefoot. It took us several minutes just to dislodge the canoe from the suction that had built up beneath it. After that, we were dogs, we were mules, we were slaves. Ten steps maximum and rest. And every step sent a jolt of pain up from the bottoms of my feet into my ankles.

After two and a half hours of it, we could go no further. So, with three-quarters of a mile to go, we lifted our heaviest equipment box and carried

it the rest of the way on its own. Then back for more. The entire opera-
tion took four hours: by the end of it, it was all we could do to limp into
the Gulf for our first baths in well over a week. The Gulf waters were not
nearly as painful to my feet as the lagoon had been, though putting on
my boots pushed me pretty close to screaming.

Our concern now is whether Israel will show up to rescue us at noon
tomorrow. If he doesn't appear, Jeff and Dana, whose feet are considera-
bly healthier than mine, will have to walk to town for help. I'm in no
shape to walk the 12 miles to La Pesca.

In spite of the tears I want to shed, I am proud of our accomplishment.
No one has ever paddled from Canada to Mexico, and I doubt that any-
one will do it again. Jeff and Dana have given their very best to my folly.
They are fine sons.

OCTOBER 12: *in La Pesca, Mexico*

Israel came, and we loaded the canoe, and were driven into town.

The pressure is off now, and we are beginning already to regain our
composure. We are temporarily camped in La Pesca, where the people
have been very hospitable. But we have no desire to stay around this
scene of our defeat, and this afternoon we decided to make our way south
by road to the coastal city of Veracruz, where we'll spend the winter. If
nothing develops there, we'll return to Winnipeg in the spring. Israel's
neighbour has a rattly little pick-up and will drive us the 500 miles to
Veracruz in the morning. His asking price of 6,000 pesos ($240) is steep
by local standards, but he knows we want out and is unlikely to give us
any bargains.

Picking Up the Pieces

OCTOBER 20: *Veracruz, Mexico*

With all we'd been through on the water, it's ironic that during the incredible drive down here last week I felt several times that our lives were about to end on land, somewhere along the tortuous Mexican highway. We left La Pesca in the early morning of the 13th and were impressed throughout the day by some of the finest scenery we have ever seen: bank after bank of rich green hills stretching far into the distance; precipitously steep valleys; tropical forest; coconut palms, citrus trees, banana plants. Our problems came at dusk, when our driver, Israel's neighbour, perversely began picking up speed, wheeling around corners, and belting down dangerous grades into oncoming headlights which, time after time, he would dodge at the last possible second.

Our real debt to Israel's neighbour is not that he got us to Veracruz but that for a day he effectively banished the dangers of the sea from our minds. We reached the city at 1 a.m. and within an hour had checked ourselves and our canoe into the ant-infested Roca Mar Hotel, surely the worst hotel in Latin America. The advertised "air conditioning" in our

Lilliputian room turned out to be a ceiling fan which, half an hour after we turned it on, seized up in a cloud of smoke. We had one thin towel, and a toilet with no seat. A single wall fixture contained a burnt-out 60-watt bulb, and our only furnishing, besides beds, was a wooden table, with a leg broken off.

During our first full day in Veracruz we visited Mexican Immigration, where we were angrily told that we should have had our visas stamped way back at Matamoros at the border. They admitted us anyway and sent us to the Port Captain, who issued a slip of paper which read: Ship – *Orellana*; Crew – 3; Captain – Donald Starkell. Now we are a thoroughly seaworthy ocean-going vessel.

We spent most of our first week in the city looking for a better place to live. But we had no luck until yesterday, when a young university student, Gabriel Delgado, sought us out at the Roca Mar, wanting help with his English. As it turned out, he lives in a large private home, where a number of rooms are rented out to students. There was a vacancy, and within an hour we were on our way to see if we could fill it. As we rode the bus, Gabriel, or "Gabby" as he calls himself, told us he studies marine engineering at the university here. His home is in Aguascalientes, several hundred miles to the northwest. He is dark and slim and athletic-looking.

The house was ideal, right on the sea, with a golden-brown beach out front. Coconut palms lined the street. With Gabby acting on our behalf, we soon had our winter home, a second-floor room with use of cooking facilities, and a balcony overlooking the Gulf.

Gabby hired a truck to bring our canoe and equipment from the Roca Mar, and within hours we were established in our new digs. What a difference it makes to be among friends and in comfortable, relaxed surroundings. I spent my first afternoon here snorkelling in the Gulf, while Dana and Jeff rambled around Veracruz.

Meanwhile, I've started to think that maybe our voyage isn't over, maybe we can return to La Pesca under better conditions and pick up where we left off. If one thing encourages me it's the state of the Gulf down here. Offshore there is a monstrous coral reef which breaks the strength of the waves, giving at least the illusion that a canoe could be launched from the beaches. We've also been told that the Gulf calms down in March and stays so until the end of June. By May or June, we could be around the Yucatán and into the gentler waters of the Caribbean.

If I have one apprehension, it's that Jeff has begun to talk about going home. Every so often he'll drop a comment about missing his friends, or feeling he's not accomplishing anything, or wanting to get back to his electronics studies. (He has two years to go to qualify as an electronics technician.) Unlike me, he sees no possibility that the trip can continue and has hinted that he'd like to be home by Christmas. I've gently encouraged him to stay.

Dana, on the other hand, is looking forward to the weeks of uninterrupted practice time. The Mexican climate is perfect for his asthma; in fact, it's been a good two months since he had any trouble.

One thing I must watch is that I don't ruin my winter with flawed and frustrating dreams of carrying on. If I can help it.

NOVEMBER 2: *Veracruz, Mexico*

I'm sad to report that Jeff's departure has become inevitable. This evening as we sat on our beds, he told me frankly that he felt he was wasting his time here. He sees no way that we can go back on the Gulf without disaster. "It's just too crazy out there. It's suicide!" he said.

As hard as it was for me to admit it, I knew in my heart that he was right – it *is* crazy out there; it may well *be* suicidal; it's certainly no place for a canoe.

"If there was any way I thought we could make it, any way at all," he told me, "I'd stay and help."

No matter how hard I tried, I couldn't dissuade him.

NOVEMBER 6: *Veracruz, Mexico*

This morning, with tears in our eyes, we said goodbye to Jeff, and he slipped quietly away in a taxi. From Veracruz airport he will fly to Mexico City, then on to Toronto and Winnipeg.

For the better part of the morning, Dana and I wandered around in semi-shock, barely able to accept that we were now on our own. Jeff had been such a part of it all, and already we missed him terribly. Any hope we had of continuing was now dashed, and I could feel myself sinking into a depression.

During the afternoon we moved into a dorm-style room with Gabby and his friend Juan Osorio of Bogotá, Colombia. The quarters will be somewhat close, but at least they will increase my obligation to work on my Spanish.

After supper, Dana and I went out for a little walk. As we came along the beach, we began talking about our predicament, and it occurred to me that if we were going to snap out of our funk we would have to give ourselves a new goal. Later, at the house, I said suddenly, "We're going to keep going, Dana. We're going to get a new paddler and keep going."

He looked at me curiously and said, "What if we can't get another paddler?"

"Could I convince you we could do it on our own?"

He gave me one of his patented smiles and said, "I'm willing to try if you are."

It was as if a crushing weight had been lifted from our backs. Even if the plan didn't come off, we could at least now look to the future with new hope.

As I lay in bed tonight, I was far less haunted by our defeat.

NOVEMBER 11: *Veracruz, Mexico*

The decision having been made, our challenge of the past week has been to find someone to take Jeff's place – not an easy task. We phoned an advertisement to our home newspaper and wrote to several canoeing friends, asking if they'd be interested, or if they knew of anyone who might be. During the past couple of days, however, we've begun to see a more immediate possibility. Gabby himself has become interested in our travels. He has been listening to our stories and has asked a thousand questions as we eat and shop and explore together. We've done our best not to misrepresent the dangers of the trip to him, but have admittedly tried to stir his enthusiasm. Last night at the table, I said to him, "If you were to come with us, Gabby, it would change your life." He agreed that it would, and if he can overcome his fears he just might join us – at least for a while. But those fears are reasonable. He's from an inland town, knows little of the sea, and has never been in a canoe. In spite of our uncertainties, we've set a definite date for the resumption of our trip from La Pesca: February 21st.

NOVEMBER 16: *Veracruz, Mexico*

A few days ago Gabby left for Aguascalientes to consult his parents about coming with us. While his friends have been advising him of the lunacy of such a venture, Dana and I have been plying him with sermons about the benefits of overcoming a challenge. At heart I'm somewhat nervous about his lack of experience, but am willing to take the gamble if he is. We've asked him to join us for the tough portion of the trip from the hated lagoon at La Pesca back along the coast to where we are now – some 400 miles.

Hovering above us is the possibility that the second attempt will be no easier than the first. Sometimes I look at the Gulf and have to work pretty hard to convince myself that it'll be any better in the late winter and

spring than it is now. In the meantime, we have three months to spend in
Veracruz. So far, I've been enjoying my swimming and snorkelling, and
Dana continues to refine his guitar skills. One night, he entertained at a
local cantina, playing five or six long classical pieces, all of which were
appreciated.

NOVEMBER 18: *Veracruz, Mexico*
Gabby returned this afternoon, at least partly committed to the trip. His
parents have given their okay, but he still has doubts about his abilities. I
spent an hour or so with him this evening, trying to convince him that
everything will be fine, that he will have to have faith in himself, and in
Dana and me.

I think we have our paddler.

DECEMBER 13: *Veracruz, Mexico*
Today the Gulf was like glass, and Dana and I looked out at it and pined.
We'd have no trouble paddling 40 or 50 miles on a day like this. It's good
to know that such days are possible, even if they're rare.

I can't seem to get enough of the sea and have been spending up to six
or seven hours a day snorkelling. I've wanted to do this all my life and am
truly in my glory. I'm ashamed to say so, but I'm finding that it beats
paddling. I spend most of my time in 15 to 25 feet of water, a couple of
hundred yards offshore, above the reef where the sea life thrives: shell-
fish, octopus, snails, plus a regular "who's who" of tropical fish. The other
day, on my 48th birthday, I got four pretty good-sized fish with my spear
gun and took them home for dinner.

This morning I made my best find to date, an ancient clay bottle in
perfect shape but heavily crusted with coral. I've also salvaged a number
of antique brass marine fittings, an ancient knife made of iron and bronze,
and, most intriguing, a two-ounce metal ingot which I think may be gold.
I've been told that my treasures are from old Spanish ships.

Our lives have become pleasantly routine, and I often feel I could stay
forever. Our biggest departure from the norm came three weeks ago when
Dana, Gabby, Juan and I took a bus 75 miles inland to Jalapa, then on to
the little village of Bandarilla from where we set out to climb Cofre de
Perote, an extinct volcano which, at 14,049 feet, is one of the highest
mountains in Mexico. It was an oppressively hard climb, mostly because
of the rain and cold that kept threatening to drive us back down the
snowcapped mountain. If the three-day climb had any positive angle
beyond sheer adventure, it was that we saw Gabby in action and now
realize he has stamina and is not a quitter. For a while on our first night

on the mountainside in the rain and cold, I was afraid we might lose him
to hypothermia, but he hung in there and finished the climb.

DECEMBER 25: *Veracruz, Mexico*
Christmas night, and our lonely thoughts are far away on the snowy Canadian prairie. It is the first time either of has spent Christmas away from
home, and we're not exactly celebrating under the circumstances. If the
house here weren't deserted we'd probably feel better, but the students
are gone for the holidays and are not expected back until the New Year.
We've at least had the pleasure of a pile of Christmas cards from friends
back home and those we've met along the route. They all assure us that
their thoughts and prayers are with us.

Last night our landlady, Señora Eloina Butt, made us a Christmas Eve
meal of chicken and tortillas, not our standard seasonal menu, but eaten
with gusto and gratitude. A little later, Browleo, the houseboy, went out
to the store and brought back rum and apple cider – *sidra* – and wanted us
to party with him, but we couldn't get into the mood. After a little cider,
we went to bed and waited in vain for the sound of reindeer on the roof.

A heavy north wind blew in this morning, stirring the Gulf into mountainous grey swells. The spray from the breakers is flying across the 8-foot
retaining wall along the beach, and pelting the houses 100 feet away. A
number of big freighters are anchored well out to sea, rising and falling
on the swells, sometimes dipping so low it seems their bows will never
rise again. Unwilling to challenge the storm, Dana and I spent the better
part of our day huddling in our room, he with his guitar, I immersed in
my Spanish dictionary.

Gabby is now a confirmed member of our crew.

JANUARY 19: *Veracruz, Mexico*
Our preparations for the trip are progressing, and today Gabby and I
refitted the aluminum tracks that secure our equipment boxes in the
bottom of the canoe. They had been jarred loose by the pounding of the
waves on the Gulf and needed to be fibreglassed back into place. We also
repaired the galvanized handles on the equipment boxes. They'd pretty
well rusted away but were quickly revitalized with a little sanding, a layer
of black vinyl tape, and an outer wrapping of nylon cord, for grip. Tomorrow, I'll apply vinyl tape to any of the canoe's wooden parts that have
suffered damage or lost their finish. We can't take a chance on the wood
rotting out.

We've moved our departure date forward and will now leave here on
February 14, hoping to be in La Pesca the following day. We'll leave

La Pesca on the 16th, and with any luck will be back in Veracruz by March 5 – a stretch of 18 days. That'll give us a big jump on the Gulf, and we'll hope to be around the Yucatán and out of Mexico by mid-May. Our plan is to leave 50 pounds of our equipment here, and pick it up when we get back. We still haven't figured out transportation to La Pesca.

Last week we met a man named Ruiz who knows a Mexican admiral stationed here in Veracruz. It occurred to us that the admiral, the *Almirante* as he's called here, might be able to give us a letter of safe passage down the coast. We got an appointment to see him, and on January 14, early in the morning, we showed up at the local naval base to meet him. He treated us with kindness and respect. When he had heard us out he told one of his men to write up a helpful letter, which was ultimately signed by the *Vice Almirante*, Jose Ponce de Léon Tirado.

All this planning is interfering with my underwater explorations, which have become a real passion with me. Diving gives me a physical and psychological high unlike any I've ever experienced.

FEBRUARY 7: *Veracruz, Mexico*
A week to go, and I'm beginning to get butterflies. It's like waiting for a race, except this time the feeling is not from excitement but from fear. Both Dana and I have been having nightmares about the sea.

This morning we bought some new tarp clips, some batteries for our radio and a few Mexican decals for the canoe. But so far we haven't been able to find other important items – for instance, a bailing pump, and liquid fibreglass for canoe repairs. The latter is an essential. When we returned from our shopping, we applied the new tarp clips and repaired our canoe cover. I managed to get its corroded zippers working again but don't expect they'll last long out on the Gulf.

FEBRUARY 13: *Veracruz, Mexico*
Some good news today: a friend of our landlady Eloina has a brother in Tampico who owns a truck and is willing to drive us from Tampico to La Pesca, if we can get our equipment and canoe to him. Tampico is about halfway from here to La Pesca, so our problem now is just to get to Tampico.

We've also learned that if we can make it from La Pesca back along the coast to Tampico by canoe we'll be able to travel south from Tampico to Túxpan, a distance of a hundred miles or more, on the inland waters of Laguna Tamihuahua.

We've done our final grocery shopping and are well stocked with eggs, cheese, ham, margarine, bread, onions, potatoes, chocolate, bananas. We simply couldn't count on the tiny stores in La Pesca.

The north wind has been blowing again, and the Gulf is in turmoil, which hasn't done anything for our confidence – but *"el norte"* has presumably made the lagoon navigable again.

A New Start with Gabby

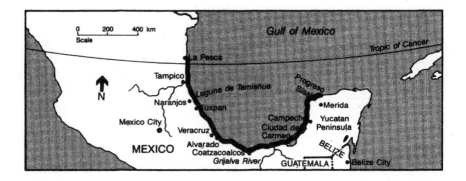

You haven't hitchhiked until you've done it with a 21-foot canoe and 700 pounds of food and equipment – not to mention a coterie of three grown men.

On the morning of the 14th, before dawn, we were picked up in a truck by Dana's 15-year-old friend, Alex, and driven to the outskirts of Veracruz, where we unloaded our gear and stuck our thumbs out. Two hours later we were picked up by a trucker from Naranjos to whom we paid a thousand pesos for what must have been the most uncomfortable ride in the history of hitchhiking. The three of us rode the back of the truck, huddling beneath the upturned canoe for over five hours to keep out of a continuous driving rain.

After four luckless hours by the road at Naranjos, we were forced to beg a restaurant owner to let us sleep on his floor overnight. Gabby did most of the persuading, earning his stripes as a member of our tattered little team.

A 500-peso ride the next morning took us into Tampico, where we looked

94

up our contact, Werner Haas, who by 2 a.m. had us in La Pesca.

By ten this morning we were loaded on our old friend Israel's jeep and heading down the sands towards the scene of October's agonies. We were determined to start from the spot where we'd broken our journey.

Luck seemed to be with us; the lagoon was full of water, and within minutes we were loaded and paddling. We hadn't gone a dozen strokes, however, when we heard the fateful scrape of mud and sand on the hull, and the canoe was as tightly aground as it had ever been. Dana's feet were still tender from our last bout with Laguna Madre, and he refused to leave the canoe. It was up to Gabby and me, and the two of us climbed into the water and hitched ourselves to the bow with towing ropes. With its decreased load, the canoe floated nicely, and we were off down the lagoon, feeling blessed merely to be moving.

By mid-afternoon, La Pesca was won. It was my fourth entry into this wearisome little town, but my first with any sense of satisfaction. I felt like a warrior who had defeated an ancient, dogged enemy.

FEBRUARY 20: *Punta Jerez, Mexico*

We are again travelling the high seas – and more successfully than ever. Which is not to say that our voyage since La Pesca has been easy. For the first day or so, we made desultory progress, part paddling, part towing our way down Laguna Morelos, a southern extension of Laguna Madre. When we could go no further, we portaged to the Gulf and were confronted by exactly what we feared most – bank upon bank of deafening 8-foot breakers. The noise alone was enough to make me wish we were back in Veracruz. Gabby was terrified. Every time I looked at him I was reminded that he had all of a single day's paddling experience. And here were waters that would have intimidated the toughest canoeists on earth.

For 24 hours we waited for a sea change, and yesterday morning awoke to a marginally calmer Gulf. We ate a death-row breakfast, loaded the canoe, and lined it up with its bow in the shallows pointing directly out to sea. Any deviation from the perpendicular, straight into the waves, could dump us.

We stood gripping the gunwales for ten minutes or more, waiting for the right moment. Just after 7 a.m., I screamed "Go!" and we were on our way – a comedy of both errors and terrors. Even before we'd got into the canoe, a wave swept along it, dumping gallons of water in through the cockpits. By the time we were aboard, the canoe was half full and was listing precariously as the weight of the water sloshed from side to side. "Turn back! Turn back!" hollered Dana.

"Shut up and paddle!" I screamed.

Gabby thrashed away valiantly in his terror.

By the time we were 200 feet offshore, the canoe was so full of water that our gunwales were dipping beneath the surface. Only the buoyancy of our equipment and the flotation chambers in the bow and stern were keeping us afloat. A canoe is never tippier than when it's full of water, and we were rolling badly. Every stroke was a balancing act, and only our forward motion stabilized us. We bulled our way through three last shore waves and into the rolling seas beyond. Out of the depths of my panic, I yelled, "Bail!"

"With what?" Gabby answered.

"With anything! With your lunch bottle!"

We carry our lunches in wide-necked plastic containers, and in no time Gabby had his open in his hands, but couldn't figure out what to do with his lunch. "Dump it!" I shouted, meaning that he should dump it on the canoe cover. Instead he gamely tossed it into the sea and began bailing frantically through the narrow zippered opening in front of him.

In half an hour, he had drained the canoe, and we were riding high. But everything was clearly not well with Gabby. The motion and excitement had got to him, and his face had gone from its normal healthy tan colour to a ghastly green. Suddenly a stream of vomit rocketed from his throat, and he began shaking and heaving. But never once did he stop paddling, although I urged him to take a rest. All day he shivered and rattled and retched, and all day he swung his aluminum Gruman paddle. I sympathized, but I was secretly thrilled by his perseverance – we had exactly the man we wanted! At about ten o'clock we surged across the Tropic of Cancer.

By the time we pulled into Barra del Tordo, it was late afternoon, and we had achieved 35 miles – some of them, I'm afraid, at poor Gabby's expense. Nonetheless, he was as happy as we were at our tremendous advance. If there was a downside to our arrival at Barra del Tordo, it was that I'd left my running shoes back up north on our launching beach. I can expect to be shoeless for some time, as my big feet are hard to fit in this land of smaller people.

Unlike yesterday's launch, today's was a masterpiece of simplicity – everything worked. Nine hours on the water gained us another 32 miles and, since landing, we've been congratulating ourselves on our progress. We're now a mere 21 miles from Tampico and the entrance to Laguna de Tamihuahua which will take us into a series of canals, then into Laguna Tampamachoco – in all, 100 miles of protected inland travel.

Gabby was healthier today, though still not entirely himself. But he

Two days before departure Don (left) and Dana Starkell check their supplies at home in Winnipeg.

Departure day. At sunrise on June 1, 1980, Don, Dana, and Jeff Starkell look like any ordinary family setting off on a little canoe trip on the Red River. In fact they will go more than half the distance around the world.

The 21-foot canoe Orellana *seen from above by its builder, Bill Brigden, as it heads south towards the American border.*

Don, Jeff, and Dana paddle up the Red River as they leave Grand Forks, North Dakota. (Grand Forks Herald)

After crossing the Continental Divide, the Starkells paddle with the current down the Minnesota, towards the Mississippi and New Orleans – and the Guinness Book of World Records *for the longest canoe trip ever.*

Under a broiling sun they head southwest of New Orleans along the Intracoastal Waterway near Morgan City, La., towards the Gulf of Mexico.

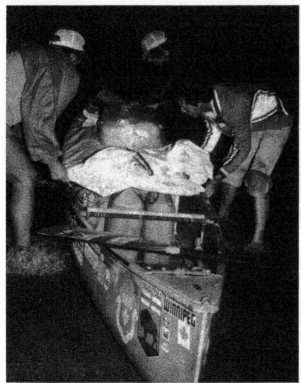

The pounding seas of the Gulf almost killed them all, and persuaded Jeff that to go on was suicide. When he returned to Canada their Mexican friend Gabby (right) helped them make it back to Veracruz. Here at dawn on March 7, 1981, he helps Don and Dana to set off again to fight the Gulf.

Two weeks later Dana looks out at the pounding surf near "the turbulent mouth of the Grijalva River", just beyond the southern bowl of the Gulf.

Always eager to practice his guitar Dana sends the music of Bach out among the coconut palms near the tip of the Yucatan.

More guitar practice, this time beyond Progreso on the Yucatan; desperate to avoid the wind-driven seas Don and Dana were soon to try ocean paddling at night which led to "six hours of torment."

Leaving Cancún, Mexico, towards the adventures in Central America that would make that part of the voyage "a nightmare." No photographs survived that section; Don and Dana barely survived.

After starving for almost 200 miles, surviving on the kindness of the local coast-dwellers, it was a relief for Don and Dana to be able to stock up on supplies in Colón, Panamá.

June 23, 1981. Safely ashore at Club Nautico, Colón, Panamá.

After over a year, Don and Dana had made it all the way to the Panama Canal. Here they pose beside the entrance and reflect on being refused permission to cross the canal to the Pacific on the grounds that Orellana was "not seaworthy."

has refused to be a damper on our spirits. The other day at Laguna Morelos he took us on a short hike and introduced us to the guayaba tree, which produces a yellowish, seedy fruit about the size of a crabapple. I ate half a dozen or more. He also showed us how to peel cactus leaves and retrieve the thin layer of core pulp, which is full of moisture and can be used as a source of water in an emergency.

We saw 20-odd dolphins today. They leap above the water in graceful arcs, like shiny grey water toys. We see them only when the weather is good and view them as well-omened friends.

FEBRUARY 24: on *Laguna de Tamihuahua*

Gabby is gaining strength and is more like a son to me every day. I'm making every attempt to treat him exactly as I treat Dana – no special favours but every respect. So far, the trip is working wonders for his self-confidence. It's not hurting our own confidence either.

We entered Laguna de Tamihuahua three days ago at the big city of Tampico, the centre of the Mexican oil industry. The first day out we were driven by tailwinds of up to 50 m.p.h., but the paddling since has been splendid. So, too, has the scenery; in the distance to our west are high purple mountains, at the base of which lies a vast apron of palms and tropical shrubs. The water supports a colourful assortment of hand-crafted wooden fishing boats, the biggest about 30 feet long. The fishermen take pride in their craft and almost invariably paint them in bright, horizontal stripes – partly for show, partly for identification.

The night before last, we camped by the tiny shack of a fisherman, who invited us to go oystering. The afternoon tide was out, and thousands of oysters were visible in the shallows. Many more clung to tree roots and shore reeds that had been submerged at high tide. We picked them like fruit – about 200 pounds, which our friend packed in burlap sacks.

The lagoon here is about 15 miles wide, but we've had no problem with cross winds or turbulence. Yesterday we spent a gruelling 12 hours on the water, gaining 42 miles, our longest advance since Texas. Gabby paddled like a veteran and staggered from the canoe, barely able to stand, when we landed. He has impressed me immensely, and I've told him that if we get to Veracruz, the aluminum paddle he's using will be his. We'll have to keep it with us as a spare for the rest of the trip, but I'll get it to him somehow.

Today, he cut the letters of the word Mexico from red vinyl tape and applied them to the handle of his paddle.

The miles fly by. A week ago at Tuxpán, we were told by fishermen that it would be insane to go on the Gulf right now, that we'd never be able to paddle it. But here we are, 116 miles later, and just 43 miles north of Veracruz. Much of our success has been in our improved launching and landing techniques. We haven't swamped once in four days – and on very high seas.

The first day out of Tuxpán, we launched easily, but by the time we were ready to land, eight hours later, we were battling 12-foot waves throwing up a formidable surf along shore. The only way we could even hope to get in was by using a variation of the landing technique that we worked out back at Washington Beach. Several hundred feet out, all three of us jumped into the water. Dana and Gabby took the bow gunwales and I took the stern, hoping my weight would act as a sea anchor and prevent the canoe from surfing or sliding off at an angle.

We successfully prevented any surfing, but did hit a snag: instead of carrying the canoe up and forward, the waves came right over the top of it, rolling down its length, flooding our open cockpits. By reaching up to keep them shut we were able to limit the intake of water, and made it safely to shore. It was the first time we'd come off heavy seas without swamping, and we've since refined our technique so that rough-water landings are no longer a trauma.

Our launchings, too, are improving, though Dana still takes an awful pounding in the bow as the shore breakers wash over him. Sometimes the waves hit him so hard the impact stops the canoe. He puts his head down for the plunge, like a football fullback driving into the line, but the waves straighten him right up and leave him gasping. He takes a few panic strokes and prepares for the next wave.

The open water, too, has given us some dicey moments. An occasional wave from the east is so threatening that we have to swing the canoe head-on into it, directly out to sea, to keep from being broadsided and tipped. It's all so strange to me as a paddler. I've never taken a canoe trip on which I couldn't say, "We'll do this today, we'll paddle so many miles to such and such a place." The Gulf tells us what *it* wants us to do – what it will allow us to do. It can chase us ashore pretty fast when it has a mind to. More and more I wonder how Dana and I will fare beyond Veracruz – and if we'll survive at all. I try to be optimistic, but am far from certain that the two of us will be able to handle the loaded canoe.

The last 100 miles have given us a gradual change of scenery. The waters are now a pretty blue-green, and the shores are thick with coconut palms, which have added generously to our food supply. The rocky cliffs we saw south of Tuxpán have given way to rich dark beaches, and a range of rugged mountains is now visible inland. For scenic oddities, it would be hard to beat what we saw the other night as we lay in our sleeping shells on the beach. As the darkness settled, the surf began to glow with a bright fluorescence that stretched as far as we could see in either direction. Row upon row of eerie walls of light rolled onto the beach. I've been told the light comes from a particular type of plankton or microscopic sea fungus.

The other day north of Nautla we landed near the villa of a young Irish-Mexican doctor, Roberto Martínez O'Hara, who urged us to stay with him for a few days and rest. We did accept the use of his shower and drank some of his tequila as we watched a televised soccer game with him in the evening. He told us he treats asthma sufferers with marijuana and asked us if we wanted some, but we politely refused.

Gabby continues to perform admirably, and the work is putting some real muscle on him. Dana and I are toughening up, too. We're all itchy for Veracruz, and won't fully relax until we see the high Spanish fortress of San Juan de Ulúa.

MARCH 5: *Veracruz, Mexico*

Sweet San Juan de Ulúa – there it was before us as we ploughed into Veracruz harbour late this morning. I shivered with excitement to see the beaches and waters and reefs where I'd spent so many pleasurable hours.

Even before landing we met a friend, Sr. Gerardo Sánchez, a venerable old citizen of Veracruz with whom I'd gone fishing a number of times during our stay here. We paddled up to him on his boat, *Iduna*, and he stared at us as if at a trio of ghosts. "*No creyó,*" he told us quietly – I don't believe it; I never thought I'd see you again.

We pulled ashore on the beach right in front of our old base at Eloina's, and were soon exulting in a loving welcome from our former landlady and housemates. Like Gerardo, they were shocked to see us. And who was among them? Gabby's parents! They had driven hundreds of miles from Aguascalientes to welcome him back. They beamed with pride at his accomplishment – and undoubtedly with relief at his safety. Gabby was about nine feet tall.

MARCH 6: *Veracruz, Mexico*

We slept the night on our old balcony at Eloina's, and today have spent all our time preparing for tomorrow's big launch. I bought a cheap 35-mm. Canon camera and will leave our damaged movie camera with Gabby. We've also decided to leave our tent, which is rotting, and our axe.

Ahead of us are 1,162 miles of Mexican coast, and we feel if we can beat Mexico, nothing will stop us. Once around the Yucatán, we'll be on the calmer Caribbean and home free. *If we can paddle the Gulf with two people.* That big if has been doing a pretty good dance on my skull as I sit here on the balcony writing, occasionally looking up into the glorious starlit sky.

MARCH 7: *north of Alvarado, Mexico*
Up at 5 a.m. and on the beach, nervous but ready to launch. Dear Gabby and Eloina had come down to see us off, and Gabby rolled up his pants and was into the water to help us with last-second adjustments. It was almost as if he were going to hop into the canoe and come with us – and didn't we wish he could! The final moments were intense, hugs all around, Eloina crying as she said her farewells.

We paddled away, petrified, at 6:30 a.m., taking numerous longing glances at the familiar sleeping city behind. Past the fishing boats in the harbour, past Isla Sacrificios and Punta Mocambo. For the first time in nearly 4,000 miles, there was no one between us in the canoe, and it felt very strange.

By 9:30, the waves had levelled, and we were making terrific progress through uncommonly light seas. If we'd wanted to, we could have paddled within 20 feet of shore. How long it would last we had no idea, but we were delirious with our success and intended to make the most of it.

We've had many emotional highs and lows, but few of the highs could top what we felt this afternoon as we slid ashore on a little sand beach just north of Alvarado. We had paddled 11 non-stop hours, and had come 36 miles. We'd hardly had time to congratulate ourselves when 20 or more people from some nearby shacks converged on us, awestruck at our presence. They were immediately at our canoe, touching it, pawing at our equipment, as if to confirm that it wasn't some sort of hallucination. An hour passed, and they showed no sign of retreating. If anything, they grew more curious as they stood around staring at our plates and mouths as we ate. At one point, I counted five transfixed faces gazing at me from no more than 24 inches away. They'd watch the food go on the fork, track it into my mouth, then watch my mouth as I chewed.

Finally we got them to leave, but only by lying down and pretending to be asleep.

MARCH 11: *Alvarado, Mexico*
Thirty-six miles the first day out; eight miles total during the next four days. Here we sit, stormbound at the sandy mouth of the Papoloapan River in Alvarado.

Our arrival four days ago was a nightmare. The seas were rough, and as we reached the jetty at the mouth of the river, the swells, which had been just manageable until then, were magnified by the action of the shallows, and by the current of the river which drains hundreds of square miles of tidal lagoon. At this point the tide was on its way out. Suddenly, a 15-foot wave rose to our left. In a fury of spray and confusion, it picked us up and flung us through the air, upside down, into the sea. My first concern was for Dana, but, on surfacing, I saw him beside the canoe about 15 feet away. Fortunately the canoe cover had stayed on, keeping our equipment in place. "Just keep cool!" I shouted. "Hang on, and the waves will carry us in!"

How wrong I was. Within seconds, we were being carried out to sea by the powerful current from the river. "Stay cool!" I kept calling, but privately I was beginning to panic, as the waves flipped us around. For the first time in my paddling career, there was nothing I could imagine doing to help myself or my crew – in that current swimming was impossible, and there was no way we could have paddled the canoe full of water. All the while, as we clung to the gunwales, this deadly current was carrying us steadily further from shore. We were certain the fishing boats at the mouth had seen us swamp, but none of them was on its way to help.

Further out we went, as I continued to call to Dana, urging him to be calm.

After 20 minutes of wild bobbing and drifting, we were a mile or more off shore (we had once been a mere hundred yards from the jetty). Just when I'd truly begun to fear the worst, we glimpsed a trawler, half a mile or so away, apparently coming toward us. We'd catch sight of it, then lose it again among the swells. Had someone seen us and relayed a message? All we could do was hope and pray. As the boat drew closer, we realized it had spotted us, and I uttered a silent hallelujah.

As it growled up to us, one of the fishermen aboard threw a strong line which I attached through our bow loop. After a minute of floundering and hesitation, the boat took off rather brusquely. But our canoe, with its heavy load of equipment and water, couldn't take the strain. "*Despacio!*" I screamed – "Slower!" But they couldn't hear me. Meanwhile, Dana was thrashing around, barely able to hold on to the stern. With every wave, the tow line went slack and jerked tight again, severely jarring both us and the canoe. "*Alto!*" I began yelling, "Stop!", but on they went. Slowly, I worked my way forward until, with the rope momentarily slack, I was able to grab a 4- or 5-foot section of it and pull it together. I would act as a cushion and absorb the shock with my arms. With each lurch I now imagined that my shoulders were going to be ripped apart. But I was determined to save the canoe, and, after repeated cries of "*Alto! Alto!*", I was able to get them to cut their diesels.

I undid the line. But, in my limited Spanish, and with all the confusion, I couldn't make them understand that we'd have to figure out a better way of getting ashore. For 15 minutes we yelled back and forth above the roar of the waves, until they must have thought we didn't want to be rescued.

Eventually, they sent down two ropes and we looped them around the canoe about 10 feet apart, in an attempt to winch the canoe onto the deck. But as the lines tightened, I could see the canoe beginning to buckle, and realized it was far too heavy for the measly support provided by the two ropes. Again, I started hollering, and didn't stop until the lines had been slackened.

At this point, one of the fishermen jumped into the water to help us. In no time he disappeared, and I was sure he'd gone down. I felt sick – here we'd caused a drowning over a mere canoe. Dana was now yelling, "*Tu hombre no es aquí! Tu hombre no es aquí!*" – "Your man is not here!" Then, as mysteriously as he'd disappeared, the guy rematerialized amid the waves and moved the ropes closer to the centre of the canoe. The weight was now better distributed. But as the winches creaked, I could see again that it wasn't going to work. Once more, I stopped them.

Eventually we removed the canoe cover and persuaded them to winch up our equipment one piece at a time. That accomplished, we flipped the canoe and had them raise it empty to the deck.

Half an hour later, we were sitting on a wharf, a mile or so up the Papoloapan River, in the heart of Alvarado. We'd lost a good deal of loose equipment, including one of the leather boots, which I'd just retrieved from storage in Veracruz. Again, I was without footwear. But *Orellana* had suffered more than we had. Her gunwales were broken; her aluminum fore bumper had been torn loose; and her hull had been badly scratched.

To add to our troubles, we were soon surrounded by dozens of onlookers, who gawked at us with insatiable curiosity. A police official appeared and demanded that we pay 500 pesos for entering port. I pretended not to understand, and he ordered me to follow him to the police station to talk to the chief. Documents in hand, I walked a quarter of a mile in bare feet and presented our letter of safe passage to a police captain who quickly released me.

By suppertime, our audience had become so large and annoying that we packed up and paddled across the river to the less populated shore.

Within minutes, dozens of new visitors had found us. Every move we made, every bite we ate, everything we said came under intense scrutiny.

Only when our last guest had drifted off late in the evening were we able to gain some peace. We moved our gear into a concrete structure that we'd been told was used for rendering shark oil. It certainly smelled the part, though at this point we couldn't have cared less. We sacked out on the concrete floor and were quickly asleep.

For two nights we toughed it out in the shark bunker, as the sea pounded the coast. But yesterday morning, unable to take our parade of gawking visitors any longer, we got into the canoe and moved to a rivermouth sand bar half a mile from the sea. Unfortunately, the sand bar is connected to land, and even here they found us by the hundreds. We were told that some of the children had walked miles just to lay eyes on us. Yesterday, I chose a responsible-looking kid named Tomás and gave him 50 pesos and a drawing of the shape of my foot. He beat it across the river on a water taxi and was back in half an hour with a pair of snappy Mexican sandals that had cost him 35 pesos, leaving 15 pesos for himself. He was happy, and so was I.

Another kid showed up this morning wearing the peaked hat I'd lost the other day a mile out on the Gulf. It was one of my favourites with its little Canadian flag, and I was delighted to see it, much cleaner than when I'd lost it. For a small reward, the kid reluctantly gave it up.

I've repaired *Orellana* and have been examining similar local craft. The fishermen in these parts use a variety of canoe-like wooden boats, one of which has a flat bottom and is similar to what the Louisiana Cajuns call a pirogue. Down here they call it a *piragua*. The smaller version of the same is called a *chalupa*. They call our canoe a *canoa*.

We've done what we can to clean up our gear, and now wait only for a break from the sea.

MARCH 23: *on the south coast of the Gulf of Mexico*
Many tough days of paddling since Alvarado, and again we are storm-bound on a little tidal flat near the turbulent mouth of the Grijalva River. We have worked our way around the southern bowl of the Gulf and are now heading pretty well due east towards the Yucatán Peninsula. We are two weeks ahead of schedule, and are ecstatic with our progress. The Yucatán will take us slowly back north along our last major stretch of the Gulf.

The big problem with travelling east is that during the morning hours, when we do most of our paddling, we get the formidable tropical sun directly in our eyes. We also get it reflected off the water and off the bright white skin of our canoe tarp. At the moment, our eyes are severely bloodshot from the squinting and strain. I tried sunglasses, but have lost two pairs into the drink during the past few days. Even when I can keep them on, the salt spray coats them, so that they need constant cleaning. I won't buy another pair. We're also without peaked sun hats, having lost ours during a hectic launch the other day. I've been wrapping a T-shirt around my head, and one day Dana wore his rain jacket with the hood up, in spite of the tremendous heat. Unfortunately we have no way of protecting our lips and noses, which are badly cracked and scabbed. Otherwise our hides are as brown as footballs. The natives know what to do – put on a sombrero and leave the sun to the *turistas*.

Other than sun, our greatest complaint is the chafing that our rear ends take from the canoe seats, which are woven of nylon seatbelt strapping. Both of us have large raw patches on each buttock. Our worst moments come when the salt water enters our cockpits and runs down over our thighs and hips, collecting in the seat fabric. The pain can be excruciating during a long day on the water.

On shore, the sandflies, or *chiquistas*, go to work on us, creating an itch pretty close to that of poison ivy. I tend to suffer more than Dana and have a number of festering bites on my ankles and between my fingers.

The land- and seascapes since Alvarado have been impressive: cliffs and mountains and an increasing variety of tropical vegetation – "lush" as the tourist brochures would have it. The beaches to the west were fouled with petroleum, but those of the past few days have been clean. Palms are everywhere, and I take particular satisfaction in the endless supply of coconuts. We always try to camp near a plantation, and recently learned that the finest treat of the coconut palm comes from the placenta-like nourishment that the parent coconut provides for the seedlings. When a mature unhusked coco finds suitable soil, it soon sinks roots and sends up rudimentary branches. In the earliest stages, a white spongy ball forms in the fluid cavity of the parent coconut; it feeds off the milk and the solid meat, and in turn feeds the developing shoots. Eventually, the fluid is gone, at which stage the spongy ball is delicious to eat, its texture like that of, say, condensed candy floss. I'm always happy to come across a seedling. Otherwise, we're happy with what we can get. The younger green cocos hold the most liquid and yield a soft jelly-like meat which makes an excellent dessert. The locals tell us that drinking the green ones is fine, but that too much milk from mature cocos, or too much of the meat, can cause the runs. I invariably eat and drink too much. We've even been filling our drinking bottles with the milk. On the average, between us, we'll consume 25 or 30 cocos a day.

Another of our natural treats is the fleshy red fruit that protrudes from the tops of tuna-cactus leaves. Gabby introduced us to it. When peeled and diced, the egg-sized fruits produce deep wine-coloured juice. They taste like strawberries, and we eat them with sugar from a bowl.

Occasionally we beg fish from the local fishermen – usually pompano or sierra. Unfortunately, Dana is allergic to most species and is unable to eat most of what we're given. I eat the rare ones, while he munches on canned sardines.

Dana has been going steadily at his guitar and is currently perfecting a piece called "Spanish Ballad". The music flows, and I call out "*Magnífico! Perfecto!*" The other day, as he practised, I took out my .22-calibre survival rifle and tried for an hour to hit some targets I'd set up 50 feet away. I adjusted the sights dozens of times, but couldn't hit a thing and used up a lot of pathetically weak Russian ammunition. I switched to good old Canadian Imperial, which was more powerful but no better for my aim. We've carried that rifle thousands of miles, oiled it and cleaned it, and it turns out to be useless. At least in my hands.

Our best news of the past few days is that the waters along the west side of the Yucatán are shallow for hundreds of yards off shore, which breaks up the swells before they get near the beach. The physical principle is that a wave breaks when it hits a depth of water equal to its own height. The further out the shallows, the sooner the waves break and lose their energy.

The other day, near Punta Buey, Dana met a beautiful black-haired señorita from the University of Mexico. He serenaded her on his guitar, and the two of them mooned over each other until sunset, when she left for home. Later that evening, in the dark, we had a long slow walk down the beach, and talked about our progress and the miles ahead, and our feelings about each other and all that we're experiencing. As I sit here writing, I can honestly say that our emotional state and cohesiveness have never been better. We are a fine tandem, Dana and I. The further we go, the more we want one thing, the same thing: to complete our trip.

MARCH 29: *on the Yucatán Peninsula, Mexico*
By the end of last week, our progress was being severely hampered by coastal currents and winds. As we worked our way into the southeast corner of the Gulf, we also hit a succession of *bocas* or river mouths which, like the mouth of the Papoloapan at Alvarado, created a fury of breakers

and turbulence. The problem arises because the river mouths deposit vast areas of silt, causing shallows which stir up the normal wave action. The powerful river currents add to our difficulties. I'm sure we'd have been grounded if we'd tried to come this way during the rainy months, when the rivers are at peak flow. The other day at the Río San Pedro y San Pablo, we went a good 6 miles out to sea to get around the *boca*, and used up well over two hours, plus a good deal of energy. At times like these, we're reminded that a two-man crew is really insufficient to our task. However, in an important way, our limitations bring us closer together and make us more determined to carry on. When we come off the water these days, we walk toward one another, embrace lovingly, and share a firm Mexican handshake.

A few days ago, as we made the gradual turn north up the Yucatán Peninsula, conditions changed. The west shore of the peninsula is well protected from the prevailing easterlies, and we knew we were in for some heady progress. By the time we reached Ciudad del Carmen, we were paddling calm, shallow waters.

Just north of Ciudad del Carmen, on Isla del Carmen, we found swarms of tourists, many of them Americans, sunning on the fine white sands. Having seen so many dark fishermen over the past weeks, and with our own skins so tanned, it came as a bit of a shock to see these sickly pale (or sickly bright red) gringos. We broke our paddling to talk here and there, and I'm afraid most of the tourists saw us as unadulterated nut cases. One pale young man in a cabaña set pointed at our canoe and said, "You mean to say you came all the way from Canadder in that thing?"

"All the way," I told him.

"On the ocean, too!" he said.

"Right around the Gulf."

"In *that* thing!" he said again.

If anything, the tourists are more amazed by our story than the fishermen. The latter are unfamiliar with maps and have no real reference for distance beyond their own shores. The North Americans know how far we've travelled – if they believe us.

Today, for the first time, we found ourselves above acres of red coral shining up from the sea floor. There are fish everywhere, including good-sized stingrays and giant rays. The other day, from about 200 feet ahead, we saw a smallish black fin coming toward us along the surface. At first we thought it was a shark but that it was too small to do us any harm, so we didn't adjust our course. But as it slipped by within 3 feet of the canoe we realized it was a pilot whale, and that it was easily 20 feet long – and at least 4 feet across the back. As it disappeared behind us, Dana turned to me with a big grin on his face. All I could do was grin back in recognition.

The water around here is a pale turquoise and exceptionally clean. At times we can see 60 feet into its depths. The beaches are pretty close to pure white. Although we no longer have the sun in our eyes, the heat is increasingly intense, and we've taken to getting on the water before dawn. Pre-dawn and night paddling are a tradition of the Canadian voyageurs. Go when the going is best.

APRIL 2: *at Isla Arena, Mexico*

Our lush shores disappeared north of Champotón, and the shoreline since has been as rocky and rugged as the set of a badlands Western. Several times we've spotted marine iguanas among the rocks. They're grey, about two feet long, and are truly not among the prettier creatures on the planet. They sit there motionless, staring at us as we slide by. Yesterday, we saw our first monkeys, tiny little things, which promptly went and hid in some dead trees. I'm surprised they can live around here with virtually no vegetation.

The day before yesterday, we reached the grand old city of Campeche, founded by Francisco de Montejo in 1540. The city is strung out along miles of steep rock, on either side of a massive fortress. We looked for a safe place to camp and eventually pulled ashore in front of a luxurious house surrounded by protective walls. We did some smooth talking (which isn't easy when you hardly know the language) and were granted permission by the owners to camp in the yard.

We walked into the city and went from store to store trying to buy glue to mend Dana's guitar bridge. We didn't know the Spanish word for glue, and it took us an hour and some imaginative miming to get what we wanted. We stocked up on food, enough we hope to get us all the way to Progreso on the northwest extremity of the peninsula.

During the evening we got talking to a local man who told us that the *Presidente* of the *Estados Unidos* had been shot. We understood at first that President Reagan had been killed, but later discovered he'd merely been injured. It's only these major items of news that ever catch up with us. Otherwise, the comings and goings of the English-speaking world are a mystery. We see no English-language newspapers, and our radio has been moody at best since its salt dunkings. If we baby it a bit, it will generally spit out a few words of crackled Spanish, but nothing halfway intelligible.

We left Campeche early yesterday morning and were soon in trouble, as the water got so shallow we had to zigzag merely to avoid getting grounded. The shallows extended at least half a mile offshore, and we spent most of our day poling our way through a foot or so of water.

Ten hours of this brought us to Isla de Piedras, the Island of Stones, where we came across an impoverished little fishing community of twelve men and a female cook – Mayan Indians. Their shelter was a bleak line of shacks along the back of the beach. In the shallows they had nine small sharks thrashing around on a stringer. We had no trouble making friends with them and were soon sharing their tortillas, cooked on a bit of flat steel over a shore fire. We were low on stove gas, and they happily gave us a quart of outboard fuel, so that we could do some cooking on our own.

Later, under the stars, we sat with them around a beach fire, talking and laughing, enjoying the camaraderie. They told their stories, and we told ours, doing our best to keep things as simple as possible. We told them about Canada, and they expressed shock to learn that we have Indian tribes up there. But when we told them that our rivers turn to ice three feet thick in winter, they were really shaken. They know well what ice is, as they buy it in Campeche for packing their fish. At one point I made a reference to the Big Dipper, which was bright overhead. They didn't seem to understand, so I pointed at each of its stars and counted, "*un, dos, tres,*" etc. – "*Que es?*" What's that? They looked at me as if I weren't too bright and said, "*Siete Marías.*" Seven Marys.

Like everyone down here, rich or poor, these people are strict Roman Catholics. Even their little shacks are festooned with crucifixes and pictures of the Mother and Child. I haven't been the best of believers over the years, but right now I'm glad to be among Christians, with their generosity and warmth.

As the night grew late and the fire turned to embers, we fell silent. What a pleasure it was to look around the circle into the serene faces of those Indians. One by one, they got up and slipped away, a couple of them returning to bring us a bedtime fruit drink and a coal-oil lantern to give us a light through the night. Instead of going to bed, however, all of them now headed for their fishing boats for a night on the Gulf.

By 4 a.m., we were up, to find our friends lying sleeping on the beach or in hammocks. We launched quietly in the darkness, and again experienced the fluorescent waters we'd first seen north of Veracruz. In the glassy calm, each of our strokes threw up a little explosion of fireworks, which remained on the water for several seconds. Occasionally, we scared up a fish, and it, too, would leave a comet trail of light as it darted away.

Later in the morning, we ran into more shallows, except that today's were reedy and fouled with endless mud bars. It gradually became clear that we were paddling in an immense coastal swamp. By noon we'd seen our first mangrove trees. The tangled roots sit above the water at low tide and often seem to be anchored in coral. These shrubby trees grow right down to the shore, in fact *are* the shore in places. Their branches send long tubes into the water, for nourishment and support. From a purely practical point of view, we don't like them, as they prevent us getting to land. In the broader equation, they make a beautiful shoreline.

APRIL 4: *Sisal, Mexico*

As we round onto the northern part of the peninsula, the winds are giving us fits. So much so that for a while yesterday we were not only slowed or stopped but were actually pushed backwards. Three days in a row the wind has come up suddenly out of the northeast just after 1 p.m. Today we were looking for it, and, sure enough, about 1:30, our slight tailwind dropped, and the air went ghostly still. Dana stopped paddling, turned to me and said, "Can you feel it?" Indeed I could. Within seconds, there was a noticeable change of pressure and a fresh scent in the air. Then came a slight wisp of breeze from the northeast – the big blow had started. These particular winds are called *brisas*, and we take them as a grim omen of what the trade winds are going to do to us when we swing due east beyond Progreso. We could sure use Jeff or Gabby in that big empty second seat.

We're seeing more greenery and palms again, and more tourists. In fact, this part of the Yucatán seems to be a kind of playground for affluent Mexicans; there are dozens of them on the beaches. There's also an increasing number of well-built beach houses among the regular array of hovels and fishing shacks.

I'm learning to love the skies. Often I lie on my back in the open at night, watching the galaxy at work. The North Star is the hub of it, hanging motionless in space as the stars and planets rotate around it like a giant roulette wheel. I understand it so much better than I used to, and am regularly reminded of the old cultures with their intricate knowledge of the heavens. The moon is our practical guide to the tides and sometimes a source of light during our pre-dawn paddles. Our highest tides come with the full and new moons, our lowest halfway between. We also see plenty of man's galactic work, the satellites coming and going as regularly as jet planes. Unlike stars, they move in straight lines, some emitting a continuous glow, others blinking like strobes as they tumble through space.

On nights when I can't sleep, I lie there watching it all happen, contemplating the mysteries. Other nights, Dana and I will get talking about the many new friends who've helped us on our way, or the old friends back home. They are with us constantly.

Out of Mexico

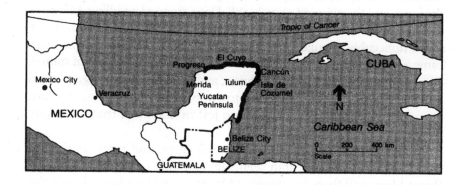

APRIL 7: *at Progreso, Mexico*

We reached Progreso two days ago, and have been unable to move since, because of the punishing winds.

Within minutes of our arrival, a pleasant middle-aged woman, Señora Gladys Marrufo, appeared beside us on the beach among the many vacationers, and gave us a heaping salad plate and a couple of icy Pepsis. She was leaving the following day for her home in Mérida, but invited us to make camp in the veranda of a nearby beach house she was occupying. So here we've sat since, in relative comfort, with far more time than we need to shop and write and kibitz with the locals. The only thing we can't do is what we really want to do: paddle.

Yesterday at noon, Sra. Gladys again brought us a fine Mexican meal: roast beef, rice, black beans, tomatoes, and radishes. Dana and I had just eaten a pile of tortillas from a local stand and were stuffed to bloating. So, after thanking our host, we quietly slipped the food under cover, to be enjoyed at suppertime. An hour or so later, Sra. Gladys left for Mérida.

No sooner had she gone than a couple of men, also from Mérida, showed up and moved into the cottage – they told us they'd rented it. They were a doctor and an engineer, and were none too happy to see a couple of Robinson Crusoes occupying their veranda. But when I'd explained our situation, their attitudes did a turnabout, and they couldn't do enough for us: beer, food, anything we wanted. All afternoon it went on. At one point, the doctor proclaimed proudly, "Soy Mayan," "I'm a Mayan," and he said a few words of his native language to prove it. They only stayed until evening, but before they left, the doctor pressed a 1000-peso note into my palm and told us to have a good meal when we got to Cancún.

Today on the beach, I met a little boy who had enormous warts on his feet. He told me they'd been there for two years, and it was easy to see how much he hated them. I remembered treating Dana for warts many years ago and thought I just might have some of the treatment, Compound W, in my old medicine box. I looked, and, sure enough, there it was. I carefully painted the boy's warts, which were truly ugly, and watched them turn white as the compound dried. I gave him our little bottle and told him over and over how to apply the stuff and how often. If he follows directions, his warts will be gone in two or three weeks. It gave me a real kick to see him walk away with a big smile on his face, clutching his precious bottle.

Back on the Mississippi at Memphis, which now seems like ten years ago, I bought Jeff and Dana new Nike running shoes. There is now nothing left of Dana's but worn soles and a few strands of greying tattered canvas. Nonetheless, he wears them proudly, and everywhere he goes people comment on their astonishing condition. In a strange way, they seem to have become a talisman for him. Yesterday he left them on the beach, and when he returned half an hour later, they were gone, which threw him into distress. He ran around looking everywhere, and finally located them neatly wrapped in a plastic bag in a nearby trash can. Someone had apparently mistaken them for castoffs and, with the integrity of the beach in mind, had discarded them. Dana quickly laced them on to prevent another mistake.

Last night as we lay on our veranda two human shapes, a man and a boy, appeared out of the darkness. Dana recognized them as the proprietors of the shop where he'd bought tortillas earlier in the day. They'd brought Dana a present, a new pair of white Converse basketball shoes. In the glow of the flashlight, he tried them on, and they fit perfectly.

Later as we lay trying to sleep, Dana said quietly, "Why is it that some people are so kind?"

I thought for a few seconds and said, "Maybe it's because of the way you've treated them."

After a longish silence he said, "How can you repay them?"

"By passing on their kindness," I said, and there was no more conversation.

Many people don't understand our trip and seem to feel that we're wasting two good years of our lives. But when I consider such things as the wonderful education Dana's getting, I privately rejoice that we're here. What's even more satisfying is that Dana understands and appreciates it all.

Before I put my pen down, I must mention one more thing, an important thing: we have discovered mangoes. We were given some today, fresh from the tree. What a treat they are! I'm reminded of Roberto, whom we met in Veracruz. Every time he saw a woman, this very macho Mexican would shout, "*Mucho bueno sabor!* – "Very fine flavour!" That's what we think of mangoes – *mucho bueno sabor!*

APRIL 13: *east of Lagartos, Mexico*
We got clear of Progreso on the 8th, but on the first day out advanced only 10 miles into the wind. We spent the better part of our time hiding behind windbreaks on shore, to avoid being sandblasted to death.

We were getting severely frustrated and needed a new plan. So that evening we decided to try a night paddle while the winds were down. We've been out paddling in the darkness before dawn, but always with the knowledge that the sun would be up in an hour to show us our route. This was going to be different.

At about 2 a.m., we slid into the water and out to sea. Our only real guidance came from the stars and the direction of the waves. The trouble was that, in the dark, we couldn't tell a dangerous wave from a harmless one, and by the middle of the night we were paranoid about every black wave that came toward us. One would roll gently beneath the canoe, the next would smack us broadside and have us scrambling to keep our balance. By the time the wind drove us from the seas at about 8:30 a.m., we had come a creditable 20 miles and felt like conquerors.

It seems that our last miles on the Gulf will be won only if we can gather all our fighting resources and continue to outwit these phenomenal winds. So last night we went back out at 11 p.m. By 2 a.m., we had paddled seven miles under ideal conditions and were well past Yalcubul lighthouse. Then the moon went down, throwing our world into impenetrable darkness. I couldn't even see Dana's outline ahead of me in the canoe.

We had intended to paddle until daylight, but now, in our blindness, we would happily have settled for a safe landing. But we knew that the coast beyond Yalcubul was an unbroken line of high cliffs offering no welcome to the sightless paddler.

We had had only four hours of sleep back on the beach, and by 4 a.m. we'd grown so weary we were dozing off as we paddled. I'd drift off, awakening abruptly to Dana's sharp rebukes – "Do you wanta die? Do you wanta kill us both?" If only we'd had something to focus on, some headland or light. It wasn't long before both of us were in a semi-coma, thoroughly disoriented, and thoroughly lost.

At about 5 a.m., there was a bright flash of light in front of me, and a wall of palms emerged from the sea; I had begun to hallucinate. I now saw rock cliffs, then palms again. At one point, unable to stand it, I laid my head back on the stern deck, but was soon jolted upright by Dana's frenzied shouting. Back and forth we zigzagged – asleep, awake, asleep again.

After six hours of torment, the first hint of dawn appeared ahead. To our amazement, we were still moving east. I could see the shape of the guitar on the canoe deck, then the colour of Dana's shirt. By sunrise, we had gained new energy, and pushed on, now hoping only to get past the cliffs before the daytime winds forced us off the sea.

By the time we were safely ashore, it was 11 a.m., and we had been on the sea for 12 hours. We had come 38 miles, and our muscles and emotions were in pretty rough shape. So, too, are my hindquarters, which are rawer and more painful than ever. At about noon, I was carefully applying seven Band-Aids to the deepest of my abrasions, which won't scab over with the constant salt and friction. Dana's rump, too, is killing him, but he doesn't want Band-Aids on it, and I can't say that I blame him. For myself, I couldn't take the open sores any more.

For most of the day we lay around in a state of low-key anxiety, unable to stay awake, unable to sleep properly. We knew we couldn't take another night like the last one, but we were also more determined than ever to get over this last stretch of the Gulf. Another 100 miles will put us in Cancún, our gateway to the Caribbean; 400 miles will take us out of Mexico entirely and into Belize, our fourth country.

APRIL 16: *near El Cuyo, Mexico*

We are back to day paddling, though not really by choice. The night before last, we had our canoe dressed up and sitting with its bow in the shallows ready to go around midnight. But as the night wore on, it became clear we weren't going to get the weather break we needed to launch. We slept fitfully, and just after dawn the wind was still strong. Dana woke up and said, "Let's do three or four miles before it gets any stronger."

This sort of initiative has been rare from Dana – he's usually so cautious – and I wasn't about to pass up the chance at a few miles. Without eating breakfast, we ploughed into the breakers, and by just past noon had covered 17 miles, every foot of which was gained with stupefying effort. We could barely take ten strokes without having to swing out to sea to avoid taking a giant wave broadside. One wave stood us right up on our stern, so that Dana was nearly 20 feet above me before he came crashing down. Time and again, he took powerful breakers in the chest and face.

We had another go this morning, but by 8 a.m. the seas were knocking us around so badly that we had to get off the water.

Our skills are one thing, our tenacity another, our faith another – but I'm constantly amazed and dismayed by the amount of unadulterated luck that has affected our survival. Almost every day, we run into some appalling new circumstance that would seem to have the potential to finish us. *But we always scrape through.* This truly makes me believe that no one could ever duplicate our trip (I'd certainly never try it again myself); they could have our equipment and planning and willpower, they could have our faith and muscles and endurance, but it's impossible to believe that anybody could ever again have our luck.

The best news at the moment is that eight more miles on these horrible seas will put us behind Isla Holbox, the first of a chain of islands forming the north boundary of Laguna Yalahua, which should offer us pretty good shelter all the way to Cancún. The water is starting to show some green, and we dare to think it's because we're so close to the Caribbean.

This afternoon, we walked a mile down the beach to a little coconut plantation. Most of the trees were pretty well dried up and stripped of fruit. We eventually found one decent palm, and Dana scrambled up it with the machete and started lopping off coconuts. As I waited, I spotted a couple of Mexican marines coming towards us in their dark blue uniforms and helmets. Each of them carried an automatic rifle and bayonet. It occurred to me that they were probably connected to the Coast Guard plane that had made a number of passes over us yesterday.

"Dana," I said softly, "we have company."

"What should I do?" he said.

"Keep on cutting – don't look guilty."

By the time they got to us, we had 15 coconuts on the ground. I smiled broadly and began telling them our story, as Dana slid down the tree. I emphasized that we were friends of the admiral at Veracruz. It was almost as if they knew about us, because they were quickly satisfied and showed no inclination to return to the canoe with us and check our documents. What they did want was a few drinking cocos, and we gladly obliged them, as it was a blistering afternoon. They carefully chose the five they wanted, dug into them with their bayonets, and drained them on the spot.

We carried our ten back to the canoe and opened them to find that only two of them were any good. Those marine bandits, with their keen eye for a good coco, had taken our best.

APRIL 19: *on Laguna Yalahua, Mexico*

We had a good day on Laguna Yalahua on the 17th and were expecting it to lead us tranquilly and triumphally into the Caribbean yesterday. But the lagoon had other ideas, and by 8 in the morning it had not only denied us the Caribbean but efficiently trapped us in what was surely the dirtiest circumstance of my canoeing career. As we headed southeast around the northern corner of the Yucatán, the water gradually decreased in depth until we were barely moving through 6-inch shallows of muskeg-like marsh.

When the depth reached 3 or 4 inches I jumped confidently into the water to do a little towing. But instead of landing on my feet I broke through the apparent floor of the lagoon and instantly was up to my arm-pits in slime – not to mention shock. What we'd thought was the bottom was nothing more than a fragile floating layer of tangled roots and lagoon debris. I laboriously dragged myself free of the suction and hoisted myself, stinking, back into the canoe.

Dana refused to enter the lagoon, as he still has open sores from our struggle months ago at La Pesca. So, after long deliberation, I propped myself on the stern of the canoe, supporting most of my weight with my arms, and did my best to push against the false bottom of the lagoon with my feet. Half an hour of this netted us 100 yards but left me cursing with fatigue.

Eventually I discovered that if I entered the water cautiously and crawled around on all fours, as if I were on very thin ice, my weight was well enough distributed that the false bottom would support me. I could move 10 or 15 yards at a stretch without breaking through. So for the next half hour I crawled along crablike at the stern, pushing and grunting for all I was worth. Dana poled hard in the bow.

This, too, soon became too much for me, and I crawled back into the canoe, dripping muck. At this point, the sun was beginning to roast us, and we had no idea how far we were from navigable water. I was despondent. The only options we could see were to carry on or to go miles back along the lagoon and out around the headlands to the sea. We might have gone to shore, but the borders of the lagoon were little more than a tangled mass of mangrove roots and muck. And they were hundreds of yards away.

I now tried lying belly down on the stern deck of the canoe, head forward, and kicking into the muck with my legs, which were dangling behind. In effect, I was an outboard motor, and we were soon skidding across the swamp at our best pace yet. But the effort was stupefying – I could go barely two minutes without collapsing in a puddle of sweat.

Three and a half hours of this took us into marginally deeper water, then quite suddenly into crystalline water some 4 feet deep. In spite of my weariness, I was quickly up onto my stern seat and paddling jubilantly. But it wasn't long before we were again in shallow water, then cut off completely by an impassable swampy landmass. Our only way out was to double back and try to escape through the mangroves to the sea.

We broke through a good mile of mangrove swamp and, as we emerged, the Caribbean appeared before us, as blue and calm as any body of water we could have hoped for. But what amazed us, as we paddled on to the ocean, was that it seemed to extend out for miles at no more than a foot or two of depth. We swung the canoe south, looking for anything resembling a camping spot. We had been on the water for 10 hours. But mile after mile of paddling showed us nothing but more mangroves and swamp.

By 8:30 p.m., our world was dark. We were soon grounded in six inches of water half a mile from the thoroughly uninviting shoreline. Resigned to a night in the canoe, we poled a few yards to a tiny mangrove plant that was growing out here on its own. Using a half-rotted shoelace, I tied us up.

With great care, we laid our foam mattress across our equipment boxes and lay down beside one another on top of the canoe. The only way to keep from rolling off was to snuggle up front to back and hold on tight.

There we lay, one peaceful pea, one peaceful pod, hoping that tomorrow would bring us better luck.

APRIL 21: *Cancún, Mexico*
The last miles into Cancún were a medley of ideal conditions: gentle seas, sugar-white sands, radiant turquoise waters.

As we paddled in along the waterfront, past the rows of hotels, we raised the flag for the first time since Texas. How proud we were, with our tarp and our flag and our bright orange canoe glistening in the sunshine. We beached the canoe in front of the elegant Camino Real Hotel.

We immediately took a bus from the tourist area into Cancún City to buy food. But as hard as we tried to obtain real groceries – rice and bananas and canned goods – all we could find were tourist treats at inflated prices. Someone told us to try Puerto Juárez, a more workaday town, which we'd passed in the canoe on the way in.

We went there by taxi and, an hour later, were staggering back to the Camino Real with 1,400 pesos' worth of groceries – enough, I hope, to get us all the way to Belize City, two weeks down the line. Except for Tulum, the coast between here and Belize City is pretty well deserted, which will make groceries hard to come by.

We spent the rest of the afternoon beside the canoe, chatting with dozens of curious tourists: from France, from Germany, Cuba, the U.S., Venezuela. Many of them took photos of us, sometimes posed with their friends and families. We lapped it up like puppies.

We slept peacefully on the beach and and were up early this morning, rousting around, swimming, reading the English newspapers. I was saddened to learn that Joe Louis the boxer had died. He was a boyhood hero of mine and a fine man.

During the afternoon, I walked out to Punta Cancún and for the first time saw the unprotected waters of the Caribbean. What we'd seen the day before was sheltered by islands and reefs, and was no real indicator of what we'd have to face further south. As I looked over the endless stretch of blue, my feelings were much like those I'd had on first seeing the Gulf back in Texas: smallness, aloneness, and outright fear. The waters here are deeper than any we've paddled, and will be nearly 900 fathoms by the time we reach Belize. The waves don't break; they just swell until they crash ashore. And they were swelling and crashing mightily this afternoon.

APRIL 25: *in the Cozumel Channel, Mexico*

Today we should never have been on the water. For eight hours, we survived 15-foot peaked waves, each one threatening to throw us into the sea, and ultimately against the high craggy rocks of the shoreline. Our fear was heightened by the presence of three wrecked pleasure boats at intervals along our route. We eventually gained land at a coral-ringed lagoon, but only by surfing in dangerously over a hundred feet of reef. Dana estimated that we'd cleared it by about eight inches.

APRIL 26: *in the Cozumel Channel, Mexico*
We are now 80 miles south of Cancún, and our canoe sits on the beach in front of us in tatters – 13 fractures and holes. We have survived the seas, if barely, but have not survived the treacherous coral reefs. This morning as we left the lagoon where we'd camped, we capsized on the same reef that we'd barely cleared yesterday coming in. There was no great damage, except that our equipment was soaked and our feet were pierced by sea-urchin spines.

Undeterred, we paddled south and were soon stroking along within 50 yards of another reef. Dana warned me several times that we were too close to it, but I told him not to worry. "Just keep paddling." Without warning, a massive wave rose to our left, bounced off the sea floor, and came at us like a train. Dana screamed the alarm, and I tried to swing the canoe to meet the wave. I managed two strokes, and the 15-footer hit us broadside, spilling us into the sea. Again we were scrambling to get out of our watery cockpits. Any delay and we'd be on the deadly coral of the reef.

We gained control, but with the canoe swamped we had no choice but to swim it over the reef to shore. As we worked our way in, we could see jagged coral protruding from the troughs of the waves. We edged up to it, hoping to pick up a swell that would wash us safely over it and into the bay beyond.

We picked up our wave, surfed in, and seemed almost clear of the reef when the wave turned suddenly to froth beneath us. We came crashing down on the coral, and our poor *Orellana* buckled and groaned. Dana and I found our footing and did everything we could to free the canoe. But with its weight of water it was too heavy to manoeuvre. For 15 minutes we struggled to empty it and free it, each of us hollering with pain as our bare feet came down on the countless spiky sea urchins that inhabit the reef. But each new wave countered anything we were able to achieve and drove the canoe harder onto its bed of nails. How it crunched and groaned, and how I suffered with it!

When we'd all but given up and were simply standing on the reef beside the canoe, bemoaning our fate, another massive wave appeared behind us, lifted the canoe and tossed it into the tranquil waters inside the reef. We went with it.

As we unloaded ashore, I was misguidedly hopeful that we'd only been badly scratched. But as the equipment came out, the tale unfolded. Each time we removed a box, Dana would gasp, "There's a hole! There's another hole!"

In my optimism, I kept insisting they were only cracks. But with the canoe empty, I couldn't deny the evidence: 13 punctures and serious fractures, one of them nearly 20 inches long. I'd never seen such a badly beaten hull. Nearly 11 months on the water, 4,800 miles, with no real damage; and now 13 holes in 15 minutes on the reef.

The challenge now was to make repairs, and I wasn't sure we had enough patching material. For hours I worked at it, straining my creativity to cut *exactly* the amount of fibreglass cloth needed for each mend. Any excess, and what little cloth we had would not go around. Never in my worst dreams had I imagined needing more than 20 or 30 square inches at one time.

Eventually I mixed our small supply of Mexican resin with hardening catalyst and applied it to the patches of cloth. The completed job was a mess. And no matter what I did, I couldn't get the resin to harden. Normally, it takes no more than a few minutes, but after several hours in the sun, the present batch was still soft. I babied it and cursed it and ranted at it. Dana sat quietly by, the anxieties of the day etched deeply on his face.

By suppertime, the resin had begun to stiffen, and we decided to test the work. I was afraid to look as we lowered the canoe into the water. The patches held. But then a puddle appeared in a spot I'd overlooked. Quickly I got the canoe back on the beach. With our last shred of material, I patched the fourteenth hole, and we left the canoe to dry for the night.

Whether we could get back over the reef in the morning without tearing my work to bits, I had no idea.

During the afternoon, Dana had grown increasingly moody. By early evening, he was thoroughly demoralized about our prospects. Several times, he abused me for my lack of caution. "The way you barrel ahead," he said at one point, "I'm starting to think this trip means more to you than our stinking lives."

As the evening wore on, I tried to cheer him up. I reminded him that on a journey this long, things were bound to fall apart from time to time.

"I know," he said, "but every day?"

"No," I said, "not every day." I had to admit, however, that things had gone badly since Cancún. The 20-foot waves of the Caribbean were no place for a canoe.

As we lay under the stars in our sleeping shells, I said, "If we're going to come out of this, Dana, we're going to have to get our spirits back up." I raised myself on my elbow and looked at him. "Both of us," I said. "I can't do it alone. I need your support."

I lay there hoping for some positive response, but it didn't come.

APRIL 29: *Ubero, Mexico*
If a graph were plotted of our emotional energy during the past few months, it would almost certainly suggest the ups and downs of a seriously afflicted psychotic. Outrageous peaks and valleys, with few plateaus in between.

When we got up the morning after our disaster, the sea was calm, and our spirits were high at the thought of reaching Tulum. We paddled off under near ideal conditions, and without a word about the previous day. Our chief concern was the patches – would they hold? Throughout the morning, I kept peeking beneath the tarp to see if there were any leaks. There weren't.

By 8:30 a.m., we had reached Tulum, and in no time were crawling over the Mayan ruins for which the city is famous. The great stone structures are officially closed to the public until 9:30 a.m., but because we came from the sea we were not blocked by the fences that prevent entry from land. We merely climbed up the rocky bank and for nearly an hour had the whole grand place to ourselves: the massive watch tower, the *castillo*, the temple of frescoes with its depictions of Mayan life and mythology. The ruins are said to be some 1500 years old, and encompass 56 structures in all.

As Dana wandered on his own, I climbed the *castillo* and walked along a narrow ledge that looks out over the Caribbean. I stood there marvelling at the view, which included perhaps a hundred square miles of green and turquoise water, as well as many miles of beaches and palms. Having arrived here by our ancient method of travel, and having suffered a near-mythic array of tests and tortures, we seem to feel a particular affinity for this place and for the ancient Mayans who built it. As I stood on top of the wall, I swear I could feel a curious energy restoring something lost within me. I felt renewed, potent, optimistic. What a high!

By this time, the official gates were about to open (busloads of sightseers were already lined up), and Dana and I were anxious to get back on the sea to make the most of our calm weather. We scrambled back down the bank and paddled off, feeling richly blessed by our ancient absent hosts.

Our only setback that morning came several miles down the coast when Dana realized he'd left his new Converse basketball shoes on a log beneath the ruins. Ah well, a little gift for the gods.

The two days since Tulum have shown us nothing but excellent paddling conditions. The sea life is our constant entertainment: sharks, giant rays, starfish, sea turtles, fish of all colours. This afternoon we were followed into a bay by no fewer than seven 4-foot barracudas. We see them frequently; they dart at our canoe, as if attacking, then veer off, undoubtedly daunted by the size of their big orange prey. This morning we saw what we think was a stork's nest – a massive pad of interwoven sticks and reeds – high atop the Herrero lighthouse.

This afternoon we had a stern reminder of who and where we are: as we came along the coast, we saw two severely mangled freighters driven hard onto the coral and left to the ravages of the sea. Tons of steel, tortured and twisted as if it were cardboard. And there we were in our little peanut shell of a boat, with its fragile fibreglass skin.

We paddled on to Ubero and are camped tonight on a quiet beach, doing our best to relax. Just down the way are hundreds of conch shells left by fishermen. I tried to find a whole one, but each has a sizable puncture where the fisherman has smashed it to break the interior suction so that the animal can be pulled out.

I'm afraid our health isn't the greatest just now. For one thing, we're still suffering from the sea-urchin spines we picked up in our feet on the reef back near Tulum. The spines are long and poisonous and can pierce to the bone if they hit at the right angle. All we can do is endure the discomfort and wait for our flesh to dissolve the calcium spines, which it will after a week or so. My hands, too, are suffering. I have a pea-sized open sore between the first and second fingers of my left hand. I've had it for days, and can't get it to heal, what with the salt and sand and the constant friction of the paddling. This morning, I could barely open my hand when I woke up. We're also sick to death of having salt all over our bodies, but we can't afford to use our precious fresh water for bathing. Our clothes and bedding, too, are saturated with salt. Last night, I agonized for hours trying to find a sleeping position in which my sleeping shell wouldn't grind its load of salt into my various abrasions and bug bites.

On the brighter side, our radio is tuned to Belize City, and we're enjoying the English-language broadcasts (Belize is the former British Honduras). The announcer tells us that the u.s. destroyer *Connally* will be in port tomorrow. No mention of our own arrival in three or four days, ho hum.

We have now come nearly 5,000 miles, including 1,700 miles on the coast of Mexico. And I must say, as our Mexican experience winds down, that the people of Mexico have been more than kind to us. They have sheltered us and fed us and encouraged us. When we doubted we could continue, one of them got into the canoe with us and paddled nearly 400 miles. Others came to our rescue when we might have drowned, back at Alvarado. Not one of them has stolen from us or harmed us. They may even have prayed for us.

We feel deeply indebted to all of them.

Stormy Belize

We said a bittersweet goodbye to Mexico on May Day, and stroked on into Central America proper.

Our passage along the first 80 miles of the Belize coast – actually along a string of cays 10 to 15 miles out – has been a paradise of favourable seas: calm and clear and teeming with life.

We reached Belize City yesterday morning and, having scanned the small harbour, paddled a couple of miles into the city on the narrow Belize River. What a parade of poverty alongshore: shack after hovel after tumbledown hut. An incredible variety of dugouts and launches lined the congested river banks. And hundreds of curious black faces grinned at us as we slipped by. Almost everybody here is black, which impresses us sharply after so many months of seeing Indians and Spaniards.

Belize City was founded in the early 17th century by British sea rowdies, who used the local cays and reefs to prey on Spanish shipping. The city's architecture is chiefly British, though much of the early architecture was lost when a hurricane hit the city several years ago. The population is about 40,000.

We soon found the Customs office, where we met a couple of young men, one of whom works on a cruise ship, the *Yankee Trader*. The ship has been working out of Belize but is in the process of shifting its home port to the Bahamas. "Do you want to go to a farewell party for it tomorrow night?" one of the young men asked. We looked at one another and, with one voice, answered, "Sure!"

Earlier in the morning, we'd met some crab fishermen down the coast. They told us to come upriver as far as Leachey's Boatworks, where we'd be able to take care of our canoe repairs and probably find a safe place to camp. Safety is a priority around here, as the city is known for its thieves; steal or starve is about the size of it.

We found Leachey's during the late afternoon and were soon sitting down to chicken dinner with Leachey and his wife Brenda. They invited us to use their boat shop as living and sleeping quarters, and late last night we spread our foam pads on the workbenches, which made serviceable beds. Unfortunately, for security reasons, the lights stayed on all night, so we didn't have the tranquillity of darkness.

This morning we were up early, as we had to lay in enough provisions to take us all the way to La Ceiba, Honduras. While we were shopping, a friendly old guy took our pots and pans to the river and by rubbing them in the sand cleaned off layers of accumulated soot. Meanwhile, Leachey was doing a charity repair job on the aluminum bumper of our canoe – it hadn't been right since our big spill at Alvarado. Leachey gave us new fibreglass cloth and resin for hull repairs.

Late this afternoon, we cleaned up and headed for our date with the *Yankee Trader*. We were ferried to the ship by a large white launch crowded with party guests. The ship turned out to be an old cruise vessel built in 1930. The two masts were said to be a hundred feet high, though I doubted that. About half the people at the party were tourists who had come on the ship from the Bahamas. The other half were guests like ourselves: businessmen, bankers, officers, so on. In the course of the evening, at least a dozen of them said to us, "Did you guys *really* paddle here from Canada?"

We had a grand dinner, then a band began to play and we danced and talked and explored the boat, managing to soak up a little wine as the evening wore on. About midnight, a launch returned the local guests to the mainland, while the passengers partied on into the night. The ship is leaving tomorrow for the Bahamas, and wouldn't Dana and I love to be aboard, free of our own risky little boat for a few days!

From the docks we hitched a ride in a Land Rover with five black soldiers and their girlfriends, all of whom had been at the party. They dropped us at Leachey's, and in no time we were flaked out on the work tables of the boat shop. But the night was so hot and muggy that neither of us could sleep. We climbed out of our sleeping shells and were immediately attacked by bugs. I thought I'd be smart and clambered up into the cabin of a launch that was in dry dock in an unroofed area of the boatyard. I shut the door to keep the bugs out, and the heat was soon as devilish as it had been on the work table. In the meantime, it had begun to rain, and I discovered that my cabin was far from watertight. The recent rains are undoubtedly a result of the sun's path being directly overhead, or nearly so, as it is close to latitude 17 here. In this part of the world, the high hot sun is known to bring on excessive rain and humidity. Until the sun moves further north, we can expect plenty of downpours.

MAY 5: *in the Colson Cays, Belize*
In all, I got two hours of sleep, but was up nonetheless at 5 a.m. for our launch.

We have been advised by a number of fishermen and sailors not to paddle directly along the coast south of Belize City but to move out into the calmer waters of a long string of cays and islands that arches south from here all the way to Guatemala. The only thing that bothers us is that the cays are anywhere from 10 to 18 miles offshore.

Nevertheless, we paddled out and began island-hopping southwards. Our protective cays – small islands formed of coral – are minuscule parts of the second largest coral reef on earth, the largest being Australia's Great Barrier Reef.

By 3 p.m., we were tired and hungry and decided to make camp on the most southerly island of a little group called the Colson Cays. The island was nothing to look at, just a little shelf of jagged coral protruding from the water. But on the north side of the island was a ramshackle fishing hut on stilts, in which we felt we could shelter for the night. The shoreline was far too jagged for a landing, so we left the canoe loaded and in the water, tied to three posts that had been driven into the coral 6 or 7 feet apart. With the sharp coral of the island so close, I put plenty of knots in the rope.

Our shack was in pretty grim shape, but we scraped the floor as clean as we could get it and moved in. But within an hour, the bugs were so bad inside, we moved back outside where there was a bit of breeze. Now, however, there was no place to sit comfortably, so we moved 100 feet to the other side of the island where a ratty little open-air biffy overhung the water. And there we spent the late afternoon, sitting side by side on the throne, Dana practising guitar, me writing.

With darkness coming on, we returned to the shack, tuned in Belize City on the radio and ate a cold supper of corned beef, spaghetti, and black-eyed peas. By 11 p.m., Dana was asleep and I was in total darkness except for a tiny dot of red light from the radio. At about midnight, the radio crackled sharply and went dead, though the red light still showed strongly, which was strange. I turned the set off and tried to sleep. But as I lay there, I began to feel uneasy.

I woke Dana, and we got up and looked out the window. In spite of the darkness, we could see an incredible wall of storm clouds coming towards us from the south. But before we could do anything to prepare ourselves, lightning cracked out of the sky, and our little world was plunged into a chaos of wind and rain, thunder and lightning.

In no time, our flimsy shelter was swaying and quivering on its 4-foot stilts. We did our best to tie down the shutters and to tie the door shut, but there was nothing we could do about the crude siding which was now flapping loose and starting to pull away from the walls.

Only after several minutes did I come fully to my senses, remembering in a panic that the canoe was in the water just a few feet from the lethal coral bank. But by this time there was nothing I could do about it. Our shack was tossing around in the gale, and Dana was frozen with fear. My only hope for the canoe was that the wind would continue to come from the south, meaning that the shallows in front of the cabin were in the lee of the island.

At this point, I tried to open the north door but could barely push it open a crack, which told me that the wind had swung fatally to the north. Peering out through the rain and spray, I could see the ghostly image of our white canoe cover. The canoe had apparently come partially loose, and had swung round so that it was taking the brunt of the waves broadside. Then a blast of wind drove the door shut against all my strength, and I was unable to force it open again.

A whole sheet of plywood siding was now ripped off the shack and whirled away, and Dana started shouting, "We're going into the sea! We're going into the sea!" Sure enough, we could soon hear a watery roar beneath us. The huge waves were now washing right across the island, tearing at the stilts of the shack. "Oh, God," I prayed aloud, "please stop the wind!" I clung to the doorjamb, trembling in the darkness.

For an hour or more, the storm raged, and the floor swayed beneath us. Then the wind died. It was all we could do to stare into the darkness in numbed silence. In time, I staggered to the door and stuck my head out. Unbelievably, the canoe was still there. I could see its outline in the shallows. But I was still too shaken to go out and check the damage. A part of me didn't care. All I could do for now was curl up and try to get some sleep.

At first light, I was out of the shack. I could have wept with joy. Not only was *Orellana* still there but her hull was not touching bottom, which meant she had not suffered any punctures. I checked my lines, and of the twenty or so knots I'd tied the day before only one was still holding, and very loosely. One of the mooring poles had been ripped out, and the others were wobbling in the light waves. Our canoe cover was missing, and the canoe was half full of water. Otherwise, everything was sound. I pulled the tops off our equipment boxes. Again, a miracle. There was no more than an inch of water in any of them.

About 40 feet away, I spotted a big pile of debris that had been blown up against some shore brush. I walked to it and started digging. A minute later I pulled our canoe cover from beneath a foot of refuse. It was dirty and scuffed, but it had not been torn.

Dana was soon up, and we dumped the water from the boxes and the canoe. As we packed up and retarped, we kept saying to one another, It's a miracle. . . . I've never seen anything like it. . . . It's gotta be a miracle. . . . It's just a miracle. . . . It *really is* a miracle. . . .

We paddled off with no desire to look back or to discuss the horrors of the previous night. Our lives had been spared, our canoe was whole. It was a miracle.

At Gunpoint in Honduras

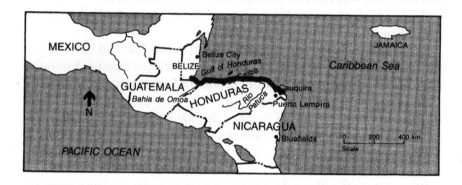

MAY 10: *Bahía de Omoa, Honduras*

We said our goodbyes to Belize yesterday at our ocean camp on Moho Cay, and made a daring 14-mile crossing of the Gulf of Honduras (much of whose shoreline is in Belize and Guatemala). The crossing was our longest open-water paddle to date, and for an hour or so in mid-crossing we could see nothing but great swells of ocean in every direction. Four hours of nervous steady paddling brought us within sight of Guatemala's Punta Manabique, our compass point on the far shore. Twenty-five more miles would take us past Guatemala entirely and into Honduras. We'd had several warnings about Guatemalan coastal dangers – mostly military – and had no intention of stopping in the country.

At about 11:30 a.m., however, as we paddled within a mile or so of the coast, a sleek grey gunboat rose on the horizon in front of us. We immediately headed for shore, hoping to evade it in the shallows where it would be unlikely to go. But it angled persistently toward us, and we knew that fleeing further was a sure admission that we shouldn't be where we were.

The boat was named *Bitol #P-655*, and as we paddled up to it, 10 armed men lined up on deck to look us over. On the foredeck were a mounted cannon and a jumbo-size machine gun. Without a word, the crew threw us two tow lines, which we had no choice but to accept. When they had hauled us perhaps half a mile into deeper water, they cut their engines and demanded our documents, which I handed over.

For an hour or more, we bobbed beside the gunboat, becoming increasingly agitated in the 95-degree heat. The crew glowered down at us, occasionally passing comments among themselves but refusing to speak to us. Some of them chuckled over our situation.

Eventually, one of them demanded that we unload the canoe. "Not here," I shouted in Spanish. "It's impossible."

"Unload!" they shouted, and I realized we weren't going to get any breaks.

I pried the tarp off at the stern and began removing the lids from our equipment boxes, explaining what was in each box. Our survival rifle and handgun were well hidden and went undiscovered, though I'm beginning to fear the day that anyone down here does a thorough search of the canoe.

By this time, we'd drifted a quarter-mile toward shore, and they threw us a tow line and once again hauled us into deeper water. When they cut their engines, I asked for drinking water, as we were sweating heavily and had been for several hours. They took Dana's canteen and filled it, and we drank it down as we ate the lunch we'd prepared before setting out in the morning.

The crew continued to gawk and snicker at us, until I couldn't take it any more and let loose with a tirade in Spanish: We're Canadians! We're a father and son! We're peaceful people! You have no right to keep us here!

As a last resort, I told them our government and Central American embassies were following our trip, and that we were reporting to them regularly. "Every country we've been in treated us with kindness and respect," I said. "And now *this* in Guatemala."

It seemed to work, as the captain now stepped forward and, with a sheepish smile, leaned over the rail and handed us down our documents. "*Guatemala es un país pacifico*," he said – Guatemala is a peaceful country. But he made no apology for the behaviour of his crew, and we paddled off in a huff, having lost so much time that we now had to spend the night in Guatemala.

This morning, as we came up to the Río Motagua which forms the border between Guatemala and Honduras, two men paddled out from shore, calling and beckoning to us. We could easily have outpaddled them and been well into Honduras before they got anywhere near us, but we didn't want to be inhospitable and slowed down. When they were within 40 feet of us, Dana said, "They've got a rifle," and sure enough, I could now see a u.s. Army automatic on the lap of the bow paddler.

"*Playa! Playa!*" ("Beach!") they began shouting as they came alongside us, but we refused to go. They told us they were marines, but they were dressed only in dirty shorts, and I had my doubts. One of them now tried to lift our tarp, but I threatened him with my paddle and he quickly stopped prying. Then he grabbed the paddle from me, and I snatched it back, so that we had a tug of war going. But, seeing that he couldn't outmuscle me, he let go. Again, they ordered us ashore, and again we refused them.

Their insistence that we beach the canoe began to make me think there was more to their actions than a document or equipment check, either of which could be conducted at sea. It was possible they were mere crooks, wanting to get their hands on our gear. We didn't even know whether they were Honduran or Guatemalan.

They held tight to our gunwales, and for half an hour we shouted back and forth at one another. Eventually I yelled, "Let go right now! We have clearance from the *Bitol*."

"*No es bueno!*" they shouted back – "That's no good!"

By this time, I was thinking about tipping their canoe away from us and throwing them and their rifle into the sea. But I would need Dana's help to carry it off and couldn't communicate with him in secret. At any rate, if they grabbed onto us from the water, we'd have an ugly situation on our hands.

At this point, I scanned the waters around us and could barely believe my eyes: there was the *Bitol* coming toward us from back to the west. Our captors now told us they'd release us if we gave them my paddle. We refused, and, at a signal, we broke away from them and began paddling frantically toward the *Bitol*, which had stopped, perhaps not wanting to get too close to Honduran waters.

Our two tormentors followed, but in no time we opened up a substantial lead on them, hoping not to hear rifle fire from behind. The seas were rolling, and as I looked back I'd lose sight of them in the swells, then see them again as they broke over a crest. "Go for everything you're worth!" I yelled at Dana as we flew across the waves. What a humiliating irony it was that we were now looking to the hated *Bitol* to save our skins.

We reached the gunboat, and, as I tried breathlessly to explain our situation, the crew stood on deck laughing at us. When our two antagonists joined us beside the boat, it was quickly apparent that they knew the crew, and were indeed military personnel of some sort. It was also apparent that they'd been told to expect us at the border. We complained bitterly to the captain, who casually dismissed us and told the two men to leave us alone.

We'd been the victims of some sort of cruel and dangerous joke, which might well have gone beyond a joke. Had we gone ashore, we firmly believe we'd have been stripped of our equipment and probably killed. We've heard enough stories to know that, where the uncontested power of the military is concerned, life can be frightfully cheap down here. The only thing we can do is paddle on and try not to think about it, which isn't going to be easy.

We camped this afternoon on a peaceful stretch of beach about 5 miles into Honduras. We're back into mountain country, and, according to our map, one of the nearby peaks stands over 7,000 feet above sea level. The shores are densely covered with palms and jungle foliage.

Tonight, an old gent paid us a visit and told us, among other things, that Honduras is the most peaceful country in Central America. I quickly thought of what the captain of the *Bitol* had told us: *Guatemala es un país pacifico.*

Ahead of us are nearly 400 miles of Honduran coastline. May every mile be as peaceful as the first few.

MAY 13: *east of La Ceiba, Honduras*

Our paddling conditions over the past few days have been better than we could ever have imagined – seemingly endless calm. Right now, we're averaging about 30 miles a day and are getting great pleasure from the mountain-jungle scenery. For the past day and a half, we've seen numerous pads of lush mauve flowers, floating well out to sea. They're anywhere up to four feet square, and are apparently carried from the rivers and lagoons by the offshore currents. They send a fabulous aroma across the water.

This afternoon, we saw the strangest disturbance, about as big as a blanket, on the water ahead of us. It was as if a large object or sea creature had dived abruptly. I steered towards it, and as we came close Dana shouted, "Stop-stop-stop-stop-stop!" I tried to back paddle but before I could slow the canoe there was a powerful thump on the bottom of our hull. We rose slightly out of the water, lurched to the right, and settled. "What is it?" I yelled, as I prepared for another jolt.

"You know what it was?" Dana turned grinning to ask. "It was a mana-
tee, a sea cow." He figured it had been a foot or so beneath the surface
when we paddled over it, and that we'd surprised it, making it plunge
and kick up at the canoe. According to Dana, it was 12 feet long.

The coast along here is alive with hundreds of dugout canoes, or *cayucas*
as the Hondurans call them (they pronounce it ky-u-ko). It's a fine feeling
to be among canoeists again, though the locals tend to treat us more as
curiosities than as fellow paddlers. As we glide by, they drop their narrow
paddles and stare. Occasionally, a couple of young men will paddle alongside us and give us a bit of a race, which we invariably win with our steady,
heavy stroke. Their paddling is excellent in technique but lacks endurance. Mind you, this morning we saw an exception, as a lone black man
paddled by our camp, well out to sea, using a long, efficient voyageur's
stroke. When we'd finished breakfast, we launched and chased him for
nearly two hours. As we were about to pull even with him, he turned
sharply right and disappeared into the narrow mouth of the Río San
Juan, probably trying to evade us.

Our biggest problem right now is the *chiquistas*, the tiny sandflies. As
soon as we touch land, they begin their merciless movable feast on all
quarters of our hides. My ankles are still elephantine from hundreds of
bites. This evening as I worked at my diary, I was obliged to walk into the
shallow water and do my writing there to protect my legs. The thought
of sitting down was pretty close to an abstraction, anyway: I'd tried sitting on the canoe, but my tattered rump had quickly given notice.

My reading tells me that the population of Honduras is about 3 million
and that Christopher Columbus stopped here on his last voyage in 1502.
Cortés came in 1525. Spain ruled the area until 1821. As we paddle the
coast, I often do a little time-travelling and can easily imagine myself
arriving with those daring explorers of the sixteenth century. In a small
way we are fellow travellers.

MAY 18: *near Santa Rosa de Aguan, Honduras*
We are now about 250 miles into Honduras, and as we round the northernmost part of the coast, we are again battling our old foe, the wind. It
comes in hard and persistently from the east, so that for the past three or
four days we've been fighting 10- and 12-foot waves, hundreds of which
have crashed right over the canoe, nearly ripping Dana from his seat. It's
so hard to describe our feelings after a bad joust with the sea. Our canoe
is so small, and the minute-to-minute concern for our lives leaves us utterly

exhausted. We get off the sea, and it's all we can do to fall into one another's arms and hold on tight.

This morning before dawn I realized that I could barely face another day of it. I'm invariably awake before 5 a.m., checking my watch, counting down the minutes to the deadly hour. At 5 sharp, I yell, "Dana!" and there are a few seconds of silence as he grunts and groans and turns over. I then say, "Time to go!" and we drag ourselves from our sleeping shells. We eat a quick bowl of uncooked oatmeal and water and within half an hour are back in the canoe.

This morning's start was as big an ordeal as ever, and all day, again, the sea gave us fits. Tonight, the entire coastline is a turbulent wall of high white breakers. It reminds me of our time on Washington Beach. I should probably make some attempt to patch the canoe, as my Mexican repairs have been leaking freely, but I'm just too tired to get at it. We'll continue to bail, as we've been doing regularly for the past couple of days.

As if things weren't bad enough at sea, we had a shocking incident on shore a few nights ago at Punta Catchabutan. The evening began peacefully enough when a tiny one-legged man and his wife walked slowly down the beach to our camp. The man had a crutch and got additional support from a machete that he thrust into the sand. He told us without bitterness that he'd lost his leg in a car accident. The pair graciously invited us for coffee at their home, which was half a mile down the beach, hidden by a stand of palms. We politely refused, as we were extremely tired, and also nervous about leaving the canoe unprotected.

Just after dark, as we lay in our sleeping shells, Antonio, the couple's 8-year-old son, materialized out of the darkness from the east with a pot of strong, sweet coffee and a little china cup from which we were to drink it. We lay on our stomachs for nearly an hour, drinking and chatting and laughing.

Antonio left, and we had just nicely drifted off when we were jolted awake by an explosion and flash that seemed to lift me a foot off the beach. Not ten feet away, on horseback, were a couple of uniformed men, with their rifles pointing down at us. One of them had fired into the sand just a few feet from our heads. We scrambled to our knees, screaming, "*Amigos! Amigos! No problema!*"

At times like this, our Spanish is reduced to a few panic phrases. Nonetheless, we were quickly able to convince our gun-happy antagonists that we meant no harm. As we regained our composure, our one-legged friend appeared on the beach on horseback, having heard the blast. He called out to the soldiers that we were his friends, and begged them not to harm us. They told him to get lost, but bravely he stayed until he was sure we were safe.

For an hour or so afterwards, Dana and I lay trembling from the shock of the rifle going off at such close range.

In spite of our traumas, we continue to be thrilled by our living nature lessons. This afternoon we saw a 10-foot black shark beneath the canoe, and yesterday we displaced a hundred or so brown pelicans when we landed on their beach. Our camping spot was surrounded for hundreds of yards by webbed footprints, feathers, and somewhat offensive droppings.

We were treated again today to a fleshy pear-shaped fruit that we first sampled back at La Ceiba. But, unlike those we'd had earlier, today's were yellow instead of red, and had a pale green kidney-shaped protrusion, with a hard casing, extending from the bottom end. Seeing the fruit reminded me of an illustration I'd included in the "tropical fruit" section of my preparatory manual for the trip. I quickly got the manual out and discovered we'd been eating the fruit of the cashew, or *maranjon* as it's called here. The little protrusion is the nut and is apparently poisonous to the lips and mouth until roasted. I can see why cashews are so expensive back home. They have to be picked by ladder from tall trees, removed individually from their fruit and casings, then roasted, shipped, packaged, whatever. The fruit is tasty and refreshing, with just a hint of citrus about it.

Last night our radio informed us that the Pope had been shot. I lay for an hour or more on the beach, listening to the surf, thinking about the state of this disturbed planet we call home.

MAY 23: *near Laguna Caratasca, Honduras*
Our days at sea remain stupefying, and the jittery Hondurans afford us little peace on shore. Shortly after we landed on a deserted beach today, the jungle erupted behind us and we were ambushed by 10 armed and noisy adults, men and women alike. "*Documentos!*" they shouted, as they waved their weapons. I tried to calm them, and one of them blasted his shotgun above my head. They seemed to think we were leftist invaders from Nicaragua or Cuba, and nothing I could do would convince them otherwise.

We argued back and forth for about 15 minutes, when one of them spotted the little blue and white Honduras decal we'd attached to the canoe back at La Ceiba. "Honduras!" he shouted in a rapture of discovery, and in no time our status had been downgraded from Enemy Monsters to harmless canoeists. Our papers had meant nothing to them, that silly little decal everything.

The countries down here distrust one another passionately, and our unexplained appearance on their beaches is just the sort of stimulus guaranteed to incite their paranoia. And we've been promised far worse when we get to Nicaragua, which has just undergone a leftist revolution and is apparently more ruthless toward suspected infiltrators than its right-wing neighbours.

Not everyone is threatened by us, of course. The other night as we lay on the beach trying to sleep, 30 or 40 people, many of them young women, came tramping down the sands. They surrounded us in a tight knot and simply stood staring, entranced to see a couple of long-haired gringos lying on their beach. We couldn't get rid of this gang, even by pretending to be asleep. Eventually the young women started pestering Dana, going so far as to ask him if he'd like to share a hammock for the night. He was embarrassed and pretended not to understand. Before long, a flock of them were giggling and badgering him to join them in their village for the night. We both began to get offers, and at one point I thought a few of the more aggressive young women were going to pick Dana up and carry him away.

After a while, a woman appeared with fresh-cooked shark meat and cassava bread for us, and we hauled ourselves from our beds, able to resist everything but the temptation of good home cooking. We sat with these gregarious beach dwellers for an hour or more, eating and laughing and chatting, until they gradually drifted away and left us alone on our sandy beds.

It's only in the past few days that we've begun to get cassava bread, a large flat bread, like a crusty pancake. It's made from the underground tuber of the cassava plant, ground into a flour called *manioc* or *manioca*. It is apparently a staple all over South and Central America, so we'll see more of it.

As I sit here writing, I'm still haunted by something we saw two days ago, a few miles east of the Río Plátano. As we prepared to call it a day, we saw a group of about a dozen local men working around a luxurious, two-masted sailing yacht, which had been grounded at the water's edge. The boat was perhaps 45 feet long and was certainly not locally owned. The men were propping the boat upright with timbers, and as we got ashore I realized they were preparing to cut the enormous keel off it, which horrified me. How could they even think of violating such a beautiful craft in such a hideous way?

When we'd established camp, I walked up to them. I suspected something illicit was going on, or had gone on. Though I had no desire to get tangled up in it, I couldn't resist trying to find out a little more.

I was told that the boat belonged to a retired couple who'd run it aground and had given up trying to refloat it. They'd apparently sold it to the locals to convert into a fishing boat. The boat must have been worth $100,000, and I really couldn't accept that anyone would sell it for the small amount of money these guys could offer. I walked around the stern of the boat to check its identity, and was flabbergasted to see that it was Canadian – the *Chaika* from the Royal Vancouver Yacht Club. It must have travelled through the Panama Canal to get here. Now even more curious, I took a photo of it, then made myself scarce before I got into trouble.

Just before sunset, as I wandered on the back stretches of the beach, I came across a litter of papers and English book pages, some of them from children's books, obviously off the *Chaika*. Would a retired couple have children's books on board? I'm determined to find out the true story of the boat and will write the Vancouver Yacht Club when we get back to Canada. Right now, I find it hard to believe that our fellow Canadians were not the victims either of a sea disaster or of foul play, perhaps piracy.

A less important incident gave me something to think about yesterday morning. As we stroked along, my paddle was seized from beneath the waves by some powerful creature, invisible in the murky water. I was so shocked, I barely managed to keep the paddle in my hands. There was a loud thump on the bottom of the canoe, and whatever had attacked was gone, leaving no teeth marks on my paddle – but giving us good reason to keep our arms out of the water.

We've developed a new technique for coping with the biggest waves. Now when they come onto us broadside, we don't turn our bow into them but wait until they're about to smash us in the left flank. At the last instant, we throw our weight hard to the right, tipping our keelless canoe bottom toward them, so that they slide beneath it, instead of crashing over the gunwales and swamping us. It's a dangerous manoeuvre, but we've employed it hundreds of times now and will stay with it until it betrays us.

The wind has been so strong that at night we've been building a windbreak out of our equipment boxes and canoe. Even so we wake up in the morning covered with sand. A few days ago the wind was so powerful that I couldn't even pour a glass of water; every time I'd get a little in the cup, it would begin to swirl like a tiny tornado and would disappear into the gale.

MAY 25: *Ticua and Cauquira, on Laguna de Caratasca, Honduras*
Yesterday afternoon, we were settled on a windy stretch of beach at Ticua,
awaiting a cooked meal for which we'd bartered at a nearby house. As I
whacked away at a pile of coconuts, two men appeared from the east,
one riding a little white horse, the other walking. We chatted casually
with them until it was obvious our Spanish was upsetting the older of the
two, the rider – he wanted us to speak English. It soon became clear that
they were drunk, and after a few minutes they all but ordered us to move
our canoe and equipment from the beach, telling us it wasn't safe by the
water. I shrugged off their meddling, trying not to create a confrontation
but wanting to let them know we had little interest in moving. We like
the canoe on the beach in the open where we can keep an eye on it and
where we can easily launch it. They persisted, until I fixed the horseman
with a look and told him, "The canoe stays where it is." We drifted into
uneasy small talk, and they wandered off, leaving me bent over my coconuts. Dana returned to his guitar 50 feet away under a tall palm. Wisps of
Bach reached me on the breeze.

For half an hour I concentrated on my work until, looking up, I saw the
same two guys standing over me, the one still on horseback, the other
now carrying a 12-gauge pump-action shotgun, aimed directly at my head.
What startled me almost as much as the gun was the sickly drunken pal-
lor on the gunman's face.

Dana was quickly at my side, and the stocky horseman, a man of perhaps 30, ordered us to carry all our equipment 200 yards to a nearby house.
"On whose authority?" I asked. Immediately the shotgun exploded above
my head, and the gunman began running around screaming, "I'm gonna
shoot your ass! Gonna shoot your ass!" He fell to his knees, waving the
gun wildly at us. I could feel my body go cold.

With our arms high, we were marched 50 yards to the canoe, against a
repeated din of "I'm gonna shoot your ass!" and seconds later, "I'm gonna
shoot it now!"

"*No ahora! Más tarde!*" the horseman screamed at the younger man –
"Not now! Later!"

"*Ahora! Ahora!*" screamed the gunman, constantly shifting his position to keep the gun on us.

We were ordered to squat in the sand while the horseman dismounted,
approached the canoe and ripped off the tarp. He picked up Dana's guitar and threw it onto the beach, then the guitar case, whose contents
went flying. Dana sat unbelieving as his emergency asthma medications
and all the other valuables he keeps in his case were scattered across the
sand. The lids from our aluminum boxes were now airborne, along with

our machete, tossed 30 yards toward the plantation. For a few frozen seconds the panic stopped as the man held up two pieces of our survival rifle. A demonic, jubilant grin crept across his face, and he growled, "*Armas! Armas! Soldados! Nicaragua!*"

"*Bombas!*" he screamed as he found our aluminum tent poles, the ends of which are sealed with rubber plugs like pipe bombs.

Our unmasking as Nicaraguan Sandinistas was ample pretext for the guy to begin stuffing things into his pockets: my Russell belt knife, my passport, credit cards, compass, watch, money. All our clothes were now ripped from their plastic bags and scattered on the sand. Meanwhile the gunman was so excited that if we moved even an inch he again set up the maniac chant, "I'm gonna shoot your ass! I'm gonna shoot! I'm gonna kill you!" At one point he begged his partner to give the word so he could do us in, but the partner cautioned, "*Más tarde, más tarde.*"

An unmarked grave in Honduras isn't exactly our idea of a fitting conclusion to our trip, and I'm not ashamed to admit that at this point we began pleading for our lives. We were quickly told to shut up and were marched several hundred yards back into the plantation.

As we passed the house where we'd bartered for food over an hour ago, Dana panicked and darted up the steps and through the door. This produced a fury of hysterical screams from the female inhabitants. Just as quickly he was back outside under the shotgun.

Again I pleaded with the drunks – tie us up! send for the police or the army! we're Canadians! "*Por favor!*" I begged, "Please!" but to no effect.

As we were marched away, the women from the house wailed out their protests: if we were harmed, they screamed, they'd report our captors to the army. The drunks yelled back that the women, too, would be murdered if they didn't keep quiet.

We trudged along a rough trail, birds squawking and screeching from the sparse trees on either side. Dana was wearing a torn T-shirt and jeans and was barefoot; I was dressed only in my shorts and running shoes. Any attempt we made to communicate with one another was met with an exaggerated "*Quieto!*" "Shut up!" The shotgun was rammed repeatedly into my spine.

Suddenly the captain shouted "*Alto!*" "Stop!" and we were forced against a barbed-wire fence and told to kneel. Our captors went into conference, then the younger one walked toward us, pumped the action on his gun and raised it to his shoulder. I averted my eyes, remorse and terror blazing through my brain. Why, why did I ever drag my son into this? Time dissolved, but the fatal blast didn't come. After what seemed an eternity, we were ordered to our feet. We rose like zombies.

That sadistic scene was played out twice more in the next half hour.

We were forced to walk faster and faster now, and as an added humiliation, the mounted captain took out my belt knife and began slapping me on the shoulders with its blade, as if daring me to try something. For a few seconds he pressed the knife point into my neck. "You're a big man," he grinned, and it was all I could do to keep from tearing him off his horse and strangling him.

I was certain they wanted to kill us and could not understand their hesitation. But now, unwittingly, the captain revealed himself, telling us we'd be killed and shipped back to Canada in boxes. "Honduras will pay your fare!" he laughed. It was our first evidence that they understood we were not Sandinistas.

As the sun sank, the horseman began to brag; he was Captain Sosa of the Honduran army and had the full encouragement of his government to kill strangers who showed up on Honduran beaches. He claimed to have killed 13 Sandinistas this week at the Nicaraguan border and would do the same to us if either of us stepped from the path. Without warning, the shotgun exploded again, further fragmenting what little morale we had left. "*Prisa! Prisa!*" was the new cry. "Hurry up!"

We were now told that we were on our way to jail in a nearby town, two or three hours away – certainly a better fate than a shotgun blast to the brain, assuming we had the stamina to make it to the town. We were exhausted from our day's paddle and had not eaten in 16 hours.

Dana began stubbing his toes on deadfall and stepping on sand burrs which embedded themselves in his feet and had to be removed as he hobbled. He was suffering severely and begged our captors to slow down. "*Prisa!*" shouted the gunman.

The captain asked Dana a question and slapped him with the knife blade when he attempted to answer.

I was ordered to smoke a cigarette, apparently so that I'd be easier to see in what was now pitch darkness. I refused until the gun was rammed into my back and the cigarette pushed into my hand. I held it far out to my side as a false target, then realized I'd be safer holding it in front of me where they couldn't see it. "Smoke!" yelled the gunman, and I blew through the cigarette to make it glow. The thought of fleeing was increasingly tempting, and Dana and I began to whisper, seemingly unheard from behind. We could perhaps run in opposite directions and meet in Puerto Lempira many miles inland. But could we find our way through perhaps a hundred miles of swamp and lagoon? I was half tempted to fall down and fake a heart attack, but feared it might make things worse for us.

Occasionally now a human figure appeared in the shadows along the trail, and I realized we were approaching a settlement. The captain had begun to soften and, in spite of his partner's continuing threats, he now said he'd see to it that our lives were spared if we promised not to tell the soldiers at the jail about all he'd stolen from us. Naturally, we agreed. "If you tell them," he growled in Spanish, "we'll be waiting for you with 15 men if they ever decide to set you free. We'll slit your throats." He said he had friends at the jail and that whatever we said would get back to him.

We reached a little hut, and he rapped on the shutter and demanded water. Dana had a drink, but I refused, partly from anxiety but also from reluctance to reveal my thirst, my insufficiency.

The little wooden military station was lit only by candles, and we were immediately surrounded by 8 or 9 armed men, none in uniform. On a table were handcuffs and cartridge clips. An interrogation ensued, and we attempted to explain our predicament in Spanish. But our interrogators' skepticism was impossible to penetrate – *nobody* paddles the ocean in a canoe! Two of the men spoke up in English, telling us to explain in our own language; they'd interpret to the officer in charge. We did so, and listened in frustration as our story was retold, in a version full of lies that depicted us as weapon-toting outlaws. "No es verdad!" I objected, "It's not true!" but I was told to shut my mouth. Our original captors stood smirking in the background.

An hour later it was over; our fate had been decided, but we knew nothing. I begged for food, and we were marched under guard to a little restaurant whose electric lights were powered by a very noisy gas generator. We hadn't seen lightbulbs in some time. We discovered we were in Cauquira on Caratasca Lagoon, 7 miles back along the coast from where we'd been arrested.

As it happened, the storekeeper spoke good English, and, as he seemed to be a man of influence, we poured out our tale to him. He was sympathetic and, having given us bread and sardines, he accompanied us back to the station. He spoke privately with the soldiers.

We were given rubber mats and told to sleep on the floor. But first I had to relieve myself and was marched out the back door at gunpoint. I was forced along a shaky log bridge to a crude toilet that overhung the lagoon. It occurred to me that we could escape by water – we are both strong swimmers. But as I completed my business, the surface began to boil with thrashing fish, which I thought might be piranhas. So much for swimming.

A few minutes later I was back beside Dana, both of us being chewed by fleas. It was nearly midnight. Including our day's battle with the sea, we had been under stress for about 19 hours.

Through all our trials and traumas, our guardian angel had not deserted us. When we awoke this morning, it was clear that the storekeeper's intervention had gone in our favour. The heavy suspicion had lifted. We were not free to go, but were at least allowed out into the little yard of the army station.

We were taken to the cantina for breakfast and found out from the storekeeper that our two captors were civilians, brothers, and that, because of our complaints, they'd been ordered to round up everything they'd stolen from us and return it to the army base. As the morning passed, our possessions trickled in: Swiss army knife, tape cassettes, wallet, compass, passports, some of our money, our radio. But some things were gone for good – machete, survival rifle, sleeping pad, and my beautiful antique knife salvaged from the reef at Veracruz. How sad I am to lose that knife.

Late in the morning, one of the brothers showed up with our handgun, proof that we were troublemakers after all. "It is a very serious offence to bring arms into Honduras," the station captain told us in Spanish. "You'll have to go to Puerto Lempira for further questioning." Although the thought horrified me, I pretended unconcern, insisting that they acknowledge my carrying permit from Winnipeg. After a lengthy debate, it was allowed that if we gave the gun to the army, or sold it, the matter would be dropped.

It soon came to light that our friendly storekeeper would be interested in buying the gun. Presently he showed up, and I dickered with him briefly, finally selling for $50 U.S. But since there was no American money in town, I had to take 100 Honduran lempiras, which was quickly snatched by the station captain as a bond against our running off. My little gem of a pistol, a .22 Hi-Standard Duramatic, which I'd treasured since 1957, was gone.

Throughout all this I'd been half desperate about the fate of our canoe, and now began to question these guys over its whereabouts and condition. We were informed it had been brought (dragged? paddled?) 7 miles back along the coast in the direction of Cauquira. Just before noon, the captain and a patrol led us a mile out to the beach where we found *Orellana* half swamped in the shallows. Our clothes and equipment were scattered from stern to bow. Many of our things were floating, including all Dana's sheet music. His guitar case had been ripped apart, and much of our gear was missing.

When we'd done what we could to sort things out, and the captain had made an exhaustive equipment check, we were led back to the station, assured that the canoe would be guarded. I had my doubts, which were confirmed on our arrival back in town, when a little boy came along carrying Dana's guitar. Dana jumped up and grabbed it back, and I demanded to be allowed to return to the canoe, which was obviously being robbed all over again. But we were ordered to stay where we were. We'd be released in due time.

An hour or so later, a gaunt American expatriate, some sucked-out prophet of disaster, came shuffling up to us in front of the station and looked at us pitifully. "I've heard your story," he said, "and if you think this is bad, wait'll you cross the border. The Sandinistas will take you for Americans – they'll cut your throats, no questions asked."

It is the third or fourth warning we've had about the horrors of Nicaragua, and Dana's despondency is deepening by the hour. I've tried to buoy his spirits, but he will not be consoled. A while ago, he said, "We can overcome the sea, Dad, but not bullets. It isn't worth it; it just isn't – well, is it?" he asked, looking up at me.

"I don't know," I told him, which was as close to the truth as I could get.

Last night, just before we went to sleep, Dana reminded me of what I'd said as we were being marched to the army station. "If we get out of this alive," I'd whispered, "the trip is over. I promise. It's definitely over."

Yet, in spite of everything, as I sit here under arrest, I don't want the trip to end. We've come too far; I've committed too much to it. I want to go on, and, deep down, I believe Dana does too, if there's any way we can do it. Maybe we could take a boat from here to Costa Rica, skipping Nicaragua. Then again, maybe Nicaragua will be a breeze, and we'll get along fine with the Sandinistas. We've certainly had other threats that came to nothing.

The longer I deliberate, the more I'm struck by the fruitlessness of weighing the dangers of the trip against our safety. We simply have no way of gauging what our real dangers will be. We were told that Honduras would be a Garden of Eden! The sea itself was supposed to have done us in long ago. We might have stayed home and been hit by a bus.

If we skip any country, it should probably be Colombia; we've heard a hundred times about the horrors of the dope trade, the killings and piracy, and the murderous Guajira Indians. . . .

As we ate our supper, our storekeeping friend, Perfidio Echeverría, issued more grave warnings about Nicaragua, strongly advising us not to go. "If you must go," he said, "you must travel to Puerto Lempira and get proper clearance."

Dana agreed with him, but I could see little hope of getting clearance for Nicaragua in Honduras. We don't even have clearance to be in Honduras! If anything, we'd get further tangled, and might never get out of Puerto Lempira. I told Perfidio we'd consider his suggestion, and we left the premises. Although the man had helped us greatly, I hoped never to see him again.

Late in the evening, we were given our 100 lempiras and told we were free to go. It was assumed we'd stay the night in Cauquira, but we had other ideas and, just after dark, slipped out of town. Dana carried his guitar, and I carried a box of mangoes given to us by some sympathetic townspeople.

We felt our way over the sand hills toward the sea, and soon located our dear *Orellana*. Although the canoe was not being guarded, it appeared to be as we'd left it this morning.

We laid out our beds, and before going to sleep had a long discussion about the confusing events of the past couple of days. We are gaining perspective and now think that the drunken Rosales brothers were initially just trying to do their duty in arresting us and turning us over to the army. But in the course of the arrest they had a good look at our equipment and decided they wanted it. The only way they could get it was to do us in, which was exactly what the younger brother wanted to do. Fortunately for us, the women in the nearby house saw them. Since they couldn't kill us with impunity, they decided they'd still get credit for our arrest. But they couldn't have us expose them as thieves. Hence their threats.

I can't help thinking that, had it not been for those women, we would have been murdered.

As we lie here tonight, we are less than 40 miles from the Río Coco and the Nicaraguan border. I think I've convinced Dana that things can't possibly get any worse, and will probably get better. On those grounds, we've agreed to carry on. Our last act before going to bed was to shake hands on our agreement.

Tomorrow at 5 a.m., we'll be back on the seas.

The Nicaraguan War Zone

MAY 30: *at Puerto Cabezas, Nicaragua*

The day before yesterday, we crossed the border into Nicaragua. Everything considered, our spirits are good – we are some 80 miles into the country, and our throats are still intact. In fact, until today, we hadn't even seen a soldier, though we've been scanning the coast for the telltale red berets of the Sandinistas.

So far, much of the landscape of the fabled Mosquito Coast has been flat and swampy, though today's has been more scenic – steep red cliffs, hung with radiant green foliage. The water today has been thick with what look like cabbages but are actually a species of jellyfish. They thud against our paddles at almost every stroke. I'd like to think they're something we could eat, but we haven't had the nerve to try them.

As we approached the pier at Puerto Cabezas early this afternoon, I couldn't help thinking we were lucky to have lost our handgun and rifle back at Cauquira. Neither of us is in any shape for another death dance. We figure our best bet is to approach the authorities here openly and ask for safe passage. We'd have stopped earlier, but there hasn't been a real port until now, and we didn't want to risk stopping at any nervous little outpost. Nor did we want to stop at Cabo Gracios á Dios on the border for fear of being sent back to Honduras, or worse.

As we came up to the pier, I spotted a lone soldier standing motionless, looking intently in our direction. His uniform was Cuban style, his hat the sort worn by Fidel. He was carrying a machine gun which he aimed our way. We headed straight for him, anxious to let him know we had no intention of avoiding him. As we drew near, we saw that a monstrous bruise covered half his face.

"*Inmigración!*" we yelled.

He said nothing, appearing to be flustered, and directed us around the east end of the pier with his gun. Even before we beached the canoe, 10 soldiers in full uniform had emerged from a nearby barracks, scowls all around.

Within half an hour, we were loaded into a jeep and driven a short distance to a military command post, where a grim-faced officer sat us down and stared at us. His first questions were inconsequential: How many nights have you been in Nicaragua? How far do you travel in a day? Who have you talked to? When were you in La Ceiba? This dragged on for half an hour, when suddenly he dropped a bomb. He looked me in the eye and said, "What ship did you come on?"

I was momentarily confused, not sure I'd interpreted his Spanish correctly. "Ship?" I said.

"Where is your ship now?" he whispered.

"There is no ship!"

The direction of his questioning gradually became clear, and again I did my best to explain that we're Canadian canoeists, nothing more.

"You can't travel this far by canoe."

"We travelled this far."

We were ordered to hold out our hands, which we did, further confusing the issue. Dana's hands are heavily callused, while mine are callus-free.

Eventually, we were accused outright of being American spies. I had little doubt that the decals on our canoe were at the root of the accusation; there are several from the u.s. Coast Guard and a couple from the military. We should have removed them, but I honestly felt no one could mistake the canoe for a military vessel – much less us for soldiers.

"Where are your weapons?" our interrogator said coolly.

"We have no weapons."

"Where is your ammunition?"

"We have no ammunition." As soon as I said so, I remembered the package of .22 shells in my valuables bag. I'd happily have got rid of them, but the zipper on the bag is corroded shut, and I'd have had to cut the leather to get at them. The soldiers had undoubtedly found them.

At length, someone brought in our brass barometer.

"What is it?"

"A barometer."

"What's it for?"

"It helps us tell what weather is coming."

"Where's the rest of it?"

"That's all there is."

"Is it aboard the ship?"

"There is no ship."

To this point, the questioning had been exclusively in Spanish, but now the officer looked up from his desk and, in perfect English, said, "Where were you in 1934?"

The inanity of the question floored me. "I was in Winnipeg, Canada; I was two years old!" (I later learned that the revolutionary patriarch, Augusto Sandino, for whom the Sandinistas are named, was murdered in 1934. Was it possible they were still looking for his murderer?)

Three hours later we were driven back to the canoe, which was a thoroughly depressing sight. Our little craft had been placed, loaded, on a pair of logs which had strained the hull, snapping several of the support ribs. A number of our fibreglass patches had been sprung, and the flotation chambers at the bow and stern had been ripped open. For the second time in a week, every bit of our equipment had been ransacked. My camera and all my film were missing; my little leather bag was missing; our maps were gone. I now remembered that several of the maps were American military issue, certain to increase suspicion.

As we combed through our belongings, a couple of soldiers approached and, without a word, began opening our food and medication containers – right down to the tiniest bottle. They held out anything that looked even vaguely like dope and demanded, "What is this?" – aspirins, water purifier, sugar, salt, flour.

When the farce had run its course, we were placed under house arrest and ordered to stay close to the barracks, where we'd been told we'd be quartered. It had now been dark for some time, and we had not eaten in over 15 hours. We demanded food and were escorted by an armed soldier to a little dance hall called the "Salon Rock" where a dozen or so tables surrounded the dance floor. Chicken, rice, beans, bread – all of which I washed down with five Pepsis. Dana had two. Total cost: $16.50 u.s., about three times as much as we'd expected to pay.

As we ate, we were approached by two young men who introduced themselves as Larabee Rigby and Samuel Juarquin. They offered to buy our meal and wanted us to visit their home. Throughout the meal, our escort had been standing by the door out of earshot, and I pointed him out to the young men, explaining that we weren't free to go. "It's all right," one of them said. "We'll arrange it."

Something didn't seem right, and I began to suspect that our friends were plants, trying to get information from us. They started talking politics, and I told them we were nonpolitical. As they were telling us about Nicaraguan seafood being exported to the Soviet Union, our escort came across to the table, and they quickly changed the subject to the beauty of the Nicaraguan beaches.

At 11 o'clock, we were taken back to the barracks and assigned bunks. All over the walls there were revolutionary posters and slogans – *Sandino Ayer. Sandino Hoy. Sandino Siempre.* Yesterday, today, forever. One poster proclaimed July 19th, 1981, as the second anniversary of the Revolution: *Por la Defensa de la Patria y la Revolución las Milicias Populares en Acción – Integrate M.P.S.*

On the wall of the outer room there was a big framed photo of Augusto Sandino himself, dressed up in khakis and a Mountie-style hat, which gave him the appearance of a slightly ineffectual scoutmaster. Sandino, was done in by the supporters of General Anastasio Somoza García who, in 1937, was installed as president of Nicaragua by the United States. In 1962, the Sandinista National Liberation Front was formed, and, in 1979, Somoza's son, President Anastasio Somoza Debayle, was chased into exile by the revolutionary forces.

Even our mattresses and pillows were done up in the red and black stripes of the Revolution, and printed all over with "Ejército Popular Sandinista" – the People's Sandinista Army.

MAY 31: *Puerto Cabezas, Nicaragua*
First thing this morning we were taken to the office where we'd been questioned yesterday. But before our dark-faced interrogator had had half a chance to go at us, I complained about all our lost articles, rattling them off like a pawnbroker's inventory: camera, film, jewellery, maps, etc. When I'd finished, he reached into his desk and pulled out my camera and handed it to me.

"The film's gone!" I barked.

"Yes," he said. "You can't take pictures in Nicaragua." He went on to explain that all our film, both developed and undeveloped, would be kept until it had been examined. If nothing was suspicious, the photos would be sent back to Canada. I was furious, knowing very well that nothing would ever be sent home. Over 100 photos were gone.

I now asked about my little jewellery bag, and he pulled it from the drawer, the corroded zipper having been cut out of it. He dumped the contents on the desk, including the 40 rounds of ammunition that I'd known were in there. "Where is your gun?" he said coolly.

I explained about the bullets, and told him our survival rifle had been stolen in Honduras. He seemed to believe me, and when I asked about our documents and maps he explained that we'd get them when we left.

"When's that?" I said, and he shocked us by saying, "Today."

In spite of our losses, our spirits were buoyed immensely. We now asked if he would stamp our passport, explaining that we still had 260 miles of Nicaraguan coast to travel and didn't want to go through another hassle of arrest and interrogation. But he refused. Nor would he give us any sort of visa.

With my confidence developing, I began nagging at him about our need for a document of safe passage. Finally, I said, "We won't leave until you give us one."

Within half an hour, he handed over a brief letter of recognition, signed by the Port Captain. At the top of the page was a tiny reproduction of the Sandinista flag and at the bottom the motto *"Patria – Libre O Morir."* Homeland – Freedom or Death.

"When will you be leaving?" the officer now asked.

"First thing in the morning."

"How long will it take you to get out of Nicaragua?"

"Ten days."

The officer looked at me balefully and said, "You must leave by noon today. You are no longer welcome here."

I explained that we needed to buy food and couldn't get going by noon. At once, a soldier was ordered to take us by jeep to downtown Puerto Cabezas to get our shopping done. We roared around to three or four dismal little stores, apparently the best in the city. But most of their shelves were as empty as Old Mother Hubbard's cupboard – not a good advertisement for the new régime. In one store we asked for sugar and were told there wasn't any. Apparently, a number of locals, who were still on the premises, had also asked in vain for sugar. Our uniformed driver intervened on our behalf, and we were quickly brought three pounds of sugar from a back room – again, not a good advertisement for the new régime, which was supposed to put an end to privilege. The looks we got as we left were anything but warm.

On the way back in the jeep, our driver advised us to get out of the country as quickly as possible. "There's going to be trouble," he said in Spanish. "You won't want to be around."

Shortly past noon, we were back at sea.

JUNE 2: *near the Snook River, Nicaragua*

Yesterday marked the anniversary of our leaving Winnipeg, but at the moment we're in no mood to celebrate. For the past two nights, the rain and tides have soaked us, and the bugs have been ferocious. The ghastly heat has been building up under our canoe cover, so that we both have severe heat rash from the waist down. Our rear ends are again raw, making paddling a torment.

The whole coast along here is heavily populated by Miskito Indians. We've talked to many of them, and they all express an abiding hatred for the Sandinistas. They can't get food; they can't get work; they can't sell their goods. The day we left Puerto Cabezas we met a frail little Miskito man and his young son, who were walking along the beach leading a cow on a rope. They told us they were taking the cow to market but wouldn't get nearly as much for it as they would have in the old days. The man had an iron cattle brand hanging from his shoulder and explained that he had to take it to market to prove to the market officials that the cow was his, that its brand matched his iron. "Miskitos are not trusted," he said sadly.

He advised us to stop further down the coast at his home town, Huahua, which we did. And again we got an earful of how the Sandinistas were persecuting the Indians, and in some cases killing them. The woman who cooked supper told us that many of the soldiers at Puerto Cabezas were Cubans from Havana, and that dozens of young Miskitos were migrating to Honduras to join a counter-revolutionary army that some day hoped to retake Nicaragua. The woman was so poor that Dana slipped out after supper and got her a couple of pails of flour from our supplies. She was extremely grateful to get the 20 Nicaraguan córdobas ($2 U.S.) that we paid her for our meal.

It was dark in her little palm shack, and when we got up from the table, I mistakenly left three chocolate bars behind. A minute later I went back for them and found a delighted smile on the woman's face. She thought they were a gift, and I wasn't about to spoil her evening by taking them back.

Tonight we met several other impoverished Miskitos. One of them gave us a couple of pineapples and refused to take the payment we offered. "You keep it, you'll need it," he smiled. Almost every one of these poor people has shown us the same kind treatment. The clothes on one fellow we met were so hopelessly patched and ragged they seemed about to turn to dust. "I'm very poor," were the first words he said to us. Yet he later brought us four boiled eggs and several boiled plantains, piping hot. He nearly flipped with glee when I gave him 25 córdobas.

Just before nightfall, a couple of young Indians from Prinzapolca, about 10 miles south of here, walked up the beach and engaged us in conversation. They asked about the military situation on the beaches between here and Puerto Cabezas. We told them what we knew, and they confided that they were on their way to catch a secret speedboat that would take them to Honduras to train as counter-revolutionaries. They told us several times that the Sandinistas were not about to drive the Miskitos from the coast. Before they left, one of them cast a hard eye at me and said, "War is coming – slaughter. The Americans will invade this week. The faster you get out of here the better."

I will say for the Sandinistas that those we've met have treated us with honesty and dignity – which is more than I can say for the soldiers of Honduras.

JUNE 6: *Monkey Point, Nicaragua*
It has been raining off and on for six days now, making our lives at sea miserable. I wasn't surprised to learn that the Nicaraguan coast gets up to 300 inches of rain a year. It certainly shows in the vegetation, which has again turned to thick jungle, running right down to the waterfront in places.

A couple of days ago, we started getting warnings about Bluefields, the major Nicaraguan port and military base on the Caribbean. We were ordered to stop there by the officials at Puerto Cabezas. A minor military official at Tasbapone told us that our piddling letter of safe passage would carry no weight with the Bluefields officials. The least we could expect, he said, was to be hauled from the water and sent packing back to Canada.

As our distance to Bluefields diminished, we considered every imaginable scheme for getting by the place undetected. We could go miles offshore and pray for calm seas; we could travel at night and hope not to be picked up by radar or fired at by patrol boats. Or we could wait for foul weather and sneak by in rain or mist.

About 15 miles north of Bluefields, we stopped for the night at the little community of False Bluff, where we met George Cuthbert, an intelligent young man of mixed black and Indian blood, who took us to his parents' home. The family was more affluent and congenial than most in this area, and soon they were telling us about their lives, marvelling at our adventures, and generally making us feel human after so many days of dismally subhuman living. They were subtly diplomatic in their politics, allowing only that things were not quite as prosperous for them under the new government.

We had a bad moment after supper when a sudden shrieking came through the window from the dark clearing outside. I jumped from the table to defend myself, only to realize that the screams were not human. We went to the door and watched, sickened, as six men held down a giant boar and castrated it. When the poor animal was released it went wailing off into the jungle, mercilessly pursued by three nasty mongrels biting at its hindquarters, undoubtedly attracted by the blood. Mr. Cuthbert noted calmly that the boar would now grow "big and fat" – just in time to have his other end chopped off, I thought.

The Cuthberts offered us a sleeping cabin for the night, thoughtfully providing mosquito nets and a coal-oil lamp so that we could read and write. Many nights had passed since we'd had clean sheets or any real feeling of warmth or security. With the light out, Dana and I lay listening to the rain on the palm roof, and talking quietly of our big plans for the following day. We had no intention of making an official stop at Bluefields.

By 5:20 a.m., under cover of heavy rain, we were off to meet our fate. Four hours of steady paddling brought us within sight of El Bluff, a huge promontory that drops sheerly into the sea and guards the city of Bluefields a few miles to the south. By this time the rain had cleared, and we were clearly visible. We hoped there was no lookout on the bluff.

Our intention had been to head far out to sea, but at this point we changed our plans, thinking that if we paddled in close to the bluff we could probably sneak by along its base, unseen from above. But as we came within a couple of miles of it we saw two tiny figures on the beach. At first they were walking, but suddenly they stopped and peered out to sea – we knew they'd seen us. There was no longer any point in trying to get to the base of the bluff, so we angled slightly out to sea, hoping to be taken for locals coming into Bluefields.

A minute later we heard the crack of a rifle, erasing any doubt we might have had over whether the figures were soldiers. We froze, then I shouted at Dana, "Let's go!" and we took off like a powerboat. One of the soldiers took off, too, running south along the beach. At this point, we felt fairly sure we could pass the bluff before the runner could get to it, thus blocking his view of us and preventing him from following us further. If he had signal equipment we were in trouble, of course, as we could easily be intercepted by a boat from the south.

For 10 minutes we paddled our guts out, expecting more shots at any moment. None came.

We soon had the big bluff to our right and were invisible to the soldiers. Immediately, I swung the canoe to the southeast and headed out to sea. The farther out we went, the higher the waves got, and the better our chances became of not being seen among the swells.

For an hour or more we paddled in abject fear, both of us bent at ridiculous angles to make ourselves less visible. Our chins were nearly on the tarp. About three miles out, we swung due south again. Isla El Venado, which is 7 miles long, was now within sight. If we could get to it, we would be shielded from the mainland. In no time, we were alongside it, still paddling frantically, half expecting to see a patrol boat at any time. By the time we emerged from the protection of the island, we were well south of Bluefields. But we didn't let up for a moment. If anything we paddled harder, excited by the possibility that we'd pulled it off.

By the time we pulled ashore at 5 p.m., we'd come an astonishing 42 miles and were 27 miles south of Bluefields. Never had we paddled so hard or long. We'd been on the water nearly 12 hours, and were understandably joyous at our achievement. We came ashore at the little black community of Monkey Point and for 20 minutes or so we couldn't stop congratulating ourselves, laughing at how they were probably still looking for us back at El Bluff. Now you see 'em, now you don't. For once, we'd given the military the slip.

A somewhat suspicious black family agreed to cook us a meal for 20 córdobas. It turned out to be a gourmet treat: smoked turtle meat, gravy, root vegetables, and lots of mangoes.

They see few white men in these poor little black villages, and we had a devil of a time explaining what we were doing here and where we'd come from. None of them had ever heard of Canada and had to be content with knowing we were from *"lejos, lejos, lejos," very* far away. Several of them told us they'd never been more than 10 miles up or down the coast, about as far as they can go in a day, round-trip, in their shallow-draft *cayucas*.

Our hosts offered a dusty little room to sleep in, but Dana decided to stay out by the canoe to guard it. It hurts us to diminish these innocent people by suggesting they're dishonest – they're not. They're just so desperately poor they have to grab what they can to survive.

All night, the jungle shook with the cries of monkeys and birds. Several of the locals keep monkeys for pets.

Yesterday, in the pre-dawn darkness, I paddled off without my sleeping shell, which had been hanging in a tree to dry. Having lost my sleeping pad during our imprisonment back at Cauquira, I'm now without bedding of any sort. It's a serious problem, as my shell has been my best protection against the nightly onslaught of bugs – as well as against the cool night air. The pad was protection from the cool and damp below. Since I can't immediately replace either item, I'll simply have to bundle up in my clothes and try not to be too resentful of Dana who still has his shell and has laid permanent claim to the remaining sleeping pad.

Past the Panama Canal

JUNE 8: *on the Río Colorado, Costa Rica*

What a relief it was yesterday as we slipped by San Juan del Norte and quietly crossed the border into Costa Rica, our eighth country. We have come some 6,100 miles, more than half the length of our trip. It's as if we'd scaled a giant mythic mountain and were now on our way down the other side.

Costa Rica (the "rich coast") was named by Columbus in 1502 when he saw the coastal natives in their fine gold ornaments. Today the country has a population of about 2 million and is said to be the most democratic country in Central America – which is just fine with us, after what we've been through in Honduras and Nicaragua. Our plan is to enter a long inland canal branching off the Río Colorado about 17 miles south of the border, and paddle the canal all the way to Limón, about 75 miles to the south.

Tonight we're safely installed on the banks of the Río Colorado, but getting in through the mouth of this flooding river yesterday was another in our seemingly endless chain of Herculean trials. The river mouth, or *boca*, is several miles wide, and in the area where the heavy breakers from the sea meet the current of the swollen river there is a boiling cauldron of turbulence, covering several square miles and stretching out along the coast to the north and south. The frightful *boca* that capsized us and swept us out to sea at Alvarado was a chamber pot by comparison. Not only was there no chance of our paddling across the *boca*, but I had grave doubts that we could even get to shore anywhere near it. We had to land on the near side of the river if we wanted to get upstream to a safe cross-ing place.

We paddled up to the *boca* about a quarter of a mile offshore and, having gone as far as we could into the turbulence, cut sharply toward land. "No matter how bad things get," I shouted to Dana, "we can't let the canoe go over. Even if it looks like we've flipped, we can't let it happen. We can't. We mustn't." I kept up a constant din as we barrelled and bounced towards shore. One false move, and I knew we were lost to the sea.

We hit the surf, struggling frantically for control, and, in less time than we might have imagined, were driven hard onto the sand, the canoe heav-ing and groaning beneath us. The strain of it all had pretty well finished our gunwales, which were now broken through in the five places where they'd been cracked, back at Alvarado. Our most immediate problem, however, was that we were still half a mile north of the river. We might have camped where we were, except that the tide was about to flood the area for miles around.

Our only course was to portage half a mile along the beach, and I calcu-lated that it would take us seven return trips to move our gear and the canoe to where we wanted to be. Three hours in all, by which time it would be dark, and we'd still have to cross the river to safety. We were already thoroughly exhausted from our long day on the sea.

Just at that moment, a wiry little black man and his young son came loping down this isolated stretch of tidal shore. Before we'd even opened our mouths, the man understood our predicament and, within seconds, had hoisted our heaviest equipment box onto his bare shoulder and was trotting down the beach with it, skipping lightly over the litter of driftwood and flotsam that covered the sand. I was afraid the metal edges of the 80-pound load would cut into his skin, but he didn't seem to notice.

Back and forth we went, all four of us working like mules, the little boy carrying paddles and water containers, and anything else that was light enough for him. We hadn't seen a soul all day, and here these visitors from heaven had shown up at the right moment on this unlikely stretch of coast. What they were doing there, we'll never know – unless the whole affair had been orchestrated by Providence.

In just over an hour, with darkness coming on, our portage was complete. I had no Costa Rican currency, and could only offer the man my last u.s. one-dollar bill, which he took happily. I gave him a big affectionate hug, lifting him right off his feet, and, when we'd shaken hands and said our goodbyes, Dana and I got back into the canoe and headed inland upriver.

Because of the flood-current, we had no choice but to stay within a few yards of the north bank, where the flow was not as great and we could pick up occasional back eddies. Debris tore by us: logs, floating pads of vegetation, small trees, stalks of bananas, all racing out to sea. We had now been going hard for 12 hours, and could barely take a proper stroke. But we saw no potential campsites; the flood water had left everything swampy.

As we pushed slowly inland, we picked up the exquisite scent of some potent jungle flower. It came drifting over the debris-infested waters and perked us up, stimulating one last good burst of paddling, which, as it turned out, was all we needed.

Just past dusk, we saw an electric light on the far bank. We accepted it as our destination, though we couldn't go straight across to it; the current would carry us much too far back downstream. We battled another quarter of a mile upstream, and then headed out across the water, drifting wildly down current in the direction of the light.

Our geometry was dead on, and in no time we pulled up at a dark wharf. Behind it we could now see the outline of a building. Even before we'd secured the canoe, two men in uniform appeared out of the darkness. They had handguns, but, ah, relief, they didn't have them drawn. They asked politely for our documents, promising to return them in the morning.

The man who'd helped us make our portage had told us to look for an American lodge owner a few miles up river. We asked the men in uniform if they knew of any such American, and they directed us to Río Colorado Lodge only a few hundred yards away. The American turned out to be a Canadian, Ken Cameron, who was very much concerned by our ghastly appearance. He saw to it that we had a comfortable room for the night, then fed us handsomely. It was exactly what we needed, and for 20 minutes before dinner I stood luxuriating in the shower as the grime and salt of many days washed down the drain.

Ken and his staff can barely believe that we came in over the mouth of the Río Colorado, which they say is the most notorious *boca* on the Caribbean. Its wide sand delta, or *bara*, has apparently claimed many lives, and has been known to destroy large powerboats. One fishing guide called it "a miracle" that we'd made it through. Ken says that if we'd come through at any point other than the one we chose, we'd certainly have been killed. We've also been told that the mouth is infested by sharks that congregate to feed on the carrion that gets washed down the river.

Our canoe is in dreadful shape, and this morning, when we got up, I asked Ken whether he thought I'd be able to get repairs done in Limón. "Probably," he said, "but you'd be better off doing them right here." This is a fishing camp (apparently famous for snook and tarpon), and there is a well-equipped repair shop right on the premises. By late this afternoon, *Orellana* had been patched and buttressed and was looking pretty much herself. I mended the gunwales with three pieces of aluminum angle track that overlap the breaks in the wood.

As I write this evening, Dana and I are feeling pretty well normal again and look forward to pressing ahead tomorrow. The 70-odd miles of calm inland waterway will be the perfect chaser to a regenerative day at the lodge. One of the greatest achievements of the afternoon was finding a slab of thick foam rubber from which I cut two seat cushions that will protect our ravaged hindquarters from the tough nylon strapping of the seats. I tested mine on land – beautiful.

There are some caged monkeys and parrots on the premises, and I spent a while this morning feeding them bananas, which grow wild around here in great numbers. I took 20 bananas back to our room and enjoyed playing monkey with them. Dana spent most of the day in a private heaven, practising his guitar.

Before I say goodnight, I should record that, for several hours yesterday, before reaching the Río Colorado, we travelled the biggest waves we've seen yet – mountainous in volume, but flat-topped and strangely unthreatening. We needed four long strokes to get up each mighty slope, and four more to get down into the next valley. We estimated the height of these slow-moving monsters at 25 feet.

JUNE 10: *Parismina, Costa Rica*

We left the lodge yesterday morning, found our canal, and were soon immersed in the dazzling world of the Costa Rican jungle: 90-foot trees trailing endless tangled vines; magnificently coloured birds and flowers; immense silences broken only by the occasional cries of birds and monkeys. The water is as black as ebony, and the jungle foliage rises straight up from the canal banks, sometimes overhanging us, nearly touching the foliage on the opposite shore.

In no time we saw our first sloth, a big bundle of sedentary fur, tucked happily into the low crotch of a tree. A few minutes later, we spotted a bright yellow bunch of bananas growing about 20 feet from the canal bank. I scrambled ashore and lopped them off with my machete. They were a smidgeon on the firm side, so we laid them out on the canoe cover to ripen.

I can hardly communicate how pleasurable it is to be back on calm, fresh water, away from the surf and the painfully corrosive salt. And it's great to be in such exhilarating surroundings. Our foam cushions are working wonders, and for the first time in months we have our canoe cover off, allowing the good fresh air to circulate around our hips and legs.

We've been taking it easy, trying to absorb as much as possible of this splendid greenhouse of nature. Today, we saw magnificent stands of bamboo, towering 60 feet above us. Many of the trees support 70- or 80-foot vines, some of which drop right into the canal, making a sinister disappearance beneath the inky water. The blood-chilling and thundering screams of the howler monkeys carry for miles through the jungle.

Surprisingly, the canal is marked with milage signs, indicating distances to various canal villages. But no sign has impressed us like the 10- by 20-foot giant that faced us as we rounded a bend this afternoon: CURVAS PELIGROS ADELANTE – Dangerous Curves Ahead. Both of us broke out laughing; the thing was as big as any sign on a North American 16-lane freeway, and the only boats we'd seen all day were a few small *cayucas*.

JUNE 12: *Moin, Costa Rica*

We finished our canal paddle yesterday at the town of Moin, and got permission to stay the night in the partially finished house of a man named Juan Lopez, who was busy carving a fine *cayuca* in the nearby yard.

We were told there was railway construction going on in town, and that a number of Canadians from the Canadian Pacific Railway were here as consultants. Having worked for the CPR for 17 years, I was intrigued, and, during the evening, we found our way to the trailer-style homes of the project workers. We introduced ourselves to a blonde woman of perhaps 35 who told us she was from Elkhorn, Manitoba, but now lived in Winnipeg. We were jumpy with excitement to meet someone from our home town. "We've canoed all the way from Winnipeg," I enthused. "We've been on the water over a year."

"That's nice," she said, and turned and disappeared into her trailer – and that was that.

This morning we took the bus into Limón and tried at two banks to get money on my credit cards. But neither would give us any. They also refused to exchange any of our Nicaraguan or Honduran currency, showing open contempt for Nicaraguan money. We're really in a fix; we're down to $7 U.S. and have no local money and very little food. La Ceiba, back in Honduras, was our last good shopping call. We can't even raise the $20 it's going to cost us to get visas for Panamá, which is now only 53 miles away. But there's certainly no point in hanging around worrying about it. We'll just have to stretch what food we've got and hope for some successful foraging. We can probably beg a few items if it comes to that. It's unlikely we'll be able to get money before our next major city, Colón, at the Panama Canal. We've been told there'll be no problem with North American credit cards in the Canal Zone. Problem is, it's nearly 200 miles away.

JUNE 15: *Crawl Cay, Panamá*

The seas have posed no real difficulties since we left Limón, and yesterday morning, in torrid heat, we reached the Río Sixaola and sliced across the border into Panamá. Our days in Costa Rica have rejuvenated us, and Dana's mood has been terrific, which does a lot for my own state of mind. The scenery, too, has elevated our spirits – unpopulated jungle, backed by heavily forested mountains which take on a purple cast as they recede into the distance.

We did have a setback yesterday, discovering that the people who cooked us dinner on our last night in Moin had stolen most of our remaining food staples. Gone were 10 lbs. of rice, 6 boxes of spaghetti, 3 lbs. of sugar, 4 boxes of biscuits, cheese, and numerous canned goods. We've been on strict rations since, and right now are waiting impatiently for the many bananas we've scrounged to ripen up. We've seen dozens of banana boats, most of which make a practice of jettisoning damaged bananas – even lightly damaged ones – into the sea. Just south of Limón, we salvaged two whole stalks that were bobbing on the calm waters. We've also harvested coconuts and guayabas, a small yellowish fruit, gorged with seeds. So we aren't starved yet, though our supplies are getting extremely scarce. At the moment, we're living chiefly on oatmeal and fruit.

I'm sad to say that this morning I left my machete and my 25-year-old scuba knife sitting on the sand at our camping spot at Lime Point. I'd been husking a coconut before sunrise and, in the darkness, hadn't done a proper equipment check before leaving. Fortunately, we still have my Russell belt knife.

We had our passports stamped yesterday at Bocas del Toro, and are camped tonight on the dock of a little store at Crawl Cay in the protected waters of Isla Bastimentos. When the storekeeper saw us eating our sparse supper, he felt sorry for us and donated a tin of sardines, a small package of soda crackers, and a couple of coconuts. He gave us permission to sleep at the end of his long wharf, which will situate us as far as possible from the bugs alongshore. We're near his gasoline storage, and as he retired for the evening, he begged us with a pained look, "*No fumar, por favor!*"

"*No fumar!*" Dana reassured him.

The guy was kind enough to give us six large plantains for the canoe; they're like big, hardy bananas, three-sided, and weigh up to a pound each. Everybody, including the knowledgeable fellow who wrote the u.s. Airforce Survival Manual, says don't eat plantains raw, you *can't* eat them raw, they'll give you problems, boil them or fry them. But we eat them raw, anyway, and they feel a lot better in our stomachs than hunger ever did. In fact, once their skins blacken, they're every bit as palatable as good sweet bananas.

JUNE 20: *at Salud, Panamá*

If you asked me how we'd survived since leaving our little store at Crawl Cay five days ago, I could easily say on strength of will, or of body, or on astuteness, or even on sheer luck, any of which answers might wash. But the truth is we'd never have got this far if it hadn't been for the incredible charity of the people who live along this coast. Everywhere we've stopped, they've recognized our situation and have befriended and fed us. And fed us. Three days back at Calovebora, a young man spoke to us on landing, then ran and got us five ripe bananas (our own were still green); a woman showed up on the beach with freshly baked buns, then a young couple brought us a big covered plate of hot rice and sardines. Further south, at Limón Donosa, we got tortillas, eggs, rice, fish, turtle, bananas, root beer, and coffee – all from different people. Just this afternoon, we sat down with the Camargo family of Salud for a superb meal of beef, rice, plantain, and mangoes.

Our meals have probably been better this week than last, before we went on starvation rations. On the few occasions we've fed ourselves, we've had to dig deep into our food box. One teensy meal consisted of two little tins of cocktail sausages and a four-ounce tin of peas – as well as a few bananas and coconuts, of course. On several occasions, I've thought longingly of turtle stew as we came upon one of the numerous giant sea turtles that inhabit the area. We slide up to them, and they slowly hiss out their air and dive. Some of them are a good 3 feet across, with heads the size of canteloupes. One old fellow we saw had a deep shag rug of moss and seaweed growing on his back. I'm sure if I put my mind to it I could take one with my belt knife, but I daren't mention it to Dana or I'll have a revolt on my hands.

Our thirst is of course as rampant as our hunger, and we'll often get talking about drinks as we paddle in the heat. "Wouldn't it be great to have a milkshake!" I'll call.

"Yeah!" shouts Dana, "a great big chocolate one!"

"Or a couple of beers!"

"Or a Coke! I could really go for a Coke right now!"

The other day, without the slightest regret, we spent our last American dollar on four cans of Orange Crush. We can't get enough fluids into us, and the sweeter the better.

We had one day of nightmarish paddling back near Crawl Cay at Punta Valiente; in fact, it may have been our worst day yet – eight grisly hours into 20-foot peaked waves, with a jagged coast waiting to tear us up if we made even the slightest miscue. But otherwise the seas have been gentle and favourable. On the 17th, we paddled 45 miles on the glassy water. Since we're into the rainy season, we try to get our paddling done during the morning and early afternoon – for some reason, it never seems to rain until about 3 p.m. We get off the water by 2, find our shelter, and down it comes, torrentially.

The other day, six big dolphins swam in close to us and accompanied us for a mile or more like a regimental guard. One led the way a few feet in front of the bow, two swam abreast on each side, and one followed. They were a new species for us, with small white spots on their navy blue skins. In the past few days, we've seen dozens of flying fish, thin little things which surprise and amuse us with their 100-foot flights.

The whole coast along here has been a continuous panorama (or should that be "Panamarama"?) of jungle, cliffs, and mountains. Some of the landscapes are alarmingly rugged. Today at Río Diego, we caught an eerie reminder of man's timeless battle with nature. Hanging over a high cliff alongshore, among the trees and rocks, was a crashed cargo plane. We were later told it was Honduran and had gone down four years ago. It startled us to see it there, and we paddled on quickly, too much reminded of our own frailty.

Last night while checking our notes, we discovered that we now have the second longest canoe trip on record. We passed the old mark of 6,100 miles back at the Río Colorado. The dream rolls on, and tonight we're just 24 miles from the legendary Panama Canal. As we came into Salud this afternoon, we could see tiny, distant puffs of smoke, surely the signs of ships entering or leaving the canal. I remember the crazy looks I got back home when I first spoke of taking a monumental canoe trip, one tiny feature of which would be dipping my paddle in the Panama Canal. And now here we are.

The other night, Dana and I had a long conversation, not entirely positive, about all the realities and illusions we've dealt with in getting here. We talked about the sacrifices and benefits and purposes of it all. Lately, however, I'm inclined to think of the trip not so much as *having* purposes but of being its own purpose, of having a rich and varied meaning in itself – the journey as the message. I remarked on this to Dana, and he seemed to accept it as valid.

Tomorrow, Colón, money, shopping, food. Maybe we'll get a peek at the Big Ditch.

JUNE 23: *at Colón, Panamá*
Our intention all along has been to take a couple of days to go through the canal, spend a day on the Pacific at Panama City, come back through the canal, and carry on. It's one of the few items on our whole itinerary that have been planned since the very beginning. Yesterday, however, we got bitter news. We will not be allowed into the canal.

We reached the Canal Commission Offices in downtown Colón at about 11 a.m. We knew that everyone using the canal must pay a fee and be assigned specific times to go through the various locks. Immediately we were given the runaround – office to office to office. We were eventually directed to the Acting Captain of the Port, E. F. Moochler, whose name I shall forever hold in contempt. He was an American, and as we approached his desk, he looked up from whatever he was doing and, before we could say a word, growled, "I don't know what you two guys want, but the answer is No!" He had a churlish grin on his face, and we first thought he was joking.

He wasn't. No matter how we pleaded or reasoned, he would not give us permission to enter the canal. His excuse was that our canoe wasn't "seaworthy", even though we explained at length how it had fared at sea, and in the locks of the Mississippi.

"Too much turbulence here," he grunted.

The ludicrous thing was that I had just been reading how, in 1970, a three-foot toy boat had gone through the canal. I'd also read that a man had *walked* through the canal, on floats of some sort.

"*I* didn't give 'em permission," said Moochler. "Why don't ya put your canoe on a ship and go through that way?"

I felt like putting him on a ship. We asked if we could speak to a higher authority, but he refused to give us any names.

How do so many of these obstructive types end up in positions of authority? Their attitude seems to be, if I haven't got the gumption or spark to do anything interesting, nobody else is going to do anything either – at least if I have any control over it. We left the aptly named Mr. Moochler chortling away on the phone, cursing a purple streak and smoking himself into what we hoped would be early asphyxiation.

We later got through to some other Canal bureaucrats by phone, but all we could get was more red tape. So the trip through the canal to the Pacific really is off. All of this is not to say that our experience of the area has been totally unhappy. I took great pleasure, for instance, in seeing the mouth of the Río Chagres as we came in from Salud the morning before. The Chagres cuts well into the Isthmus of Panamá and was the route used by the gold seekers from the east as they headed for California in the Rush of '49. They'd go some distance up the Chagres in small boats, then trek through the swamps and over the hills to the Pacific shore. Many of them lost their lives en route. During the 1600s the old pirate, Captain Morgan, had used the same route to bring his booty through from the Pacific. He built a fort on the north shore of the river mouth, but it was destroyed and rebuilt as Fort San Lorenzo by the Spaniards in 1751. The vine-covered remains of San Lorenzo looked benignly down on us from the cliffs as we passed within a quarter of a mile of the wide river mouth.

We'd had numerous warnings about thieves, but have had no trouble with them. The most disturbing thing about the city is the poverty – which is superficially masked by the enormous volume of international retailing that goes on here. The city is a duty-free port, and is crawling with bargain hunters and beggars. One poor old black fellow, who volunteered to show us to the Dairy Queen, told us that his son had been killed the previous day in an industrial accident in the u.s. and that he was headed for the funeral if he could raise any money. It may have been true.

The Bank of America gave us $500 u.s. on my visa card, and we went out directly and bought a new machete, our Panamá visas, a new set of guitar strings for Dana, and a bear's helping of junk food: milkshakes, ice cream, French fries and hamburgers. We waited till yesterday to do our proper food shopping, and are now well stocked for the next couple of hundred miles.

One of our stops was at the Colombian consulate, and after many delays we managed to get three-month visas for Colombia. In the end, we were so grateful to the woman who finalized the transaction, I opened up a big bag of buns we were carrying and gave her several for her lunch. We then told her we'd been hearing terrible stories about Colombia and its dope smugglers and pirates. "Do you think we'll get through?" I asked her in Spanish, and she started laughing. "Of course you'll get through. You'll have no trouble with the people at all." Unlike others we've met, she stopped short of declaring *her* country the most peaceful in South or Central America. But she made us feel better, and we can only hope she knows what she's talking about. A small voice inside tells me to suspend judgement for the time being.

We've been staying at the Club Náutico, a Colón yacht club on Limón Bay. We've struck up a friendship with the club Commodore, Hubert "Pretty" Webber, who lent us five dollars when we arrived, broke, on Sunday. We're sleeping on a 2-foot-wide concrete section of the club wharf, with water on either side of us. It's not comfortable, nor is it the worst mattress we've had. At least it has a roof over it, which protects us from the nightly rains. From our wharf, we can see dozens of international vessels at anchor out on the bay, each awaiting its turn in the canal.

Today an attractive young American woman named Susan Stabbler who writes for the Panama Canal *Spillway*, the Canal Commission newspaper, showed up to interview us. She was the most energetic reporter we've met, and took elaborate pains to get our story down, enthusing all the while over what we'd accomplished. It was a pleasure talking to her, and I was pained to think she worked for the same organization as E. F. Moochler. She took a good 30 photos of us in various poses, making us feel like a couple of grubby fashion models.

Yesterday, we phoned our hometown newspaper and talked to Richie Gage, who told us he couldn't make it to Panamá but might get to Cartagena, Colombia. He'd relayed our last call to Jeff and to Dana's mother, who he said had seemed disturbed by the news of our difficulties. Jeff expressed disappointment that he hadn't stayed with us. It'd be wonderful to see him if he ever decided to rejoin us.

JUNE 29: *Mansucun-Comarco de San Blas, Panamá*
We're beginning to get psyched up for Colombia, which is now only 40 miles away. In the meantime we're enjoying the delights of the San Blas Islands, which form a 100-mile chain along the eastern Panamanian coast, about 12 miles offshore. Our route has been marvellously protected, and

it's wonderful at the end of a day to be able to write it all up without having to describe some new threat or trauma.

The wildlife, too, seems to appreciate the protection. In some areas, thousands of bright orange starfish, a foot or more in diameter, shine up at us from the clean sand bottom. We're seeing more giant turtles than ever, and the other day decided to try to get close to a particularly big one bobbing on the surface. Dana froze in the bow, and I paddled soundlessly to within 20 feet of it, then just let the canoe drift. We were soon within 3 feet of it, and still it didn't dive. I thought perhaps it was sick, then Dana shouted, "It's made of wood!" I edged up to it, and, sure enough, it was a great big wooden replica, perfect in every detail, right down to the moss growing on its back. I prodded at it and could see several bamboo poles hanging beneath it, and some sort of suspended net. We thought it must be shark bait but were later told it was turtle bait, intended to lure and trap giants like itself, presumably for food. It certainly lured a couple of naive gringos.

Yesterday afternoon we camped on a fine island beach backed by a luxurious stand of coconut palms. As we ate our supper, a small motorized Indian canoe approached, carrying two men. One of them introduced himself as an island Sahila or Chief. He was polite but told us firmly that this was a Cuna island and was not to be used for camping. We later learned that the Cunas consider the entire San Blas chain their territory and not that of the Panamanian government. They have their own flag of independence and are apparently disposed to check the passports of visitors to their islands, though no one has yet asked for ours. The Panamanian government goes along with this, and has officially named certain islands (apparently not as many as the Cunas would like) exclusive Cuna property.

Our two visitors told us we'd have to go to their community at Playon Chico and might be able to sleep there. They offered us a tow, and we explained that we'd prefer to paddle, which we did for half an hour, as their canoe motored alongside us, trailing a fishing line.

Within minutes of our arrival at the village, at least 200 Cunas of all ages were out to greet us. The men and boys were dressed like most other coastal villagers, but the women wore gloriously coloured costumes and jewellery and were the first natives we've seen with gold rings through the fleshy septum between their nostrils. Their skirts were substantial-looking wraparounds, in striking red, blue, and green patterns. Many of them wore equally bright shawls over simple garments called *molas*, which are nothing more than embroidered cotton panels, one for the back, one for the front. The most intricate parts of their costumes were the tiny single-strand rings of beads, which they wore by the hundreds on their legs and arms, sometimes forming anklets or bracelets 8 or 9 inches wide. All the women wore their dark hair bobbed short, just below the ears.

We were escorted by the crowd to a nearby church whose front door was padlocked. One of the men who'd led us in the canoe, Filio Misselis, smashed open the lock with a hammer and let us inside. He then barred the door with his arms and told the crowd to leave us alone, explaining that we needed some peace. But as soon as he'd gone, the door and windows were filled with dozens of curious faces.

Filio was soon back, asking us to follow him to a small stand-up washing area enclosed by a woven bamboo fence. We went in, took off our clothes, and began sloshing buckets of water over ourselves. However, the bath had been constructed for the much shorter Cunas, most of whom are less than 5 feet tall, so, from the chests up, we were entertainment for the numerous villagers who stood around as we scrubbed away at our filthy hides.

We were subsequently led to a small, dark house, where Filio and a couple of others treated us to a cold chocolate drink, then fresh fried fish and hot buns. Well fed, and feeling honoured by all the attention, we were now led through a maze of alleys between several dozen thatched houses. A crowd of kids followed along, chattering and laughing.

At the far end of the village, we came to a massive structure made of palm leaves and local wood. We entered the black interior and were escorted by hand to a number of hammocks, all of which were occupied by male members of the tribe. We were introduced to a very old man who, as it turned out, was the Sahila. The others seemed to be lesser tribal officials. A crowd had followed us in and now stood around, watching and listening.

As the Sahila swung slowly in his hammock, I used my best Spanish to explain our voyage. He said little – just listened, nodding casually as I talked. Eventually, he seemed satisfied and told us to take our documents to a small desk at the other end of the lodge to be checked by one of his officials. From his hammock he held out his hand; we shook it and quickly had our papers confirmed.

What marvellous hospitality it all was – and everything in the ideal order: accommodation, cleansing, food, then business.

Halfway back to the church, in the middle of the packed road between rows of houses, we got a surprise. In front of us, though certainly not for our benefit, a ceremonial dance was about to begin. Twelve people in costume formed a ring and started stomping and shaking gourds in time to an exotic tune played on reed pipes by three musicians. The dance was quickly over, and we never discovered its significance, though we appreciated seeing this aspect of Cuna tradition.

Tired from the day, we retired to the little church to sleep. But in no time we had visitors, including a number of children. Dana responded by taking out his guitar, and the youngsters soon produced a guitar of their own. The kids plunked away, and in the course of an hour or so Dana was able to teach them a few simple skills – a gentle souvenir of our visit.

When our last guest had left, we settled quickly to a deep, pleasurable sleep.

. . . Again, tonight, we're camped in a Cuna village, except that this time our home is the main community hall. And once again we got visitors as the day drew to a close – 50 or more of them. Again Dana took out his guitar, this time putting on a proper concert. The shy Indians listened to piece after piece without so much as a clap or a sound, though their fascination was obvious.

When Dana stopped for a break, the crowd swarmed in on us, many of them touching our arms and hands, I suppose to see if our skin felt the same as theirs. Some of the children reached up and touched our long hair, especially the parts that have been bleached by the sun and salt.

Again we slept well, confident of our safety in the hands of these honest people.

At 4 a.m., we were wakened by the powerful voice of the village crier: "*Cuatro en día! Cuatro en día!*" – "Four a.m.!" Immediately, we could hear the village awakening: the coughing and clearing of throats, feet stamping, pots and pans rattling. Work while the day is young – especially if you have no electricity to work at night.

Into Colombia

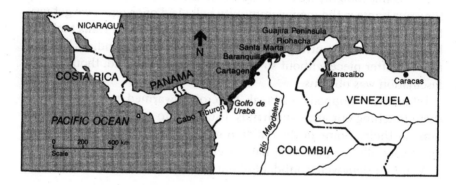

JULY 2: *Punta Goleta, on Golfo de Uraba, Colombia, South America*

We've had intensifying warnings about Colombian coastal pirates, who are said to travel in speedboats and to exact ruthless penalties from their victims. So it was with some trepidation that we slid across the Colombian border at Cabo Tiburón yesterday morning. The fact that *tiburón* is the Spanish word for shark did little to bolster our courage. Nor did our brief conversation with a couple of Panamá National Guardsmen we met at Puerto Obaldia just before crossing into Colombia. "They'll take everything you have," one of them told us. "If you're lucky they won't kill you." We paddled far more slowly than usual – why hurry toward disaster?

But by early afternoon we'd seen nothing but our own paranoid shadows and decided to call it quits at the village of Zapzurro, where we immediately gave a young black kid an American dollar to get us some bananas. He returned with 30, we gave him another dollar, and he quickly got us 30 more, most of which were gone by this afternoon.

Yesterday was Canada Day, and we spent the evening in quiet celebration of being the first people to reach South America by canoe from

Canada: 6,730 miles. By nightfall, however, it had begun to rain, and the rest of our night was miserable.

I had an intense scare in the hours after midnight when Dana woke me up yelling, "The canoe is gone!" The beach here is very low, and the tide had come in higher than we'd expected and had flooded the sands. I jumped up and went tearing down the beach to grab the canoe about 20 feet offshore. Only the slight onshore wave action had prevented it from floating away entirely.

I must say we're not impressed by the Colombians we've met so far. A few hours ago we watched a cruel teenage boy repeatedly throw a long pole into a flock of brown pelicans that was quietly fishing offshore. He eventually hit one on the head and stunned it, though it recovered after a few minutes and resumed its fishing, if groggily. A while later a young man came down to the beach with a rifle that he fired by pulling a bit of cord where the trigger had once been. In no time, he'd shot and killed a pelican, which he hauled away. Why we don't know; they're supposed to be terrible eating.

As the rain came on this evening, we asked a local homeowner if we could sleep under the overhang of his roof. We got a quick refusal, so asked if we could sleep in a crummy little tin-roofed structure that we could see a hundred yards down the beach. "*Siiii!*" he said enthusiastically. When we got there, we discovered it was a pig pen, full of skinny little oinkers and ankle-deep manure.

JULY 10: *at Isla Baru, Colombia*

On July 3 we made a desperate 18-mile crossing from Punta Goleta to Punta Caribana, saving over a hundred miles' paddling around the mighty Golfo Uraba. We are now well over 200 miles into Colombia and have still experienced nothing in the way of a serious confrontation. One night at Puerto Rey we were wakened by the police, who shone spotlights in our faces, but who turned out to be as polite as British bobbies, efficiently checking our documents, then leaving us alone. On the 8th, in a little restaurant at Berrugas, 50 miles west of here, we were given a bit of shake-down by a stubborn army sergeant who wanted to sell us Colombian money for American at a highly profitable rate. I told him we didn't have any money, American or otherwise, and that we travelled exclusively on credit cards. As we returned to the canoe, three armed soldiers came down the beach, and we psyched ourselves up for a rough time. But they were fine young men and wanted only to see our canoe, having heard it had come all the way from Canada. After a few minutes, they shook our hands and left, disappointing the 40 or so locals who had gathered behind them, hoping for a little action.

Our worst trauma so far has been strictly of our own making. The day before last, in the late afternoon, I ate several small green fruits that looked like unripe crabapples, but were sweet to taste. I was painfully overtired at the time and, right after eating them, went and lay down in a grove of trees. When I wakened an hour later, it was raining, and I felt curiously drugged – nothing seemed to matter. Eventually Dana wandered over to ask if I was okay, as it was now pouring and I was simply lying there in the rain looking up at the sky. As I roused myself, my mouth and lips began to burn, and nothing I could do in the way of drinking or salivating or eating would quench the sensation. Half an hour later, the burning stopped as quickly as it had begun.

But for the past couple of days, I've been woozy every time I try to sleep or relax. The feeling clears when I paddle, probably because of the increased circulation, but it returns when I slow down. Dana has warned me a hundred times that one day my curiosity about potential foods will poison me.

The bugs are after us as usual, and now that I'm without my sleeping shell, I wrap myself at night in the only suitable covering I've got – a number of mesh fertilizer bags given to us by Ken Cameron back at the Río Colorado. I put one on each limb and put my mosquito hat on my head. I wrap towels around my neck. It's not Eddie Bauer, but the bags keep the bugs out, and that's what matters.

We're no longer seeing the elongated, diamond-shaped paddles that we saw along the entire coast of Central America. The Colombian blade is a circle, perhaps a foot in diameter, and slightly concave, like a giant porridge spoon.

JULY 15: *Cartagena, Colombia*
This is our fifth day in the majestic city of Cartagena, and I'm only beginning to get over my stomach problems and occasional woozy feelings. We had no intention of staying here so long, but we'd half planned to meet Richie Gage, our reporter friend from Winnipeg, so that he could do a series of stories on our trip. It took us two days of sporadic frustration to reach him by phone and to establish that he's not coming. This is the second aborted attempt to meet him, and we're getting a little fed up with the business. Nevertheless, we've agreed to meet him in Trinidad, where we'll be staying for a while in the fall.

Cartagena was founded in 1533 by Pedro de Heredia, a Spanish imperialist, and is still partly surrounded by its original fortress-like walls. The modern city is full of tall hotels that stretch for a mile or more along the beach. As we paddled into the harbour on the 11th, we were hailed by the crew of a big anchored freighter, the *John*, which was flying the Panamanian flag. We tied the canoe alongside, climbed the ship's ladder, and were enthusiastically greeted by Captain Pollio Giovanni of Italy. The Captain lapped up our story, translating it into French for the benefit of his Tunisian first mate. "I know your St. Lawrence Seaway like the back of my hand," he told us proudly.

Eventually we mentioned that we were hungry, and within minutes two bottles of Italian beer and two submarine sandwiches appeared from the kitchen. Ten minutes later, we were presented with an international treasure chest of food to take with us: Russian salad, sausage, and sardines, Italian beer and canned goods, Dutch canned milk, Polish and Egyptian jams.

We were so hungry that, before we left, we asked politely for another sandwich. "No problem," said Pollio, and he led us to the kitchen – where the cook immediately blew his top at the request. The crew had apparently been wasting his bread, and if he used another loaf on us, he'd have to bake again. He and Pollio went at it in a dramatic standoff, screaming at one another in Italian, their noses inches apart. A few minutes later we got our sandwiches and quickly retreated, uttering nervous thanks.

We paddled into the city and made camp on a quiet lagoon that fronted several elegant hotels. Dana quickly met a young man who invited us to dinner at his parents' restaurant. Meanwhile I made friends with a family from Bogotá, the Sarmientos, who invited us to meet them this evening at their hotel suite a couple of blocks away.

We had an excellent dinner at the restaurant and, an hour later, went off to meet the Sarmientos, a middle-aged couple with a grown son and daughter. The four of them welcomed us and invited us to join them for a room-service dinner in their hotel suite. We had *another* fine meal, whose *pièce de résistance* was a little bowl of unidentifiable, crunchy brown nuggets, salty and tasty.

"Do you know what you're eating?" asked Mr. Sarmiento as we scoffed up the delicacy.

"No," I said, "what?"

"*Hormigas*," he smiled – ants.

Back at the suite, Ricardo, the son, brought out a beautiful Brazilian guitar, and he and Dana took turns demonstrating their various skills. We questioned Ricardo about the Colombian coast and he told us to be careful between Santa Marta and the Guajira Peninsula, where much of the country's dope smuggling takes place. We'd heard that the Guajira Indians could give us a rough time, but Ricardo said he'd recently done a photography shoot on their part of the coast and had had no trouble with them.

I left the party early to get back to the canoe, and laid out my bed on one of the hotel wharves. I lay there in satisfied tranquillity, tolerably full after my two dinners, staring up at the towering hotels, which were lit like Christmas trees against the dark sky. We see so few electric lights that the effect was something of a festival for me. When I awakened later, a young man and woman on the third-floor balcony of the nearest hotel were embracing passionately. I put my head under our tarp, to preserve their privacy – I was sure they wouldn't be there long, as they seemed on the verge of something more intimate. But when I looked an hour later, they were still there, hugging and kissing as passionately as ever.

Twice during the past two days, the female manager of the nearby Galeon Hotel has sent us packages of food, one including an array of chicken parts: gizzards, hearts, livers, wings and feet. With the first package, she requested that we do our best to stay as far as possible from her hotel. She's apparently "*nerviosa*" that we'll frighten the clientele. I won't deny that we're an appalling sight with our burnt and cracked lips, our scabbed noses, our rawhide skins, our straggly bleached hair – all accentuated by our tattered and dirty clothes. It's as if we'd stepped out of some prehistoric tableau. When we went to see the Sarmientos in the hotel the other night, everyone who saw us seemed shocked. Occasionally, we try to explain to people – we've been living in a canoe for 13 months, things have been a little rough, and so on – but it's not easy to put them at ease.

Last night when Dana returned late from the Hilton Hotel, he dug into one of the food bags from the *nerviosa* hotel manager. Suddenly, we were set upon by a couple of plain-clothes policemen with flashlights. They'd apparently been watching us for some time on our well-lit dock, and the sight of Dana sifting through a plastic bag brought them swooping into action. One of them reached into the bag, undoubtedly expecting to extract drugs, and pulled out a handful of soggy rice. He asked to see another bag, a big orange one. "*Mi ropa*," Dana said to him as he handed it over – "My clothes." The policeman snatched it open, then recoiled in horror at the stench of Dana's mouldy canoe apparel, which had been in the bag for several weeks awaiting laundering. "*Mi ropa*," smiled Dana, as he reclaimed the bag.

Though we were disappointed that Richie wasn't coming from Winnipeg, we were at least able to tell him we were safe, and to ask him to pass the message along. His relays are a great help, as so many of our friends and loved ones are anxious for news.

JULY 17: *at Santa Veronica, Colombia*
The Colombian coast is as jagged as a saw blade, and I like to save miles by jumping from point to point. The danger is that, when the bays are deep, we're often left far from shore. Dana prefers the safe route closer to land.

Yesterday morning, as we paddled a couple of miles offshore, heading for Punta Hermosa, Dana grew particularly angry at my risk-taking. A storm was rising ahead, and an offshore wind was stirring up the seas. "Just keep paddling!" I said. "We've only got a couple of miles to go!"

"We've got *six* miles to go!" he objected; he had consulted his maps and was pretty sure of his distances.

A minute later he shouted, "We're too far out!" In no time the storm was on us, and I realized he was right. We immediately headed for a near *punta* on our right, trying to reach a little settlement that we could see beyond it. The point itself was far too rocky for a landing.

We struggled for ten minutes against increasing wind and sidewaves and managed to clear the *punta*. But about 200 yards out a rushing 6-footer caught us obliquely, and our many days without capsizing were over. In an instant, we were hanging upside down in the surf, still tied in our cockpits. Dana got out quickly, but I was held in by a well-tied knot. I'd been struggling frantically for a good 30 seconds when another wave ripped into the canoe, tearing me free.

When I surfaced, gasping, Dana was with the canoe some 30 yards away. He was fighting to right it, and I was amazed to see him succeed – an all but impossible task alone in deep water. The surf quickly carried us to shore, crashing the canoe on the beach.

We bailed like machines, then lifted the lids from our equipment boxes, astounded at what we found. Except for about a cupful of water in each, they were dry. Dana's quick action had saved them. We had a new crack in the canoe, although it was only 3 inches long and I doubted that it would admit water.

Soaked and embarrassed, we were greeted by a family who seemed to be caretaking a nearby beach cottage. We were soon sitting inside, drinking hot coffee and calming our nerves. A middle-aged woman brought us a couple of mangoes. Our maps had been soaked, and Dana began unfolding them and draping them out to dry. He was in the kitchen when I heard him yell. Barefoot and still dripping, he had draped a wet map over the top of the refrigerator and had been belted with a shock. He was all right, though he said the jolt gave his feet and wrists a lingering burning sensation.

Each community we visit sends out its vibrations. We had been befriended here, but as the afternoon wore on the people around us seemed to become increasingly detached and calculating. When I took out my plastic money bag, six or seven pairs of eyes followed everywhere it went. When Dana asked a young man what he did for a living, he said simply, "Contraband – marijuana."

We are now seeing a new breed of suspicious and calculating Colombians. We can feel a strangeness from them.

We paid our hosts $2 to cook us a meal, and as soon as we'd eaten we spread our tarp on the concrete floor of the veranda and sacked out. The canoe sat loaded and tarped about 300 feet away where we'd crash-landed. We felt reasonably secure, but had nonetheless taken our valuables to bed with us: money, maps, documents, radio, compass, binoculars, and, as always, my diaries, which have gained increasing importance to me since the loss of our cameras and film.

About 9 p.m. we were shaken awake. Eight uniformed soldiers surrounded us, armed with machine guns. They had apparently been tipped off by the locals, perhaps one of our hosts. We put up with a good hour of hassling before being left alone.

It rained throughout the night, but I took a number of walks down to our lonely canoe to make sure it was safe.

This morning when I went to check it, however, I found the tarp loose. We had been robbed. I was livid. Much of our clothing was gone and most of our important provisions, including all the wonderful canned goods we'd been given by Captain Pollio of the freighter *John*. Normally, the food wouldn't mean much, but down here it's terribly difficult to replace.

Dana ran off in wild frustration, checking around the nearby houses for any sign that might betray the thieves. I told him he was wasting his time, but he was too enraged to listen. What bothered me almost as much as losing the food was that I'd ruined a night's sleep getting up to check the canoe – at least four times – and it hadn't worked.

We paddled off, cursing, heading northeast for Barranquilla, a city of perhaps a million people and an important centre in the drug trade. We've already decided not to stop – in fact will make as few stops as possible in populated areas along the remaining 400 miles of Colombian coast.

JULY 20: *at the Río Magdalena, Colombia*
Almost everyone we meet these days is a self-appointed cop and demands a
complete explanation from us as to who we are, what we're doing here,
where we're going, etc. They don't merely ask, they *demand to know.*
Last night as we slept no fewer than three separate delegations of beach
walkers shouted us awake, shoving lights into our faces, and firing insensitive questions as we groggily tried to figure out what was going on.

Things are pretty bad here just east of the *boca* of the Río Magdalena.
The wind is howling, the seas are crashing, the sand is whipping us, and
the tidal waters are swirling like boiling soup. We've been here for over 24
hours, making this the first time since Tulum, Mexico, that we've lost a
day to the weather. Our campsite is surrounded by acres of 3-foot sand
dunes, apparently the former bed of the Río Magdalena, which has since
been diverted by concrete embankments and jetties. In the distance,
upriver, we can see Barranquilla.

I hardly need repeat that we've had some tough times at sea, but getting around the *boca* of the Río Magdalena yesterday morning was un-
questionably our worst yet. The river's mouth has been artificially narrowed by two jetties that extend a mile to sea and are half a mile apart.
They narrow the flow and thereby increase the speed of the current, so
that river silt won't settle until it's well offshore. The *boca* must be kept
open for shipping. The trouble is, the accelerated current causes massive turbulence where it meets the incoming waves a few hundred yards
beyond the ends of the jetties.

At 10 a.m., we attempted to cross from one jetty to the other. But we
seriously underestimated the strength of the current. By the time we
were a few hundred yards out we were careering sideways across the water,
groping to stabilize ourselves. The only thing I could do to prevent our
being carried broadside into the worst of the turbulence – an area of deadly
standing waves – was to turn the canoe seaward and run with the current.
We skirted the standing waves, but were soon above the great sand bar,
or *bara*, created by the Magdalena's silt. Here, for as far as we could see,
the waves were bouncing off the sea floor to heights of 20 feet or more.
Our only hope was to get out onto calmer waters, but a persistent wind
from the northeast was holding us in the same place no matter how hard
we worked. Up and down we rocked, sometimes barely aware of our direction, as we were now out of sight of land.

When we'd been tossed about for several hours and were exhausted
and almost drained of hope, a motorboat appeared out of nowhere, carrying five fat Colombian tourists. They had somehow seen us as we rose
on the swells and had come to save our lives. The problem was that their

boat was already crowded — the sea was within 6 inches of their gunwales. What's more, any tow they could have given us would have restricted the rise and fall of our bow, which would have swamped us in no time. At any rate, I wasn't sure their boat was any more certain to make it to shore than our own.

We could hardly ask them to stay nearby to rescue us if we tipped, so, against their puzzled protests, we ordered them to return to land. Slowly they turned their boat, and, a mere 50 feet away, vanished among the swells. We never saw them again.

For five hours we battled, without ever escaping that few square miles of fury. But by 3 p.m. we had manoeuvred far enough east to make a desperate run at the shore beyond the *boca*. When we were a quarter of a mile out, a breaker caught us from behind, sending us into an uncontrolled rocket ride. It was all we could do to keep the canoe pointed to shore. Twice our bow dipped; the third time, it dug into the surf, wrenching us sideways. In an instant, we were back in the water, and the guitar and our paddles and various pieces of our gear had been tossed free. It took me several minutes of panic swimming to round everything up, as Dana clung to the canoe. We were 300 yards out, but soon were washed ashore.

How terribly discouraging it all was. Twice in three days. If it's not the thieves, it's the seas; or the rain; or the bugs; or the sun; or the police or the army. We're nearly 1,400 miles from Trinidad, and more and more I wonder if we'll ever make it. It's impossible to stop and rest, as we have to get there before December, when the northeast winds make the coast impossible to travel.

We spent the five hours between landing and sunset laying out every piece of our sea-soaked equipment. In the dismal process, we discovered that we'd lost more than we'd thought: hats, clothes, plates, pots, running shoes. About suppertime, an old man came wandering down the beach with one of our drinking cups, which I had to buy back with a couple of guayaba candy bars.

We had a fitful night on the beach, as the wind-driven sand banked up around us. This afternoon, even my mouth is full of grit, so that my teeth grind when I move my jaw or talk. Our slow-drying equipment is a ghostly array of petrified sand and salt. All day we've prayed for a break, but I'm afraid we're in for another Sahara night. Down the beach there are two deserted houses, heavily banked with you know what. They remind me of houses I've seen in photos of the dustbowls during the Great Depression. It's them and us and the wind, and that's about it.

The Evil Coast

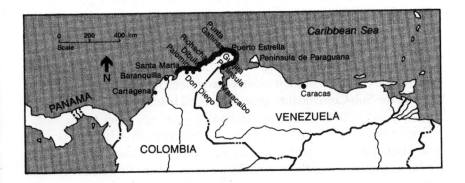

JULY 24: *east of Santa Marta, Colombia*

About the only constant these days is the enormous swings in our fortune and our mood. We pulled away from the Río Magdalena on the 21st, elated to escape the sandstorms and wind. We enjoyed a fine day on the water, and for the first time in nearly a week got an excellent night's rest. Great. The next morning, however, near Laguna Ciénaga, we were accosted at sea by a gang of 13 pie-eyed Indians, doped or drunk beyond reason. They cut us off in their *cayucas*, made a blundering attempt to pirate us, and were only driven off by my machete bravura and a blustering warning that the Colombian government and police were behind our trip. We carried on so brave, so mad, and terribly shaky.

That night, in the tourist centre of Rodadero, we were befriended by a stubby American expatriate named Bronco, who put us up in his hotel room. As we sat around talking, he told us that Rodadero, which is flourishing, had been built on "marijuana money" and that "everything goes on here." Although he stopped short of saying so, he implied that he knew the drug trade from the inside, which was easy enough to believe:

several times that night, a young Colombian named Carlos visited and left the hotel suite either delivering or picking up packages.

Normally, we wouldn't have taken up with a character like Bronco, but when we met him he showed genuine interest in our trip, and he spoke English, which is invariably a drawing card for us. At first we had no inkling that he might be tied up in illicit activity. In the end, he made us somewhat nervous, but we had no arguments with his generosity. And he was certainly right about the bedrock of Rodadero's economy: during the course of the day, we had a dozen or more offers to buy marijuana or cocaine.

Yesterday in Santa Marta we got shelter from yet another unexpected source: The Santa Marta Maritime Police. Thinking we'd get to them before they got to us, we reported to their headquarters when we got into the city. We were introduced to the Sub-Comandante, Gabriel Fernando Rojas Ortiz, who listened to our tale and happily offered us the full services of the headquarters, which houses perhaps 150 men. We could eat with the residents in their cafeteria and sleep in their barracks. At our request, the Sub-Comandante gave us a signed letter of safe passage which *may* help us get to the Venezuelan border, some 350 miles to the east.

Secure and well fed, we headed into the steaming city, where we bought new white hats, eating plates, and a pair of blue track shoes for me. Then we hit a snag – none of the ten banks we were able to find would give us money on either my Visa or Mastercharge cards. And our next major city, Caracas, is nearly a thousand miles away. It's an impossible financial situation, but, having discussed it for an hour or more, we decided there was nothing we could do but carry on and hope – and scrounge when we have to. We bought $65 worth of groceries and are left with $40 u.s.

Our more immediate fear, of course, is the treachery that we're assured awaits us over the next couple of hundred miles of coast. We've had continuing warnings that our lives will be endangered. Even the police are reluctant to give us encouragement. "I can tell you anything you want to hear," said a young officer, who sensed we were looking for some sign of hope. "I can tell you it's scenic and safe and friendly, but it won't change the truth – it's a very dangerous area."

And thus this morning we set out with heavy hearts in the direction of the Guajira Peninsula.

About two hours out of Santa Marta, we heard it coming behind us – the faint whine of an outboard motor. We were soon overtaken by four dark-skinned Colombians, all in their thirties, and each wearing a silly grin of combined curiosity and contempt.

"*Donde va?*" they hollered – "Where are you going?"

"*Lejos!*" we hollered back confidently. We have no desire these days to tell anybody anything about our destinations. Now they *demanded* to know where we were going, but we said nothing. They offered us a tow but we refused, and in no time they swung their boat and disappeared behind us.

But a few minutes later they were back, this time ordering us to shore. Several times we paddled calmly away from them, and each time they roared up behind us again, giving me increasing fears that they were going to ram our canoe. As they passed us for the third time, one of them jumped onto the front deck of the boat wielding a 12-gauge shotgun and screaming, "*Playa! Playa!*" – "Beach! Beach!"

In no time he was yelling, "*Ploma! Ploma!*", then "*Ploma o vida!*" – "Lead or life!"

Through it all we masked our panic, meeting their screaming and threats with a good deal of screaming of our own. When they claimed to be the police, we shouted back that we'd just left the police station at Santa Marta, and that we knew they were lying. If we gave so much as an inch, I knew they'd be on us like wolves.

For half an hour, we yelled back and forth, at which point I was fed up and decided to take a chance and up the ante. I reached beneath the tarp for my machete, and began waving it threateningly. I substantially increased the intensity of my screaming.

"*Plata! Plata!*" they now screamed back – "Money!"

"*No plata!*" I hollered, continuing to wave my machete.

At this point, Dana flipped out. I had never in my life heard him use profanity, but he now unleashed a volley of English curses that turned the air between our boats to a thick blue smog. And I joined right in, practically frothing at the mouth.

Before our eyes, their determination disintegrated. They began looking at one another as if to say What are we supposed to do now? Suddenly, the gunman jumped down from the deck, shook his head, and they swung their boat back toward Santa Marta.

We watched in shock as they disappeared from sight.

An hour later, the seas had grown rough, and we swung into a tiny mountainous bay and flaked out on the beach.

JULY 26: *Bahia Confusa, 19 miles east of Santa Marta, Colombia*
We've made no progress since I last wrote. We attempted a launch yesterday, but the seas were too high, and we were flipped and thrown back on the beach.

At least I've had time to do some work, installing new tarp clips and repairing a couple of thwarts. When the canoe was made, I asked our builder to use nothing but brass fittings and screws. But for some reason, he fastened the thwarts with steel screws, which have now rusted and loosened.

We've decided that, in spite of our losses, we're still carrying too much stuff, and Dana has been going wingy, trying to knock off every unnecessary ounce of baggage weight. He's gone so far as to cut away any portions of maps that we won't need. Our map of Colombia looks like a tapeworm – a long line of coast with a half-inch of paper on either side. A bit excessive, perhaps, but we've come to the conclusion that we just won't make it with anything extra on board. We'll also have less to worry about when we swamp, as we've done three times in the past week and are likely to do many times more on the tough seas to come.

The night before last, I gave our big Sony radio to one of four fishermen (at least they *said* they were fishermen; there wasn't much evidence of it) who paid a visit to our deserted beach. The guy looked at me as if he'd just won the 64-thousand-dollar prize. I explained to him half a dozen times, and in considerable detail, that he'd have to dry it out and clean the salt out of it, as we've had to do many times ourselves. Although I liked the old thing, I'm relieved to be rid of it – with its spare batteries it weighed 5 pounds or more.

Nearly everything we started with is gone, taken by thieves or the ocean: binoculars, tape recorder, two cameras, guns, ammunition, tent, sleeping pad, tools, boots, most of our pots and cutlery, our gas stoves. Dana has even trimmed the rims off our plastic food containers. One thing that pleases me is that, after 7,000 miles, we still have our original paddles. Mine is so heavily bound with string it's beginning to look like a tribal artefact. More and more, I copy the natives and use string or twine to make my repairs – even on the canoe, where I've stabilized the thwarts with tough cord.

Late yesterday afternoon, I got into an exploring mood and set off down the beach toward the rocky promontory at the western boundary of the bay. A few hundred yards from camp, I found a well-hidden path that led up into the jungle. I followed it across a stream into a man-made clearing where someone had recently camped. Normally, I'd think nothing of such a thing, but on this isolated strip of coast, where the mountains rise behind and the surf crashes in front, I was surprised by it. I continued into the jungle, where for some reason I began to feel uneasy. Telling myself it was nothing but the gloominess of the surroundings, I carried on and, within a few yards, experienced a real adrenaline rush. Across the path in front of me, at waist level, was a red plastic tape which extended hundreds of yards through the trees, seeming to encircle some forbidden place beyond.

Incurable explorer that I am – fool that I am – I ducked beneath the ribbon and kept walking. In no time I came to a clearing where I spotted a sturdy little palm hut with what appeared to be a small bed alongside. Nearer to me was a wooden table-like structure that must have been 20 feet long. I stood at the edge of the clearing for nearly a minute, listening and watching. The faintest wash of green light sifted through the trees. Convinced I was alone, I walked as far as the table, intrigued to find it spread with a couple of inches of hard-packed soil. I tiptoed to the hut, peered in and was relieved to find it was nothing but a storage shed – no weapons, corpses, whatever. But on the floor were dozens of burlap sacks. I counted 50, each filled to bursting. There were also twenty 45-gallon drums of gasoline. I hefted one of the sacks and figured it weighed 100 pounds or more. Noticing a rip in one of the bags, I reached in, withdrawing a handful of tiny greenish-brown seeds, perfectly clean and dry. I examined them closely, slipped them back into the bag and left the hut. I walked silently from the clearing, taking care to step only on dry ground so as not to leave footprints.

Intrigued by my find, and now feeling more confident, I persuaded Dana to return to the hut with me. When we got there, he picked up some seeds and immediately identified them as marijuana – 5,000 pounds of clean marijuana seed.

We beat it back to the beach, our only thought, now, to get out of the area as quickly as we could. But the surf was still impossible – if anything it was worse than when we swamped in it during the morning.

The visit of the four men the night before now made some sense. They told us they were fishermen and that they'd come from down the coast. I'd been perplexed by the wretched condition of their equipment, and couldn't imagine it would even be functional. Of course, it didn't have to be; we were the only fish they'd see that night. They'd walked up the beach and disappeared, perhaps along the very trail I'd found. We'd told them we'd be gone first thing in the morning; and here we were, still.

We waited anxiously for a break, but by sunset the waves were still high, giving us no possibility of escape.

Early this morning we launched, and succeeded in getting a few hundred yards onto the water. But out beyond the protection of the bay we were badly tossed about by the east wind and the swells. We looked along the coast ahead for landing sites and could see nothing but steep black rock, sending 20-foot fountains of surf into the air. Dana was being walloped, nearly drowned, by every wave we hit.

Weary and paranoid and soaked – and at great risk of capsizing – we swung the canoe and headed in the direction we'd come. For the first time in a year, we were undoing our progress.

This time we paddled a couple of miles back past our campsite and into another bay, remarkably like the one we'd left. In this one, however, we have a couple of houses and a small plantation behind us in the bush.

Early this afternoon, a young man from one of the houses came along and introduced himself as Jesualdo. A little later, he brought us a gift, a big bag of *yuca*, the staple carbohydrate of the area. We boiled some of them up, doused them in lemon juice, and went to work. Jesualdo hung around, and I asked him the name of the bay we're in. He wouldn't tell me.

"I want to find it on the map," I said.

He now looked at Dana and said jokingly, *"Bahía Confusa"* – the Bay of Confusion.

I didn't press the point but began to wonder if we're just as badly off here as we were up the coast. I must say we saw some unusual activity this morning shortly after our arrival. Six black men from the plantation began carrying out fruit and vegetables and loading them into a red boat anchored in the shallows a few hundred yards down the beach. When they had loaded seven or eight bags, they carried out a live goat and put it aboard. We walked toward them, gradually realizing that their boat was no off-to-market tub but a stylish fibreglass speedboat, perhaps 25 feet long and with a monstrous engine.

The six men, each of whom wore several pieces of gold jewellery, waded out from shore and jumped aboard the speedboat, which roared out of the bay. I asked an old man on the beach if they were going to Santa Marta to sell their produce. He told me they were going to Miami.

"Miami, *Florida?"*

"*Sí*," he said quietly.

This evening as we made our beds, a trawler appeared a few hundred yards offshore, just visible in the twilight. It battled upwind, apparently on the verge of foundering. A few minutes later, a small powerboat appeared from the east, and the trawler sent up several alternating blasts of black and white smoke. Abruptly, the two boats changed course and headed into our bay.

When the trawler was within 200 yards of us, it cut its engines and dropped anchor. I could now see that one of the men in the smaller boat was carrying a rifle. Another powerboat now appeared and positioned itself on the east point of the bay, from where its crew could see down the coast toward Santa Marta. The first powerboat glided to shore, disappearing into an inlet up the beach. In no time it reappeared, towing a huge dugout canoe. In the light that remained, we had no trouble seeing the crew of the dugout loading large wrapped bales onto the trawler.

Unlike yesterday's scene, this one seemed strangely benign – more like a movie than real life. We were soon called back to reality, however, as our friend Jesualdo appeared, insisting we leave the beach immediately. "You must come to my house," he said. "You must come and sleep there – *venga acá.*"

I explained that we didn't want to leave the canoe, and he proceeded to warn us about the many poisonous snakes that infest the beach at night; earlier in the evening he'd told us that tigers would get us if we went into the jungle. I showed him my machete and told him I'd fix any snakes that came our way. He grew increasingly agitated, and when it was clear we wouldn't follow, he got up and walked briskly away. I tried to call him back, but he did not return.

From out of the darkness, the look-out boat began sending signals with a spotlight. The trawler was now showing lights, including a floodlight which it used to illuminate the loading. At a signal from the lookout, the trawler suddenly went black. There were a few minutes of inactivity, then the dugout made another trip. During the next hour, it made half a dozen more. By this time it was totally dark and the only sounds were the waves and the purring of marine engines.

I lay thinking how odd it was that all this was going on within a few miles of the police station at Santa Marta. I was musing that perhaps the police were involved, when I fell into a half-sleep – and was snapped awake by the trawler's searchlight, which was sweeping across the beach toward us. Everything was as bright as noon. I shut my eyes as the light passed over us and moved on. A few minutes later, I was asleep.

JULY 30: *Bahía Confusa, Colombia*

The winds howl, and the waves crash. This is our fifth day windbound at Bahía Confusa, and both of us are racked with frustration. Since leaving Santa Marta seven days ago, we've advanced only 18 miles. We watch the seas obsessively, but have no idea what is happening beyond the mountainous *puntas* that guard our bay. We need a good eight hours of paddling time to get us past the next 30 miles of coast, for which our maps show no protective havens. Weeks ago, Dana predicted we'd have trouble along here. I knew it, too, but more or less ignored the threat, being far more concerned about the smugglers and pirates along the way.

At least the trawler hasn't returned, and in the absence of obvious drug activity, Jesualdo and his friends have been a lot more relaxed toward us. They seem to enjoy having us – we're such an oddity.

One thing's certain: we're not going to starve. The place has 75 sheep, 100 or more turkeys and hens, several cows and steers, and all sorts of fruit trees and vegetables. The women of the bay have cooked us excellent meals, lots of beef and onions and tomatoes. Several times, I've helped out with the plantation work, anxious to repay the many kindnesses we've been shown. The other day, I carried 20 pails of water from a nearby stream to water foot-high coconut saplings. I was more or less under the supervision of a 60-year-old man, whose steady pace of work I greatly admired. At one point he walked me to a hole at the edge of the clearing to show me a 9-foot black and yellow snake he'd killed with his hoe. He told me matter-of-factly that it was deadly.

Last night we helped put out fishing nets, which is done from an 800-pound dugout. Just pushing the thing across the beach nearly gave me a hernia. And paddling it was worse – there were no comfortable seats, and it was extremely difficult to control. It made me thankful for sweet *Orellana*. This morning we retrieved the nets, harvesting five good-sized fish – three days' supply we're told.

As I sit here writing, the driven clouds are moving as fast as ever above the mountains.

AUGUST 4: *at Don Diego, Colombia*

By July 31, we were so frustrated with Bahía Confusa that we were ready to launch at even the hint of a sea change. And when the hint came on August 1 we were off like buccaneers. We rounded the eastern *punta*, and were smacked immediately by heavy swells and chop, as well as fierce headwinds. But as we fought on conditions improved, and our confidence grew. In no time we were tearing off the miles.

We were welcomed back to the seas by the biggest turtle we'd ever seen – it must have been 4 feet across and had a head the size of a man's.

By mid-afternoon, we'd come 30 difficult miles, passing Cabo San Juan Guija and Buitaca, and were relieved when Dana spotted what looked like a narrow beach on the hazardous shores near Don Diego. As we headed in, we could see that the beach rose steeply from the water, so that the waves crashed onto it instead of rolling across it. What we didn't see until it was too late was that the beach was strewn with spherical boulders, some the size of ten-pin balls, which tumbled up and down with the action of the waves. About 50 feet from shore, I jumped into the water to act as a sea anchor and keep the canoe straight.

We hit the beach perfectly between a couple of boulders, but as I tried to haul the canoe up the steep sand, I was knocked over by a wave. In seconds the canoe was awash and too heavy to pull up the incline. Wave after wave battered it, and again our equipment was being carried off in all directions. By the time we were safely onto the beach, the canoe had suffered another 6-inch crack, two broken support ribs and several minor fractures.

We were soon surrounded by locals who, in spite of our pleas, were onto our equipment like scavengers, casting sly glances to see if we were watching. To impress them, I told them that in Honduras a man had tried to steal something from us, and I'd cut his hand off. I gave them my wildest look, pulled out my machete, and showed them how I did it.

We've been camped on this awful beach for four days now, listening to the boulders tumble in the surf. Some of the locals have befriended us, though even the friendliest have tended to wear on us, as their conversation runs invariably to the dangers that await us down the coast. "Es muy peligrosa!" they say again and again – "It's very dangerous!" They tell us that, at all cost, we must avoid Palomino, just five miles away, and Rio-hacha, the capital of Guajira State, as well as of the Colombian mari-juana industry. Both places are said to be full of thieves and Mafiosi. We don't take all of it seriously, but are somewhat rattled by the constant gloom. The Guajira Indians, we're told, are specialists in murder and theft.

By the end of our second day here, I'd managed to get the canoe repaired, and the following day, with the help of two Colombian fisher-men, we attempted a launch. We aimed the canoe out to sea, and the four of us stood beside it for 20 minutes, waiting for just the right moment. Suddenly, one of the fishermen yelled "Adelante!" – "Forward!" – and we charged into the breakers. The fishermen pushed us successfully through three waves, but the fourth, a heartbreaker, set us off course, and the fifth tossed us back into the brine. Again the canoe was punctured in several places, and this time the second seat, Jeff's, had been torn out by the force of the waves.

Again we patched, and again, today, we tried to launch. And again we were thrown into the sea. This time, as we hauled the canoe out, a wave caught it and dropped it on Dana's foot, lacerating him badly. My ankles are severely swollen from bites, and as we hobbled along the beach tonight, trying to get the canoe into a better launching location, we looked and felt like a couple of weary old men. We wanted a better location, because we really can't handle another crash – we're almost out of repair material. Fact is, we can't handle much of anything any more – we are discouraged beyond description; the more we give of ourselves, the more we get hurt. Although I hate to say it, I've been wondering tonight if we should simply quit and get out while we can. Here we are killing ourselves to get further into Colombia where all the trash of mankind seems to be waiting to prey on us.

If we've had one reason to smile since we got here, it's that the other day a man came from some distance to bring us a pineapple and a stalk of green bananas. He'd heard we were stranded and wanted to help us out. We gave him a tin of jam in exchange, which pleased him immensely. The same day, I threw away an empty tomato paste can, and a couple of little boys, 6 and 8, came along and picked it up. They studied the pictures on the wrapper, pried open the lid, and sniffed at the inside. We spoke to them, and they admitted they'd never seen a tin can. The area isn't all that isolated – there's a highway here; it's simply that the families are too poor to afford canned goods.

AUGUST 8: *at Punta de la Vela, Colombia*
I won't go into the details of our return to sea on the morning of the 5th, except to say that we had a difficult launch and that we're indebted to the two young fishermen who pushed us out through the initial breakers into more manageable waters.

We scooted by Palomino, and the dangerous La Punta and Dibulla, feeling good about our progress. But our luck was short-lived, and at Río Lenea we were caught up in yet another wearisome hijacking. This one involved nine senseless cowards, each armed with a rifle or pistol. After the usual orders to get to shore, the screaming and denials and demands for money, two of the pirates actually jumped into the water and grabbed our bow and stern. Another two, unbelievably, jumped right onto our canoe where they did a gun-happy balancing act as one of their two motorboats hauled us to shore.

In no time, they had our tarp ripped off and were shoving item after item into their pockets. As this was going on, three newcomers appeared, one of whom had obvious authority. Immediately, we were on him, begging that he acknowledge our letter from the police in Santa Marta. We'd hesitated to give it to the others, feeling they'd only rip it up or throw it into the sea; we weren't even sure they could read. But in the hands of this new character, it was magic. Within seconds, the nine thugs were humbly putting our possessions back in the canoe. It wasn't long before we were being treated like guests, and someone appeared with a gift of plátanos and cheese for us. We asked for permission to camp on the beach and it was granted immediately.

But no matter how well we come out of these incidents, there is a lingering effect; and that evening Dana was still so shaken that he couldn't get his supper down. For several hours, both of us walked around in a kind of trance, talking in abrupt, strident voices, saying all sorts of silly, unnecessary things. At times like this, we seem to be trying desperately to reassert ourselves – or maybe we're just filling a deep, nervous void.

We have reason to be nervous. The next day, further down the coast, we were lured ashore by friendly Guajiras. Walking along a crude road, which we were told was used as a landing strip for small planes, I noticed a large blackened area and picked up a piece of melted aluminum mixed with mica. My guide calmly explained that two American marijuana smugglers who were cheating the local drug barons were caught by the military when they flew in, shot, then thrown back into their plane, which was set on fire.

AUGUST 12: *Punta Coco, Colombia*

We survived Riohacha, and are slowly struggling northeast up the Guajira Peninsula. Several fishermen told us that we'd never make these past 30 or 40 miles – not because of pirates this time, but because the east winds and waves would overwhelm us. I must say it hasn't been easy. But here we are at Punta Coco, just 29 miles from the famous Punta Gallinas, the most northerly point of land in South America.

We've been paddling at every opportunity, including a couple of tough night paddles, when the air was cooler and the water calmer. The area is so dry, and the shortage of drinking water so acute, that we've been on limited water intake for several days. We're down to eight gallons at the moment, which isn't much if we get marooned. The other day, a healthy young Indian asked for some of our water, and we had to turn him down, indicating our cracked lips and skin and explaining that we needed the water more than he did, which was true. He subsequently asked if he could have my green squall jacket, then a T-shirt of Dana's, and we only got free of the guy when Dana began demanding *his* shirt and went up to him and started unbuttoning it, which sent him on his way.

Our *punta* here is ironically named; *coco* means coconut, and there isn't a palm tree, or any other kind of tree, within many miles. The whole eastern peninsula is a moonscape of arid rock and red clay, sometimes flat and low, sometimes rising into precipitous red cliffs or weathered hills. Cacti are everywhere, some of them 20 feet high. The place is a paradise for lizards, many of which have fluorescent blue and green skins, like sequined gowns. We've seen wild dogs and surprising numbers of birds, including big green parrots and smaller parakeets, which screech away at us as we pass or as we infringe on their nesting grounds. The other day we saw a floating island of large pink water birds, perhaps flamingos but more likely spoonbills. We see the shells of sea turtles, cleaned out for food by the Indians.

Our prayer for a breather from the pirates and dope trade has been answered. Our only human company in four days has been the Guajira Indians, who greatly impress us with their ability to survive on such a godforsaken corner of the planet. Every mile or so, we see one or two of their pathetic little stick houses, their roofs designed to keep out sun but not much else. Of course, there isn't much else to keep out around here, with so little rainfall.

The only Guajira industry we've seen, apart from a little fishing, is salt production. To extract the salt from the sea, they allow the tides to flow into extensive foot-deep lagoons, which quickly evaporate in this arid climate. The crystallized salt is then scraped up and put into 100-pound bags which, according to an old Guajira salt miner, sell for 100 pesos, or $2 U.S. No wonder some of them grow and sell marijuana.

The other day we had a close-up look at both Guajira ingenuity and Guajira poverty. We were camped on a sheltered beach by a lone shade tree, with a wretched old fishnet under it. At about 4 p.m., a fisherman and his young son came along, claimed the net, and rolled it out on the beach. They had two bags, one full of old bricks, which the father proceeded to break into pieces for weights, and one full of scavenged beach sandals, which he cut up for floats. Next he took out a pathetic old ball of string made of hundreds of little scraps knotted together, many of them only a few inches long. The ball reminded me of my childhood when I, too, collected scraps of string and rolled them into a big useless ball. I couldn't see how his string could possibly support a fishnet in the ocean, so I dug into our supplies and gave him a large tightly wrapped roll of waxed nylon cord which should last him for years. He was almost embarrassingly grateful, flashing a big yellow smile that he could barely erase. He gave the string a couple of good tugs, and within minutes was stringing it happily through his weights and floats and net.

Contrary to warnings, the Guajiras have given us no difficulties whatever. The only time I expected a problem was a few days back, leaving

Riohacha, when we saw a spectacular fleet of about 30 Indian *cayucas* under sail coming down the coast toward us. They looked like an Arab pirate flotilla, with about five men to a crew. We got a good curious stare as we blasted by, but no one showed any inclination to interfere with us. I wish all coastal people were as dangerous as these.

AUGUST 14: *at Puerto Estrella, Colombia*

The east winds during the past couple of days have been merciless. They rise with the sun, whipping the sea into turmoil, and don't calm down until dusk. Although we hate night paddling, we realized a few days ago that our only hope for getting out of Colombia was to avoid day paddling altogether – we'd get as much sleep as we could while the wind was up, and shove off at dusk.

Yesterday, unfortunately, we got very little sleep. Eight Guajira archers showed up on our beach about noon and spent the better part of the day shooting nail-tipped arrows in a long high arc over our camping spot, which was hardly conducive to slumber.

We set off regardless at 7 p.m. as the sun and winds dropped. Our first goal was the Punta Gallinas lighthouse, which marks the northernmost tip of the continent. During the morning, we'd had a visit from the lighthouse keeper who, on hearing our story, exclaimed in English, "You guys are very lucky to be alive!" Apparently, the local Guajiras are engaged in a murderous feud, knocking one another off with some regularity. The last thing he told us was, "You may not be here tomorrow."

We muscled our way past his lighthouse and, in the failing light, could see miles down the coast as it dropped to the southeast. We were over a mile from shore, staying well out to avoid any coastal currents that might be sweeping the *punta*. We paddled hard until perhaps 1 a.m., figuring we'd come 20 miles or more. A few miles ahead lay Puerto de Chimare, tucked in the bay of a small river mouth. We hoped it would be our escape from the sea.

But just after one o'clock, the full moon, which had guided us thus far, disappeared behind a heavy cloudbank. It was as if a lightbulb had been switched off. Instantly, we were paddling blind. Using the direction of the waves as a guide, we did our best to angle toward shore. We'd been told that the *boca* at Puerto de Chimare was ringed with coral and that its *bara* or sand bar threw up a heavy wash. But it was still our best hope for shelter, and as we drew closer to shore we peered into the black line of cliffs, looking for any gap that would signal the *boca*.

The wind was negligible, but for some reason the swells now began to build and soon were reaching heights of 10 feet or more. We struggled along, increasingly tense and weary, until, from a mile or so out, we saw what we thought was our *boca*.

As we drew closer, however, we could hear the sickening roar of breakers smashing the shoreline. There was little hope of getting in safely, and capsizing would be disastrous in the dark. We had a frantic conference – it was either take our chances here or paddle on to Puerto Estrella, 10 long miles down the coast. Dana and I seldom agree entirely on anything, but it was clear that we couldn't get in here. So off we paddled toward Puerto Estrella, guided only by the sound of waves hitting the reefs and rocks.

Within a couple of hours, the rolling waves had risen to 15 feet, and we could no longer take them broadside. I had no choice but to swing the canoe directly into them – *straight out to sea*. We had no idea where we were or how far offshore, but I knew that if we didn't keep moving we'd lose control of the canoe and be swept back onto the rocky coast.

One mighty disturbance after another rose and crashed around us, and our fear of being carried ashore increased. By this time Dana was issuing panic instructions – Go left! Go right! Straight ahead! Then, out of the darkness, like a vision from another world, came the dim lights of a massive ocean vessel, a mile or so away. Then came another, and I knew at least that we were well away from land. I uttered one silent prayer after another and shouted countless encouragements to Dana, who by this time was sick with fatigue and fear. About 50 feet to our left, the sea now broke, and a huge shape rose from beneath the surface. At first I thought "Submarine!" but a loud hiss and whoosh quickly told us it was a whale. "Get us outa here!" screamed Dana, and we angled away from it, fearing it might dive and surface beneath us, or approach us out of mere curiosity. But it quickly submerged, and we didn't see it again.

For five hours we fought the waves, until I was sure we'd never see dawn. But now off to our right I detected the faintest glimmer of light. I thanked God. As the sky brightened, we were shocked to realize that we were only 2 miles off shore. All along I'd imagined we were at least 5 miles out. The treadmill of waves had kept us penned against the coast.

All I wanted now was solid ground beneath me. As we paddled within a mile of the coast, however, we could see the waves battering the high red cliffs as powerfully as ever. At this stage I didn't care; I wanted off the seas, whether we crashed or not. "Pick your spot!" I shouted to Dana.

"We'll get killed in there!" he shouted back, and before I could say another word, he had seized the initiative and had virtually ordered me to head further down the coast. For 15 minutes, we sat arguing our course, when suddenly Dana shouted, "Estrella! There it is, Puerto Estrella!" In the distance he could see a few faint shapes on the horizon.

Two hours later, with the waves building, we paddled into a large wind-protected bay, surrounded by cliffs, on top of which sat the houses of Puerto Estrella. In no time, we were besieged by townspeople, several of whom offered us drinks and fruit. None of them believed we'd come from 13 hours at sea. We barely believed it ourselves.

As we sat by the canoe in a stupor, Dana looked at me and said softly, "When we reach Venezuela, I'm going to cry. I'm just going to sit there and cry." For myself, I could have broken into tears on the spot. The tension has all but overwhelmed us; it's difficult to believe that neither of us has cracked. I've come to expect perseverance from myself, but for Dana the demands are new, and there's little I can say that adequately conveys my admiration for him. Very few older, stronger men could have borne up as well.

I'm particularly proud of the leadership role Dana's assumed. He plans our days in advance, chooses landing and launching sites, sorts out various paddling problems, reads the maps, and issues responsible commands at sea. Without his constant watchful concern for our wellbeing and safety, we probably would not be alive. I often think that without his guitar he couldn't have held up; on many occasions it's been his only sanctuary from the madness.

Within an hour of arriving, we were fast asleep in the shade of an old wooden barge that was rotting on the beach. When we awakened in the early afternoon, I looked at our maps and realized that last night was a historic occasion in more ways than one: somewhere on the seas in the darkness, we surpassed the record for the longest canoe trip ever. We have now come 7,557 miles.

AUGUST 15: *Parajimaru, Colombia*

I can only explain our decision to go back on the sea last night by saying that we were desperate to conquer this last stretch of Colombia, and couldn't do it while the wind was up during the day.

We ate a mighty supper of spaghetti, peas, and watermelon, lingering over every bite, and set off. The moon was full, and for the first couple of hours on the water we slid along through ideal conditions. Our problem was that we'd had only three hours' sleep during the day. Before long, our eyelids and paddles began to droop. By the time we'd gone 10 miles, we were paddling in our sleep, drifting away for a minute or more at a time before snapping back to consciousness.

By 2 a.m., my periods of sleep were ablaze with hallucinations: palm trees, cars, massive logs, walls, sailing ships. I'd be barely beyond con-sciousness when an explosion of white light would occur. Out of nowhere, an enormous sailing schooner would be racing at me from just a few yards away, or the canoe would be about to strike a brick wall, or a stand of palms. I'd be jolted awake, trying desperately to steer away from an obvious collision. Or I'd jam my paddle into the water in an attempt to stop the canoe altogether.

Dana, too, was having queer visions: a snarling pirate face, mountains, objects from our canoe, a brilliant sunset. At one point, dangling before his face, he saw the 1-gallon food container in which we keep our rice. Time and again, he was awakened in terror by the grinning face of a pirate. At one point, he screamed out in shock.

Fortunately, the seas were kind as we paddled and slept and hallucinated.

After dawn, we paddled 10 miles, fully awake, and at 9 a.m. glided ashore on a gentle desert beach. Except for our hallucinations, neither of us had any recollections of our first 30 miles at sea.

In three nights of paddling, we've advanced over 100 miles, on a total of eight hours' sleep. It is now nearly 10 a.m., August 15, and, as friendly little Guajira kids wander around our campsite, I can no longer hold my pen to keep writing. My weary eyes are now focused on the words *La Mano de Dios #1*, the name of a tiny boat in *Orellana's* colours that attracted us to this site. *The Hand of God, #1.* We are truly here only by the hand of God.

Venezuelan Feast and Famine

AUGUST 16: 20 *miles into Venezuela*

This morning at about 9 o'clock we pushed across the border into Venezuela. Notwithstanding my respect for the wild seas of the past few weeks, I can only agree with Papillon's assessment of the country we've just survived: "From what I've seen of Colombia and Colombians, the sea is a joke."

You'd think that crossing the border would be an occasion for jubilance, and I, at least, am ecstatic to be where we are. Dana, however, is irritable beyond belief. This afternoon, I asked him the spelling of *Adriena*, the name of a ship we'd seen wrecked in the shallows near the border. He spelled it out rather quickly, and I had to ask him again, then again, as I couldn't hear him very well and wanted to make sure I had the spelling right. He seemed to think I was baiting him, and suddenly he picked up our plastic map container and swatted me across the face with it, roughing up my cheek and gashing my nose. He then took off down the beach like a jack rabbit, and I was left boiling in frustration. I only wish that I, too, could blow off steam as directly and effectively.

This evening as we lay on the beach, we had a bit of a chat about the bad feelings, and it turned out he'd been annoyed at me all day over my insistence on paddling so close to the various *puntas* with their surf and rocks. I'm only trying to save a few hundred yards here and there, but he seems to think I'm deliberately trying to irritate him. We made up tentatively before going to sleep, and I've resolved to be more responsive to his wishes and advice.

As we drifted off, the full moon shone above us, and a light breeze cooled our wounds.

AUGUST 22: *Punta Capana, Venezuela*
We thought we'd had it with guns and arrests, but on the 19th, our fourth day across the border, we got a pretty good dose of Colombia revisited. At about 11 a.m., a motorboat with seven male passengers closed in behind us. Two of the men were wearing khaki pants, and as their boat pulled alongside us one of the two, a fat little porker with an ugly scowl, produced a rifle and ordered us brusquely to shore. Incensed by his rudeness, I shouted, "Why?" and right away the roar of his gun shook the air. A shell cleared my head by what couldn't have been more than 2 feet.

Another gun now appeared, and we were quickly on our way to shore, where five of the men picked up the canoe and carried it 30 feet onto the beach. When I complained that we had Venezuelan visas (we couldn't get them at the moment), Fatso quickly fired two more rounds over my head. "For God's sake, Dad," yelled Dana, "listen to the guy! Don't argue with him!"

We had obviously been taken for dope smugglers from Colombia, and were ordered into the seatless back compartment of an old Mercedes-Benz that was parked on the beach. We sat like convicts on the metal floor, as the two soldiers drove us recklessly toward Paraguaipoa, which we'd passed on the coast about 10 miles back.

Just before noon, we rattled through the gates of a large military base whose sign read: "Armadas de Cooperación Destacamento No. 30 Cuarto Compañía." For four hours, we were left sitting outside in the high desert sun – no water, no shade, no food. From time to time, soldiers came up and grilled us with hostile questions. It was soon apparent that we were wasting our time trying to make them understand who we were; when we told them we'd come from Canada, they seemed to think we were making fun of them. Our documents meant nothing to them. It was as if they were assumed to be fake.

The worst of it at this stage was that we hadn't eaten in 20 hours. We

were also getting increasingly worried about the canoe, which was supposedly now being guarded by the two guys who had arrested us.

We sat, we paced, we sweated, we sat some more. What was doubly
frustrating was that this had been the best paddling day we'd had in a
week or more of high winds and waves. And here we were frying in a
desert army compound.

In the mid-afternoon, a three-star officer showed up and asked us a
few silly questions. An hour later, our documents were returned to us,
and we were told we were free to go — *free to walk ten miles back down the
beach*. I raised a stink, and the officer who'd questioned us ordered a
soldier to flag down a passing vehicle for us.

We arrived back to find Fat Boy sitting on our canoe, with our two
machetes in his hands, clanging the blades together as if preparing to
carve up a turkey. I walked directly toward him just wild with rage. There
were half a dozen fishermen standing around and a couple of sluggish
military types. When I had claimed our machetes, I stepped back and, in
my loudest clearest Spanish, so that everyone would hear, told our cap-
tor, "You are the worst soldier and the lowest human being I have ever
met!"

It took him about half a second to pick up his rifle and blast another
shot over my head — my first thought had been that he was going to kill
me on the spot. "Shut up, Dad!" cried Dana. "The guy's crazy!"

We checked the canoe, and found that every one of our equipment
boxes had been turned upside down. Then I noticed that Fatso had placed
a nice neat little plastic bag of our valuables behind the canoe – binoculars, camera, film, jewellery – so that he could have them for himself. I
snatched up the bag and, unable to control myself, cursed him one last
time. In a matter of minutes we were back on the water. The rifle stayed
silent.

By way of contrast, we've met some very fine Venezuelans, too. The
other day at Cojua three little Guajira boys led me a mile or so back across
the sand dunes to what they said was their water supply. But when we
got there I could see nothing but more sand. One of them fell to his
knees and uncovered a wooden disc which he removed, revealing a secret
desert well, from which I was able to fill our big blue water container. I
started back, stopping every so often to switch the heavy container from
one hand to the other. The boys thought this was a big joke. Unable to
stop giggling, one of them, who couldn't have weighed more than
70 pounds, ordered me to give him the container. He hoisted it to his
shoulder, telling me that this was the way to carry water, and the three

of them carried it the long mile back to the canoe. Another labour-saving lesson – out of the mouths of babes.

That afternoon, I found an old abandoned *cayuca* from which I was able to pry a good-sized lump of caulking tar. I spread it across *Orellana's* weakening patches, and it partially staunched the leaks. I'll make stronger repairs in Caracas.

The day before yesterday we passed Bahía Tablazo, the entryway to giant Lake Maracaibo, whose bed has for decades been one of the richest sources of Venezuelan oil. Although we couldn't see the lake in the distance to the south, I clearly remembered pictures in my school books during the 1940s, showing hundreds of oil derricks pumping away on the surface of the shallow lake. On the shore of the nearby Isla de San Carlos, facing out to sea, we saw a lonely World War II cannon, whose job it must have been to protect the oilfields. A great quantity of Venezuelan oil went into the allied war effort.

We're still pretty frazzled from Colombia, and Dana continues to go at me. One of the problems is our perpetual exhaustion, which leads nearly every day to some little mishap. Yesterday, I lost my concentration and allowed the front of the canoe to veer into a breaker that washed over our bow and drenched poor Dana. "What do you care if I get soaked!" he yelled, proceeding into a diatribe about how I couldn't care less about his welfare, etc., etc. On he went, until, frustrated myself, I shouted, "Dry up and paddle!" Almost before I realized it, his paddle was winging toward me, glancing off my arm into the sea. This evening he was on me about our poorly executed launch this morning, and ended up giving me a sharp kick in the leg. It was my ridiculous idea to paddle to the Amazon, and, until conditions improve for us, I won't be allowed to forget it.

Dana is at least back at his guitar, after several days away from it during our final stretch in Colombia. He's also celebrating a full year of freedom from his asthma medications. For ten difficult years, he tried to break the dependence, and now he seems to have done it. I remember the days, years ago, when he couldn't walk home from school without having to stop and sit on the curb for a while to catch his breath.

One of our most uplifting recent experiences was the sight, this evening, of thousands of brown pelicans flying above us from the west and landing on the tidal flats down the coast. I've read that they're an endangered species; if it's true, we must have seen a pretty fair portion of the world's population tonight. For half an hour they came – an endless D-day convoy of graceful flying boats. By counting them in groups of a hundred, we estimated there were more than 20,000 of them – far more birds than either of us had ever seen in one place.

For a while, the sight took our minds off the fact that we're running short of food. We did our last major shopping in Santa Marta 27 days ago. Tonight we had to supplement our supper of rice and peas with the hearts of a couple of rotting onions I found washed up on shore. We still have our $40, which is taped in plastic beneath our centre thwart where it won't be discovered by thieves. It should buy us a couple of weeks' worth of supplies, though not nearly enough to get us to Caracas, where we'll next be able to get money. Unlike the Colombians and Hondurans, the Venezuelan coastal dwellers have shown little interest in getting their hands on our food – what's left of it. We did wake up back at Cojua, however, to find several pigs and goats nuzzling around our supplies – presumably not to check our documents.

AUGUST 27: *on the Golfete de Coro, Venezuela*
Since I last wrote, we've worked ourselves into a frightful situation. But to explain what has happened I must first describe the section of coast we're on. Immediately to our east is the huge Peninsula de Paraguaná, which thrusts into the Caribbean in the shape of a giant frying pan, the thin handle of which is attached to the Venezuelan mainland. The distance from the tip of the handle (at the mainland) to the end of the peninsula is perhaps 50 miles. To save the many miles it would have taken us to go around the peninsula, and to avoid having to brave the seas at the end of it, we decided to approach the narrowest section of the peninsula's handle, the Isthmus de Medanos, which is about 4 miles across, and portage it. To get to the isthmus, however, we had to come into the Golfete de Coro, a shallow bay that is perhaps 30 miles across and surrounded by vast low-lying tidal flats.

The Golfete has been our downfall. We'd no sooner entered it than the winds rose, sending the shallow water into a frenzy that has kept us stormbound for three days now. Our water is down to five gallons, our food supplies have dropped to starvation level, and our resolve is just about gone. Before sitting down to write, I routed through our food box, seeking any items we might have overlooked. But I could find only what we already knew was there: a few canned goods, some rice, and some powdered milk. For breakfast, we had half a bread roll each and a teaspoon of jam, which was all we had left of either item. An hour later, I took a stroll up the beach in search of food and found a dead fish that had washed up. It was well over a foot long and had lost its tail. I poked at it, and the meat seemed firm, so I cut it up and put it in our aluminum pot. I should imagine the ultra-salty water of the *golfete* would keep a dead fish looking edible for a week or more. If we don't get out of here soon, we may have to take our chances and eat it. We'll boil it well and hold our noses – it's bound to be more exciting than last night's boiled rice and sugar.

It's almost impossible to convey how isolated and desolate it is here – or how *persistent* the surf and winds are. Our camp is a pathetic little mud bar amid the endless swampy tidal flats that surround us. For miles around *there is simply no dry land.* To keep the tides at bay, we've erected a 6-foot-diameter ring dike of mud and sand around our sleeping spot. Yesterday the surf was beginning to eat at it, so I shored it up with driftwood and sticks, which successfully kept us dry last night. Several times during the night I woke up and stuck my hand out over the foot-high dike to test the water level, then went back to sleep, reassured at least that we wouldn't be washed away.

At this time of year, the sun is directly overhead. During the day, the heat, combined with the wind, quickly draws the moisture from our bodies. With so little water remaining, we're on rations of three cups a day (the water may last longer than we do). To combat moisture loss, I've been wearing a full set of clothes and have been wrapping a T-shirt around my head. It would help if we could get out of the sun, but our only shade is a crummy little flooded shack half a mile back across the flats. Dana sloshed over to it yesterday to practise his guitar. Just getting to it takes so much energy, however, that, for relief from the wind and sun, I've just been curling up beside the canoe and trying to keep covered. At any rate, walking through the brine irritates the salt sores on my legs. Mere hours after being driven onto the tidal flats, I could feel the heavy salt affecting the bug bites on my legs. By yesterday morning, full sores had developed, and today the sore on my ankle is as big as a fifty-cent piece and is growing like a cancer. In one spot it has eaten right through to the ankle bone, a disgusting sight. It's beginning to scare me, as well as giving me severe pain. Curiously enough, it doesn't bleed – it merely seeps a bit of yellowish fluid. Somehow the salt and sun have cauterized the blood vessels. I apply bandages, but they quickly get soaked in sea water which only makes things worse. A little fresh water would probably cure the wounds, but we can't afford to use drinking water.

Under the circumstances, Dana has been holding up remarkably well. He's depressed, of course, but he's been fairly relaxed toward me and has done his best to show a bit of optimism. He's spent hours poring over our maps and has marked every mile between here and Trinidad with a tick. It seems to be his way of reducing our tenuous future to a manageable scale.

This morning while I was going through our equipment, I noticed that the number indicator on our camera was back at zero, which means the soldiers back at Paraguaipoa opened the camera in their search of the canoe. I have no way of knowing how many pictures are left or whether the film is still good. The next cop or soldier who goes for that camera is going to lose his hand.

More and more, our situation reminds me of Laguna Madre and La Pesca. We haven't seen a boat or plane or human being in three days. The only dry land we've seen is the mountain peaks out on the main body of the peninsula and a few peaks about 20 miles behind us on the mainland to the south. We still have 30 miles to go to reach the Isthmus de Medanos for our portage. It makes me laugh to say so, with our survival in the balance, but if we could get to a telephone somewhere, we do have an ace in the hole. Four days ago at Puerto Gutierez we met a fine young professor, Dr. Douglas Jatem, from the National University at Coro, about 30 miles east of here. He showed genuine interest in our trip and told us to telephone him if there was anything he could do to help us on this part of the coast. If we last long enough, we certainly will.

In the meantime, I sit here sweltering, wanting nothing more than to tear into what little food we have left – and to drink our water bottles dry. One minute I have hope, the next I don't think we'll make it. Our nerves are shot.

AUGUST 29: *Guasare, on the Istmo de Medanos, Venezuela*
Yesterday morning we were up early, but there was still no possibility of getting on the water. The sun was as relentless as ever, and as we ate our ration of rice for breakfast, I had a craving for water that nearly drove me crazy. It was as if I'd run a marathon on a day of 100 degrees and had been given a few drops of water with which to refresh myself. If I hadn't stood up and walked away from the canoe, I might well have grabbed the water container and been extremely irresponsible.

We languished through the morning, afraid that we were going to be trapped here forever. But just before noon I had a curious feeling that the wind had altered. I felt it first on my skin and in my ears. I stared out to sea and, within minutes, detected a slight reduction in the rush of waves onto the flats. I shouted at Dana who roused himself from where he was resting by the canoe. He confirmed the sea change. It was all the encouragement we needed, and minutes later we were packed up and on our way. Having safely launched, we were too excited to take the slow shore route, heading instead east across the south end of the *golfete*, attempting to save a few miles.

Three hours of desperate paddling brought us to the little settlement of Cocuy, partially hidden in a shallow bay. We zeroed in on it like predators and were met on shore by a few villagers, who were obviously shocked by our condition. My hunger by now was unbearable, and, on landing, I dived into our gear for the aluminum pot which still held our fish from yesterday, when we'd been unable to bring ourselves to eat it. I tore the top off the pot, and a ghastly, nostril-stinging odour exploded into the air. One of the villagers grabbed the pot from me and threw the fish into the sea. The others took this as a signal, and within minutes we were inside a tidy little house eating corn cakes and fresh fish. I must have downed a gallon of ice water. Dana sat for ten minutes shoving food into his mouth with both hands.

Villagers gathered, until there were eight of them sitting with us. All of them were concerned about my salt wounds, which were leaking badly. I've counted 20 sores in all. One man brought me some peroxide, and I poured it into the raw flesh which fizzed like seltzer, as I groaned with the pain. I was then taken to a community bath house where two men washed me down with bucket after bucket of fresh cold water. For the first time in weeks, I was free of the terrible burning salt.

Next I was brought a white ointment which I slathered over my lower legs, bringing a stop to the itching. Dana has not had a single salt sore – perhaps because he spends his nights in a sleeping shell and, on account of it, has fewer insect bites than I have; the bites let the salt in.

Early in the afternoon, we were brought more food – tuna and tortillas, or *arepas* as they're called here. I ate three of them; one would have made a normal meal. A little boy came in and gave us two bananas. When we finished eating, we asked the woman of the house to cook us a dozen *arepas* to take with us when we go. We wanted to pay for them, but she wouldn't hear of it.

I don't know what gets into us, but as Dana and I rested late this afternoon we began talking about moving on, gaining a few miles before dark – we're obsessive about progress. But the thought of ending up on another tidal flat was too much for us, and we opted for the safety of the community.

Just before sunset, we were shown to a little sleeping hut made of clay and sticks with a roof of cactus cuttings. A young man brought us a pair of hammocks and hung them for us, then led us back to his house. As the sun sank, we were joined by half a dozen dark-skinned Indians who sat talking quietly in a language of their own, occasionally breaking into Spanish. They passed around a bottle of rye whisky until it was empty, then brought out another, then another. Dana drank nothing, and I took the smallest possible sips, knowing that my ravaged body couldn't take the shock of the alcohol.

We were drained beyond telling. Nonetheless, as I lay in my hammock later, my first thought was not to get to sleep. For a few minutes at least, I wanted to savour the comfort of our little hut, and the warmth and grace of these generous villagers. With my hammock swaying gently, I drifted into a satisfying sleep.

SEPTEMBER 1: *on Istmo de Medanos, Venezuela*

We left our little village on the morning of the 29th and proceeded along the south shore of the Golfete, then north up the Isthmus de Medanos to another little place called Guasare, where our friends had told us the isthmus was narrowest and where we could best make our portage. We'd been told to look for, and soon found, an elderly fisherman named Chimo who welcomed us with a big smile and invited us into his poor little home for *arepas* and fried fish. When we'd eaten, he gave me two small bottles, one of alcohol, one of Mercurochrome, with which I treated my salt sores. At this point, I'd have been quite happy to slack off for the afternoon – we'd paddled 22 miles. But we couldn't ignore the magnitude of the portage that lay ahead, and, soon after lunch, we set out on a reconnaissance mission across the 4-mile isthmus. It was important to find the shortest possible route, as we knew we'd need four or five return trips to transport the canoe and all our gear.

What a surprise we got! We'd expected the isthmus to be sand, but it was mostly tidal flats. For 3 miles we slogged through brine varying from 6 inches to a foot in depth. My salt sores raged.

A mile or so from the far shore, we came to a modern restaurant on the well-paved highway that runs the length of the peninsula, north and south. Our final mile took us across high sand dunes, and when we got to within a few hundred yards of the sea, we could hear an old familiar sound, the thunder of breakers hitting the shore. We walked over the final dunes, and our hearts shrivelled: 10-foot waves were crashing onto a low shelf of squared-off rock, which extended as far as we could see. There was no way we could launch here.

As we walked back over the dunes, we decided to make our launch at the port of La Vela de Coro, to the south, where the isthmus meets the mainland and where we knew there was a proper harbour. But to get there we'd have to haul the canoe some 20 miles down the highway. We'd need a trailer – could we get one through Dr. Jatem at Coro?

We stopped at the restaurant we'd passed earlier and persuaded the owner to let us store our equipment in his fenced-in compound. As there were no phones in the area, we had no idea how long it would take us to get hold of Dr. Jatem.

That night, back at Guasare, our friend Chimo introduced us to Rafael Parades, a sport fisherman from Maracaibo, who owns a fishing shack here. Rafael invited us to stay with him and cooked us an excellent supper of pig's feet, onions, and peppers. Late in the evening, we were given guest hammocks, adjusted to just the right angle by Rafael's knowing eye. But no sooner had we bedded down than our host began snoring – began *snoring*. He then started calling out in his sleep in Spanish. Every few minutes, all night, we were wrenched from our slumbers by Rafael's outrageous snorts and yells.

The following day we borrowed a stout 12-foot pole from Rafael, slung two of our equipment boxes from it, and hoisted it to our shoulders. Off we went, sloshing barefoot through the swampy flats of the isthmus toward the restaurant 3 miles away.

We made the trip in just under two hours, stopping many times to switch the pole from one side to the other. The restaurant owner, who now introduced himself as Eustoquio Betancourt, immediately opened the outside enclosure for us. It's a perfect storage place, safely surrounded by a high wooden fence, and paved with concrete. We went into the restaurant for a soft drink and were at once questioned by five or six patrons: who were we? where were we from? had we been shipwrecked? how many days had we been lost? We know we're not in the best of trim, but it's always a shock to be reminded of how bad we really look. A tourist from Germany bought us an order of *yuca*; another bought us a beer and a soft drink. One man, seemingly overcome by our story, gave us 30 bolívars, about $7.50 U.S. I tried to give it back to him, but he wouldn't take it.

We limped back through the flats to Guasare and again hung two equipment boxes from our pole. This time our trip took nearly three hours, and when we reached the restaurant the owner himself bought us a beer and a soft drink.

Again we returned to Guasare, tired now to the point of collapsing. Rafael had returned to Maracaibo but had given us permission to use his shack, which we did to the fullest – good big supper, good big sleep, with no snoring.

We were up early yesterday morning, this time to transport our empty canoe. Luckily, the tide had been high during the night, and we were able to float the canoe across the first quarter-mile of tidal flats. From that point, it was a gruelling two-and-a-half-mile carry.

We spent the better part of the day hanging around the restaurant, writing notes to Dr. Jatem. We gave them to anybody who was willing to take one into Coro (the restaurant is patronized by dozens of travellers on their way up or down the peninsula). All day, the Betancourts fed us, and by late afternoon we'd become something of an attraction in the dining room. Unfortunately, not all of those we met believed our tale, and by dinner time, a couple of doubters had reported to the Betancourts that we were frauds and couldn't possibly have come all the way from Canada. One of them got out an atlas and scoffed openly when he saw the distance involved. By bedtime, Sr. Betancourt himself had begun to have doubts.

We went to bed in the compound with our canoe, and just after we fell asleep, one of Sr. Betancourt's sons woke us up. "Señor," he whispered, "Dr. Jatem is here from Coro. He's here to see you."

I sat up groggily and began mumbling in my half-sleep to Dr. Jatem. But as my eyes adjusted to the dim light I grew confused; the man I was talking to looked nothing like the man we'd met at Puerto Gutierez. Then Dana said sharply, "You're not Dr. Jatem. You're a phony – now leave us alone!"

Sr. Betancourt's son had apparently persuaded a friend to pretend he was the doctor. If we'd acknowledged the impostor, we'd have been caught out in our supposed lies. But Dana had beaten them at their small-minded game.

If anything, their machinations worked in our favour, as they were now obliged to accept at least part of our story. Nonetheless, we felt badly that they'd thought it necessary to try to trick us.

Right then, we decided that something had to be done, and that Dana should hitchhike the 15 miles into Coro in the morning to locate Dr. Jatem in person. I'd have been willing to go myself but the sores on my leg have become severely infected, so that my ankle is nearly twice its normal size, and the glands in my groin are grossly swollen. Anyway, Dana was happy at the thought of a day on his own.

So at 6 this morning he was off to Coro. I spent the better part of the day catching up on long overdue chores like washing clothes and installing new tarp clips on the canoe. Late in the morning, I repaired a hole in the bow that had been leaking for weeks.

As I was standing looking down the road at about 3 p.m., a blue truck pulled up, and a stranger got out. He was looking for me, and on the back of his truck was a good-sized boat trailer, sent by Dr. Jatem. One of our notes had obviously gotten through, as the driver knew nothing about Dana's visit to Coro.

My credibility with the Betancourts shot back up, and I set to work equipping the trailer for our haul. I found some old lumber and built a bed that would support the canoe and its load, then cut a 7-foot pole and tied it crossways to the hitch as a pulling bar. I then manufactured two yokes of heavy rope that would fit over our shoulders. As I worked, I drew disparaging comments from onlookers who said what we were attempting couldn't be done – one man told me we'd kill ourselves in the hot sun. I smiled through my resentment, and by the time Dana returned in the late evening, having found Dr. Jatem and enjoyed the day in Coro, I had the trailer loaded and ready to go.

My only worries now are over the state of our health. My legs have shown no sign of healing, and one of Dana's feet has a number of slow-healing cuts that have been bothering him for several weeks. He's been limping noticeably, angling the foot sideways, as if it had been broken or malformed. Nevertheless, we're excited to be going.

SEPTEMBER 3: *La Vela de Coro, Venezuela*
The first few miles of hauling went faster and more easily than I'd expected. I'd balanced our load, so that all our energy was going into forward motion, not into lifting. The road was smoothly paved and flat, and was bordered by unrelieved sand dunes and tidal flats – not a tree, not a shrub in sight. We were well fuelled for our work, having eaten a magnificent breakfast with the Betancourts before leaving the restaurant.

A few motorists sped by us as if the ridiculous sight of two men pulling a boat trailer along a desert highway were an everyday occurrence. But many, too, waved and shouted encouragements as they passed. Five times during the lunch hour, well-wishers stopped to give us food and drinks. Among the good Samaritans were three men from the little village of Cocuy where we'd been taken in after breaking away from our tidal beach on the Golfete. They'd apparently been talking to Chimo, and he'd told them we'd be coming this way. They drove up in a silver-coloured jeep, greeted us like long-lost brothers, and presented us with a dozen fresh walnut buns. Seeing that I was suffering in the sun, one of them then took off his red hat and placed it lovingly on my head.

An hour or so later, we were met by a TV crew from Caracas who were on their way to do a story on the oil refinery further out on the peninsula. Their cameras whirred as they ran along beside us firing questions. The interviewer, Julio Camacho, explained that they were from Venevisión, the country's largest television station. Before leaving, he offered his card and told us to look him up when we get to Caracas and he'll do everything he can to help us out.

True to form, not everybody we met was encouraging. One carload of young men stuck their heads out and shouted *"Burros! Burros!"* and laughed and hooted, making us feel about as silly as we undoubtedly looked.

We limped on like a couple of cripples, sweating profusely. Eventually we reached a military checkpoint, where we suspected we'd be in for a grilling – we weren't even sure whether it was legal to travel as we were doing on a major highway. But news of our trip had preceded us, and we were welcomed not only with courtesy but with cold drinks and food, sent by Sr. Betancourt from the restaurant. The man's continuing generosity seemed like an apology for having doubted our word. The guards at the checkpoint told us the television crew had also been there and had put in a word for us.

About 5 p.m., we reached the junction where the road splits, one branch going west to Coro, the other east to La Vela. By this time, we were severely fatigued and were looking for a place to stop. Dana's foot was practically dragging behind him, and my salt sores were oozing and fiery. The one improvement in our route was that we were now among trees and shrubs. We'd come 15 miles.

Not far down the road to La Vela, we came to an unusual park surrounded by a high iron fence, like a zoo. A sign over the arched gate read: Parque Exposición Don Pablorsaher-Coro. It was as good a stopping place as we were going to find, and we shucked off our harnesses, limped to the fence and broke open a watermelon that had been given to us by a considerate motorist.

A security guard invited us into the locked park, and as we pitched camp near the fence dozens of curious faces peered in at us. A couple of men brought us soft drinks and hamburgers, which they passed in through the iron rails. We later found out that the park was for agricultural and livestock shows. Last night, they had two weary Canadian draft horses on display.

We trudged the final 6 miles into La Vela this morning, and were no sooner there than a couple of newlyweds offered to drive us the 10 miles into Coro to change our American money into Venezuelan bolívars. The couple told us they got their kicks out of meeting and helping strangers; we couldn't argue with their pastime. We stocked up on food for the 300-mile paddle into Caracas.

We next visited the Port Captain, Miguel Quintero, an elderly gentleman who was sympathetic and asked a friend to drive us a few miles east
along the coast to the ferry terminal at Mauco, where we could get our
passports stamped, to extend our Venezuelan visas. When we returned,
Sr. Quintero wrote us a kind letter of reference which he told us to show
to anybody who gave us hassles, or from whom we needed a favour. We
asked him to keep our boat trailer until Dr. Jatem could pick it up, and he
happily agreed.

In the late evening, we went down to the beach and laid out our beds.
After what we've been through in the past few days, our launch tomorrow should be easy.

SEPTEMBER 8: *San Juan de los Cayos, Venezuela*
Venezuela is determined to make schizophrenics of us. We left La Vela
four days ago with a budding sense of success: we had our letter of support, and, for once, our passports and visas were in order. We were high
on our recent friendships and on the reappearance of coconuts and sand
beaches on the east side of the peninsula – clear sailing.

But by late morning of the second day, near Sauca, we were caught up
in the predictable old scenario: suspicious boaters, commands, refusals,
threats, and guns. At the height of the fray, our ten captors suddenly
snatched us from the canoe and threw us bodily into their boat. One of
them held a handgun to Dana's temple, another a rifle to my stomach.
Dana's guard was so drunk and shaky I was afraid his gun would discharge
from vibrations alone. On shore, he began pawing and slobbering over
Dana, who quickly lost his cool and threw him heavily to the ground. But
before anyone could react, wily Dana went into an exaggerated charade,
jumping around, pretending the man had stepped on his bare foot and
injured him, thus inviting the retaliation.

The Guardia Nacional were summoned, but didn't arrive for four hours
to check our documents and free us. We just can't get used to this crude
sense of justice by which you're detained (for no crime) and are guilty (of
no crime) until you can prove yourself innocent (of no crime).

The same night, at San José de la Costa, we were again hassled for our
documents by a local government official. After taking two hours to decipher that we weren't dope smugglers or child murderers, the guy at least
had the courtesy to treat us to a meal at the local restaurant.

Last night at Punta Aguide, we were met on the beach by five friendly
young men from Valencia who insisted that we join them for a meal. We
reluctantly left the canoe and drove inland with them to a little commu-

nity where they left us while they went for food. In their absence, we drew a crowd of suspicious locals, who quickly let us know they didn't want us around. Our friends returned and embarrassed us by attempting to persuade the locals to accept us. Nothing doing.

At this point, we went and sat in the back of the truck, and our driver and his friends eventually got in and drove us away – but not back to the canoe, as we'd hoped. Off we went for miles along the darkest of roads until we reached another ramshackle village, La Pastora, where we were escorted into a grubby *cantina* lit by candles and oil lamps. But here, too, we were stonewalled by the locals – in particular by ten young black men who gave us every indication that they'd as soon lynch us as share a meal with us. Back into the truck, insisting now that we be returned to the canoe.

By this time, our hosts were nearly frantic to show us some hospitality; again they ignored our requests, and were only persuaded to comply when we started banging on the back window of the truck and shouting that we wanted to return to the beach, which was now 7 or 8 miles back.

Tonight we're camped at San Juan de los Cayos, after a tough day at sea. The coast is becoming increasingly hazardous as we move towards the mountains ahead. The next 50 miles are flagged on our map as "dangerous navigation" – dangerous for ocean-going ships, let alone our fragile little craft.

Dana is again showing the stress, arguing constantly with me over every little difference of opinion. This afternoon after landing, we couldn't agree on the choice of a campsite, and he suddenly threw our maps into the water, and I had to wade in and retrieve them. Later he dumped one of our supply boxes into the bottom of the canoe. It's all so discouraging and wrenching. Here we are, father and son, isolated in South America, 8,000 miles from home, and what are we doing? – fighting instead of supporting each other. I've reached a point at which anything that separates us is unbearable for me – far more draining than any of the other hazards of the trip. Without each other, there's just no reason to go on.

To the Dragon's Mouth

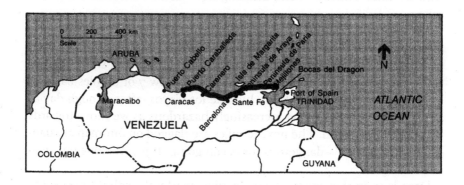

SEPTEMBER 14: *at Caraballeda/Caracas, Venezuela*

The emotional roller coaster is as unpredictable as ever, and over the past few days our spirits have bounced around, building gradually to tonight's stupendous high. We have reached Caracas. It is a milestone in our trip, and we are comfortably installed in the home of the Port Captain at Puerto Caraballeda (Caracas proper is 10 miles inland). We are 100 yards or so from the exclusive Sheraton Yacht Club.

Last night at this time we weren't at all convinced that our stay was going to be a happy one. We were camped at Macuto, a coastal suburb of Caracas, where we found the people tough and cynical, and several times we were taunted openly by those who gathered around us on the grimy beach. The astounding density of population that fans out along the coast from Caracas had begun to work on us earlier in the day as we paddled in. The air traffic alone was unsettling – one jet after another coming in over the canoe. We get to a city and have to reverse our entire approach to survival – although I must say that our current circumstances augur well for a good stay in Caracas.

Our gradual recovery from the depression that had gripped us when I last wrote began on the 10th at Puerto Cabello, a fine old Spanish city amid the coastal mountains. It's the third largest port in Venezuela and is geared exclusively to major shipping, so that when we arrived we had trouble finding a suitable landing area in the harbour. When, finally, we beached on a little strip of sand, we were informed by a patrolman that it was the property of the Venezuelan Navy and that we were to move on. But Dana was intrepid (not to mention tired and hungry – we hadn't eaten breakfast and had been on the water nearly 12 hours). "I want to speak to the top official here," he demanded.

Within minutes, we were in the presence of a bright young lieutenant who went well beyond granting us permission to stay: he had us chauffeured to a nearby base camp, where we were fed an excellent beef dinner and given a luxury guest cottage for the night.

The next afternoon, after a long battle with 15- and 20-foot swells, we were beckoned ashore by a group of fishermen at the tiny settlement of Cabo de San Andrés, which sits in a precipitously mountainous bay. Our friends fixed us a hearty meal of *arepas* and fish, and, as we ate, I noticed that each of them wore a delicate, hand-woven anklet, from which a tiny woven cross was suspended. They told me these were for good luck, and I was reminded of the commercial beach fishermen at Veracruz. When their loaded nets were nearly to shore, each of the foremen would place a (lucky) starfish between his teeth and keep it clamped there until the final fish was landed.

All afternoon, the fishermen lazed around the beach, their boats set up ready to go at the edge of the sea. In the mid-afternoon, I asked a few of them when they were leaving, and each of them gave the same mysterious answer: "When the Man in the Sky tells us."

In the late afternoon, they all jumped up and ran yelling to their boats. I thought they were about to launch, but they merely hauled the boats a few yards back out of the rising tide. They returned to their lounging, and one of them told me that the Man in the Sky had told them to move the boats.

An hour or so later, they jumped to it again, and this time were quickly out on the water, racing away from us in a mile-wide arc, dropping a seemingly endless net. Apparently, the Man in the Sky had again given the word. Dana and I discussed all this privately and decided that these guys, with their anklets and their messages from above, were just a grandly superstitious bunch with some rather poetic notions about fishing. But just before sunset, when the fishermen had returned, a stocky middle-aged man appeared among them, and was introduced to us as the Man in the Sky. We soon learned that this guy was the owner of all the boats in the settlement and split the daily catch, 50-50, with the 22 fishermen we'd met. He has a tiny house away up the mountain, where he can see out over a vast area of water. All day he sits up there, and when he sees the fish coming (nobody told us exactly what he could see of them from that distance) he sends down a signal, and the men fly into action, encircling the fish with their nets. Nothing is left to chance. Although the men get only half the catch, none of them seemed unhappy with the arrangement, and one man told us they make a lot more money this way than if they fished on their own.

After dark, a young fisherman from the Dutch island of Aruba, just off the Venezuelan coast, helped us fix a canoe thwart, working at it for over an hour with only the dim beam of his flashlight to guide him. We slept with the fishermen in a long, open-walled shack facing the sea. Our beds were nothing but elevated boards, but when you've been sleeping as we have even a piece of flat dry wood can be perfectly conducive to a good night's sleep.

Tonight's sleep should be even better, as the Port Captain, Vicente Larez, has installed us in bunk beds in his air-conditioned guest room. The poor man was befuddled when we got here – he wasn't sure he liked the idea of a couple of dirty gringos calling on him for assistance. But he couldn't ignore our visas and passports – and particularly our letter of safe passage from La Vela – and quickly drove us to have our documents approved.

If there was still any doubt in his mind that we were legitimate contenders, it was wiped away when our old friend Julio Camacho and his television crew pulled up as we left the Immigration building. Julio had filmed us on our long haul to La Vela and I had phoned him from the Port office this morning. In an instant, television cameras were rolling, and Vicente was the co-star of the show.

The crew followed us back to Vicente's, and we launched the canoe so that they could get some shots of us on the water. We paddled out, then came in past the yacht club, leaving a number of its members in some confusion. Most of them had turned up their noses at us when we'd paddled in to their docks a few hours earlier, and now our little craft was getting a bear's helping of attention while their million-dollar yachts got none. When we reached Vicente's dock, there he was, the old showman, reaching out to welcome us for the benefit of the cameras, a big pot of coffee in his hand.

One of the most comforting things about being here is being able to have freshwater showers, which will surely ease my salt sores. At the moment, I look like a leper from the knees down, and people are justifiably intimidated by the condition. I've also developed a fluid-filled cyst about the size of a ping-pong ball on my elbow. I'd like to lance it, but don't want to risk an infection. More importantly, the rest will be good for my eyes, which have failed since we left home. The combination of the sun's glare and the constant focusing on distant objects has taken its toll on my close-up vision. Sometimes, I can barely read or write. It is now past midnight, and I must put my pen down and get some rest. Dana is still going at his guitar.

SEPTEMBER 16: *Caraballeda/Caracas, Venezuela*
Our three days in Caracas have blown by, and tonight we're preparing for another raid on the seas. We were up before dawn yesterday, and by 8 a.m. I was ministering to the many ailments of the canoe: leaks, loose thwarts, missing tarp clips, loose stowage tracks, broken gunwales and seats. I wasn't doing much of a job with my materials, and eventually a local man, Timo Nenonan, who clearly knew something about boats, came up to me and suggested very discreetly that there might be a better way of doing things. "I don't think your repairs are going to last," he said.

I couldn't have agreed more, and when he suggested we take the canoe to the boat-repair shop where he worked a quarter of a mile away I was all for it, as long as we didn't have to let the canoe out of our sight. We ended up carrying it by hand to the shop, where for six hours Timo applied all his healing skills to it. Timo's boss, Manuel Coello, pitched in, and when we were about to leave, instead of asking for payment, he gave us a couple of T-shirts and a 100-bolívar note ($23 U.S.).

Right now, the canoe is healthier than we are, and we're convinced that only a total disaster can do it in.

We had chicken dinner with Captain Vicente, and shortly afterwards met a man who introduced himself as Dr. Jean de la Chesnais, Vice President of the Instituto Biotécnico in Caracas. We chatted for a while, and then, out of the blue, he asked, "Which do you like best, Argentine beef or Venezuelan beef?"

"I like all beef," I said, and within minutes he had whisked us away to a little seaside restaurant in Macuto. We enjoyed our second fine meal in 45 minutes – Argentine beef as it turned out. A few yards away, however, we could see and hear the heavy breakers, which tended to take the pleasure out of our relaxation. We're like Pavlov's dogs: we've had so much of the sea, and are so shell-shocked by it, that we only have to get near it and we start to shake. I mean that literally.

After dinner, Dr. Jean took us to the Caribe Yacht Club, where he keeps his sailboat. I'd never seen such a lavish collection of pleasure craft. One man told us that to become a member of the place you must buy a share at $100,000 American. I'm privately appalled by the concentration of wealth here, but am not so innocent as to reject it out of hand when it's been such a blessing to us. Then again, the poor have blessed us, too.

This morning at 9, our TV friend Julio Camacho picked us up and drove us 20 miles into Caracas, where the heat and humidity overwhelmed us. We'd barely left the Captain's when we were hit by torrential rain, which flooded the roads, bringing traffic to a halt. Kids ran around the streets splashing water into the cars' tailpipes, attempting to stall the engines so that they could help restart them for a fee. Julio's Maverick took 4 inches of water over the floorboards, and we had to stop and bail.

Caracas is an impressive monster. Founded in 1567, the original town is in a deep valley among the mountains, but its suburbs and slums range for miles up the lower slopes. The white skyscrapers of the business district stand like futuristic missiles awaiting launch. The population of six million is a broad mix of Latins, Indians, and blacks, many of them extremely poor.

The second secretary of the Canadian Consulate, a man named Eduard del Buey, had contacted Julio, asking him to bring us to see him. We went to the consulate, but were refused entrance to the elevator because we were wearing short pants, which are against the building's dress code. Julio quickly intervened, and had us cleared on the grounds that we weren't "normal people". Fair enough.

Del Buey greeted us cordially, but when we made an official complaint about the soldier who'd fired on us at Paraguaipoa, he merely shrugged his shoulders and said, "These things happen down here." I couldn't help suspecting he'd have raised quite a stink if a Venezuelan soldier had drifted a few shots over his own well-groomed head.

Julio showed us around handsomely, buying us groceries, restaurant meals, writing supplies, even providing a new pair of Venezuelan blue jeans for each of us – and I was able to get $150 U.S. on my Visa card at a downtown bank.

When we got back to Puerto Caraballeda, we found ourselves locked out, as Vicente had left the house and had locked our door to protect our equipment. While we waited for him we walked over to the yacht club and were invited to watch the Leonard-Hearns championship boxing match on television. It was an excellent fight, the perfect distraction from our anxieties about returning to the sea.

The whole coast along here has been a paradox for us; it's as beautiful as any we've seen – the mountains rise straight up from the sea, some as high as 9,000 feet – but it scares the daylights out of us. We've been told that these mountains are the northernmost peaks of the Andes, which extend thousands of miles down the west coast to the tip of the continent.

SEPTEMBER 20: *Caracas, Venezuela*

When we left Caracas on the 17th, we never dreamed we'd be back, but here we are, and in far more luxurious circumstances than on our last visit.

For three days we fought heavy seas and breakers, averaging no more than 12 or 13 miles a day. By this morning at 11 o'clock it was stiflingly hot, and we were drawn into a pretty bay at tiny Puerto Frances. The bay is supposed to have been a haunt of the legendary French pirate, Lafitte, who made his unscrupulous living up and down the Caribbean coast and the Gulf of Mexico during the early 19th century.

As we approached shore, we were hailed by the crew of a big white sailing yacht, flying the French tricolour. We paddled up and were welcomed aboard by Martial Beau de Loménie, a man of perhaps 60, and his blonde wife, Edith, whom I'd judge to be in her late 30s. Their two daughters, aged 11 and 15, seemed particularly excited to see us. Martial was born in France and is a top executive of the Banque Nationale de Paris in Venezuela. Edith is from Germany, but has lived most of her life in Argentina.

Like many others, they had seen us on television and wanted to do what they could for us. We were immediately served a gourmet lunch, after which Edith brought out a medical kit and went to work on my salt sores, which won't stop leaking. For fifteen minutes I had the full attention of this attractive Florence Nightingale, who not only washed and salved my wounds but bound them with bandages, so that I looked like a casualty of the Crimean War.

In the mid-afternoon, our hosts surprised us by asking us to drive with them 60 miles back to Caracas and stay as their guests for a week. Trinidad is very much on our minds, and our initial instinct told us to keep clawing our way along the coast. But as we got thinking about it, we remembered St. Louis and Houston and Barranquilla and many other places that we'd whisked through without stopping for a proper look. We're still ahead of our original schedule, and wondered if this was an opportunity we shouldn't pass up. We had a brief conference and, against all our normal inclinations, decided to go back – but for three days only.

We paddled nine miles further along the coast past Cabo Codera to Martial and Edith's yacht club at Carenero, where we'd agreed to meet them at suppertime and where we'd store *Orellana*.

When they got to the club, we had already been there for an hour, and they could barely believe we'd beaten them, since the coast along here is one of the most hazardous stretches in Venezuela. Few people, even intelligent sailors, have any idea what skilled paddlers can accomplish in a canoe. We stowed our belongings and climbed into our friends' luxury sedan.

As I write, I'm hoping that the extra days in Caracas will give us the rest that our first visit couldn't possibly offer, with all its running around and excitement. We've been at one another constantly since we left, and this morning before dawn at Chuspa had our most explosive disagreement in weeks. I'd been talking to Dana gently as we prepared breakfast, trying to persuade him that we should try to get along a little better, that our communication problems were robbing us of energy. It was an honest attempt to promote understanding. But Dana took it as a personal attack and went into a tantrum, first dumping the better part of a bag of sugar into my cereal bowl, then dumping his own cereal on the ground.

"Cool it, Dana," I said, but my superficial calm only seemed to enrage him, and he picked up one of our water containers and started draining it. Again, I told him to cool it, but he went right on with his petty destruction. This was too much for me, and I jumped up and tussled with him, giving him a sharp whack with the back of my hand, which threw us both into brief emotional paralysis. We're so terribly worn out, both mentally and physically. We work hard, and when we get a chance to relax, it seems we're invariably harassed by all manner of hangers-on and officials. Time and again, they ask the same wearisome questions; they watch us eat; they report us to the police; they sit on our fragile canoe, so that we constantly have to ask them to get off. We're as polite as possible, but we're just about nuts with it all, and there doesn't seem to be any solution.

I apologized sincerely to Dana, but it was only later in the morning that he warmed up to me and we were able to reclose the circle.

SEPTEMBER 22: *at Caracas, Venezuela*

As I hoped, our days with the Beau de Loménies have given us a wonderful respite from our toils. Our home here, "Mi Casa", is the fanciest place we've been in yet, a big concrete estate perched high on the mountainside, with a vast view of the city. The place is fanned day and night by mountain breezes, and since we arrived the night before last we've been making good use of the hammocks in the high-walled yard.

As we sit down at mealtime, Edith sounds a little silver bell, and the help appears with the food, always served with fine European wine. Almost anywhere you look in Mi Casa, you see evidence of Martial and Edith's respective backgrounds, French and German. They are both collectors and have, for instance, French and German military helmets on display. On the wall is a series of World War I French military posters which depict the Germans taking a thrashing. They even own a German Doberman pinscher and a French poodle.

This morning, after Edith dropped off one of her daughters for a ballet lesson, she took Dana and me high into the mountains for a spectacular view of the city. The red tiled roofs make an impressive sight against the foliage.

When Martial got home from work, he announced that he'd sent a telex in French to Prime Minister Pierre Trudeau, commending us on our achievement. This pleased us, as we're planning to request government assistance in getting our canoe home from Belém. If we don't get help, we're considering an incineration at sea, Viking longboat style. When a Viking chief died, he was placed in a longboat and set out to sea ablaze – supposedly for a better transit to Valhalla.

Our time in Caracas has been full of everything we could have hoped for – rest, affection, good company. The only drains on us have been our recurring nightmares and fits of anxiety about going back to the sea. Just as in Veracruz, we know it's out there waiting, and that before long we'll have to face it. Last night Dana woke up several times, having dreamt he was being swallowed by a tidal wave. He tells me he has similar dreams almost every night. My own nightmares are not so well defined but are every bit as persistent.

Tomorrow morning, Edith will drive us back to the yacht club at Carenero. She and Martial have begun loading us up with food and have given us two hammocks they're convinced will be useful to us. In return, we gave them a big Canadian flag for their yacht. They've been ever so kind and have provided a real boost for the tough miles ahead.

SEPTEMBER 27: *at Barcelona, Venezuela*

Looking back at the last line of my entry from Caracas, I have to admit that the five days since have been far from tough. We've had remarkable accommodations, favourable sea conditions, and scenery out of God's own painting book. The sands are white, the palms high, the mountains a photogenic spectacle in green, grey, and blue.

On our first night out of Carenero, we were grandly entertained in the Club Isla de Oro, which we happened on by chance. The coast east of Caracas is a kind of diamond necklace of wealth, but this was the most ridiculously posh establishment we'd seen yet: swimming pools and tennis courts, gourmet restaurants, fantasyland architecture. The club's members and staff were mostly Colombians, and we couldn't help suspecting that some of the wealth was connected with the dope trade.

The next night we stayed in a less affluent club, better suited to common types like ourselves. The hospitality was as generous as ever, though the accommodation – a cupboard-sized hut with a 40-watt bulb and a half inch of dust on everything (the atmosphere nicely heated and humidified to about 110 degrees) – left a little to be desired.

The following night we were back in luxury at another *club privado*, the Playa Pintada, near the mouth of the Río Panapo. During the evening, two of the club members grew concerned over my salt sores and urged me to try "*yodo*" on them. They drove me inland to a pharmacy to get some of this mysterious drug, and it turned out to be good old iodine. I've never in my life had sores as persistent as these. But as much as I want to get rid of them, I hated to douse them in iodine, fearing it would burn the tissue and leave me with lifetime scars. But I did it anyway, figuring it was better to be scarred than to risk blood poisoning and the possible loss of my legs.

Tonight, we're camped in a little beach settlement on the outskirts of Barcelona, less than 300 miles from Trinidad. We'd intended to get to sleep early, but were rousted from our evening slumbers by three weekend partyers who wouldn't leave us alone and eventually dragged us to a little seaside cantina which was crazy with Saturday-night drinking and music. We drank nothing stronger than soft drinks, but were nonetheless drawn into the spirit of the evening, and Dana went for his guitar. Three more guitars appeared, and as the songs rang and the breezes drifted in from the sea, I slipped into a kind of trance, imagining that we were all off in some isolated corner of the jungle, invincibly protected by our music and laughter and drink.

At about 10 o'clock, a strange thing happened. The music suddenly stopped, and a ghostly silence enveloped the room. The merrymakers froze for a few seconds, then, three or four at a time, stood up in slow motion, placed their hands behind their heads and spread their feet. It was as if they were performing in some freakish movie.

Dana and I had no idea what was going on. Finally we were the only ones still seated – were we supposed to play along? was it a joke on us? Then, from beyond the open sides of the cantina, four men in blue jeans appeared, each carrying a machine gun. Thinking we were being robbed, Dana and I stood up like our buddies and raised our hands and spread our feet.

No one moved as one of the gunmen frisked the men around us. Then it was our turn. I was carefully searched for weapons, and nearly screamed as the searcher kicked at the legs of my jeans, battering my salt sores. Then Dana and I were taken outside, and our canoe searched and our documents closely examined. After an hour of suspense, the gunmen gave us the okay, and they were gone as quickly and mysteriously as they'd appeared.

Our friends explained that these were secret government agents, whose job it was to uncover anti-government guerrilla activity; there is apparently a fair bit of it in Venezuela. Raids of this sort are apparently quite common, though we hadn't heard a whisper about them in all our time in the country. I guess because we're gringos and a little weird looking, we were singled out as possible disturbers. Maybe we were reported by someone. I couldn't help wondering what trouble we'd be in if we'd still had our handgun and survival rifle.

SEPTEMBER 28: *at Puerto La Cruz and Santa Fe, Venezuela*
Nearly two years ago, a friend in Winnipeg gave me the name of a man in Puerto La Cruz, Walter Low, whom we were supposed to contact when we got here. To cut a long story short, we did so, and when we phoned he promptly offered us the use of his beach house. In fact, he immediately suggested that he meet us there in a few hours to welcome us and to help us settle in. We were to have the place for as long as we wanted it.

The beach house was at Santa Fe, 17 miles to the east, and as we paddled along the scenic mountain shoreline, through numerous little islands, we were hit by a tropical downpour which bathed and soothed us for an hour or more. The rains down here are heavy but not cold and energy-sapping like the rains up north.

When we got to Santa Fe, we asked around and quickly found Walter's haven, which was very much a beach house – from its concrete patio you could step directly into the clear shallow water. The whole bay was protected by Punta Gorda, four miles to the northwest, and by a number of islands, including the popular tourist retreat, Isla de Margarita. Our Winnipeg friend had promised us we'd like the place if we ever got here, and we'd already gone him one better: we loved it.

Ten minutes after our arrival, Walter showed up with his young wife Lila who welcomed us warmly and went to work cooking, while Walter showed us around. He's 63 years old but has the bearing and zest of a man of 30. He told us he's had three wives, and that they just keep getting better. When we'd showered, Lila gave us a big meal of chicken and rice, with freshly baked *arepas*, and with juicy slices of canteloupe for dessert.

Before Walter and Lila left, they went through their cottage supplies and made up a generous food hamper for us: sardines, corned beef, peas, asparagus, butter, sauces, cooking oil–everything we'd need. Then these good people were away, and we were on our own in Lotusland.

OCTOBER 5: *Carúpano, Venezuela*
We holed up for two days at the beach house, doing little more than lying around in hammocks. Although I thought I was well rested after our first night's sleep, I succumbed easily to four hours of hammock sleep the next afternoon – and the next. The sum of our work here consisted of a gunwale repair and a bit of coco picking and meal preparation – Dana made *arepas* for the first time. The locals stopped by regularly to take a look both at us and at our canoe, which they figure must possess special powers to have come so far. More and more, we're inclined to agree with them.

I spent some of my time browsing through my extensive notes on the great German explorer, Alexander von Humboldt, who, in 1800, explored the Orinoco, the Río Negro and the Casiquiare Canal, all of which we'll be travelling. Humboldt went overland from Caracas to get to the Orinoco, whereas we'll be entering it from its mouth. But the greater part of our travels will overlap, and even though we're 182 years behind him we'll be using his writings to guide us.

By yesterday, we'd made it as far east as Manzanillo where, for the second day in a row, we had minor difficulties with the locals. Two days earlier at El Rincón we'd been besieged by beach dwellers who refused to leave us alone. Even when we retreated for a rest, they crowded in around us, staring from close range as we sat motionless on the veranda of a beach shack. At supper time, they pressed in so persistently that we hardly had space to lift food to our mouths. Finally, I couldn't take it any more and turned my back on 50 or so of them, eating my meal with my face about 6 inches from the wall of the beach shack.

At Manzanillo, our problem was the opposite – we couldn't get the people to trust us. Normally, in situations like this, we look for someone of intelligence and leadership, and key on this person, usually offering him or her a little gift, such as one of our gold maple-leaf pins. If we can win the person over, we have an ambassador to make our case to the others. After we had spent half an hour getting nowhere with a surly crowd of locals, a bright young man named Luis Jesús Rivas appeared on the waterfront, and we knew we had our man. He could understand our Spanish, and in no time he was interpreting our trip to his countrymen, who gradually came round.

For the past few days we've been paddling the rocky and barren Peninsula de Araya, much like the Guajira Peninsula. We've temporarily lost our supply of coconuts and fruit, which is both a physical and a psychological deprivation; I get such pleasure out of foraging and adding to our food supply.

Tonight we're camped at Carúpano, a good-sized port about 120 miles from the tip of the Peninsula de Paria from which we'll make our crossing to Trinidad. Back at one of the private clubs we visited, we met an army officer who told us to look up Captain Osorio when we got to Carúpano. As soon as we arrived, Dana went looking for the man, returning shortly in an army vehicle with dozens of little boxes of army rations, compliments of the captain. We moved our canoe from the pier to a nearby beach, where within an hour a number of high-ranking officers had come to visit us. They'd heard our story and apparently doubted its authenticity. I could certainly understand their puzzlement. I try to imagine what I'd think if I met a couple of canoeists on Lake Winnipeg who claimed to have paddled all the way from Venezuela.

Eventually, a truck showed up and transported us and our gear to the local Guardia base, while 10 soldiers carried our canoe there by hand. We were given a big concrete room, empty except for a couple of mattresses on which we'll spend the night.

The soldiers here have issued severe warnings about the Bocas del Dragón, the Dragon's Mouths, which is the 12-mile gap between the tip of the Peninsula de Paria and the island of Trinidad. The gap funnels tides and currents and is a legendary hazard to navigation. Columbus remarked on its fury in 1498. All we can do is pick a time when the tides and winds are down and then challenge the Dragon as we've challenged all our other tough transits – and hope for the best. I don't mean to sound cavalier; we're nervous, and getting more so.

OCTOBER 10: *Mejillones, Venezuela*

We spent a rest day at the Guardia base, and that night I dreamt of Papillon. I'd talked earlier to a couple of elderly coastal dwellers who said they'd met him on his heroic travels during the 1930s.

The coastline since the base has been as treacherous as any we've paddled. The vegetation and lushness have returned, but there are no beaches, just mile after mile of sawtooth *puntas* and rock ledges. If it weren't for our maniacal ambition, there's no way we'd be out there. Fishermen pass us in their boats and look at us as if to say, You guys must be from outer space – you're certainly not earthlings out here in conditions like this.

Sometimes, for miles, we can hear the breakers ripping into the rocks with a sound uncannily like claps of thunder. The spray shoots 40 feet into the air. In places, massive rocks, shaped just like deadly black icebergs, protrude from the sea several hundred yards offshore. A clear testament to the treachery of the shores along here is that we haven't seen anything like a canoe or dugout for hundreds of miles. It's all motorboats – which also says something about the relative prosperity of Venezuela. Fortunately, we're getting co-operation from the weather or we'd be landbound.

One wise old seaman came up to us the other day on shore and examined our canoe with great interest. "We've come 8,500 miles in it," I told him with my customary pride. He continued to peruse the canoe, then lifted his eyes to meet mine and said softly, "*Tú es muy loco*" – "You are really crazy."

We have just heard that during the past six weeks there have been nine hurricanes on the Caribbean. The news made me truly relieved that we have no communication with the weatherman – we'd be more terrified than we already are.

Yesterday, after a frightful eight hours on the sea, we pulled into little Puerto Viejo, hoping desperately to find a safe landing spot on the bay that shelters the port. No luck. The entire shore was a 5-foot-high wall of boulders that had fallen down the mountain over the years and been tumbled smooth by the waves.

Down the shore some fishing boats rode at anchor about 200 feet out. We paddled there and hung on to one as we reassessed the shoreline, knowing that it was our only hope for a landing on many miles of coast. In minutes, a crowd of locals had gathered on the waterfront, apparently discussing our situation.

Presently, a couple of middle-aged men waded into the water and swam out to us, signalling that we were to follow them. We trailed them toward a rocky part of the bay that gave no hope of a safe landing. But as we approached shore ten men came briskly along the bank and surprised us by jumping into the water. In no time, they were on either side of us and were lifting the canoe right out of the water. I screamed at them to stop, as the canoe with its load was about to break in two. They put us down, and Dana and I jumped out and helped them lift *Orellana* over the boulders and 50 feet up onto the sand.

We needed their friendship (we had nowhere else to go), so we quickly handed out gold maple-leaf pins, which did the trick. Even in this remote corner of Venezuela, we soon had icy Pepsis in our hands.

Further up on shore, a rich variety of fruit trees and plants grew, including cocoa and a fruit we hadn't seen before, *manzana agua*, or water apples. I tried the fleshy pulp of the cocoa pod – a yellowish fruit, anywhere from 8 to 10 inches long – and found it much like lemon in taste, except sweeter. The mother of one of the men who'd swum out to us went into her house and brought us a container of frozen natural fruit-juice cubes, extraordinarily tasty.

I was led up through the jungle behind the beach to a mountain stream, the community bathing facility, where I shucked off my salty clothes and had a refreshing bath. Just around the bend, some women were bathing in their own private area.

During the evening we were entertained in a well-built concrete house. The owner had a gas generator, the only source of electricity in the community. Dana played his guitar, but the drone of the generator pretty well obliterated the subtleties of the music.

This morning we were returned to the sea in the same fashion we'd left it: five strong men on each gunwale – up and over the rocks, into the surf. Beyond the shelter of the bay, we began another lunatic battle with the wind and waves. This afternoon as we were about to call it quits at a little settlement just east of Mejillones, three men roared up behind us in an open 30-foot fishing boat, powered by two big Yamaha engines. We recognized one of them as a man we'd met yesterday when we put ashore for a while during a rainstorm. As he passed us on his way to shore, the man waved to us, and we waved back, happy to have an ambassador who would pave the way for us in our new community.

We watched from about 200 yards out as the three men landed and were greeted by five local men who came to meet them. In no time a fight had broken out, the whole eight-man commotion staggering up and down the beach as first one side gained an advantage, then the other. Soon rocks were flying, then one man picked up a two-by-four and swatted another across the head, felling him like a statue. The poor guy staggered to his feet, bleeding, but not before his opponents had gotten in a few good body kicks. Knives appeared, then more two-by-fours, and in a matter of minutes, the invaders, our buddies, were running for their boat in the shallow water.

Meanwhile, Dana and I, horrified and mesmerized, clung to a fishing boat 100 yards offshore. Was it possible we were the cause of the fight? If so, we didn't imagine our reception was going to be particularly hospitable. We'd happily have fled, but the seas were high and the coast for miles around was impenetrable. Our sincerest hope now was that we wouldn't be taken for friends of the three outsiders.

Once in their boat, the three began taunting the locals, challenging them to continue the battle on water. Two men took up the challenge, and soon two boats were racing around the bay at full speed, trying to ram each other, with us smack in the middle of the drama. Eventually the invaders, who had more motor power, made a head-on strike into the locals' hull, leaving their boat awash, its engine flooded and useless. For a minute or so, the visitors tore around the foundered boat, while the two locals watched in terror, trying frantically to get their engine restarted. Then the visitors zeroed in at high speed for the *coup de grâce*. At the last possible moment, the two local men leapt overboard and swam toward shore as if chased by sharks. In the meantime, the visitors rammed repeatedly into the half-sunk boat, doing an excellent job of wrecking its engine and hull.

Only when four more local boats roared out of the far end of the bay did the victors scoot off back down the coast.

The whole battle lasted maybe 15 minutes and left us drained and shaking. Were we going to get the same reception? No. When we reached shore, we were treated respectfully, if distantly, until a few of the villagers warmed up to us and took us in. They fed us and offered shelter for the night.

Soon after landing, Dana found a shiny new hypodermic needle near the water, which led us to believe that drug activity was responsible for the big battle.

Just before I sat down to write, Dana showed me a pair of pea-sized salt sores that have developed on his hands. I'm not glad to see them, but do feel a sense of small-minded justice, as all along he's been teasing me about my poor resistance to salt. Now he knows what it's like. Sometimes when I look at him, I despair – he can get so drawn and run-down looking. His lower lip is one big scab from the sun, and his nose is thick and brown under its layers of baked skin. He's still got his discouraging limp. My own latest ailment is a painfully poisoned first finger on my left hand. The nail is throbbing with the swelling. On the brighter side, the cyst on my elbow has disappeared. What we really need is a good long rest in Trinidad, which is now only 30 miles away.

Interlude in Trinidad

OCTOBER 13: *on Isla Monos, Trinidad*

We spent our last night on the Venezuelan mainland at the lush little coastal town of Uquire, about 11 miles from Punta Penas, which forms the tip of the Peninsula de Paria. Our sole aim once we were there on the 11th was to get as much rest and information as possible for the challenges of the following day. During the afternoon, we lazed around the sun porch of an unoccupied house we'd commandeered, and at suppertime were generously fed by the wife and daughters of the town Comisario, whom we'd met earlier (many of these little Venezuelan communities are headed by a government-appointed comisario). After supper, a kindly middle-aged man, Juan Salvador Jiminez, came to our veranda with a small bottle of clear medication which he said would help my salt sores. He sat me down and, using a bird's feather, patiently applied the viscous fluid, then placed a little piece of cotton batting on each sore.

As I sat there, I grew nostalgic for all the wonderfully kind people we've met in Venezuela. In Papillon's book, *Banco*, he says, "these Venezuelans are dangerous, with their generous hospitality. Kindness and good will turn you into a prisoner if you let yourself be caught."

Just after we got to sleep, at about 8 p.m., we were roused in the darkness by the Comisario's family who'd prepared another meal for us: *arepas*, fish stew, fried bananas. We began stuffing it in, but after nine or ten mouthfuls, both of us experienced something exceedingly rare – we were full, we couldn't eat another bite. Later, as I lay in my hammock, fretting about our date with the Dragon, I developed an uncomfortable case of indigestion. As if to join the party, my sore finger began to throb. I squeezed it, held it high, held it low, but it gave me no peace.

At about midnight, a drunk began wandering around the community yelling, "Othello! – Othello! – Othello!" Hundreds of times he called out, first from one corner of the village, then another, sometimes close, sometimes far away. For hours it went on, until I began to seem a player in some mysterious Shakespearean drama. My stomach burned; my finger throbbed; "Othello" rang through the air. In the meantime, two other drunks had wandered onto the veranda, lain down within a few feet of me and begun to snore.

In the morning I made the discovery that Othello was a lost dog. By this time, I'd happily have strangled dog and master alike.

I was understandably listless as we set out from Uquire, but as we made our way along the peninsula toward the Dragon's Mouths my adrenaline started to pump. The warnings swam in my head: Your boat is too small, you'll be swallowed up, or swept off to Grenada, 100 miles offshore.

After 3 miles of paddling we knifed precariously between Punta Mejillon and a small rocky island about 15 feet off its point. For a minute or so, we were absorbed with the hazards of the narrow pass. But as we rounded the point, Dana hollered, "There it is!" and I began to shiver with excitement. On the distant horizon, behind a number of islands, lay the hazy mountainous shape of what could only be Trinidad. Emotion tightened my chest, and I came close to weeping. But the demands of the moment allowed little time for tears or celebration, and in seconds we were again focused on the dangers of the coast to our right.

Our plan was to round Punta Penas at the tip of the peninsula and to paddle a few miles back west along its south shore in the Gulf of Paria, which is better protected than the waters of the Caribbean. From the south shore, we'd jump four miles out to Isla Patos where we'd stay the night before making the seven-mile jump across the Boca Grande of the Dragon's Mouths to Trinidad's Isla Chacathacare.

We made our way cautiously around Punta Penas in 12-foot swells, feeling just the edge of the Dragon's teeth as we headed south into the Gulf of Paria. I was ecstatic; heroes like Columbus, Drake, Raleigh, Orellana,

After surviving the dangers of "the evil coast" of Colombia, the Starkells almost died on the Golfete de Coro, Venezuela. Here, trapped by the wind on a tropical sand bar as food and water supplies run out, Don Starkell shows the marks of salt burns and heat prostration.

A passing tourist, Anthony Lamb, took these photos of sun-roasted and salt-caked Don Starkell, and of the canoe heading across the empty ocean north of Venezuela, on the way to Trinidad.

After crossing the Dragon's Mouth, Dana and Don celebrate their arrival at Port of Spain, Trinidad.

On the Orinoco. Dana with two friendly boys in a dugout cayuca, *near the point where Colombia meets the west bank of the river.*

After hauling the canoe 45 miles past the rapids Dana is glad to pose beside 22 friendly Indians – all from one dugout canoe.

"The day marked the first time we'd erected our mosquito-netting bug house since leaving the U.S. As we prepared our camp we were plagued by plaga."

On the upper Orinoco Dana poses beside one of the river boulders that were havens for the swarms of bats that darkened the sky – but were preferable to the thousands of bees that swarmed over the Starkells in search of salt.

The fateful crocodile sand bar. "For an hour or so we sat in the river just cooling off. This wasn't entirely relaxing, however, as we'd just chased a good-sized crocodile from our campsite and were pretty sure he was lurking in the water nearby."

"Tonight, thank God, we are safe in Tama Tama." After an attack of food poisoning that left them struggling 50 upstream miles to the mission, Dana and Don stand, shaved, washed, and well-fed, at the end of their voyage up the Orinoco.

On the Casiquiare Canal: "After 175 miles on the canal, we came to the first house we'd seen." Here Juarita Gonzales and her children sit with their pet pacas, astonished by the white strangers who have paddled into their lives.

"Now it's just a matter of 1800 miles or so on the Rio Negro and the Amazon." In Brazil, looking south down the Rio Negro, to the mountains on the other side of the equator.

Journey's end, May 2, 1982. Don and Dana framed by the spires of Belém, where the Amazon meets the Atlantic. In their 12,000-mile adventure they had learned a great deal. But most of all Don and Dana, father and son, had learned about themselves.

and even Papillon had all travelled through these same gates. Even better, we were off the Caribbean; we had survived its wildest coasts. As we worked our way west, conditions improved, and when we'd paddled 8 miles we swung south across open water towards Isla Patos.

Within an hour and a half, we were working our way along the island's north shore, an impenetrable flank of volcanic-like rock in shades of red, black, and grey, and crowned with thick foliage and palms, even cactus. We rounded the southwest end of the island, straining for a glimpse of beach or harbour that would afford us a landing. As far as we could tell, the island was deserted.

A mile or so further along, we came to an abandoned fish camp with three little buildings and, to our great relief, a bit of beach. A Venezuelan flag streamed from a beacon light, as if to remind us that we hadn't reached Trinidad yet.

One of the most interesting features of our camp was an ancient deciduous tree which I couldn't identify but whose trunk was a good ten feet in diameter. There were dozens of names and dates carved into it, some going as far back as the early years of the century. I looked in vain for Papillon's name among them, for I knew that he visited this island; in fact later as I lay in the darkness in my hammock, I had an uncanny sense that his spirit was close by. He was quite a man, Henri Charrière. A convicted forger, he escaped from prison in French Guiana in 1933 and sailed to San Fernando, Trinidad, where he was arrested by British officials and taken to Port of Spain. He was released and sailed to Curaçao, off the north coast of Venezuela, then on to Castilletes, Colombia. At Río Hacha, he was again arrested and jailed, but escaped to the southeast Guajira Peninsula where he spent six months with two Indian sisters, Lali and Zoraima. In Santa Marta, he was arrested yet again, shipped back to French Guiana, and thrown into the penal colony at Devil's Island. He escaped from there in 1941 by putting together a raft of coconuts which carried him to the South American mainland. He had several more scrapes with the authorities and ended up in jail in Ciudad Bolívar on the Orinoco River in Venezuela. In October of 1945, after 14 years of battling for his freedom, he was set free and given residence in Venezuela, which he had grown to love and where he lived until the end of his life.

In no time we'll be in Port of Spain, Trinidad, then on to San Fernando where Papillon first made landfall after his initial escape in 1933.

We were up early this morning, our hearts in our mouths as we prepared for our seven-mile crossing of the legendary Dragon's Mouths. The Dragon's main channel, the Boca Grande, is a 7-mile-wide funnel for the deep tides of hundreds of square miles of the Gulf of Paria. This incredible flow of water reduced to a 7-mile opening creates such powerful currents that we'd be committing suicide to travel at any time other than absolute low tide when the waters are at their least violent.

Unfortunately, our ability to judge the rise and fall of tides wasn't as sharp as it might have been. We left camp at about 8 a.m., and as we rounded the northeast tip of the island were immediately caught in the grip of an incredible force of water moving north. I'd initially thought a little current might help us on our way, but this was ridiculous. We were moving sideways almost as fast as we were moving forward, and it was getting worse.

We'd paddled about a mile when Dana yelled, "We have to turn back! We'll never make it!" I knew he was right, and, after a short debate, we turned the canoe 180 degrees and started pulling for our lives against the heavy current.

It took us nearly an hour to struggle back to the safety of last night's bay, where we were astounded to see that the waters had dropped a foot and a half in the little time we'd been gone.

At 12 noon, when we were sure the tide was as low as it would go, we made our second attempt. We aimed well to the right of Isla Chacachacare to compensate for the current, and paddled like demons. After two hours on the tricky waters, we made land for the first time in Trinidad. We had slain the Dragon.

From the island of Chacachacare, which functioned as a leper colony until recently, we made a two-mile jump to Isla Huevos, then another short jump to Isla Monos. Not far from Monos, we were trailed and passed by a whaleboat manned by smartly dressed sailors from the Trinidadian Navy. They pulled alongside us and – wonderful to hear – spoke to us in English. After so many months, we were back in a country where we could use our own language.

We're camped tonight in front of a string of luxury vacation homes in Turtle Bay on the south shore of Isla Monos. It's still difficult to believe we're here. Just over a year ago, we were high and dry in La Pesca, convinced that our trip was over. What I'd really like to do right now is let out a wail of relief – we've survived, we've been blessed, we owe thanks to so many. Though we still have more than 3,000 miles to go, we've never been more confident. We're all but done with the sea.

As I browsed through my journals after supper, I calculated that it's taken us 378 travel days to get here, not including our four months in Veracruz. We've come 8,930 miles.

As I mentioned, Richie Gage of the *Winnipeg Free Press* told us he'd do his best to meet us in Port of Spain to do some articles on our adventures. The other day in Carúpano, we telegraphed him to say we'd be in the city by the 15th, which gives us plenty of time to cover the 13 or 14 miles that will put us there. We do hope the plan works out this time. It'd be wonderful to see someone from home.

OCTOBER 14: *Williams Bay, Port of Spain, Trinidad*
This morning, before leaving to make the 2-mile jump from Isla Monos to mainland Trinidad, I cut a flagpole from some wild brush and hoisted our Canadian flag in the rear of the canoe, for the first time since Cancún, Mexico.

We made the jump easily and, as we followed east along the shores of Chaguaramas Bay, we could see a number of naval and Coast Guard boats at anchor ahead. On a nearby pier were a number of uniformed naval and military personnel, all waving at us. Among them, I noticed a rather misplaced-looking civilian in a red plaid shirt. He had either binoculars or a camera around his neck and seemed to be taking particular interest in us. As we passed, he began beckoning us towards him.

We headed in, and when we were still some 20 yards from shore, I recognized what I thought was a familiar smile on the face of the man in red – could it be? "Don!" he shouted, "Dana!"

"Is that you, Richie?" called Dana.

In no time we were on shore, rejoicing not only at our arrival but at the presence of Richie Gage, who'd come all the way from Winnipeg to welcome us. What a thrill it was to see this friend who'd been writing about us since May of the previous year and keeping our family and friends advised of our travels.

Almost immediately, we were fielding his questions, which came chiefly out of his concern for our wellbeing. He obviously saw things that shocked him: our exhausted bodies, parched skin, scrapes and scars and scabs, most of which we've grown inured to. He was especially impressed by the thick scab on Dana's lower lip.

Richie had come out along the coast to find us, intending to accompany us into Port of Spain in the canoe. To accommodate him, we had to pull back the tarp to free the second seat, as Dana had long ago sewn its cockpit shut. But Richie was soon established there, and we began what was supposed to be a triumphal entry into the city.

But from the outset, we had too much weight up front, and as we headed out along the coast, we met such tough tidal currents that we were soon taking waves over our front gunwales. Without the tarp in place, the canoe began filling up. It was a serious predicament. If we capsized, all our equipment, normally held in place by the tight-fitting tarp, would be lost. Richie was soon bailing frantically, working his passage, and he continued to bail for nearly half an hour as we struggled along rocky Punta Gourda and into the calmer waters of Williams Bay, where we docked at the Trinidad and Tobago Yacht Club.

We stored our canoe and equipment; then Richie took us by cab to the Canadian High Commission, where we met briefly with the high commissioner, Paul LaBerge, and one of his senior officials, Ms. Jean Blanchard, the acting military attaché, both of whom were very friendly. As we sat waiting to meet Mr. LaBerge, I poked through a pile of books and magazines on the table in front of me, and pulled out a 14-year-old book covering the highlights of Canada's Centennial in 1967. There on pages 37 and 39 were pictures of me, as a participant in the cross-Canada Centennial canoe race. It was as if they'd known I was coming.

During the mid-afternoon, we checked into Richie's room at the Kapok Hotel; then Richie took us out for a celebration dinner at the Hilton-Trinidad, where we gorged ourselves on a majestic poolside smorg: steaks, fish, vegetables, salad, fruit. Richie gazed awestruck as we put away plate after plate. We toasted each other with German champagne, then, glowing like sparklers, returned to the Kapok for a warm, two-hour interview. Richie is to do three long features on us, the first to appear on page one of next Saturday's *Free Press*.

Richie had a bit of a cold and went to bed early while Dana and I sat up and worked our way through the pile of mail he'd brought us. We had long letters from Dana's mother, from Jeff, from my daughter Sherri, from Dana's grandmother and aunt and uncle, as well as numerous letters from friends and well-wishers. All the news was good, and it felt wonderful to know that they were all pulling for us. Dana's mother had sent two white T-shirts with Canadian flags on the fronts. And a Winnipeg outfitter, "The Happy Outdoorsman", had sent two green rain suits which should come in handy during the wet season in the tropical jungles ahead.

OCTOBER 17: *Port of Spain, Trinidad*

Richie left for home on the afternoon of the 15th, but first he accompanied us back to the yacht club, where a photographer he had hired took several dozen shots of us mocking up an arrival and landing in *Orellana*. As we sat around the yacht club that afternoon, trying to figure out where we were going to stay for two or three months, we were again the beneficiaries of a well-timed act of grace. As we talked, Jean Blanchard, the acting military attaché from the High Commission, drove up and invited us to move into the guest quarters at her home until we got ourselves established.

Her home is really something – a white colonial-style bungalow, surrounded by lawns, fruit trees, and palms, the whole business enclosed by a concrete wall with wrought-iron gates and embellishments. We have twin beds, private kitchen, and bathroom, as well as the use of the house at large, with its living room, library, colour television, stereo system, etc. We also have the companionship of Jean's beagle-like pooch, George, who waddles around the house with his stomach about an inch off the floor. Jean has invited us to store our canoe here for as long as we're in Trinidad, which means we won't have to move it around as we ourselves move.

I'm determined to get some serious reading done during the next few weeks and am already well launched on Albert Speer's *Inside the Third Reich*, which I've borrowed from Jean's library. I want to sharpen my mind after the numbing it's taken in recent months and, if possible, to bring my vision back to normal.

Shortly after we got here, I took a good look in the mirror – the first in some time – and was startled at how my beard had spread. I couldn't help thinking of Robinson Crusoe, or Ben Gunn in *Treasure Island*. I cherished the beard for all the protection it had given me from the sun, but it does tend to be wild-looking, so this morning I took scissors and razor and hacked it off. From savage to human being in 15 minutes. Trouble is, my upper face now looks as if it had been painted brown, while the lower part is ghostly white. Dana was jolted to see me when I emerged from the bathroom. I'll start a new beard when we get on the rivers.

OCTOBER 24: *Port of Spain, Trinidad*
We've been enjoying the comforts at Jean's for over a week now and are hoping we'll be able to stay here for as long as we need accommodation. We're having trouble deciding exactly when to leave Trinidad. December 1 is a possibility, although we fear that will put us on the Orinoco while it's still pretty high; the lowest waters come during the dry season from February to April. The beginning of January would probably be better, though we don't want to get too complacent. We'll be doing a thousand miles of upstream paddling on the Orinoco, 210 miles downstream on the Casiquiare Canal, 850 miles down the Río Negro and nearly a thousand miles downstream on the Amazon. The Amazon, much further south

than the Orinoco, is rainy from February through June, which means we're bound to hit its rainy time if we hope to take advantage of the dry season on the Orinoco.

OCTOBER 31: *Port of Spain, Trinidad*
This morning, Dana and I hitchhiked into downtown Port of Spain to pick up his guitar, which had been in for a repair. The owner of the repair shop was a fascinating 70-year-old named Pat Fortune, who has spent the better part of his life teaching and playing classical guitar. He was interested in our story and in Dana's playing, and, after chatting with us awhile in his cluttered shop, he took us to his equally cluttered home, where his wife made us lunch. Afterwards, Pat and Dana took turns playing guitar while I routed through the *Encyclopaedia Britannica*, looking for information on the Orinoco and Amazon. Pat's eyes sparkled when he played, or when Dana played, and, before we left, he told Dana, "You've got a good future in music."

We've set our departure date at January 1, and, when we mentioned it to Jean, yesterday, she offered us the use of her home until then – exactly what we'd been hoping for.

NOVEMBER 2: *Port of Spain, Trinidad*
This morning I went on a scouting mission to find bamboo support poles for our bug house and rain tarp. Our steel and aluminum poles had pretty well corroded away with the salt, and I've decided to trash them. Bamboo grows like a weed here, and I found a good stand in a little clearing and cut nine stout green lengths, which I dragged home to dry. I've been told they won't last long in the jungle, as termites apparently get into the closed compartments of the bamboo and eat it from the inside out.

The high humidity here sucks the life out of me, and when I returned from my expedition I was soaked with sweat and in need of a rest. I'm a little worried about what we're going to meet in the way of heat and humidity in the jungle. We're accustomed to having the sea breezes to keep us cool, though I must say I'd far rather have the heat than the sea to deal with. What a blessing to be done with the sea! If we had to go back to it, I could barely endure our time here. Actually, we'll have a few days of sea paddling as we go down the west coast of Trinidad to the southwest corner where we'll jump the Columbus Channel to Venezuela, but it's nothing to worry about; the west shore is well protected. Once we make the jump, we'll have 10 more coastal miles on the Gulf of Paria before heading up the Manamo Canal, one of dozens of waterways that make up the mouth of the Orinoco at its delta.

I've been getting around a bit and am impressed by the Trinidadian gaiety. Everywhere I go I hear music – calypso, African, Indian, occasionally one of the local steel-drum bands. The Rastafarians, with their big heads of frizzy, braided hair, are another feature of the streets. Some of their mops look like storks' nests, tufts flying off in all directions. They have a bad reputation for drugs and theft and are spurned by the local establishment as some sort of Caribbean hippies; but we've found them nothing but friendly and gentle. And we really enjoyed *Divali*, the Hindu Festival of Lights.

NOVEMBER 16: *Port of Spain, Trinidad*
I've been monitoring my health pretty carefully and am concerned about my weight – I'm up around 200 pounds, about 35 heavier than when we got here. Dana, too, has put on weight and is nearly bursting the seams of his jeans. We'll have to cut down on the starches and sugars we've become accustomed to, and still crave.

Dana's sores and wounds are pretty well healed, though my own continue to give me problems. My two biggest salt sores, though vastly reduced in size, are still oozing fluid and, sometimes, pus. In my years of research for the trip, I read about tropical infections, and am determined to have my sores healed by the time we go into the jungle, where the heat, humidity and foreign germs can turn a mere scratch into a major medical problem. We'll have to doctor all our bites and wounds no matter how small. Malaria and dysentery are other problems that have stopped many more experienced jungle travellers than ourselves. I have pretty good resistance to disease, but that's probably what they all say – I can see it on my tombstone: "He had pretty good resistance to disease."

Dana has been invited by the local Classical Guitar Society to give a recital at the University of the West Indies here on the 24th, and he's been spending extraordinary amounts of time preparing. Sometimes he practises from nine in the morning until after midnight. We're excited about the recital but won't anticipate too big a crowd.

NOVEMBER 24: *Port of Spain, Trinidad*
The recital came off better than I'd expected. More than a hundred people, including a number from the Canadian High Commission, showed up and were much impressed by Dana's playing. He gave a fine performance (if I do say so myself), mostly of pieces he'd either learned or improved during the course of the trip. It was an excellent opportunity for him, and I could see in his eyes that he knew he'd come a long way.

We've temporarily moved our headquarters, and are currently house-sitting the mansion of the Canadian high commissioner, no less. We were driven up here by chauffeur on the evening of the 19th and could barely believe our peepers as we drove through the front gate. The place is surrounded by remarkable lawns, with all sorts of shrubs and exotic trees, many in flower. The mansion looks like a big white birthday cake, set amid the green slopes behind. It's where the high commissioner entertains prominent visitors and dignitaries (like ourselves). The interior is a maze of reception rooms, guest rooms, living rooms, dining rooms, bathrooms – more space than anybody could want or need. Our severest deprivation is that our bedroom is in the maid's quarters at the back, though we've been given the run of the house and pantry. Within an hour of arriving, I attacked the well-stocked library and started in on Bernal Díaz's *The Conquest of New Spain*, which recounts the daring march of Cortés through Mexico and his conquest of Montezuma and of Mexico City.

DECEMBER 16: *Dana's 21st birthday, Port of Spain, Trinidad*
The other day, we went to the Brazilian consulate to get permission to enter Brazil. We also need special permission to travel on the Amazon River. The consulate has telexed Brasília, the capital city, to get authorization, and we're awaiting approval. Our departure is now two weeks away, and we're beginning to get excited. We're still a little worried that we're going to hit the Orinoco too soon and find it in flood as we fight our way upstream. The rains here are falling heavily twice a day and showing no sign of letting up. We've been replacing our ruined equipment, and yesterday Pat Fortune, our old guitar friend, gave me a nice little alcohol stove, one burner, no moving parts. It'll replace the last of our three gas stoves, which is corroded beyond repair. The new stove is said to be able to boil four cups of water in ten minutes, and Jean has given us the perfect thing to boil water in, a nice old copper-bottomed coffee pot. Both of our aluminum pots are corroded through by the salt. What I want now is a small kerosene lamp for those long nights in the jungle. And with my extra pounds, I'm feeling a real need for some good canoe activity.

DECEMBER 21: *Port of Spain, Trinidad*
As Christmas creeps up on us, I'm getting quite sentimental about home. This evening, we were invited to a neighbourhood Christmas "Parang" party at the home of a black Anglican clergyman, who lives across the

street. We got to the party early, so I decided to go out for a little walk on Lacroix Avenue. The darkness was soft and close, and, as I walked under a sky full of stars, I could hear Christmas music seeping out of the houses. At one point I heard the beautiful strains of "Away in a Manger" and had to swallow a lump in my throat. In almost every window, a candle flickered.

When I returned to the party, it was going full tilt. I'm not quite sure what "Parang" means, unless it refers to the winter solstice, which is today, or to the homemade music that is played on such occasions. Everybody at the party had some sort of instrument: bottles, scrapers, cans, triangles, a bass fiddle, five guitars, anything that would make any sort of music. Dana joined in, and we had a rousing and expressive evening. Lots to eat and drink.

DECEMBER 24: *Port of Spain, Trinidad*
This morning, Steve Agard and Russell Benjamin, a couple of young black fellows we've been friendly with, picked us up and drove us to the local zoo where we hoped to learn something about the animals we'll be encountering in the months to come. We got an eyeful: flamingos, ibises, monkeys, tapirs, agoutis, pacas, ocelots, wild pigs, crocodiles, pumas, and more. What interested me most were the tropical snakes, of which I want to be fully aware when we enter the jungles. We saw a couple of big boas and anacondas, which are impressive in size but won't pose much of a threat to us, as they're easily seen and avoided. The two I was happy to get a look at were the fer-de-lance and the notorious bushmaster, both of which I'd read about in my preparatory research. They're relatively large and are highly poisonous, though we're unlikely to see the bushmaster, as it generally lives in dry upland country. The fer-de-lance is brownish in colour, with a lance-shaped head; I made a mental note of its appearance, and hope never to see one again.

On the way home, we had a drive through Port of Spain, bustling with last-minute shoppers. We've noticed a lot of Canadian apples for sale and were told by Steve that they're a Christmas specialty down here.

We've had a little more of the Christmas spirit here than we had last year in Veracruz. The use of English has opened things up to us, but we're also affected by the easy-going ways of the Trinidadians. Everywhere you look, you see people smiling and laughing and moving with an infectious gaiety. I've heard numerous people humming Christmas tunes as they walk down the street. I see them, and I can't help but think of all the blank, sad-looking faces I'm used to meeting on the streets and buses of Winnipeg.

This evening, we were invited to the home of a fine Trinidadian family, the Keillers, whose son, Phillip, is an exceptional guitar player. We were met at the door by Phyllis Keiller who greeted us with a big hug and said, "Call me Mums." After a splendid dinner, she played the piano for us – a mixture of jazz and pop and classical – and Phillip, who has studied under world-class guitarists, showed Dana some techniques which he says will improve his playing. Dana was all eyes and ears and respect. Phillip's wife gave me a big envelope of used stamps, mostly from the West Indies, for my collection back home. We left around midnight, and I stayed up until 1:30 sorting my philatelic windfall. Then I bade Dana a Merry Christmas and crawled into bed.

DECEMBER 25: *Port of Spain, Trinidad*
The morning dawned clear and bright, and by eight o'clock, it was 75 degrees outside. Just before Christmas breakfast, I was sitting in the living room when the house began to move in a long slow oscillation that set the walls and floor shaking. I looked outside and could see the large overhang on the roof flapping in slow-motion waves. This went on for five seconds or so and was over before I'd realized an earthquake had hit. Dana came out of the bedroom and said, "Did you feel that?" He'd been lying on the bed and had thought someone was underneath, shaking him.

Dana went back to the Keillers' for more instruction from Phillip, and I sat around, feeling a little lonely and pensive, and sorting more stamps. I hate to admit it, but for a while in the late morning I watched the Osmond Family Christmas show on television from the U.S. – it made me feel deeply nostalgic. We miss home so much. Only Christmas makes me miss the crunch and squeak of snow crystals beneath my feet.

One of the nice things about Christmas in Port of Spain is that the poinsettia shrubs and trees, which grow naturally here, are in bloom all over the city. Some of the trees are over 10 feet high and are covered with blossoms. Quite a show compared to the little potted plants we get at home at Christmas.

At three o'clock, we were picked up by new Canadian friends. Roy and Ruth Beatty, who had invited us for a family Christmas dinner. One of their three children lives here in Port of Spain with them, and the other two flew down from Canadian universities for the holiday. They put on a fine traditional Canadian feast: turkey, cranberry, Christmas pudding, everything. Afterwards, we sat around talking and reminiscing, mostly about our homeland, which means so much to us. What a pleasure it was to be there with these generous Canadians, all of whom contributed to getting us through what could have been a pretty lonely day.

DECEMBER 27: *Port of Spain, Trinidad*
Tonight as I watched television, I saw an old friend, Phil Scott, who was
the subject of a news clip, having won the world logrolling championship
for the 13th or 14th year in a row. Phil paddled for Nova Scotia in the
cross-Canada canoe race in 1967, and we got to know one another over
the 104 days of the competition. Seeing him got me thinking about how
I'd quit my job of 17 years to compete for the Manitoba team. It was one
of the best decisions of my life. So often, as the years go by, I think of how
happy I am to be a planner and a doer, and not let life pass me by.

DECEMBER 29: *Port of Spain, Trinidad*
The hours are ticking down, and today we did a good food shopping for
the canoe, adding milk powder, cheese, margarine, oatmeal, bread, among
other items. Dana visited the Venezuelan consulate to pick up our visas
for the next two months. He also bought Franol tablets for his asthma –
not because he intends to use them, just for emergencies. He's now been
off medication for 16 months. Several times lately he's mentioned stomach pains when he finishes his meals, though he doesn't seem particularly worried about them. I'll have to keep an eye on him.

Farewell to the Sea

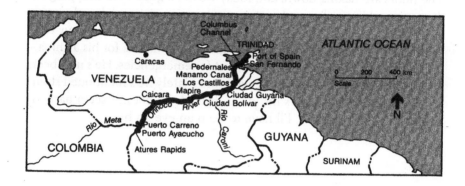

NEW YEAR'S DAY, 1982: *Pointe à Pierre, Trinidad*

Yesterday afternoon at two o'clock, Jean's son-in-law drove us to the Motor Yacht Club with our canoe and equipment. We had said emotional goodbyes to many of our friends earlier in the day, while others came to say farewell during the afternoon and evening as we relaxed by the docks. Eventually we were alone under the dock lights, unable to sleep, as the sounds of New Year's parties floated over us from shore or from boats on the water. Dana took a bed in a covered yacht, and I sacked out on a padded chaise longue. But I soon got up and spent a lonely half hour standing by the water, staring at the fish that swam into the dock lights. Nothing seemed quite real – except that I was lonely in the shadow of the many revellers and wasn't particularly happy to be leaving our good friends in Trinidad. I started thinking about home, and about Jeff and Gabby, and missed them terribly. I was also extremely anxious about returning to the sea. To tell the truth, I could barely stand the thought of it.

Sleep or no sleep, we were up at 5 a.m. and on the water within 45 minutes. Conditions were calm as we paddled past the lights of the still sleeping port, out onto the gulf and south down the coast.

By 2:30 this afternoon we were camped at Pointe à Pierre, having come 31 miles. We fared pretty well physically for our first day back on the water, though I was pretty well played out by one o'clock and had to paddle the last few miles on guts alone. We'd been too nervous to eat this morning, which undoubtedly affected our stamina. Dana seems to have lost his resistance to the sun during the long weeks of living in houses in Port of Spain and picked up a pretty fair sunburn on his legs and face. Other than that, he has only a little blister on his hand to complain about. I, as usual, am blister-free.

JANUARY 3: *on Columbus Bay, Trinidad*
We advanced another 23 miles south yesterday and, tonight, are camped on palm-ringed Columbus Bay from which we'll head out tomorrow for our 9-mile crossing back to Venezuela.

Strange occurrence last night at Point Fortin: About 4:30 a.m., I was wakened by the sound of bells and faint chanting from down the beach. I looked around but could see nothing, as the foliage of a fallen palm was blocking my view to the south. I crept along as far as the palm, some 40 feet away, and from there I could see lit candles about 60 feet further down the beach. As my eyes adjusted to the darkness, I made out several people who seemed to be participating in a cult ceremony – perhaps Rastafarian. About 10 feet from the water, two people in white robes knelt before a candle-lit altar made of sticks. The two held candles which they rotated as they chanted.

A figure in a dark robe came onto the scene and stood before the couple. It occurred to me that it might be some sort of Voodoo ceremony, and I tiptoed back and woke Dana who returned with me to the palm. But now I wanted a better view, so I crawled around the fallen tree and sat invisibly in its shadow on the close side. From here, I could see that the altar was actually a cross set in a frame of sticks.

The dark-robed person now picked up the cross, with its several candles, and walked into the water with it, planting it in the sand about 50 feet from shore. Two people who'd been standing in the background came forward and gently took the elbows of one of the kneeling people, a woman, I think. They ushered her through the shallows toward the burning cross, rotating her in slow circles as they walked.

All of them disappeared into the sea for a minute, then they reappeared, left the water, and formed a compact group on the beach. Presently they headed toward a car parked well up on shore.

At this stage my curiosity got the better of me, and I walked to the car and spoke to the man in the dark robe. He greeted me cordially, and explained that he was the pastor of the Spiritual Baptist Church and that what we'd witnessed was a baptism, Trinidad style. I thanked him rather sheepishly and told him we'd found the service very beautiful, which was the truth.

Our beach here tonight is one on which Columbus came ashore on his third voyage in 1498. He complained in his log that he lost an anchor in the bay here, and, indeed, an ancient anchor was found here in 1877. It now rests in a museum in Port of Spain.

Our 9-mile crossing tomorrow will take us across Columbus's route, as he came along the south coast of Trinidad. He had been a long time at sea when he reached Trinidad in 1498, and it's said that he vowed his next landfall would be named to honour the Almighty. When he sighted the island, he saw three peaks on the south-east coast and named the place La Trinidad, the Trinity.

Columbus was also the first European to see the muddy waters of the Orinoco, which he said coloured the sea for 150 miles along the South American coast. Two years later, Vicente Pinzon visited the Orinoco and called it *Río Dulce* or Sweet River, but very little was done to explore this mighty waterway until 1531 when Diego de Ordaz travelled a fair distance upstream.

Even in modern times, the route we're to follow remains relatively untravelled. Before leaving home, I read a book called *The Last Great Adventure*, about a British Hovercraft expedition that started at Manaus, Brazil, moved north up the Río Negro, through the Casiquiare Canal and on down the Orinoco to its mouth. Quite a trip, but accomplished by motor on a cushion of air, and with plenty of sponsorship and aircraft support.

In 1909, Joshua Slocum of Nova Scotia, already famous for sailing solo around the world in 1895, set out from the eastern u.s. for a South American river trip. His aim was to take our route exactly – up the Orinoco, through the Casiquiare Canal, down the Río Negro and the Amazon to Belém. But as he sailed to South America he was lost at sea and never heard from again. Even if he had reached the Orinoco, he would have failed: his boat was 37 feet long and weighed 9 tons, and even Captain

Slocum would never have made it up the 30 or 40 miles of rapids south of Puerto Ayacucho.

Orinoko is a Guarauno word which means "the place where one rows". We feel the Indians knew what it was about and have given us the secret for the successful navigation of their fabled river. We will be the first travellers to navigate the route from North America.

Today we passed the 9,000-mile mark.

JANUARY 4: *Pedernales, Venezuela*

At 6 this morning we set off nervously, and paddled 2½ miles of coast to Icacos Point, the extreme southwest corner of Trinidad. From there, in the distance to the west, we could see the faint shore of the Venezuelan mainland. We checked our tarp to make sure it was well anchored, tied ourselves tightly into our cockpits, and headed out across the Columbus Channel at a compass hearing of 242 degrees.

Our muscles strained and our adrenaline pumped as the low strip of trees on the horizon came slowly into focus. I was particularly alert to the possible presence of dolphins or whales which might cause us to make a sudden move and which in the tricky waters could cause us to capsize. But in under three hours we had reached the swampy Venezuelan shore, where we swung to our right and paddled northwest up the coast towards Punta Tolete, maybe 10 miles away. Gone were the rocky shores we'd seen in October; now we were in delta country. We paddled hard past the trees and swamp, searching for the Boca de Pedernales, the entrance to the Manamo Canal, our route into the Orinoco.

We soon passed the famous Soldado Rock, a large, protrusive rock formation, 6 or 7 miles offshore, named by Columbus in 1498. We passed Punta Tolete, and, just beyond it, on the near side of Isla Cotorra, spotted our *boca*. I've seldom seen Dana more exultant. We swung southwest, and slowly left the sea for the last time.

We were surprised by the lack of current flowing against us on the first few miles of inland waterway. We've since found out that the Orinoco is dammed 15 miles the other side of Tucupita, which should give us over 100 miles of relatively easy paddling on the canal and on our first few miles of river. All we'll have to contend with until we reach the dam will be the tides, which greatly influence the flow of water through the delta. We'll try to paddle with the incoming tide.

One of the thrills of entering the delta was our first sight of scarlet ibises in the wild. There they sat in the trees, with their brilliant red plumage and long curved bills, so many of them that the trees appeared to be in flower.

Tonight we're camped at the Guardia Nacional base at Pedernales, which is occupied by 12 soldiers, 7 of whom are currently out on patrol boats. When we pulled in here, one of the soldiers looked at my sunburnt nose and called out, *"Payaso!"* which I knew meant clown.

JANUARY 7: *on the Manamito Canal, Venezuela*
Three days of canal paddling have brought us 81 miles into the interior of Venezuela.

When we awoke at the Guardia base the day before yesterday, we found our loaded canoe, which we'd left floating nicely the night before, sitting stranded and dry on some large rocks and logs, a hundred feet from the water. The tide had gone out. What a chore we had getting to it in the pre-dawn darkness, through the foot-deep muck and debris of the tidal flat.

As we pulled away I noticed that, in our grogginess, we'd left Dana's guitar in our sleeping quarters. We went back for it, and, as Dana reached for the case, a thin brown snake, with the telltale lance-shaped head, plopped off it to the floor. A soldier ran up, warning us to keep away from it. I picked up a push broom and dispatched the thing with a well-aimed polo shot to the head.

Our first day of canal travel took us past many little Indian shacks, set on stilts at sporadic intervals along the shores. The dwellings are crudely constructed of logs, sticks, and palm thatching and are apparently spaced so that each family has a good-sized area for foraging and hunting.

We hadn't been on the canal long when we saw a strange new species of fish that lives in an inch or two of muddy water at the edges of the canal. They're anywhere from 3 to 8 inches long and have a pair of bulgy eyes that protrude above the water surface. Every so often, they'll propel themselves up and forward and go skipping across the mud, then resubmerge. We saw thousands of them; I believe they're called (appropriately enough) mudskippers. We also saw dozens of green parrots and hundreds more red ibises, one flock numbering over 200. When they took flight in front of us, the jungle seemed to burst into flame.

We'd been told at the Guardia base to make camp at a little settlement on the south end of Isla Tigre and to look for a man named Juan Suarez. We reached the settlement at about 2 p.m. and in no time found Juan, who owns a small store on the canal bank. He fed us and invited us to make our home in a dusty palm-thatched room attached to the back of his store. It wasn't long before our canoe was surrounded by friendly Indians, who were fascinated by our different-shaped craft and paddles and, surprisingly, by our long trip. They're real canoeists and travel great distances through the hundreds of miles of waterway that dissect the great delta.

As we loaded in the early hours of yesterday morning, Juan watched us with utmost curiosity. He's seen many river travellers over the years and couldn't believe how big a load we could cram into our canoe without significantly lowering it in the water. He kept shaking his head and muttering, "Caramba – caramba – caramba."

Yesterday we were pleased to realize that we hadn't lost contact with our friendly dolphins. Over the past couple of days we've seen many of the freshwater variety – toninas they're called down here. They're silvery in colour and are more playful than their ocean cousins. We're now seeing fewer ibises, but have met a species of big brown peacock-like birds, with fan tails and tufted crowns. They're pretty but slow and stupid – and loud; they squawk away at us as we pass. We've nicknamed them "turkeybirds".

Every mile we go south brings us drier land, and we're already into the famous cattle-raising area of the delta. In some places we can look out over miles of prairie-type grassland or llanos and see cattle and horses by the hundreds.

Before retiring tonight, I took a walk and came across a squealing pig which was feasting on a nice stalk of bananas that it had pulled from a low plant. I figured the pig was fatter than I was and needed the food less, so I took the bananas and stashed them in the canoe. It was the first time I'd taken food from a pig.

JANUARY 8: *Tucupita, Venezuela*

Just before we reached Tucupita this morning, our canal opened up and we paddled happily out onto the Orinoco River. Right away, we noticed more boats on the water, particularly dugouts, some as long as 40 or 50 feet.

We pulled up for the day in Tucupita and met an old priest, Padre Baral, whose faded black robe dragged along the ground as he walked. He told us he'd preached in Tucupita for 50 years and had written three books about his life with the Indians and his extensive travels by dugout on the Orinoco. Dana went to visit his church and returned with the books, which the old man said were a gift from Tucupita. Not an hour later, Dana ran into a pretty girl who took a shine to him and bought him salve for his lower lip, which has again turned to scab after its weeks of healing in Trinidad.

The local police watched us closely during the afternoon, seemingly envious of the attention we were getting on the river bank. Several of the cops were women, with 3-foot stainless-steel machetes on their belts. At about 4 o'clock, they'd had it with our little sideshow and swooped in – two men, two women – for a shakedown. They marched us off to the police station, where their superiors were floored by our extensive documents and immediately stamped our passports and freed us.

Just after dark, as we chatted with some friendly locals, four more cops, all male, came along, wanting to search our canoe. "For what reason?" I demanded in Spanish, explaining that our documents had been thoroughly checked during the afternoon. Against my loud objections, they started opening every last one of our packages, some of which had been sealed to keep out moisture. Everything went into a heap, hopelessly scrambled.

When they ripped apart the two tiny boxes in which I'd sealed the stamps I'd been given in Port of Spain, I saw red. "*Estúpido!*" I yelled.

"*Quieto!*" one of them yelled back.

"*Estúpido!*"

Again the guy yelled "*Quieto!*", this time with his hand on his gun, looking me menacingly in the eye.

One of them now picked up a clear plastic bottle containing six or seven red survival candles. He tried to get the top off, but it had been corroded on, and he couldn't budge it. He peered in through the plastic, and asked me what was inside.

"*Bombas!*" I blurted out.

He looked again, then looked at me angrily (and a little foolishly) and said, "*No es bombas – es candeles.*"

"*Sí,*" I hissed.

They eventually gave up their search, but not before they'd left us with an hour-long clean-up to perform. We'd just finished the job when, as if to atone for the idiocies of his countrymen, a local restaurateur came along and invited us to his restaurant for dinner. He had a couple of pet toucans, a pair of tortoises, and a cute little monkey on the loose among the tables. He told us he'd made his money smuggling liquor between various Caribbean islands. And the cops are after *us*.

JANUARY 11: *on a sand bar in the Orinoco River, Venezuela*
Paddling has changed greatly for us since we left Tucupita. We've passed the outlets to the Macarao Canal and to the Río Grande, which, together,

carry most of the volume (and current) of the Orinoco's flow across the delta to the sea. We're now dealing with the full current of the river and are obliged to stay close to the banks to take advantage of the slacker current and back eddies.

The river here is about 3 miles wide, and its banks remind me of those of our own Red River back home – clay, grass, not particularly tropical-looking. The water, too, is like the Red – muddy grey-brown. We've been told that the river has dropped between 10 and 20 feet since the rainy season ended and is expected to drop a good bit more. In the distance to the west we can now see a long string of low purple mountains. One thing we're especially pleased about is the appearance of big white sand bars in the river, much like those of the Mississippi. They make terrific campsites, convenient and private, and we're stopped on one tonight just south of Los Castillos.

An hour or so ago I had my first swim in the river, a little wary of piranhas, even though local fishermen have told me we'll have no trouble with them. My fear is exaggerated by what I've seen of the jungles of Hollywood, in which piranhas can reduce a man to a skeleton in a matter of seconds. The real threat, here, is from freshwater stingrays, whose spinal barb, we've been told, can go right through your foot, crippling you for months. A fisherman has told me always to shuffle along the bottom on the way into the water, and not to lift my feet, so as to avoid coming down on the stingray's barb. I recall that Humboldt himself wrote about the dangers of stingrays and played down the piranhas. He also warned of the electric eels in these waters, claiming they could knock over a horse with the power of their shocks. The locals have also mentioned the eels, which live near shore amid the mud and rocks. We'll be on the lookout.

Dana and I are in good health. Paddling muscles have tightened up, and our spirits are high. We were a little worried about our drinking water, in terms of both quality and availability, but have been watching the locals drink right out of the river and have tried it a couple of times without harmful effects.

I've been keeping my eye on the North Star. I read somewhere that it would no longer be visible when we got south of latitude 7°. I intend to test the claim. We have an attachment to the North Star, as it's one of our last daily ties with home. Childish as it may seem, I get comfort out of seeing it as I lie awake at night, knowing that our people back home can see it and might even be taking a glance at it at that moment.

Yesterday, for the first time, we had a chance to use the green rain jackets that Richie delivered from Winnipeg. They worked well, and we know they'll be a big help further south during the rainy season.

JANUARY 13: *Isla La Ceiba, Venezuela*
I felt sad as we passed the mouth of the Río Caroni before sunrise this morning. I knew that way back on its waters were Angel Falls, the world's highest waterfall at 3,297 feet. How I would have loved to travel to them, through the area in which Papillon found his fortune in diamonds. But our obsessive urge to advance drove us on.

JANUARY 17: *Ciudad Bolívar, Venezuela*
The current is getting stronger as we go upstream. We've been resting at Ciudad Bolívar since the 15th, but had some pretty tough paddling getting here. We can't always stay in the calmer waters close to shore these days, as in many areas the shallows are strewn with boulders, some of them 20 or 30 feet high. In other areas we're hampered by sand bars, which can occupy so much of the river that the flow is narrowed and the current vastly increased. Many of the sand bars are joined to the mainland by narrow strips of sand. Occasionally we'll make the mistake of trying to pass one on the blocked side and will have to go back and around.

We're seeing fewer big ships and less heavy industry now that we're west of Ciudad Guayana. Perhaps correspondingly, we're seeing more wildlife. The other day, Dana sighted our first Orinoco crocodile, a stout little 5-footer relaxing in a foot or so of water alongshore. It eyed us keenly from 6 feet away, but didn't budge, probably figuring it was well camouflaged – and that we were too big to eat. Our scarlet ibises have left us, but we've seen plenty of black ibises over the past few days. Like their cousins, they have distinctive down-curved bills. The natives call them *coro-coro*, perhaps because of their strange call, which sounds like someone screaming out of a hollow log. We're seeing a little more jungle these days, and the other night as we slept on Isla Bongo we were awakened by the bizarre screams of howler monkeys. They were at least a mile away on the shore to our south but were still able to fill the air with the fantastic power of their cries. Howlers indeed.

A couple of days ago, west of Puerto Ordaz, we were trailed for over an hour by five dolphins, or *toninas*, whose silvery skin was blotched with pink patches and whose dorsal fins were small and soft-looking, unlike the more prominent fins we're used to. From time to time, one of them would rocket toward us on the surface, then veer away sharply as it got to the canoe, doing its playful best to give us a good splash. They seem to

love our canoe; perhaps it's the orange colour or the bright Canadian flag
– or maybe just the repetitive plop-plop of our paddles. Earlier that day, I
was startled when a foot-long fish, closely pursued by a dolphin, flew from
the water and bounced up my arm, hitting my chin and throat before
returning to the water on the other side of the canoe. One *tonina* was a
good 8 feet long and must have weighed several hundred pounds.

Our camp here in Ciudad Bolívar is on a narrow beach at the base of a
towering concrete restraining wall that prevents the city from being
flooded during periods of high water. The river level here varies up to
65 feet from season to season, and we're told it still has 15 feet to drop
before hitting its low point in March or April. The beach on which we're
camped is joined to the city by a great set of concrete steps, like something
the Egyptians might have engineered. Ciudad Bolívar is the Orinoco's
main city, with a population of about 120,000. The city was once called
Angostura, but its name was changed decades ago to honour Venezuela's
liberator and national hero, Simón Bolívar. Angostura bitters was made
here until late in the 19th century, when its inventor packed up his kitchen
and moved to Port of Spain, where the product is still manufactured.

Today, our old friends Walter Low and Lila drove down from El Tigrito to
give us good maps of the Orinoco that they'd found for us. We'd arranged
the meeting by phone from Trinidad. Generous as ever, they also gave us
a good-sized bag of groceries, then took us out for a fine restaurant dinner before leaving for home. The new maps are far better than any we
had and will serve us all the way to the Río Negro.

There are plenty of speedboats on the river, and today, just before Walter and Lila arrived, a fat speedboat driver of about 45 pulled in to shore
by our camp and presented us with a cantaloupe and a watermelon. He
also offered us a big ugly river iguana which was lying dead in the bottom
of his boat – even offered to cook it for us. But we refused the kindness;
we'd have had to be pretty hungry.

Later, another speedboat pulled up, this one driven by an old man I
recognized as the hardware merchant who sold us a couple of machetes
yesterday. He had a German shepherd dog with him and wanted me to
go for a ride. I did. He wound up his big outboard, and we roared across
the river at a harebrained speed. What a ridiculous experience after a
year and a half of crawling along at 3 or 4 miles an hour! The dog and I
were both relieved to get our feet back on land.

Tomorrow, as we leave Ciudad Bolívar, we'll pass under the mile-long
Angostura Bridge, the only bridge we'll see in 3,000 miles of river paddling. It's a marvellously lit suspension bridge – in red, yellow and blue,

like the Venezuelan flag. We hope to go under it before dawn, for the
magic of seeing it twinkling above us.

JANUARY 21: *at Isla Infierno, Venezuela*

Our last couple of days have been our most challenging since entering
the Orinoco. We're nearly 400 miles inland, and the currents and sand
bars and boulders are so entirely unpredictable we can no longer plan
our days in advance, as we like to. Every bend has to be faced for what it
throws at us. But far from getting us down, the unpredictability stimu-
lates us. We feel like readers, always wanting to turn the next page in an
exciting book.

At times the river is like an enormous conduit through the desert. Some
of the sand bars extend a mile out from shore and rise to heights of 10
feet or more. Of course, they wouldn't even be visible during the rainy
season when the water is 40 or 50 feet higher. During the day, we thread
our way among them, cursing them as we fight the current; but, at night,
we're happy to pitch camp on them. They're dry and private and, above
all, they shelter no insects – or, at least, very few. The other night we did
have a visit from some hard-shelled beetles, many of which crawled over
us and under our clothing, apparently trying to find warmth on a cool
night.

The landscape, high beyond the clay and sand, is a variable mix of
jungle and grasslands, and away to the south we can now see a range of
low green hills. We don't need a reminder that we're working our way
upland; the current grows stronger every day, and our average canoe speed
is down from about 3.5 m.p.h. to about 2.5. In rare instances, we're able
to gain no more than an inch or two with each long stroke.

This afternoon, nearly the entire river was blocked by sand, and we
had to plough along within a few feet of a large island; the current further
out was impassable. The clay bank rose 30 feet above us, and, as we crept
along under its shadow, high winds began tearing off pieces of the bank
and sending them down around us. We didn't like risking our lives but
couldn't land and couldn't move further out for fear that the current
would carry us away. Suddenly, just 100 feet ahead, a giant block of clay
and sand, weighing many tons, broke loose and plunged into the river,
creating a temporary 50-foot island which was quickly dissolved by the
current. We were white with shock, knowing that if we'd been 30 seconds
further along we'd have been crushed.

This evening we were visited at our sand bar by a couple of motorized
dugouts, one driven by a man of about 60, the other by a father with his
two boys. They tell us we're camped on Isla Infierno (Hell Island) and

that the route along the far side of the island is the notorious west channel of the Boca de Infierno, hazardously strewn with boulders, around which the water flows in terrible currents. We had chosen to travel the east channel, the passable one, quite by chance, with no thought that we were avoiding trouble. The *boca* itself, a few miles upstream at the tip of the island, marks the furthest recorded penetration of the explorer Ordaz when he navigated the Orinoco in 1531.

JANUARY 22: *southwest of Mapire, Venezuela*
We reached the *boca* early this morning, and could see why Ordaz had decided to cash his chips. Boulder after boulder, some as big as houses, clutter the channel. It rattled us to think what the area would be like during high water. But at this time of year it's navigable, and we fought our way upstream, winding and angling among the rocks. One thing that impressed us was the shiny, almost coppery surfaces of the boulders, which seem to have been glazed in a kiln. The effect is undoubtedly caused by the scouring of thousands of years of rushing sand and water at flood time. These historic sites continue to give me a sense of kinship with the great travellers of the past. I wouldn't feel the same if we hadn't come by our quaint means of travel; a Hovercraft or speedboat just wouldn't do it for me. It took Ordaz 20 sailing days to reach the *boca*. We took 15, not including our two-day layover at Ciudad Bolívar.

We're camped tonight on a sand bar near the north shore of the river, a couple of miles upstream from Mapire, a small city where we stopped to shop this afternoon. A while ago several of our friendly *toninas* gathered around the campsite, poking their noses and eyes above the water to see what we were up to. Today, off and on, they leapt from the water around us, sometimes two or three at a time, obviously showing off. We realize that some of them have been following us upriver for three or four days or more. Many of them have distinctive pink blotches, so that we've come to recognize them as individuals. The day before yesterday, we were surprised to see one that was entirely pink.

We've been seeing increasing numbers of iguanas, some of them three feet long. They have terrific climbing capabilities and can dart up a 10-foot cliff in a matter of seconds. Some of them stare at us from their hot clay perches as we paddle by; others feel threatened and scoot into the grass and shrubs at the top of the banks. We also see good-sized crocodiles in the shallows, and the other day on shore we saw a couple of catfish heads, each a foot and a half wide. The whole beasts must have been as big as good-sized sharks.

Dana is happier than ever and has been pursuing his music with near-religious fervour. He surprised me the other day by telling me that all the paddling, with its heavy demands on hand strength, has improved his touch and dexterity. I'd have thought it would hamper dexterity, as seems to happen with me. Sometimes when I wake up in the morning my left hand is virtually paralysed from being wrapped around the top of my paddle. Occasionally it's so locked into the paddling position that I have to pry it open with my other hand.

As I sit here tonight in this hot desert-like place, I feel hundreds of years removed from Trinidad, 500 miles back. We are worn out, yet our progress on this remote waterway keeps our spirits jumping. We've changed our routine somewhat and now, instead of eating our main meal as soon as we land, hold off for a couple of hours. We weren't getting the most out of our meals while we were exhausted. A few minutes after 6, the sun sinks and the wind dies, and for a few minutes at dusk everything is frozen into a photograph. This is our special time to talk, think, and share our feelings. We light our little coal-oil lamp, ignite our alcohol burner, and boil up our evening treat, a big pot of tea.

We no longer unload the canoe at night, haven't done so in weeks. We simply pull it up sideways three or four feet onto the beach and take what we need from it. This gives us an extra hour or so for the more important things – like enjoying our tea and watching the sun go down.

Note next day: During the night, our sands finally got the better of us. A wind came up after dark, and by dawn it had blown 100 pounds or more of sand over me – in my ears, hair, clothing, eyes, everywhere. I could barely haul myself out of it, and had to dig 8 inches to find my paddle and machete, which I always keep beside me as I sleep. We paddled off, a couple of dusty iguanas in the faint light of dawn.

JANUARY 27: *near Caicara, Venezuela*
We had a magical experience as we left camp this morning. Several big *toninas* were swimming along in front of us, half watching us as we stroked. Every so often, one of them would break away from the rest and power in toward us, jumping into the air a few feet from the canoe and doing a complete somersault, sending a high spray of water over us. A second or so later, a delicate rainbow would appear out of the spray and hang for several seconds before disappearing. I've decided that the vapour necessary to produce such rainbows could only have come from the exhaled breath of the diving *toninas*.

These majestic mammals are by far the dominating wildlife of the river. What puzzles me is that none of the other river adventurers I've read has mentioned them. We've begun to suspect, incidentally, that they don't follow our canoe merely for friendship, but because we tend to scare smaller fish out from along the banks. The dolphins make easy prey of these unfortunates once they're in the main stream. Last night, we watched them working in pairs to catch 2- and 3-pound fish which they would bring to the surface to eat. Even as I sit writing, they are hanging around offshore, some swimming back and forth (pacing?), others just looking in at us, waiting for us to resume our trip.

The most unusual-looking animal we've seen in the past few days was a turtle of about 15 pounds with prehistoric-looking spikes on its shell. I pulled it out of the shallows and set it on the canoe, thinking it would head back into the water as soon as possible. But it just sat there enjoying the ride, and I had to dump it back myself. I guess when you're armoured with inch-long spikes and aren't particularly bright, you don't tend to worry much about predators.

We continue to see crocodiles, mostly about 5 feet long and not terribly threatening – or interesting.

We have developed enormous affection for this great river, even though its islands and sand bars and winding channels can give us fits. Almost every way we turned this morning, we got blocked. Eventually we stopped so that Dana could climb a 30-foot dune to get perspective on the water ahead. For a mile or more, he walked along the dune toward the southeast, looking for open channels. Even after all this, the route he chose took us into a dead end. Our calculated advance for the day was 18 miles, though I'm sure we paddled 30 for that 18.

Early in the afternoon, we pulled into the town of Caicara, and found the Guardia waiting for us, seemingly aware that we were coming. We paddled right up to them, and were surprised by their respect and courtesy; there was no talk of a canoe check. It seems we're better off when we go to them.

We'd expected to stay the night, but the place was dirty and hot, and the locals distrustful, so at 4 o'clock we packed up and paddled to a sand bar about a mile and a half upriver.

We're tired at the moment and know that the next couple of weeks, when we turn almost due south, are going to be even tougher than the last. We're 225 miles from Puerto Ayacucho, and between here and there our maps show hundreds of sand bars and islands, plus four sets of rapids.

It is now dark, although Dana's guitar continues to sweeten the air. Before I put my pen down, I must mention that, last night at dusk, when everything had gone calm (the winds always go down for a few hours at sunset and rise again during the night) we were puzzled by a massive whirring sound, as if a million leaves had begun to vibrate. The whirring got louder from the south, and a few bats appeared. In no time, there were thousands of them, swarms of them, *clouds* of them, rushing past us, some about 30 feet up, others skimming the surface of the water and land. For several minutes they passed, apparently heading north for a night's insect-hunting. Then they were gone, and the air was as still as ever.

Tomorrow we'll pass the mouth of the Río Apure, where Humboldt entered the Orinoco on his travels from the north coast of Venezuela. It will be interesting to compare our own observations with those Humboldt made in 1800. I have copies of many of his notes; I was never able to find anything modern that was better or more detailed.

Our only health problem at the moment is my lower lip, which is severely sunburnt and has been for several weeks. It generally forms a thin scab during the day, but as I eat my supper it breaks open and begins to bleed into my food. At night as I sleep the scab seals my lips.

JANUARY 28: *on the Orinoco River, Venezuela*
Dana left our campsite late this afternoon for a walk down the sands. He came back a while later with a long face which told me something was distressing him. He'd relieved himself, and said he found evidence of intestinal parasites. He was inordinately upset, but all I could do to comfort him was urge him not to worry and tell him that we'd get to a doctor as soon as we get to Puerto Ayacucho. He's been complaining about stomach pains since we left Trinidad, and this is probably the reason. We've been eating pretty much the same foods, so I, too, probably have parasites.

FEBRUARY 2: *near Isla Gallo, on the Orinoco River, Venezuela*
Sometimes it seems as if our days have been cranked out of a duplicating machine: paddle, current, paddle, sand bars, camp, dinner, sleep, paddle, paddle. We have our wildlife for distraction, of course, though we don't have much contact with humanity. We'll often paddle 20 or 30 miles and see only the occasional Indian woman, or pair of women, doing their laundry on the rocks along the river bank.

At sundown two days ago we had another storm of bats, this one ten times as impressive as the first one. For half an hour, they whirred past us in an incredibly dense cloud, all moving north for the night's feeding. Dana happened to be eating watermelon as they went over, and almost every time he spat out a pit a bat would dart in and catch it well before it hit the ground. The bat would immediately discard it, realizing it wasn't an insect. We've seen few *toninas* over the past couple of days, though the local reptiles are as numerous as ever. This morning as we paddled, Dana said to me quietly, "Dad, do you want to see a snake?" I back-paddled quickly, and there under water was an 8-foot anaconda about 5 inches thick. I gave it a nudge with my paddle, and it slid peacefully beneath the canoe.

We're camped tonight on yet another sand bar, from which I can see a long chain of mountains off to the south. To the east is another chain, many of whose peaks we passed on our lengthy travels today. The river is narrowing, and the climate is more humid as we move south. We're seeing more and more jungle foliage atop the river banks.

Tomorrow, about 15 miles south of here, we'll pass the Río Meta, which marks the Venezuela-Colombia border. For the next 150 miles, we'll have Venezuela on our east bank, Colombia on our west. We don't have Colombian visas, but have no desire to enter the country anyway.

The books are wrong. We're now south of latitude 6° 34′ N, and can still see the North Star at night.

FEBRUARY 5: *Puerto Ayacucho, Venezuela*
This morning at about 11 o'clock we paddled into Puerto Ayacucho. The *puerto* is not really a port at this time of year with the water so low; but at flood time, with the river 50 or 60 feet higher, it is the most southerly point on the Orinoco that can be reached by ocean-going vessels. It is the capital of Territorial Federal Amazonas and has a population of about 35,000 people. Across the river is the Colombian town of Cazuarito.

During the past couple of days we've come through four minor sets of rapids, and when we leave here will face what are probably the most ferocious and extensive rapids on the continent – three sets of them in succession, 40 miles in all. The annals of travel in these parts are studded with tales of how this missionary or that explorer was flummoxed by the insurmountable waters south of Puerto Ayacucho. We may be able to paddle parts of them, but we're mentally preparing for some exhausting portages. At worst, we'll have to portage the entire distance along a back-country road.

Predictably enough, the Guardia were waiting for us as we arrived here this morning. They seemed certain we'd come from Colombia and did an immediate search of the canoe. Finding nothing, they ruffled around, looking for another angle on us, until one of them growled in Spanish, "Take that flag down!" and we removed the Canadian flag from our stern.

While I guarded the canoe, Dana got started on the many chores that
await us before we can move on. His first call was at the nearby Port
Captain's office to get our documents updated. Then he was to get medical attention for his parasites. We also need maps of the Río Negro and
information on the rapids and on boat trailers, in case we should need
one for our portage. As much as anything, we need accommodation and
a couple of nights of good rest. To set off south of here in anything less
than peak condition would be beyond foolishness.

Dana returned at noon to tell me that the Port Captain was going to
take him to the hospital to be checked over. He left again and came back
an hour later with a prescription for himself and one for me; the doctor
told him I most likely had parasites, too, which is what we'd imagined.

A few minutes later, a military official came down to the dock and gave
us stunning news: we've been refused permission to carry on into Territorial Federal Amazonas. The immigration office has refused to extend
our visas, which expire in three days, 30 days after they were validated at
Tucupita. For some numbskull reason, the Venezuelan consulate in Trinidad stamped the visas "improrrogable", which means they can't be
extended.

Apparently, our only hope is to leave the country and reapply for visas
at a Venezuelan consulate. The closest consulate is at Puerto Carreño,
Colombia, which we passed about 50 miles downriver. The problem is
we have no visas to enter Colombia and could well get arrested if we
enter the country illegally. If we get there and can't get our visas reissued,
we'll be unable to get back into Venezuela. The problems of getting around
and of what to do with our equipment in the meantime are maddeningly
complicated. Beyond all this, we've been told we'll need a separate letter
of permission from the governor of the Territory to travel the Orinoco
from here. What complicates things most right now is that it's Friday,
and everything is going to shut down for the weekend in a few hours.

In my notebook, I happened to have the name of a local man, Mata
Paratima, whom we'd been told about way back west of Caracas, months
ago. In the middle of the afternoon, I phoned Sr. Paratima, who kindly
offered to meet us at the docks and to drive us to see the governor. In no
time he was there, a tall man, about 60 years old, with a thick European
accent. Mata is a chicken farmer and owns a number of barbecue units
which he leases to local cafés.

We visited one of his barbecue outlets for a chicken dinner, then went on
to the office of the governor. There we were told to return Monday morning at 8:30, when the governor *might* feel disposed to issue us a travel
document for the upper Orinoco.

We've talked to a number of people about the rapids ahead and are getting grossly conflicting reports. Some say the first and second sets are passable but that the third will necessitate a jungle portage. Others say the second and third sets are the easier ones. The confusion seems to lie in the ever-changing level of the river from month to month. Dana wants no part of any of the rapids and is determined to tow the canoe from here to Samariapo, 40 miles away, which would be possible only with a decent trailer. I'd rather go as far as we can on the river – *if* we can get out of here.

SUNDAY, FEBRUARY 7: *Puerto Ayacucho, Venezuela*
Late Friday, the Port Captain offered us the use of his office reception area as a sleeping space. We were happy enough to have shelter, but have spent two dismally uncomfortable nights on hard benches in the perishingly hot room. We've been obliged to keep the windows open, which of course brings the bugs in (screens are far from universal down here). Give us back our sand bars.

Early yesterday morning, we were picked up in a jeep by a young man named Christian whom Dana had met the previous night. He drove us a short distance south of town to a lookout site, from which the Orinoco and the Ature Rapids (the first set south of the city) were visible in a grand panorama. I put my binoculars to my eyes and just about fainted. I had never seen such an intimidating, wild-looking stretch of river – boulders and whirlpools and white water, apparently extending forever. I spent half an a hour trying to determine whether there was any way at all we might find a passage through, but I saw nothing to encourage me.

Christian took us to his home to meet his family, who came from Chile after the right-wing takeover in that country a few years back. His mother made us a fine lunch of tuna salad and *empeñadas Chilenas* – pork and eggs in a thin wheat-flour wrap.

I was particularly interested in an array of Indian weapons hanging on the living-room wall, and after lunch Christian took down a blowgun and some darts, and we went out into the back yard for a demonstration. The jungle Indians dip the tips of the darts into the powerful drug *curare*; a very small amount can paralyse man or beast, and I'm told it's been adapted for use in heart surgery. We took turns shooting the slim 21-inch darts, which flew at an incredible speed and lodged deep in the thick trunk of our target tree. I was highly impressed by the silent efficiency of this famous weapon.

Christian knew some American missionaries and seemed to want us to meet somebody who spoke English. So, in the early afternoon, we drove to the office of the *Misión Nuevas Tribus*, the New Tribes Mission. We met a couple named Larry and Susan Fyock who told us they knew a Manitoba man, Elmer Barkman, who works at their mission site in Tama Tama, which will be our last stop on the Orinoco before entering the Casiquiare Canal. The Fyocks invited us to their church service this morning, and for the first time in my life I felt I wanted to go to church. Our past 20 months have humbled me and, in many ways, deepened my sense of gratitude.

About 8 o'clock, we went to a rousing birthday party for Christian's 15-year-old girlfriend. What a night! A hundred or more people; endless amounts of good food and drink; music; camaraderie – everything under a clear tropical sky, with a faint breeze sighing through the mango leaves. Throughout the evening, we were swamped with questions about our trip, which we hope won't end in this hospitable town.

We didn't get to bed until 4 a.m., but were nonetheless up by 8 for our 9:30 church service this morning. When Christian hadn't shown up by 9 to pick us up, we set out on our own, going from one side of the street to the other as we walked, trying to stay in the shade of the city's many mango trees and out of the equatorial sun. We missed part of the service, but arrived in time to join in a hymn and enjoy the simple sermon.

The Fyocks invited us to their home for a noon meal and laid on an exceptional spread in North American style: roast beef, mashed potatoes, cooked vegetables, and so on. Susan is a nurse and gave us a four-month supply of malaria pills and strongly suggested that we start taking them as soon as we leave here. The Fyocks are flying to Tama Tama in a few weeks in the mission plane and may well be there when we are – if we are.

MONDAY, FEBRUARY 8: *Puerto Ayacucho, Venezuela*
Big day at last, and we were up early and off to the governor's office. But after a long wait there, we still didn't have our travel permission. We decided to try the immigration office, but our luck there was no better. The only thing to do, apparently, was to go back downriver and cross over to the Venezuelan consulate at Puerto Carreño, Colombia. So, just past noon, Christian and his girlfriend and Dana and I climbed into Christian's jeep and headed north.

After a tedious 55-mile drive over poor roads, we checked in with the Guardia at Puerto Burro on the Venezuelan side. We were told we'd have to rent a motorboat and driver to cross the river, and within an hour we'd left Christian and his girlfriend and were careering across the river, pushed by a 40-h.p. motor.

At the guardhouse at Puerto Carreño, a couple of Colombian soldiers played cool with us until we hauled out our old letter from the Maritime Police in Santa Marta. This softened them up, and we were on our own in Colombia. But by the time we found the Venezuelan consulate on the main street, it was 4 p.m., and to our consternation the place was closed. As we stood there racking our brains over what to do, a smart-looking man in a light blue suit appeared on the street behind us. "May I help you?" he said politely in Spanish, and we immediately poured out our tale.

"Well, I'm the consul," he smiled. "Give me your passports."

We handed them over with shocked gratitude, and he disappeared behind the building. But when he didn't reappear after 20 minutes, we began to get nervous – was he really the consul or just some con man who'd come along at an opportune moment? There is apparently a lucrative international trade in stolen passports. A few worried minutes passed, then he appeared, not with the 30-day visas we'd requested, but with 45-day visas, much better. The extra 15 days should get us all the way to Brazil.

In no time, we were back across the river to rejoin our jeep, and within a couple of hours were sitting under a mango tree eating barbecued chicken in a quiet street restaurant in Puerto Ayacucho. Mission accomplished.

FEBRUARY 12: *Puerto Ayacucho, Venezuela*

By 11 the next morning we had our travel letter from the governor and spent the remainder of the day kibitzing with friends and stuffing ourselves with food.

We'd decided to paddle as far upriver as we could and to portage when we had to. So the day before yesterday, at 7 a.m., we loaded the canoe and headed out, happy to be moving again. But within a few miles the waters had become difficult and were beginning to give us serious doubts. By 10 o'clock, we'd done more towing and poling than paddling, and by noon we'd been obliged to conduct four brief but strenuous portages.

At the 10-mile mark, well into the Atures Rapids, we met our Waterloo – a frantically turbulent stretch of water, which seemed to extend upwards for miles among the huge boulders.

We had a conference and decided that Dana should scout ahead. Off he went, alternately picking his way through the fast-flowing shallows and climbing over the 20-foot boulders like a mountain goat. For three long hours, I waited for him to return; I was sure he'd fallen and been carried off by the whirling current. Then I saw him, slumping toward me from a half mile away. I was overjoyed. When he got to me, he was dripping with sweat. His face was pale with fatigue, and his eyes were badly bloodshot. He'd walked miles and had seen nothing but more rocks and turbulence. We had no choice but to return to Puerto Ayacucho.

We picked our way painstakingly back downstream, repeating in reverse the four portages we'd made earlier, and shooting some remarkable stretches of white water. We spent the night on a sandy beach 4 miles south of Ayacucho, and by 9 yesterday morning were back at the Port Captain's office.

All day we scoured the city for a trailer, without luck. Several people owned trailers – not particularly suitable ones – but when they heard what we wanted to do with them, they turned us down, obviously assuming we were crazy. One man said outright, "You'll never be able to walk that far." If we'd intended to tow the trailer with a vehicle, he'd have lent it to us.

At about 7 p.m., I saw a couple of familiar faces go by on the street; they were people I'd seen at the mission office. It hit me like a bullet – the mission would have a trailer, or would know about one. And they trusted us. Dana went immediately to the home of the mission pilot, and returned shortly wearing a weary smile. The mission owned a trailer. Within 15 minutes, we had been granted the use of what was by far the best boat trailer we'd seen all day. It was light and well balanced and, above all, available. Christian agreed to drive to Samariapo in a few days to pick it up and return it to its owners.

We had a wonderful night's sleep, and early this morning I cut a river tree and fashioned a 7-foot towing bar, complete with a rope shoulder harness padded with a couple of borrowed pillows. The Port Captain was in a good mood when he got to work and volunteered to pick up the trailer with his jeep and pull it to the waterfront.

By 10 o'clock we had the trailer loaded, and by noon had begun to psych ourselves up for our long haul tomorrow. We've decided we'll do it over three days, so as not to kill ourselves with the burden. The 45 miles will be more than twice as far as our towing trek back at the Golfete de Coro.

I might mention that, since returning from the rapids yesterday morning, we've suffered a fair bit of ridicule from the locals, who regard it as a big joke that their rapids have defeated us. They assume the road will defeat us, too. One young guy said to me with a guffaw, "We'll see you in a few days." Even Christian and his buddies have had some laughs at our expense. Nevertheless, I'm optimistic. Puerto Ayacucho has been good to us, but it's not going to see us again.

Up the Orinoco

FEBRUARY 15: *near Isla Ratón, Venezuela*

Tonight, as I write, we're triumphantly back on the river. The past three days have been hell.

We got out of Ayacucho by 4 a.m. the day before yesterday, pulling our 1,200-pound cargo over a gently rolling asphalt road. But the little rises and valleys that had seemed so insignificant when we drove over the road with Christian quickly got the better of us. By daybreak, it was almost as if we were hauling through the mountains. As the sun rose our T-shirts soaked through, then our shorts, and, by 8:30, our shoes. I was sweating so hard that my feet left wet tracks on the baking asphalt.

About 9 o'clock, the soles of my running shoes began working themselves loose from the uppers, so that I had to stop and wrap them with nylon string to hold them to my feet. We trudged on through the dry countryside: massive rocks, half-dry creek beds, occasional patches of trees. In several places, we saw herds of water buffalo. These mean-looking creatures, which seemed as curious about us as we were about them, were imported from Asia decades ago and are said to be ideally suited to

257

the Venezuelan climate. One big bull backed away from the road as we approached, then planted his legs, daring us to try to scare him off.

By 1 p.m. we'd come about 18 miles, and had reached a little food stand by the roadside. I yelled out in Spanish, "Do you sell soft drinks?" and the answer came back "*Sí!*" – ample reason to call it quits for the day.

Only our stopping made us realize how weary we were – I limped away from the trailer like an aged cripple and practically inhaled a couple of cans of pop (by two o'clock, I'd consumed six more cans). The place was owned by a family of Colombians who had a little house behind and a pretty fair agricultural spread. They warmed to us quickly, fed us a fine lunch, and invited us to stay the night. During the afternoon, both Dana and I had long siestas, and later in the afternoon were again well fed by our hosts.

Yesterday morning I was painfully stiff, and for the first few miles in the darkness, at 4 a.m., I hobbled along with a severe limp. Dana was better off. He doesn't have my strength, but his younger body renews itself much faster than mine. I'll forgo reporting any more of the agonies inflicted on our bodies by the trek, except to say that every step was a battle. At times, it was all we could do to gain the next 50 yards, let alone the next 10 miles. We'd pick a tree or a rock or a culvert 50 or 60 yards up the road, and that would be our goal. Only our insane sense of purpose drove us up the hills.

Through the morning, we passed numerous Indian communities, none of them named on our maps. Most of the dwellings are apparently government-built and reminded me of many of the buildings on our Canadian reserves. At one community, a hundred or more Indians swarmed to the roadside to watch us pass.

In mid-morning, a man stopped his truck and offered ice cubes, which we accepted gratefully, though they really didn't do us much good. We chatted with him, and he told us that the river at Samariapo was exceptionally low and full of rocks. He said we wouldn't be able to navigate it and should carry on to Venado, another river community four miles further upstream. "I'm sorry," he said when he saw the dejection on our faces. He seemed knowledgeable, however, and we reluctantly accepted his advice. Venado or bust.

After pulling for 17 miles, we spent the night in the roadside home of a rather strange pair whom we knew only as Caesar and Anna. Caesar was about 60, Anna perhaps 30, and their chief occupation seemed to be lying around in a kind of perpetual siesta. During the afternoon, Caesar killed a good-sized bottle of La Palmita liquor, mixed with lemon juice from his own trees. He'd lie in his hammock, drinking and smoking, talking to himself, snoring a little, then get up for a few minutes, squat Indian-style on his heels, and launch a long-winded monologue aimed at no one in particular. He'd go back to his hammock, then get up again and launch another monologue. Anna, too, seemed a little unglued, but she and Caesar were kind to us, and we were certainly happy to accept their oddities along with their hospitality.

Three hours of brute trudging this morning brought us to the road into Samariapo, just four miles from our destination. The proximity of our goal perked us up, and it didn't seem long before we were standing on the river bank at Venado, overlooking the sweet Orinoco.

We presented our documents at the local Guardia base and, in return, were given a yellow pass, which we were told we'd have to have stamped at every Guardia base between here and the Brazil border. (Late this evening, we were visited by a soldier who strongly emphasized the importance of this pass – if we missed having it stamped at one base, we could be sent back.)

We were a little worried because we'd told Christian we'd leave the trailer at Samariapo. We felt he'd be able to figure out what had happened and would come the four extra miles upriver, but we couldn't be sure. The Guardia agreed to look after the trailer in the meantime and also took the address of the mission.

At the Venado docks there were two mighty dugouts, each a floating grocery store. At one, we bought 15 platanos, at the other four giant discs of cassava bread. Each disc was about a quarter-inch thick and a yard or more in diameter. Cassava bread will keep for months if dry, so we broke the loaves into chunks and stored them in plastic bags, then in boxes.

By 10:30 we were back on the river, paddling like gleeful kids. Although our legs were rubber, our arms and shoulders were begging for a workout. The Orinoco isn't nearly as wide down here as it was north of the rapids, but its thick tropical shores are far more romantic than the clay and sand we've seen so far. The rocks are still with us, but they're easy enough to sneak around in the relatively slow current.

We paddled 15 miles, one of the pleasantest stretches of water we've paddled in weeks, and made camp on a convenient sand bar extending out from Isla Ratón. We saw very little wildlife on the water but are making up for it now, fending off hordes of insects, which have been with us like a plague since Puerto Ayacucho. Most of them are what the locals call *plaga* or mosquitoes, but they're more like what we know as sandflies or no-see-ums. What we call mosquitoes in North America are called *zancudos* down here, and we haven't seen any of them south of the rapids. *Plaga* can give a sharp little bite, and the sting lasts for ten minutes or more before turning to a powerful itch. I get them all over my legs, and, before I know it, my ankles are as big as fenceposts – and as colourful as a sunset. Our real fear of the bugs is that they might be carrying malaria. We've started taking our pills, which for the first couple of days made us a little groggy.

We were told back at Ayacucho that the best defence against bites is to cover ourselves with a mixture of insect repellent and baby oil, which we've been doing. The combination seems not only to poison the bugs but to drown them, so that an hour or so after we apply the stuff our bodies are heavily polka-dotted with bug corpses. We tried the mixture during our trek, but our sweat washed it off as fast as we could slather it on. Actually, I think my sweat itself repels the bugs, or at least drowns them. Sometimes it nearly drowns me. Fortunately, the bugs usually disappear after dark, leaving us in relative comfort for sleeping.

FEBUARY 19: *at San Fernando de Atabapo, Venezuela*
The 16th was a red letter day for us. Exactly a year earlier, Dana and Gabby and I paddled away from La Pesca. Six months before that, on the Red River, Dana took his last medication for asthma. The day also marked the first time we'd erected our mosquito-netting bug house since leaving the u.s. As we prepared our camp, we were plagued by *plaga*, which we fended off for nearly an hour before taking the big step. Hundreds of the little predators clung to the netting as we sat inside, but as usual they disappeared at sunset, and we took the thing down for a peaceful night in the open.

Today's paddle was brief, 10 miles to San Fernando de Atabapo where the Orinoco meets the Atabapo River coming from the south, and the Guaviare River from the west in Colombia. From here, the Orinoco swings due east, so that tomorrow we'll have Venezuelan soil on both shores again.

We were obliged to check in at San Fernando to have our yellow document stamped, but the town is located a couple of miles up the Atabapo River, which we had a little trouble locating amid islands and the generally mixed currents of the confluent waters. Some Indians in a couple of dugouts had to show us the way. What surprised us when we got onto the Atabapo was its tea-coloured water, which is apparently the effect of run-off from the jungle soil. The heavy concentration of tannin is said to prevent insect breeding, so that such rivers are generally free of *plaga* and mosquitoes.

The Guardia did their customary canoe search (we wouldn't *stand* for such constant harassment at home) and said we could use their compound up the bank as a headquarters. The canoe will stay grounded and tarped on a mid-river sand bar. Venezuelans have a great respect for property – or at least a respect for the ever-present Guardia – and we've learned that we can leave our canoe pretty well anywhere without having it touched.

We walked through town with a couple of soldiers and had a refreshing swim in the cold, black waters of the Atabapo, whose beaches are pure white. The local Indians and Latins have been gawking at us as if they'd never seen such creatures; perhaps they haven't; our blue eyes and long bleached hair are a particular attraction. As Dana practised his guitar in the compound, 25 or more kids lined up along the fence beside him, gripping the wire mesh, peering in, bug-eyed and silent.

The soldiers gave us a fruit we haven't seen before; it grows on palms and is about the size, colour, and taste of a purple grape, but with a larger single pit. I later found a guayaba tree and snared a couple of the yellow fruit, which we ate voraciously until Dana noticed that the seedy centres were crawling with tiny white worms, hundreds of which are now inside us.

Something has been on my mind tonight, and I haven't been able to shake it. My research mentioned several cases in which river travellers have been refused entry into Brazil on the Río Negro at Cucuí. They've apparently been turned back because their craft weren't considered safe or seaworthy, or for any number of other reasons. What can we do but hope for the best?

FEBRUARY 22: *near Cerro Yapacana, on the upper Orinoco, Venezuela*
Every mile we paddle takes us further into remote jungle country. We see very few people now, and the animal life is a constant reminder of how far we've come and where we are. Yesterday, for example, we saw our first big group of monkeys. They were a small, light-brown species and did a quick disappearing act as we passed beneath them. A little later, as I was towing the canoe through some shallows, I was startled to see the outline of a stingray just beneath the sand where I was about to plop my foot down. I must remember to shuffle.

On the same stretch of river, we had an experience that wouldn't have been out of place in an eerie jungle movie. Paddling close to the south bank in the silence of the afternoon, we heard a strange rustling high in the trees, as if a number of small animals were suddenly on the move in the foliage. The noise increased to a thrashing sound, then quickly to a thunderous roar, as an enormous tree fell out of the jungle, dragging hundreds of vines with it and several smaller trees. The whole collection crashed on shore just 20 or 30 yards from us.

Today's thrills were better yet. We made camp during the mid-afternoon on a pleasant sand bar which, within an hour, had been invaded by thousands of bees, which are still with us. We can only hope they aren't the famous South American killer bees. As I write, I have 20 or more bees crawling all over me, including one on my pen. Dana, too, is covered with bees as he sits gently playing his guitar. Shortly after they appeared, we noticed them swarming over the salty seat pads in the canoe and realized that it was probably salt they were after more than us. In ultra-slow motion, we removed our salty T-shirts and pants, threw them in a heap, and walked into the water up to our necks. Sure enough, as we watched from the river, the bees congregated by the hundreds on our clothes. Unfortunately, by this time, I'd already picked up three nasty stings; the *plaga* had also been bad, and I'd made the mistake of swatting at them, riling the bees. Dana pulled the stingers out for me – one from my hind end.

After an hour in the water, we gingerly emerged in the nude, hoping that our now saltless bodies would no longer be an attraction. The bees weren't nearly as interested as they'd been, though there are still a fair number on us, so that all we can do is sit quietly as they explore our naked hides. The gentle motion of writing or guitar playing doesn't seem to bother them. Actually, we have two species with us, one about the size of a honeybee, the other like a bumblebee; there are far more of the honey type. Dana says that when the sun goes down they'll take off, because they can't find their way in the dark. Right now the temperature is dropping, and we can't even get to our clothes, as the bees are still swarming over them.

Just north of the Santa Bárbara rapids today (which had me out of the canoe and towing), we saw our first *toninas* in some time, a couple of little ones, which were much more cautious than the bigger ones further north. We miss the groups, and assume that this is the area in which the young ones grow up and prepare for their careers in the larger hunting grounds.

Looking about 20 miles to our southeast from here, we can see Cerro Yapacana, a towering single mountain, clearly marked on our maps. It's by far the highest peak we've seen on the Orinoco, and we should pass it sometime tomorrow or the next day; it promises to be in sight for some time.

Our goal now is Tama Tama where the Orinoco meets the Casiquiare Canal, about 130 miles of fairly even uphill ride from here. From that point on, our route will be all downcurrent. We'll take two or three days to rest at Tama Tama, where we hope to meet our mission friends again.

It is now dark, and I'm relieved to report that our bees have finally left us in peace, after four hours of siege.

FEBRUARY 24: *on the upper Orinoco, near the Puruname Canal, Venezuela*
Again, the bees have claimed our salty clothes, and I'm standing here on a sand bar, writing my notes in the nude. Today, we were a little smarter with our wee adversaries and immediately gave them everything we own – clothes, canoe, equipment, whatever they wanted. They've thanked us by not stinging us. For an hour or so, we sat in the river cooling off. This wasn't entirely relaxing, however, as we'd just chased a good-sized crocodile from our campsite and were pretty sure he was lurking in the water nearby. His footprints are all over the beach.

Apart from our bees and the croc, we've had a safe, exhilarating day. The bird and animal life has been spectacular: 4- and 5-foot storks, both black and white; big red and yellow macaws; hundreds of kingfishers; parrots; and more *coro-coro* birds. At several points, the whole river and rain forest shook with the bellowing of the howler monkeys; you'd swear there were lions or gorillas out there. The howlers stay pretty much invisible, but we did catch a glimpse of 30 or so smaller brown monkeys with black-tipped tails. They saw us coming and waited for a peek before leaping out of sight.

The jungle here is a massed tangle of large-leafed plants and vines – and towering trees. What we see of the vegetation often strikes me as a theatre curtain, behind which a remarkable drama is constantly being played out, and of which we get the merest glimpses. I guess the same might be said of the surface of the water. I'm particularly impressed by the sucker or parasite plants which live high in the trees, trailing 60- and 70-foot water lines into the river.

All day, again, we could see the formidable Cerro Yapacana which sits about 10 miles north of the river. It will undoubtedly dominate our view for another day yet.

We have now come 10,000 miles.

Note: Our big crocodile stayed around all night, grunting and snorting on the surface of the water, 20 or 30 feet out. A couple of times I picked up a bit of pink light reflected from his eyes. We slept fitfully, with our machetes close at hand.

Struggling to the Mission

FEBRUARY 28: *Misión Nuevas Tribus, Tama Tama, Venezuela*
Tonight, thank God, we are safe in Tama Tama. I have made only the briefest notes over the past few days, and with very good reason: The evening after I last wrote, at Kirare, just past suppertime, my head started aching, I grew dizzy, and my muscles and stomach began to cramp. I began shivering. I lay down on the tarp in the sun and, even in the heat, had to ask Dana to cover me. To add to my miseries, a few bees got under the tarp and into my clothing, and I got a severe sting on the leg as I tried to roll onto my side.

Two hours later, Dana, too, began to complain of shivering and cramps, and then he was up and vomiting. As he staggered back to his bed on top of the canoe he moaned something about our having malaria.

"We haven't got malaria," I told him. "Don't get carried away." But there was nothing I could do to prevent him taking a couple of extra malaria pills, even though they're strictly a preventive measure and do no good after the fact. I have to admit that we hadn't been taking them as regularly as we should have; they tend to give us headaches and to

264

weaken us. I laid off them, but, for the first time in many years, took aspirins to try to allay the terrible pain in my temples and skull.

Just after dark, it began to rain, but we were too weak to set up any sort of shelter, and simply lay there shivering and sweating, as our tarp soaked through.

The next eight or nine hours were an agonizing blur of half-sleep and fear. Our alarm went off as usual at 5:30, but Dana couldn't move. I was in no shape to get up either, but was too scared to lie there, convinced that, if we didn't get to Tama Tama for help, we'd die.

The pain and tremors and weakness were now more severe than anything I'd ever experienced. Although we couldn't be sure, we now suspected we'd picked up a case of water or food poisoning – maybe from a can of Venezuelan sausages we'd eaten at supper the night before, maybe from the river water, which we've been drinking liberally for weeks. The river bottom around our sand bar was slimy with what was probably crocodile waste.

I was determined to move, knowing that, if we didn't, our condition might worsen, so that we wouldn't be *able* to move. I knew the story of Captain Scott and his men, all of whom starved and froze to death while returning from the South Pole in 1912. They became stormbound just 10 miles from a known food depot, and decided to wait until the storm improved before carrying on to their much-needed nourishment. The storm got worse, and they never moved.

We were 50 miles from Tama Tama – 50 upstream miles.

I bullied and prodded Dana into getting up, and, soon after 6 a.m. – unable to eat, barely able to stay upright – we launched the canoe and angled into the current. It was the beginning of two days of torture, particularly for Dana, who, by this time, was far worse off than I was. I had actually begun to feel marginally better as I got up and moving.

All day, Dana lifted his paddle as if it were lead, constantly begging me to stop. All I could do was keep at him to do his best, to keep pulling, even though his weak stroke was of very little use; several times, he slumped in the bow, and I was afraid he might fall overboard. But I knew if I gave him any sympathy, he'd probably quit altogether and I'd have to paddle myself, a nearly impossible task into the stiff current. As it was, we were gaining less than 2 m.p.h. "We can't quit," I kept hectoring. "We have to keep paddling; we've gotta keep going – just a few more miles." Meanwhile, the sun burned down at equatorial strength. We were precisely 3 degrees north of the equator.

By about 2:30, we were all but unconscious. A flat rock island came into view in the middle of the river, and we dragged the canoe onto it, stretched out the tarp, and fell asleep. We had come 17 miles.

At suppertime, Dana was able to eat half a can of green peas, his first nourishment in 24 hours. I didn't feel like eating, but forced down a fair quantity of food, knowing that, if I could keep it down, I'd be better off for it.

The night air soothed us, but the morning brought no noticeable improvement in our condition. If anything, Dana was weaker, and I had lost my appetite altogether. When we had each forced down a single platano, we headed off on a grim re-enactment of the previous day's travels. Our goal was to get past the mouth of the Río Cunucunuma, maybe 20 miles away, which would put us about 10 miles from Tama Tama. Again I was forced to harass Dana almost constantly to keep him functioning. We were eventually forced into our old last-ditch game, choosing a branch or rock upstream, fighting our way to it, choosing another branch or rock, and so on. By late morning, Dana's complexion was a pale but distinct green.

We passed the Río Cunucunuma during the mid-afternoon, and just when everything was at its lowest ebb a strange event lifted us briefly from our miseries. Suddenly, without speaking, Dana pointed to shore, leaving his arm extended for several seconds. "Look," he said softly. At first I saw nothing but a thick fallen tree angling from the river bank down into the water. But as we inched forward, a massive snake came into view, lying draped and twisted on the tree trunk, apparently sunning itself. I took it for a boa constrictor and frantically dug into our #4 equipment box, searching for my camera. In my excitement, all my cramps and weakness vanished.

We paddled until our bow was within a dozen feet of it, and I snapped a picture, keeping Dana in the frame for size comparison. "Jump out on the log," I said. "I'll take your picture with it!" But he refused to budge.

We then paddled right up to the fallen tree and, when the snake showed no interest in us, I decided to get out onto the trunk for a better photo. This upset Dana, and he began scolding me for taking stupid risks. But I knew that a boa, being primarily a land snake, would shy away from water and that I'd be pretty safe with the water behind me.

As I stepped slowly up the log, Dana pulled the canoe ahead ten or twelve feet. "What are you doing?" I demanded.

"I don't want to be anywhere near that thing," he said.

Despite my arguing, he wouldn't come back. I was determined to take another picture, a close-up, and continued up the log, amazed by the snake's great size. It was as big around as a man's waist and easily 20 feet long. I'd estimate its weight at over 300 pounds. It had several long gashes on its skin, as if it had been fighting, and, as I got closer, I could see a heavy swelling in its midsection – undoubtedly the animal with which it had done battle. Perhaps the most incredible thing was the relatively small size of the snake's head – about as big as two closed fists. It seemed impossible to think that it had swallowed an animal that must have been as big as a medium-sized dog. Flies swarmed over the congealed blood of its cuts. "I think it's dead!" I called to Dana, and took a quick photo of it.

"No," he called back, "I can see it breathing!"

Part of the snake's body was draped over a small branch that angled toward me, which I now grabbed and jiggled, to no effect. "It's dead!" I called. But when I shook the branch harder, the massive creature slowly raised its head and swung it my direction, throwing me into an adrenaline panic. For a few seconds, I stared at it from 4 feet away, and it stared back, occasionally flicking its forked tongue. I took another step toward it, feeling that I could bluff it back into the jungle. Again, I grabbed the branch, this time giving it a good tug. But instead of retreating, the snake started ever so slowly down the log toward me. It was then – too late – that I realized it was not a boa at all but a deadly anaconda; only an anaconda would move toward water with such confidence.

Dana was now hanging onto a branch some 20 feet upstream and in no position to rescue me. The only thing I could think of doing was to stand up on the log – I'd been crouching – and to make myself seem as big as possible by throwing my arms in the air. I did this and began roaring like a grizzly bear (in spite of my knowledge that snakes are deaf). The snake advanced about 4 feet. Then, when I repeated my grizzly act, it stopped 2 feet in front of me and plunged into the water below. Its splash reached Dana 20 feet away. My camera and I were soaked, but I had my pictures. My legs shook, as I climbed into the canoe, feigning calmness.

For a couple of hours during the late afternoon we searched for a camping spot, but could find nothing on the steep 8-foot river banks. By 6 o'clock, with darkness coming, we had no choice but to tie up alongshore, beneath overhanging vines, and prepare for a night in the canoe. Dana opened a can of tuna, saw some bubbles in it, and refused to eat it. "It's poison," he said, "just like the sausages." I tasted a bit which seemed fine; I told him he was paranoid. But when he persisted in his complaints, I, too, got suspicious and reluctantly threw the can in the river.

Dana ate half a cup of raisins. I wasn't hungry, but forced myself to eat. Then we moved some equipment from my end of the canoe to Dana's, so that I had a little sleeping cocoon beneath the gunwales. Dana stretched out on top of the equipment boxes, and we prepared for a painful night.

This morning Dana looked awful – his face was flushed, his head ached, he couldn't bend his back. He was crankier than he's been for months. When we were about to leave, he refused to untie his end of the canoe, showering me with abuse as we sat there. When I went to untie it myself, he threatened me with his paddle.

For the first mile or so, he refused to take a stroke, complaining that I'd exhausted him yesterday with 12 hours on the water. And I couldn't refute it; I *have* worn him out; he *is* exhausted; he *is* too sick to paddle. But how else could we have made it to where we are?

He eventually picked up his paddle. For four hours we crawled up-current, and about 10 a.m. we saw what should have made us throw our arms in the air and shout for joy – or weep for it. But we were too tired for any display of emotion. On the far shore, amid the trees, the bank gradually fell away into a broad channel that signified the beginning of the Casiquiare Canal. Our battles with the current were over.

The Misión Nuevas Tribus is located on the Orinoco a couple of miles beyond the opening to the canal, and we had reached it within an hour. We staggered up the banks and onto the park-like grounds, among well-built houses and meeting halls. What puzzled us was that there didn't seem to be any people around. Then we saw two young Indian kids, who disappeared behind a building when they saw us. We walked to the building and peeked through the screens, surprised to see several dozen Indian kids sitting around with a few adults. At this point Dana felt too weak to walk and returned to the canoe. A hundred yards away, in the trees, was a large hall, from which I could now hear singing. As I walked toward the hall, it dawned on me that it was Sunday morning; the mission was at church. I sat down in the shade waiting for the service to end, and was soon spotted from inside by Larry Fyock who had befriended us in Puerto Ayacucho. He rushed out to welcome me to Tama Tama.

As I write this evening, I can already feel the life and health returning to my body. Dana, too, is feeling better and *looks* better, as I'm sure I do, after a shave, shower, and shampoo. We're staying in the home of Fran and Laura Cochran, who divide their time between here and the mission office in Puerto Ayacucho, where we first met them. We're still pretty weak, but I don't think we're going to need any special medicines – just lots of shade and rest and plenty of the same healthy food we've had since arriving. What a relief it's been just to be out of the sun. We had dinner this evening with Elmer and Tina Barkman and their family. Elmer is a Canadian from Blumenort, Manitoba, about 40 miles from Winnipeg. So we are not only among friends but among neighbours.

MARCH 3: *Misión Nuevas Tribus, on the Orinoco River*
For the past three days, these good people have done everything in their
power to bring us back to health. They have cared for us and fed us (at
least five different families) and shown us an abundance of good will.
And we're more than grateful. The missionaries take a lot of heat from
the skeptics and leftists, who decry their cultural and religious influence
on the Indians. Perhaps I'm naive, but I'm sure I could name a hundred
20th-century influences that must have an infinitely worse effect on native
cultural survival.

My strength is pretty well back to normal, although my psyche is still
suffering from our long days of paddling. Last night, hour after hour, I
had a nightmarish dream of bucking impossible river currents. I woke up
several times, relieved to be safe in my little mission bed. Dana, too, is
better, and yesterday afternoon felt well enough to play a brisk game of
soccer with the locals and mission kids. He says he's ready to go tomorrow, and so am I.

This morning, young Matthew Cochran presented me with a perfect
departure gift, a Guaica bow and two seven-foot Guaica arrows, plus some
wooden arrow tips, two of which had been dipped in *curare*. He also gave
me a slim blowgun dart – wonderful souvenirs. A man named Gary Dawson
gave me two giant harpy eagle claws given to him by a local Indian.

We had a farewell dinner this evening at Elmer Barkman's, and as we
sat around the table, I felt a rush of affection for these people. Their
warm-hearted spirit has really affected us, and we know their prayers and
caring will help us on our way.

On to Brazil

MARCH 6: *on the Casiquiare Canal, Venezuela*
The Casiquiare Canal is not a canal at all since it is not man-made. It was discovered in 1744 by Jesuit missionaries, and is the only natural waterway in the world connecting two major river systems. As it leaves the Orinoco it is about 50 yards wide, but by the time it dumps its waters into the Río Negro it has expanded to nearly 500 yards. It is notorious for bugs, which probably explains why its 210-mile length is virtually unpopulated.

We entered the canal on the morning of the 4th, and for the past three days have been enthralled by its flora and fauna. Most of the trees and plants bear exotically coloured flowers that send an almost constant heady perfume out over the water. During our first two days of paddling we saw no human beings. But early this morning as we flashed along we saw four little Indian kids up to their necks in water, apparently escaping the bugs. There was no sign of a house or building.

At this dry time of year, the canal is well dotted with rocks and sand bars and has a current of 1 or 2 m.p.h., which keeps us moving at quite a

clip. Today we came an astonishing 60 miles, our longest one-day advance
of the entire trip. We've come about 120 miles since leaving Tama Tama.
The heat has been torrid, though we've had to keep heavily clothed to
avoid the swarms of hungry insects.

We've seen several new forms of wildlife on the canal, including a little
coral snake, which, during our first day out, crawled out of the water
onto the flat rock of our campsite. It was ringed with bright bands of red,
yellow and black and had a distinctive black nose, which, according to
the snake literature I'm carrying, identified it as deadly. When it headed
for our sleeping area I had to kill the little beauty with a stick not wanting to
take a chance on its being around as we slept. The same day we saw our
first family of capybaras, five of them, which took to the water as we
passed and smartly eluded us. For a second, one big head appeared above
the surface, then it was gone. The capybara is the biggest of the rodents
and quite common in these parts. It's about 4 feet long and is apparently
hunted for both its meat and its hide. It's an extraordinarily good swimmer and diver, as we saw. Its feet are webbed.

The bird life has been abundant, with dozens of parrots and parakeets
and what we'd been calling "turkeybirds" until Matthew Cochran at Tama
Tama gave us their real name, hoatzin. They're like a prehistoric cross
between a turkey and a peacock, and have claws on the mid-joints of
their wings when they're young. We stir them up regularly on the canal
banks, and they go squawking and flapping through the shore foliage.
We also see plenty of snake birds, which swim with only their heads and
necks above the water surface. They resemble snakes swimming upright
on their tails.

MARCH 7: *on the Casiquiare Canal*
One thing that has surprised us about the Casiquiare is the easy availability
of good campsites on the flat rocks and sands (which are almost certainly
flooded during the rainy season). I'd read in at least a couple of books
that we'd find no place to stop. But here we are again tonight, comfortably situated – except for the bugs, of course, which, as usual, are driving
us nuts at this time of day. For a while after supper, we were forced into
the water to avoid them.

This morning, we saw our first tapir, a big long-nosed brute of maybe
300 pounds. We surprised it in the shallows, and it crashed up onto shore
like a wounded bull and disappeared into the foliage. Any occurrence of
this sort always comes as a shock to us, as the canal is generally so quiet.
We often go for miles hearing nothing but the sounds of our own pad-

dles. Then something will alert the birds or animals, and for a minute or so the jungle will rattle with life. This morning, for instance, I let out a terrific sneeze, which touched off a long barrage of roars from the howler monkeys.

Our food supply is holding out well, though we're doing nothing to supplement it. We've been eating a lot of manioca, which bears a close resemblance to grape-nut cereal. The Cochrans gave us a kilo of it. We mix it with river water, swelling it to three or four times its dry volume, and add sugar and bananas or platanos.It's an important part of the local diet and a good travel food, as it will keep for months.

MARCH 8: *Porvenir, on the Casiquiare Canal*
This morning at about 11 o'clock, after 175 miles on the canal, we came to the first house we've seen since leaving Tama Tama. The Indian inhabitants could barely believe we'd paddled into their lives. When we arrived, the woman of the house, Juarita Gonzales, was up to her knees in the canal, skinning and cleaning a paca – an animal that looks like an overgrown guinea pig – for butchering. Even though our advance for the day had been only 20 miles, we decided to call it quits and were welcomed ashore by Juarita and her husband Gabriel and their three young children.

What an existence these people have way out here on their own! Their little house is made of bamboo and palm branches and is so porous that birds fly right through it. One of the interior walls is papered with pages from a Venezuelan magazine. Gabriel told us they call the place *Porvenir* – Future. We soon realized that our friends were desperately poor and were getting by on what little they could hunt or harvest from their bug-infested surroundings. Yet they were determined to share their paca with us, and we gratefully accepted. We supplied cooking oil and a pound or so of corn flour for *arepas*, as well as sugar for coffee. Juarita did her best with the paca but didn't get it quite fully cooked, so that it was rubbery to chew. It tasted like chicken.

After dinner, Dana played with the kids for a while. They seem unhappy away out here in their remote world – there was almost nothing we could do to get a smile out of them. They're perpetually swatting bugs, and the scars from hundreds of bites over the years have left the skin on their legs covered with large grey blotches (each *plaga* bite leaves a little black dot). The kids' chief enjoyment seems to be their pets, eight skinny dogs, two pacas, and a three-toed sloth.

The sloth is the strangest animal I've ever seen. He's got longish grey hair and is extremely docile. His chief aim in life seems to be to rest and hang – from rafters, railings, branches, anywhere he can find a perch. The kids show him tremendous affection; they pick him up, and he wraps his long arms around them and hugs them like a teddy bear. I picked him up myself, and he did the same to me. I noticed that his eyes were always closed, and Gabriel told me the poor thing is blind. Apparently the ants came down out of the trees one night and attacked his eyes. How touched I was to think of these poor little kids away out here in the wilderness with a blind sloth for a pet.

We talked through the early evening, and Dana did some entertaining on the guitar. Then the two of us retired to a couple of open-air benches under a stand of fruit-laden cashew trees where we sacked out.

At midnight, I was jolted awake by fierce nips at my skin. I realized that I was covered with big black ants which were making their way down out of their daytime roosts in the trees for a night of foraging. They were all through my clothes and hair and bedding. What was amazing was that they all seemed to take their bites at once, then there'd be a lull and they'd bite again, seemingly at a signal. It's quite possible, of course, that this is the way they subdue a larger prey, by biting simultaneously. This was presumably the type of ant that blinded the poor sloth, and I did my best to clean them out, but finally they drove me from my spot.

I stumbled around in the dark, found a wobbly 8-foot-high structure, and crawled up on its flat roof of poles. Here I lay for another half hour, sweeping off ants. But by the time I had peace, I'd begun to feel uncomfortable on the hard poles. Then, in the quiet, I began hearing the ripe cashew fruits dropping from the trees, each making a plop as it hit the clay below. Every 20 seconds or so, a little alarm – and still the odd ant bite.

MARCH 9: *near Buena Vista, on the Casiquiare Canal*
This morning, as we were about to leave, Gabriel and Juarita presented us with the back leg of the paca they'd cooked yesterday. Then they gathered up their two best hunting dogs, a shotgun, and a longbow, jumped into their dugout, or *cayuca*, and followed us onto the water. Gabriel was determined to show us his hunting skills, and, when he reached the far bank, he let the dogs out on shore, where they scampered excitedly into the jungle. Their job was to find a paca and flush it out into the water where Gabriel would be waiting to shoot it with either his gun or his bow.

We lingered in the early-morning silence, staying close to shore as the dogs thrashed through the bush. Gabriel gave occasional whistle signals to let the dogs know where he was. But it wasn't his day, and after a fruitless half hour we decided to pull away, in spite of Gabriel's disappointment. He wanted so badly to demonstrate this important talent of his.

We said fond farewells and had paddled only a few strokes when Gabriel called us back with something important to tell us. He could barely bring himself to utter the words, but managed to tell us that he and his family were desperately short of food – could we spare a few cups of manioca to get them through the day? We gladly handed some over and again pulled away. About 300 yards downstream, however, we were alerted by a commotion behind us. Gabriel's dogs had chased a big paca into the water, and within seconds Gabriel had shot and wounded it and was preparing to put an arrow through it, which he did with ease.

We paddled back to find him radiant in his triumph. The paca weighed 20 pounds or more and would undoubtedly feed the family and dogs for the next couple of days. We congratulated him on the fine show and again pulled away, only to be called back yet again. They wanted us to have the paca. These poor, primitive people, who live on the edge of starvation, wanted us to have their best food. Naturally, we refused, explaining that the unbutchered meat would go bad in the heat.

This morning when Juarita gave me the cooked paca leg, I stuffed it in a pot and put it under cover, where I thought it would stay coolest. But late this afternoon, as I prepared supper, I found it crawling with maggots. I couldn't afford to waste the meat, so I quietly scraped it off, gave it a good wash in the canal, then cut it up and boiled it extensively with our rice and spaghetti. I didn't tell Dana, as I was sure he'd never eat it if he knew. I might as well have announced it with a bullhorn – he took three bites at most and exclaimed that he'd found a maggot. "Don't be silly," I told him, "it's only rice," and I was sure it was. But he insisted it was a maggot and proceeded to lambaste me for my insensitivity to his health. "You just don't care, do you?" he said disgustedly. But he ate the paca and seemed no worse for it.

The canal where we're camped is several hundred yards wide, and across from us, in a clearing, is what looks like the remains of a house. A few minutes ago, I heard a disturbance over there, got my binoculars, and saw a dozen or so wild pigs ravaging the shore, apparently fighting over food. They appear to be peccaries, which have a reputation for viciousness and have been known to attack man. I could see their tusks from here, and hope they don't decide to go swimming.

MARCH 11: *near Cucui Rock on the Río Negro*
Yesterday at Solano, about 10 miles from the end of the Casiquiare, we passed the canal's most significant landmark, a 400-foot-high rock forma-

tion whose shape resembled a monstrous rabbit's head. "Bunny Rock," we called it, later learning that its Indian name is Curimacare. Humboldt climbed it in 1800.

Three hours later we said goodbye to the canal and joined the mighty flow of the Río Negro. The first things that struck us about the river were the blackness of the water (which, given the name, shouldn't have surprised us) and the astonishing whiteness of the beaches and sand bars.

We swept past a number of pretty sand bars and islands near the junction and hadn't gone more than a few miles when we heard the roar of rapids ahead. We approached them gingerly, assessed them as navigable, and shot down them like a fragile, floating rocket.

Ten miles downstream we reached San Carlos, high on the banks of the east shore. We stopped to get our documents checked and our yellow paper stamped, and were surprised at the friendliness and efficiency of the Guardia. We decided to stop for the day and took some food and supplies up the bank to an unoccupied *charuata*, a shelter with a conical palm roof and no side walls. We weren't long installed when three young men came to visit, having heard via the jungle grapevine that we were on our way here. One of the men is a student at the University of Georgia and is in Venezuela studying the effects of jungle clearing and slash burning. Another is studying anthropology – and probably us.

One of the most pleasing things about our new river is the absence of bugs. As I've mentioned, the tannin that darkens these jungle rivers keeps insects from breeding. Not so good is that we're back in border country, so that the far bank is again Colombia and will be for the next couple of days until we reach Cucuí. From there on, both banks will be Brazil.

We left San Carlos at daybreak and paddled across glassy, black waters, sped on our way by a variety of small rapids. The river along here is about half a mile wide, and its jungle shores and islands are among the prettiest we've seen.

This afternoon, as we paddled within a few hundred yards of the Colombian bank, three young men in white T-shirts and military pants started yelling at us, apparently ordering us to shore. We immediately picked up our stroke, angling across to the safety of Santa Rosa, Venezuela, which we could see a couple of miles ahead. In no time, the young men had scrambled down the bank and were on our trail in a *cayuca* powered by a small outboard. Unlike other chases we've had, this one was tailored to our advantage; all we had to do was beat our pursuers to Santa Rosa, where they'd be unable to land.

We stroked for all we were worth, and reached the docks narrowly ahead of them. But they pulled right in behind, shouting angrily at us for not stopping. It turned out they were Venezuelan soldiers, who for some reason had been visiting Colombia. I did my best to cool them out, explaining that we wanted no part of Colombia and didn't have Colombian visas. "We much prefer Venezuela," I said in Spanish, which is no lie.

In fact, this will be our last night in Venezuela, and, from our camping spot, we can see miles downriver to the famous Cucuí Rock, which stands in Venezuela, close to where Venezuela, Brazil, and Colombia come together. The rock stands 700 feet high and has three distinct peaks, much touted symbols of the three countries. It has been mentioned by numerous explorers over the centuries, and is visible for dozens of miles around. It's another landmark which, as I look at it tonight, gives me a stirring sense of connection with the great river travellers of history.

MARCH 12: *on the Rio Negro, south of Cucuí, Brazil*
This morning at about 11 o'clock we passed quietly but excitedly between two white markers, one on either side of the river, and entered the thirteenth and last country of our trip. We were so excited to be entering Brazil that we pulled ashore and took each other's pictures at the boundary marker.

But as we got back into the canoe to paddle the few miles to Cucuí, where we'd have to clear Customs and Immigration, an old fear began to nag me. What if we couldn't get through? I'd read so many times of how tough it was for foreign craft to get clearance to travel the Brazilian rivers, unless they met the Brazilian authorities' ideas of safety standards. Although Dana and I feel perfectly "safe" in *Orellana*, our standards are by no means the sort likely to impress the permit granters.

If we had an ace, it was a letter written for us in Port of Spain by the Brazilian ambassador to Trinidad:

> To the Brazilian authorities, Cucuí, Brazil – Mr. Donald Starkell and Mr. Dana Starkell, Canadian citizens, are doing a sportive and recreative trip. They are to enter Brazilian Territory in Cucuí, in the Federal Territory of Roraima. I would ask that due and necessary assistance be given them.

We covered the two miles to Cucuí in a matter of minutes and were escorted by three soldiers up the steep bank to a military office. Inside, we were surrounded by four officials, who quickly confirmed our worst fears. We would not be allowed to enter Brazil by canoe. In fact, we wouldn't be able to enter at all without proper papers, which we could only get at the Brazilian consulate in Caracas.

We'd warned ourselves many times that this could happen, but we were nonetheless stunned when it did. To make matters worse, we couldn't even argue our case properly – Brazilians speak Portuguese, not Spanish. The languages have plenty of overlap, but these guys were in no mood to decipher what we were trying to say. I pulled out our letter and handed it to the officer in charge. He took a look at it and handed it back, thoroughly unimpressed.

For an hour, we did what we could to communicate with these guys – I thought maybe we could wear them down.

Our only chance seemed to be to try to contact the Canadian embassy in Brasília, the capital. We told the officials we wanted to do this. "Have you got a phone or radio?" I asked.

"No," said the official in charge, whose impatience with us had been mounting.

At this point, crafty Dana drew out our map of the area, opened it on the desk and pointed slowly to Cucuí. Beside the name of the town were two radio call numbers, 5610 PVG and 1698 PVG, as well as a Morse-code signal. The official who'd said "No" quickly picked up our map and stared at it in embarrassment; he'd been caught out in his lie. But still he would not acknowledge the presence of any radio on the base.

He now told us we had two hours to leave Brazil, and I told him we wouldn't leave until we'd contacted our embassy. No way were we going to paddle hundreds of miles back upstream without putting up a fight. As if to finish us off, the official now told us it would take minimally seven weeks to gain clearance. Refusing to respond to this new silliness, Dana again brought up the radios, forcing the guy to admit they existed, further embarrassing him in front of his fellow officers.

In our frustration, Dana and I had been using a good deal of English, most of which was meaningless to the guys we were dealing with. Unknown to us, a couple of men who spoke English – a senior officer and a civilian – had been listening in the background. They now stepped forward, and the officer, Edison Pena, a military engineer, asked us politely in English to follow him outside. "I'd like to see your diaries," he said as we left the building.

In the course of our confused arguments, we'd made numerous references to where we'd been and when, and this intelligent officer now wanted to check our story against my writings. I pulled out the diaries, and he glanced quickly at several entries, comparing them with the dates and occurrences I'd mentioned inside. In no time, he smiled and said, "Don't worry, everything will be fine." He told us he'd phone Manaus for clearance and that we should be free to go within a couple of hours. I shook the man's hand with fierce gratitude.

We had lunch at the base canteen and had a good chat with Edison's civilian friend Laszlo Szabó, who lives in Manaus, about 800 miles downstream, and has promised to show us around when we get there. Laszlo gave us the name of a man who has a waterfront business in Manaus, where he says we'll be able to leave the canoe. We bought 12 kilos of manioca from a merchant, and, at about 4 o'clock, our clearance came through, and we were free to go. The only stipulation was that we report to the military and police at Manaus.

We paddled jubilantly away. As far as I know, we've cleared our last major obstacle. Now it's just a matter of 1800 miles or so on the Rio Negro and the Amazon.

Down the Rio Negro

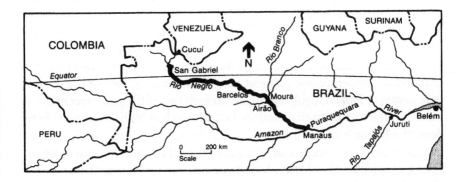

MARCH 14: *near Aru, on the Rio Negro, Brazil*

What has surprised us most during our first few days on this wild stretch of the Rio Negro is the number of houses along the banks. Every mile or so the jungle will open, and a little thatched dwelling will reveal itself. At first there'll be no sign of life, but as we pass a family will generally materialize along shore, straining their eyes to see us. Occasionally, they'll jump into their rickety dugouts and paddle out to get a better look.

Last night at Madia we camped with an Indian family at one of these clearings – what an industrious bunch they were. The grandfather was making paddles when we got there; he carves one enormous paddle about 8 inches thick, then delicately splits it into three or four thin paddles. We hadn't been there long when a couple of family members arrived in a dugout, carrying two big pots of white liquid. I mistook the stuff for milk until they told me they'd been gathering sap from the hundreds of nearby rubber trees. They took me into the bush to show me how they cut deep Vs into the tree trunks, then ram in spouts just beneath the Vs. Some of the trees were gouged with long vertical nests of Vs, with a deep groove

279

down the centre, presumably to facilitate the flow of sap. The spouts drip into little cups made of palm leaves. The harvesters prepare this liquid latex by pouring it on a stick which they rotate over a fire. As the latex grows viscous, more is added, until a big spool of crude rubber forms. The spools are sold to river traders.

Our friends also produced manioca, which has become a staple of our diet during the past couple of weeks. It's made from the cassava plant, which is peeled, boiled, and ground up, then run through woven wicker strainers to allow undesirable acids to drain out. The moist grindings are then spread on metal sheets and roasted above a fire to produce manioca. I asked about a pot of fluid that was sitting near the house and was told it was cassava juice being made into tapioca. All my life I've eaten tapioca and have never had a clue what it was or where it came from. As the cassava juice evaporates in the sun, it crystallizes into hard little nuggets. Tapioca!

Just before sunset, I walked out through the fruit trees and garden and discovered the family graveyard in the jungle. I counted more than 50 unpainted wooden crosses, almost all of them rotting. Few of the graves bore names or looked regularly tended, though two of the more recent ones were covered by a palm-thatched shelter about 6 feet high. Some were bordered by liquor bottles whose necks had been stuck into the clay a few inches apart. The tragedy was that 30 or more of the graves were those of young children – tiny little plots three or four feet long. It was a sad reminder that fever and catastrophe and poor diet still claim many in these outlying regions of the planet. The people here work hard and have little; there's so much they don't know. We've passed dozens of homes like this one, and undoubtedly each has its own little cemetery full of the bones of children.

At about 7 o'clock, we joined the family for their daily river bath. We all waded in together and scrubbed away the dirt and heat of the day. I felt better for the cleansing, but couldn't get my mind off those little graves out behind the house.

We've seen very little wildlife on this stretch of the river, though yesterday a 4-inch hairy spider crawled from under our canoe tarp as we paddled. I imagine it had been with us for several days. Our hitchhiker at the moment is a good-sized frog which has been living in the canoe since it came aboard at San Carlos.

MARCH 16: *São Gabriel, at the Uaupés Rapids, on the Rio Negro, Brazil* We've been counting down degrees of latitude for nearly two years now, and yesterday morning, just after sunrise, our count reached zero. As we passed the south end of Ilha Guia, we put our paddles down so that we could savour the moment. On glassy calm water, we drifted across the equator into the southern hemisphere.

As with most of our other attainments, there was no fanfare or celebration except what we could generate ourselves. So, to mark the occasion, I arched my back, lifted my face skyward, and screamed out a salute to the heavens. We drifted for a minute, till our pride began to dissipate; then it was back to the salt mines.

For most of the day, we shot gentle rapids, which sped us on our way to the town of São Gabriel, where the military at Cucuí had ordered us to stop for clearance. We would undoubtedly have stopped anyway, as we were sorely in need of food and maps. While Dana was off looking for the police, I climbed the bank and bought 20 lbs. of bananas and 3 kg. of coarse white sugar. When I returned, I watched several men unload hundreds of plugs of crude rubber from a low flat riverboat, or bongo. Some of the plugs looked like sea slugs or footballs, some like big dirty watermelons.

Dana returned after a five-hour absence, with permission from the military to carry on. He hadn't been able to buy maps, but had at least seen some maps at the military base and had been given tissue paper on which to trace our route from here to Barcelos 300 miles away.

Immediately south of São Gabriel we came smack into the Uaupés Rapids. They weren't particularly extensive but were far too hazardous to shoot. We twisted and turned among the upstream rocks, then dragged the canoe on lines until we were at the brink of the most turbulent stretch of water. A 250-foot portage took us past the main drop to an immense swirling pool, beyond which was a lesser set of rapids that we knew we could safely shoot.

By this time it was nearly dark, and we decided to leave the canoe on the shore of the pool and camp for the night on the high bank. I found a nice little teepee-shaped cave in the rocks and, in spite of the bats that populated it, made my bed on its floor. Dana walked up into São Gabriel to see some friends he'd met earlier.

As I lay in the darkness, the bats whisked by within inches of my face. But what affected me more was the rapids, whose unearthly roar took me back to our long nights on the seacoast. I managed to doze off for a few hours, but awoke around midnight, nervous, and stepped out of my cave. In the dim light I could see the canoe below me. I had no sooner located it, however, than an inordinately large swell boiled up onto the sand where it rested, and yanked it out into the rapids. I froze in panic but could do nothing but watch as it was dragged into the current and smashed to pieces on the rocks. I screamed for Dana, but to no effect against the din of the rapids. Our equipment floated away.

But as I floundered at the door of the cave, the scene in front of me began to re-create itself, like a photo developing, and there by the water's edge, slowly coming into focus, was the canoe, as sound as when we'd pulled it ashore. I was passionately relieved, but also disturbed that my imagination had run away with me as it had. Or had I even been fully awake? Again I called for Dana and was beginning to worry about him, when it came to me that he'd gone into town. I crawled back into my cave, where I belonged.

This morning, we shot the remaining set of rapids with ease, and entered a 20-mile stretch of river in which the current raced past the rocks and islands at what must have been 6 or 7 m.p.h. For three hours we sped downcurrent, getting thrill after thrill as we blasted between the rocks. At times, I'm sure our speed reached 10 m.p.h.

For the next four days, we'll have the sun directly overhead, and are expecting a good baking.

MARCH 23: *south of Tomar, on the Rio Negro, Brazil*
Increasingly we're beckoned from shore by people who want a visit. They scream away and wave their arms or clothing – anything to get our attention. Most of them are undoubtedly innocent and well-intentioned, though far more of our problems in the past have come from these solicitous types than from people we approach by choice. When we see them, we generally pick up the pace.

Two odd little incidents last night. As we lay in the darkness, a *tonina* swam up and down the shore of our sand bar. Suddenly it darted in close, and with a bit of a commotion worked a live fish onto the sand within reach of where Dana was lying. "Dad! Do you want a fish?" Dana called.

"Grab it!" I yelled, but as he reached out it slithered back into the water. It was a good foot and a half long, and we know it had been intended as a gift by the smart little dolphin.

Later, as I tried to sleep, I got running my fingers through my matted hair, which hasn't seen a comb since Tama Tama. I found a particularly thick clump and began slowly to untangle it. When I finally got to the centre of it, I found a good-sized black beetle, which had set up house-keeping in there. He decamped agreeably, and I drifted off to sleep.

Today as we paddled I saw a flash of red in the flooded shrubbery along-shore and persuaded Dana that we should go back and check it out. It turned out to be a hand-carved native paddle with a spade-shaped blade. I can never see a lost paddle or empty boat without feeling concern for the owner and whether or not he's safe. But neither can I deny my pleasure at getting this wonderful souvenir of the river.

At the moment, we're finding the personality of the river a paradox – so helpful to us in its powerful current but so perplexing in its sheer size. For the past couple of days it's been anywhere up to 7 or 8 miles wide and crammed with long twisting islands. Three or four islands often run parallel to one another, some of them 10 or 12 miles long. Our best bet for navigation has been simply to stick to the south bank and let the river be our guide.

MARCH 25: *south of Barcelos, on the Rio Negro*
Yesterday afternoon, we pulled into Barcelos, a town whose small population of about 4,200 belies its importance as a trading centre around here. We got permission to establish base beside a good-sized river freighter that was anchored at the docks. When Dana went up into town to look for maps, he met an English-speaking lawyer, Anita Katz Nara, who teaches night school. She invited us to speak to her class that evening about our trip.

At 8 o'clock, we walked in the dark up to the school. As we approached, we could see that the dimly lit classrooms were packed with adults of all ages and backgrounds. The more we found out about the school, the better we understood that education in this part of the world is still seen as a privilege. I spoke briefly to Anita's class, and she did her best to translate our adventures into Portuguese. Then Dana played a classical piece on the guitar, which went over every bit as well as my narrative. The class applauded warmly as he finished.

We spent the rest of the evening kibitzing with a Belgian couple in the "Mercadinho Barcelona" cantina. English rock music blared from the cantina's stereo, giving me a dose of reverse culture shock. Our daytime music had been screaming macaws and howler monkeys.

We slept aboard the river freighter, and pulled out early this morning. We hadn't gone far when we began to see changes in the riverscape. The stable shores and islands of the upper river gradually gave way to lower, swampier shores. In places, the river had flooded well back onto the mainland. We've had plenty of rain in recent weeks and knew the river would rise, but we didn't expect to see it happen so suddenly.

By late afternoon, we were on a stretch of river that offered nothing but swampy shores to a couple of would-be campers. We eventually found sanctuary on an island at a rickety collection of huts, occupied by some desperately poor families. What an odd group they were – blacks, Indians, Latins, a few whites. They say they're collecting rubber and are here only temporarily. Dana dug into our supplies for candies for the kids, and when he took the lid off one of our food boxes, a young girl let out a gasp. She couldn't understand why we have so much food. When these people want to eat, they go to the earth or trees or hunting grounds, and here we are carrying all this food in packages.

We couldn't possibly feed the whole settlement, or even part of it, and I felt guilty as we prepared our supper of corned beef, sardines, and peas. Not that the people were hungry – they were cooking a good-sized wild boar of their own – but it wasn't hard to see that they longed for a taste of some of the items from our boxes. However, there were no hard feelings. When their boar was cooked, at about 9 o'clock, they willingly offered us some, as well as servings of wild gourd and manioca. The meat tasted just like domestic pork, juicy and delicately flavoured.

For several hours we sat around the fire, exchanging a few words of Spanish with our new friends and filling in the gaps with laughter and nodding and bits of creative sign language. The night air was soft and fresh, unlike the steambath of the daylight hours.

MARCH 27: *near Moura, on the Rio Negro, Brazil*
The further downriver we go, the more extensive the flooding. In one spot today, a poor little howler monkey was stranded up a tree, surrounded by water. There he sat about 60 feet up, staring sadly down on us. I only hope he can swim.

Between Carvoeiro and Moura, the clear black waters of the river changed suddenly to crystal green, and we knew we were passing the Rio Branco, the biggest of the Rio Negro's tributaries, although we couldn't see it entering from the north.

We're camped this evening with another little group of impoverished river dwellers. And, like so many of the others, they've taught us something. An hour or so after we got here, one of the men came up the bank from his *cayuca* carrying a burlap sack, from which he dumped seven or eight big brown nuts about the size of grapefruits – "*castanha*" he called them. He broke one open with his machete, and out tumbled 15 or more brazil nuts. He dumped them in a pail of river water, and two floated to the surface, which he discarded. Then he split another ball, and gave me the nuts. I've stored them in the canoe for future treats.

We've been making great speed, averaging better than 40 miles a day and 5 m.p.h.

MARCH 30: *near Airão, on the Rio Negro, Brazil*
I imagined that, as we got closer to Manaus, the river population would increase. But for the past 100 miles we've hardly seen a single dwelling. With houses denied us as stopping spots, and with our sand bars and rocks now submerged, we've had no choice for the past couple of nights but to make our beds on the floor of the jungle. Today, like yesterday, we were driven off the water during the late afternoon by the torrential rains of the season. We could hear the deluge coming from a mile or more away – first as a distant hiss, then a percussive, snare-drum clatter as it moved onto the heavy canopy of foliage where we'd taken shelter. At the first distant sounds, the howler monkeys set up an intense whine and roar, which increased as the rain got closer. It was the first we'd known of their anxiety over getting wet, and probably explains the reluctance of the little guy in the tree the other day to jump into the flood.

It rained for an hour, and the thick leaves were an efficient umbrella. But when the rain stopped, the water that had collected in the nooks and crooks of the foliage began falling in cup-sized dollops from 100 feet up. Every so often, a little water-bomb would crash onto our heads or shoulders.

At dusk, we crawled beneath our tarp. But it wasn't long before I had to roll it back because of the stifling humidity. As the darkness deepened, our little jungle enclave came alive with the sounds of nocturnal birds and animals – mostly just peeps and rustlings but the occasional squawk or cry in the distance. Flecks of light from hundreds of fluorescent insects shone on the ground around us. In the quietest moments, I could hear very tiny footsteps moving within 10 or 20 feet of us – all a bit disconcerting.

This morning, in heavy rain, we reached the famous Arquipelago das Anavilhanas, a 15-mile-wide conundrum of islands, thousands of them, stretching for miles downriver. If we were confused before, we were *hopelessly* confused now. All we could do was follow the current and the odd river boat heading for Manaus, knowing they'd eventually lead us through the maze.

MARCH 31: *Manaus, Brazil*
About 20 miles northwest of Manaus, all islands vanish, and the Rio Negro becomes one great open freeway as it bears down on the Amazon. In

places, it is up to seven miles wide. Manaus is not on the Amazon, where it's sometimes said to be in tourist literature, but on the north shore of the Rio Negro about 10 miles from the forks. It's a city of about a million people, and as we approached it yesterday morning boat and jet traffic picked up appreciably. The volume of airliners wasn't nearly as heavy as it had been at Caracas, but, considering the jungle location, the effect was impressive. Our first glimpse of the skyline set our hearts pounding, and we figured we were only two hours away. In fact, it took five hours of paddling to bring us in.

We'd never seen a waterfront like it: *cayucas*, launches, bongos, tug-boats, great ocean vessels. The whole base of the cliffs alongshore is over-run with shacks and shanties, many of them built right in the river on stilts – or floating! Further up the banks, the shacks are stitched precari-ously to the clay, seeming to defy gravity. The poverty and filth are aston-ishing, and sad, suspicious eyes peered at us from almost every hovel. Twice I saw people drinking the river water, which is thoroughly pol-luted. We've since been told that the cliffs are not stable and that occa-sionally huge chunks of them will fall into the river, taking houses and people with them. Above all this degradation and poverty stretches the modern city, with its banks and businesses and wealth.

It didn't take us long to find the boatworks where Laszlo Szabó had told us we'd probably be able to make camp. The owner made us wel-come and offered sleeping space on the riverboats being repaired in the yards. Our plan is to stay three days here, do our chores, and try to get some rest for our big haul down the Amazon.

We went to bed early on the deck of a riverboat but, by midnight, had been driven into the workshop by heavy rains. We slept in until 8 this morning, by which time we've usually paddled 10 miles or more.

Our schedule today has been an exhilarating runaround, beginning with a visit to a big Chinese grocery store, where I bought $180 worth of Brazilian cruzeiros, at rates considerably better than the bank rate. I spent a fair chunk of the money on the store's inventory, which was impressively inexpensive. I was surprised to see cans of corned beef for 100 cruzeiros, about 60 cents. Even the cheapest foods are beyond the means of many Brazilians, however, as the wages here are very low.

Late this morning we returned to the boatworks and were met by Laszlo, whom we'd phoned. He immediately walked us downtown to a place I'd heard about for years and had longed to see, the legendary Teatro Amazo-nas, the Amazon Opera House. What surprised me as we approached the Teatro was the drabness of its outer walls, which rise to a coloured dome, but otherwise give no hint of the splendours within. But as we entered the foyer the world was transformed. I could hardly credit my senses.

The place was built in 1896 on the vast wealth of the rubber boom, when the rubber barons were obviously as ambitious about their culture as they were about their profits. The theatre's hand-painted dome was imported from France, as was the enormous hand-painted stage curtain. The central chandelier came from Portugal, some of the plaster pillars from England. The great Italian tenor, Enrico Caruso, gave the opening-night performance. It intrigued me to see that one side of the stage curtain bears the painted inscription "Rio Negro", while the other side is lettered "Rio Solimoes", the local name for the Amazon River. The curtain is the same one that rose on Caruso's performance nearly nine decades ago.

Next to the 700-seat theatre, there is a reception room as impressive as the theatre itself. On entering it we were required to put on guest slippers to protect the hardwood inlays of the floor. The ceiling and walls were lavishly painted with Brazilian jungle scenes, interspersed with depictions of 19th-century theatrical productions.

The Teatro was one of those landmarks around which my fantasies of the trip had taken shape over the years, and after an hour or so of browsing I felt reluctant to leave the place and return to the heat and obligations of the day. I glanced back several times as we left it.

Everywhere we've been today, we've been stared at – not only by the Brazilians, who seem impressed by our height, but by the European and North American tourists. Again, we've been reminded of how bleached and sun-scorched and weathered we are. The equatorial sun has been so strong, it's burnt right through our tans.

With Laszlo's help, we managed to get through to Richie Gage at the *Free Press* back home. He says that the *Free Press* is likely to send him to Belém to meet us at the beginning of May. He also says they'll probably pay to fly our canoe home, in appreciation of our stories. I told him we'd be in Belém on May 1st, no ifs or buts.

APRIL 2: *Manaus, Brazil*

This afternoon, Laszlo showed up with a big tin box of manioca, playfully explaining that when we reached the bottom of it we'd find a present. He also brought us a Brazilian flag – yellow and blue and green, with 23 white stars. I immediately attached it to our flagpole above our larger Canadian flag.

This evening I'm sitting in an open-air restaurant on top of the cliffs, enjoying my last night in Manaus. I've just finished four cheeseburgers and a couple of big bottles of my favourite Brazilian soft drink, Guaraná. Dana stayed behind to practise guitar and to finish work on some river maps he began copying this afternoon aboard a docked tugboat. The maps are far from ideal (40 feet of tissue paper) but are better than anything we had, and are certainly better than what Orellana had when he embarked on the Amazon 440 years ago. A few feet from me, along the edge of the cliff, there's a curious tiny trail about 6 inches wide, and embedded perhaps 2 inches in the hard-packed clay. It runs off in both directions for several hundred feet. A while ago I approached it for a closer look and discovered dozens of big black ants striding purposefully along it in both directions, many carrying chunks of leaf and greenery up to three or four times their size. Tiny feet. Many years.

From up here, the river is visible only in contrast to the hundreds of twinkling boat lights that are moving on it or docked alongshore. I feel like a spaceman, gazing out onto the stars and planets. Somewhere below me, our little canoe is floating, packed and tarped, waiting for sunrise.

On the Amazon

APRIL 4: *at the Nuevas Tribus Mission, Puraquequara, Brazil*

The confluence of the Rio Negro and Amazon – the Meeting of the Waters it's called – is a great marbled swirl of black and brown water, black from the Negro, brownish-yellow from the Amazon. At about 9:30 yesterday we crossed that swirl and entered the mythic river that will take us to the end of our journey.

Curiously enough, one of the first thoughts I had as we paddled out into the current was that the great river wasn't as big as I'd expected it to be. Not that I was disappointed – in fact, I was extremely excited; the river is *huge*. The warp in my expectations lay in the incredible fantasies I'd built around the Amazon over the years; no mere earthly flow of water could match them.

The facts about the Amazon are staggering: it is 4,000 miles long and has a flow about 11 times as great as that of the Mississippi. One day's discharge into the sea is said to be the equivalent of a nine-year supply of fresh water for New York City. The river supports over 2,000 species of fish, and the plants and trees along its banks supply half the world's oxygen. It is the largest river on the planet.

The current moved us briskly along the north shore, and in three hours we'd reached Puraquequara, one of the schools of the Nuevas Tribus Mission. (Puraquequara means "home of the electric eel".) The Americans and Canadians who teach here seemed glad to see us and we didn't hesitate to accept a couple of nights' accommodation from them. The rest will be beneficial after our hectic days in Manaus. All along, we've made the mistake of thinking we'd be able to rest in the cities, but we invariably leave them more drained than we'd entered.

Other than a whopping meal of spaghetti and meatballs, the highlight of my afternoon was a visit from one of the schoolboys who brought me a live 6-inch piranha he'd just caught. "Are these guys dangerous?" I asked him.

"Naw," he said, "they swim in the deep water; they don't bother anyone."

He pulled the fish's lips back to show me its frightful triangular teeth. "Watch this," he said, and he pulled a thick piece of wicker out of the back of an old chair. He placed it crossways between the piranha's jaws, and, *snap*, it was clipped as neatly as if it had been cut with a knife. Today, a boy gave me the skull of a piranha as a gift. He said he'd filleted the fish and placed the head on an ant hill, where it had been gnawed clean in hours. I was also taken to see a pet toucan. A boy peeled a banana almost as big as the toucan's beak, and gave it to the bird, which, like something out of Ripley, swallowed it whole.

There are rubber trees all over the grounds of the school, and every few minutes you hear a little explosion as one of the rubber nuts heats up and pops open, sending its seeds in various directions – often onto the tin roofs of the school buildings. The nut casings are like giant walnuts, enclosing three seeds, each as big as a good-sized grape.

APRIL 9: *São Agostinho, on the north shore of the Amazon, Brazil*
One thing that has impressed us about the Amazon is the density of population along its banks; every day we see dozens of homes and ranches. Compared to the Rio Negro or the Orinoco, there's relatively little jungle or animal life. Certainly little romance. I imagine things are different on the isolated upper river, but on these stretches we see far more trade boats than *toninas*, far more cattle than crocodiles.

The river is so big in parts that the locals refer to its shores as *costas* or coasts. The other day at the mission, I thought I was seeing its entire width and that the far bank was about 3 miles away. It turned out I was looking at an island some 26 miles long and 11 miles wide. The far shore was 15 miles off. Meanwhile, our one navigational problem is that we're forced to paddle well out from the banks if we want to claim the benefit of the current. The backcurrents alongshore (the same currents that were such an advantage to us on the Orinoco) would slow us to a crawl around here.

Because of the flooding, our strategy has been to get on the water early and get off early, so that we have plenty of time to find dry shelter. Yesterday, we found a half-completed house on stilts near the river bank and, since no one was home, decided to claim it for the night. Every time we go into one of these places, we're afraid that the owners are going to show up and take us for criminals or thieves. Many of the people around here carry shotguns, which doesn't help our confidence. Our apprehensions were particularly strong yesterday, though by suppertime no one had shown up, and we began to relax, even going so far as to lower an elaborate four-walled mosquito net that hung from the rafters.

At about six o'clock, just as we had supper going, a *cayuca* came gliding along a small canal that ran behind the house. Sure enough, it was the owners, a man and wife and two daughters, humble river Indians. Naturally, they were shocked to see us in their new house, and we were highly embarrassed as we called out our sheepish hellos and assurances from behind the mosquito net. We're so much bigger than these tiny Indians and know how we must frighten them. Fortunately, most of them understand what it is to share, and also what it is to travel the river and need accommodation.

It didn't take more than a few minutes for this particular family to accept that we weren't there to harm them or steal from them. Even so, they weren't about to join us for the night. As soon as they were at ease, they paddled back up the canal to a small house that we could see in the distance. "*Muchas gracias!*" I shouted. "*No molesta nada!*" – "We won't bother anything!" I hoped they understood my Spanish.

After all our months and miles of heading south, we're now heading slowly north toward home. Three days ago, at Iracema, we hit the most southerly bend on the Amazon, the southernmost point of our trip – latitude 3°20′ s, about 250 miles south of the equator. As we travel, I often think of Orellana, who in 1541 made his incredible Amazon voyage, all of it uncharted, from the Andes in the west to the river's mouth at present-day Belém.

APRIL 10: *Parintins, on the Amazon, Brazil*
It has been raining off and on for weeks now – to such a degree that in places we see creeks and small rivers that would normally be flowing into the Amazon but are actually flowing backwards because of the great vol-

ume of river water. The floodwaters tear up chunks of shore vegetation and send them out onto the river as floating islands, often 30 or 40 yards square. The other day we pulled the canoe onto one where the grass was about 2 feet high – we ate our supper as we drifted along. Flotsam is every-where – trees, logs, driftwood, all racing downcurrent to the sea.

One good thing about the rain is that it's given us a ready supply of drinking water. We're still carrying water we got way back at Manaus, though that's running low. Here and there, I've been drinking Amazon water, trying to condition myself to it. So far, so good. The Amazon is the colour of weak coffee, with skimmed milk.

As I write this evening, I'm still deeply affected by something we saw this afternoon. We were travelling the south shore, and had just passed Ilha do Caldeirão when we saw a few tiny shelters, and thought we might stop for the night. A number of men were at work in the shallow water, and as we drew close we were horrified to find that they were butchering *toninas*. There must have been several hundred pounds of bright red meat in big tubs – dozens of our beautiful friends had been either shot or speared. Heads and carcasses were strewn for 20 feet around. We have to accept that these people need to eat and to make what living they can, but it was an awful scene to witness. The guys doing the butchering weren't at all friendly, and when we asked them if they'd sell us some bananas they looked at us as if they'd just as soon add us to their butch-ery. We didn't hang around.

Actually, we have plenty of bananas, but none are ripe. Just this after-noon, I spotted a flooded stand of banana plants, with one big stalk of red-skinned bananas hanging just above water level. We weren't sure whether they were wild or domestic or even good to eat, but we weren't about to pass them up. We paddled in as close as we could get, and, with my machete in hand, I jumped into the water up to my neck and slogged through 30 feet of submerged and floating shore debris. So at the moment, on top of our canoe, we have 105 red bananas which we hope will ripen in a week or so.

APRIL 12: *east of Ilha das Marrecas, on the Amazon River, Brazil*
Things have certainly not been easy since I last wrote. Yesterday, we battled a ferocious wind from dawn until late afternoon. At one point, for the first time in my many years of paddling, I could see by the shoreline that we were actually being driven *backwards* — this in spite of the strong current in our favour. During the afternoon, the wind loosened our flag-pole, dropping our Brazilian and Canadian flags briefly into the river. We

did have a bit of a pick-me-up as we passed the town of Juruti on Ilha Juruti. A festival was going on – fireworks, rock music, canoe races; there must have been a thousand people in the dock area. As we came onto it all, Dana called back to me, "I think it's a religious holiday or something." Holiday, indeed. It was Easter Sunday, and we'd been so entirely wrapped up in our affairs, we'd been oblivious to it. I'm surprised we didn't pick up an inkling of it at the mission school. I certainly remember Easter Sunday last year. We were on the northeast Yucatán and got bogged down in that awful swamp, and I had to drag the canoe all day.

Today, it was the rain that tortured us – eight hours of it. But we had a good strong current, especially at Obidos, where the river is only a mile wide, as narrow as it gets between Manaus and Belém. With the entire flow of the Amazon so restricted, the current gets up to 5 or 6 m.p.h.

The closer we get to the big population centres and "civilization", the less we're trusted. Yesterday, in our search for a place to sleep, we were turned down at three different dwellings. Today, it was four. It's beginning to seem like Texas – everybody in paranoia about their property and their safety, everybody with a gun. Yesterday, we finally set ourselves up in an open shelter by a Catholic church. But we'd no sooner erected our bug house than three men and three boys appeared out of the jungle. One of the men had a shotgun and was brandishing it in a way that suggested he expected to use it. It took us 45 minutes of intense debate, plus a thorough display of documents, to convince them that we hadn't come to burn down their church.

Today, after our thwarted efforts to find a place, and with darkness coming on, we saw a man and woman on shore in a good-sized banana plantation. We paddled in and for ten minutes did our best to convince them to put us up for the night. No dice. We began pleading with them (we'd been on the river 12 hours and had come 74 miles; we were gassed), and in the end they consented to let us stay.

The next trick was to get to their home somewhere back in the jungle. We tied the canoe and followed our hosts along a submerged path. The water was waist-deep in parts, and at one point I slipped and went sprawling in the floodwater.

We walked about 400 yards to a little house, where the couple became confused. They'd allowed us to stay, but now didn't seem to trust us to be inside with them. As it happened, there was a 4-foot-wide storage shed alongside the house. It was filled with equipment, and with bales of jute, like almost every house along the river. "Can we sleep in there?" I asked in Spanish.

"*Sim!*" They brightened, and we quickly moved out some of the horse-hair-like jute, and swept the floor. It was dark by this time, and as we lit our lamp and nestled down a quiet knock sounded on the door. It was the woman, and she invited us in for a meal. For an hour or more, we sat eating and talking, enjoying the firelight and hospitality. As I write, we are back outside, crouched in our little shelter in the lamplight.

APRIL 13: *east of Santarém, on the Amazon River, Brazil*
We seem to have lost the ability to sleep in. The alarm sounds at five, and we're out of bed like programmed jack rabbits, into the day's routine. I'm reluctant to say it, but in some subliminal way we probably want the trip to be over; we've been at it too long. In another way, I'm a little afraid of the ending. For me more than for Dana, it's going to be difficult to replace.

By 8:30 this morning, we reached the expansive mouth of the Rio Tapajós, which enters from the south shore. The river is at least a mile wide and is by far the biggest tributary we've come across on any of the South American rivers. Its waters are a rich greenish black, and they enter the Amazon with such force that the muddy waters of the main river are forced well back out to the north. (Normally, the Amazon does the forcing.) For about 3 miles along the south shore, by far the greatest volume of water is that of the Tapajós, not the Amazon. Santarém, a major shipping port, sits on the east side of the forks. Its importance for us is that it's halfway between Manaus and Belém.

About two o'clock this afternoon, a good 35 miles east of Santarém, we heard a clanging noise and turned to see a 40-foot launch coming up behind us. There were five men aboard, and they were yelling in Portuguese, apparently trying to get us to stop. The old fears took over – we had no intention of stopping for them – and we headed into the shallows, where we thought they wouldn't be able to follow. But they followed us right in and made a couple of unsuccessful attempts to cut us off. They then dropped back a few yards and came roaring in again from behind, as if to ram us.

Our stubborn behaviour may seem unaccountable at times – why couldn't we just give in and make things easy? But I know very well that if it weren't for our obstinacy we'd never have come 12,000 miles. If we'd allowed ourselves to be bullied by guys like this, we'd probably still be in Colombia.

When they again threatened to ram us, however, we decided it was time to pull up and at least show them our documents. But when they tried to get a rope onto our canoe, I pulled out my machete and began waving it.

Four of the men were young fellows, but the fifth, the leader, was a man of perhaps 60 with thick white hair and beard – he was a pretty fair ringer for the aging Ernest Hemingway. When this older guy saw the machete, he calmly reached for his shotgun, and I immediately placed my weapon across my lap. But within a minute the younger guys were again trying to rope us, and I had the machete up and flashing. They were determined to haul us back to Santarém.

Our escalating argument with them took a course that we've known far too many times – demands, threats, counterthreats, hollering, until the energy of the thing began to wind down. In the face of our stubbornness, there was little they could do but shoot us or leave us alone. They seemed to think that if they tried to take us captive, they'd lose their hands to my machete, and I was glad to have them think that way.

After 45 minutes of harassment, they began slowly to back away from us, muttering and shaking their heads. Refusing now even to look at us, they coiled their rope, put their shotgun away, and swung back up river, convinced we were crazy. Our wilfulness had carried the day.

We're huddled tonight in a frightful old shack set on wobbly stilts above the floodwaters. The place is truly a wreck. Within an hour of our arrival, a heavy planting frame that had been sitting on the veranda crashed without warning through the floor 2 feet from where we were standing, leaving a table-sized hole where it had been. We walk carefully. On the floor of the interior are two snake skins, apparently recently shed by their owners. At the moment, it is pouring rain and the wind is doing its best to tear our roof off. The stilts beneath us are shaking, and the waves are spurting up through the floorboards with increasing regularity. In the meantime, Dana is lying calmly beside me in the lamplight reading the Bible he was given by the missionaries at Tama Tama. He intends to read both the Old and the New Testament by the time we reach Belém. He just may do it – right now, he's at Second Chronicles 2:5, a rather ironic verse for our current situation: "And the house which I build is great..."

Dana saw two snakes in the water today, a 6-foot anaconda, which floated by on a thick pad of water plants, and a little flesh-coloured snake swimming with the current.

The more our house rattles, the more I'm reminded of our nightmare off the coast of Belize. Sweet dreams.

APRIL 14: *near Monte Alegre, on the Amazon River, Brazil*
Our little house shivered and shook until about 1 a.m., when the wind went down and we could get some proper sleep. Several times I imagined that we'd come unstuck and were floating down the Amazon.

The river is getting wider, and this afternoon as we passed the Cucari Islands and came out onto the Costas dos Brocas, we could see nothing to the east but water and sky. The river is at least 5 miles wide here, and there are fewer islands to obstruct either our view or our navigation. We're seeing an increasing number of floating islands, as well as a few big *toninas* again. The curious thing about the islands is that they're often moving at a better clip than we are. We figure they have hanging roots that pick up the sub-surface currents, while our high-riding canoe allows much of the strength of the current to slip beneath us. Paddling into headwinds, we'll often pull in behind one of these islands, getting both the advantage of its slipstream and a bit of protection from the wind. One island we saw today was about 100 yards square and covered with 20-foot cane-like trees.

During the past couple of days we've seen several good-looking herds of Brahma cattle stranded on submerged islands. In some cases, the water is as high as their stomachs, though they don't seem particularly concerned – in fact most of them seem to be enjoying themselves as they nibble the tops off the long grasses and shrubs. We've also passed numerous Asian water buffalo, mean-looking creatures, which seem even more at home in the river than do the Brahmas. Some of them go in up to their necks.

We quit early today and have just finished tidying up the canoe and making a few repairs. The screws in the stern seat had pretty well rusted away, and I had to rig the seat to the frame with waxed nylon string. While we were unpacked I took the opportunity to examine my souvenir collection, which has taken a beating over the past few weeks. A bleached turtle skull and long-fanged payara skull that I picked up back on the Orinoco got wet one day on the Río Negro, and I put them out to dry. Along came a hungry dog and ate them. My piranha jaw from the mission school lost its teeth. My rubber-tree nuts swelled up and rotted. I still have my Indian bow and arrows and two eagle claws from Tama Tama. I also have a little jade relic from Marijuana Bay in Colombia and the brass bottle opener from Christian at Puerto Ayacucho. Today, incidentally, we added a new souvenir. At the bottom of the tin of manioca given to us by Laszlo Szabó, we found a pretty little oil painting in a plastic bag. It's a still life of flowers in a vase, and is Laszlo's own work.

APRIL 17: *Ilha Oroboca, on the Amazon River, Brazil*
After two years of not knowing whether we were ever going to get to our destination, we're finally beginning to relax and let up a little. Dana seems to be taking our success in stride, but I'm afraid I'm a little more vulnerable to it. In fact, there have been several times during the past few days

when even a brief consideration of where we've been and where we are has brought me pretty close to tears. It's ironic that, now that we don't need big advances every day, the power of the Amazon is almost forcing the miles on us. We get out there in the big current, and away we go. We don't want to get to Belém before May 1st, which means that, with 300 miles remaining, we have only to travel a little more than 20 miles a day. Today, however, we came 37 miles and still quit early.

From our perspective on the river, we see very little unflooded land. Last night we stayed at the community of Porto de Moz at the mouth of the Aquiqui River; every house in the community was sitting on stilts above three or four feet of floodwater. The only movement from one house to another was in dugouts, of which there were hundreds. Coincidentally, yesterday's route also showed us higher ground for the first time in weeks. Perhaps 10 miles west of the Rio Aquiqui, a group of hills rises beyond the north shore of the Amazon. Some are plateau-like, while others have rounded or cone-shaped tops. The highest is probably not much over 800 feet, but it was impressive to see them after hundreds of miles of flat river basin between Manaus and here.

Today we had a new and powerful reminder that our trip to the sea is winding down. As we passed Ilha Comandai, well out in the main channel, we felt the canoe being ushered forward on a greatly increased current. In no time, we realized we were riding an outgoing tide – we have reached the Amazon's tidal basin. We've since discovered that the twice-daily tides alter the river level as much as 6 feet, which will necessitate some changes for us. We'll have to avoid paddling when the tide is coming in, as well as watch where we leave the canoe at night. If we tie it in the wrong spot, we may find it sitting on the bottom in the morning. Right now, it hasn't been out of the water since Manaus – partly for convenience, partly because there's so little dry land on which to beach it.

We're situated tonight in a fair-sized frame house on Ilha Oroboca. When we arrived, the tide was out, and the house was surrounded by mud, heavily pocked with the footprints of 20 or more good-sized pigs and a few dozen chickens and ducks. On the elevated dock was the stretched skin of a 10-foot water anaconda. Nearby, the hide of a freshly-killed white Brahma had been pegged out to cure. The poor animal's tail and ears lay close by, covered with feasting flies.

Our host, who had been reluctant to give us shelter, soon warmed to us and invited us in, treating us to a lunch of manioca, beef broth, and roasted meat from the Brahma whose hide was outside.

The interior of the house was a single enormous room, an Amazon curiosity shop, replete with bamboo shrimp traps, baskets, fish nets, floats, line, gas tins, motor parts, paddles, bows, spears – all the paraphernalia of jungle-river survival. Half a dozen hammocks hung in various parts of the room. The only item that gave any sense of the 20th century was a battery-powered transistor radio. No electricity.

When I went outside in the mid-afternoon, three skinny dogs were chewing on the Brahma hide. I called our host, who shooed them off, though they were soon back, gnawing on the Brahma's tail and ears, which they quickly polished off. People don't feed their dogs around here. Pets, like people, must fend for themselves.

News got around about our presence, and, by late afternoon, as the tide rose, visitors started appearing in dugouts – *cascos* as they're called in Portuguese. One of them was a tiny old lady who scrambled nimbly up the ladder into the house, carrying a dripping paddle. She couldn't have weighed more than 80 pounds and must have been well over 70 years old. She pulled out a rock-hard plug of tobacco, chopped a bit off, and lit up her pipe.

"Do you paddle?" Dana asked her in Spanish.

"I have to," she said spryly in Portuguese, "I don't have a motor." We all had a good laugh, and, out of some bone-deep sympathetic instinct, I snatched her off her feet and gave her a big hug.

I should explain that Portuguese is often so close to Spanish that we understand it without difficulty. At other times, there seems to be little similarity between the languages. This may have as much to do with the accents and dialects on different parts of the river as with the words themselves.

Darkness came at 6 o'clock, and for the next couple of hours, we sat around in the lamplight. This is the perfect time of day here – the heat is gone, and there's no longer enough light to work. As I write, it is perhaps 9 o'clock, and people are coming and going in the shadows. I believe there are nine male visitors in the house right now, most of them sacked out in hammocks.

I don't think I've mentioned it, but our river for the past couple of weeks has been aflutter with hundreds of brilliantly-coloured butterflies of many shapes and species. Some are as big as a stretched-out hand. Today, as we paddled well out from shore – the river today was 10 miles wide in places – we saw a hairy spider about 5 inches wide swimming downriver. So many forms of life here are wonderfully adapted to the water.

APRIL 18: *Gurupá on the Amazon River, Brazil*
The 200-odd bananas we've been carrying are finally ripening, and today
I ate 18 of them as we paddled. Dana had a dozen or so, and, between us,
we'll eat another dozen at supper.

It's Sunday, and for a good part of the day we just sat back and drifted,
taking in the scenery, eating and resting. We had something of a hassle at
Gurupá, where an ignorant young soldier forced us to shore for a document and canoe check; but, before things got out of hand, the comissário
of Gurupá showed up and had us on our way.

This evening, again, we're in commandeered quarters – a little thatched
house by a flooded creek a few hundred feet from the Amazon. The owner,
who has another house nearby, discovered us here about an hour ago
and gave us permission to stay. At the moment, I'm lying here on my
stomach, wearing a dirty T-shirt and a pair of gym shorts. It is raining, and
I'm looking through our open door and down the creek to the river. If I
stretch my neck and look up, I can see monstrous trees, the forebears of
which lie beneath them on the wet soil, in various stages of decomposi-
tion. Everywhere, there are glistening leaves, some as big as table tops,
others as small as microbes.

I'm afraid that during our first few days in these parts I may have down-
played the Amazon and its jungle. What with the rains and flooding and
our re-entry into populated territory – not to mention our weariness and
language problems – I couldn't seem to generate much enthusiasm for
the river or its surroundings. For the past week, however, the Amazon
has shown us a far more impressive version of itself; it has certainly been
our benefactor, and we feel somewhat chastened. At its best, it is everything its myths hold it to be.

APRIL 20: *in the canals of the Amazon Delta, Brazil*
Unlike the mouth of the St. Lawrence River in Canada, the Amazon's
mouth is congested by a massive delta, intricately traversed by hundreds
of narrow canals. Today we paddled into the southern reaches of that
delta and are no longer dwarfed by the great, open waters of the main river.
For the moment, we're on the narrow Tajapuro Canal, which is about a
quarter of a mile wide and richly bordered by jungle. Within a few days,
we'll have paddled into the larger Rio do Pará, which forms the southern
boundary of the delta and will carry us our last 150 miles to Belém. Our
hope will be to find decent accommodation on the big Ilha de Marajó,
which sits like a cork in the Amazon's mouth, and which, for perhaps 160
miles, forms the northern shore of the Rio do Pará.

The tides in this area rise as high as 10 feet, forcing the inhabitants of the delta to live most of their outdoor hours on water. Everyone paddles – grandmothers, grandfathers, pregnant women; we've seen youngsters no older than 5 or 6 paddling solo, like veterans. Most of them are shy and pretend lack of interest in us, though we can tell by their expressions that they've never seen gringos quite like us, or a canoe like *Orellana*. When we pass a house, as many as eight or ten people will crowd a window or door to stare at us.

Like their countrymen upriver, the people are largely dependent on the bounty of the soil for their food; but, unlike people upriver, they do most of their gardening in flat wooden planters set high on stilts. We've seen several old dugouts propped up and planted with vegetables and herbs, or flowers.

Not everyone is a successful gardener. Occasionally we'll go into a house where there doesn't seem to be any food at all – and no money or fishing equipment. We've been puzzled that more Brazilians don't fish – perhaps because they can't afford the equipment. Last night we stayed with a family whose breadwinner spent most of the afternoon standing by the window, staring out into the rain. In the meantime, the only food in the kitchen was a bit of manioca and some salt. Had it not been for the rice and onions and sausages we supplied for supper, I guess they'd have eaten manioca and salt. As I lie at night trying to sleep, my mind often wanders back to all the thin and hungry people we've met over the months.

Our shelter tonight is a beaten-down old shack, whose only selling point is the stand of coconut palms behind it. The place is crawling with 8-inch green and brown lizards. They evidently have no fear of man, as one of them just leapt onto Dana and is walking all over him, placidly poking and sniffing. Today on the canal, we passed a hundred or more transport boats, carrying logs, cars, trucks, tractors, oil, clay pots, anything that can be floated. We're only 50 miles from the port of Breves, our last planned stop before the final push to Belém. My feet have not felt shoes in over three weeks.

APRIL 22: *Breves, Brazil*

We plough relentlessly on towards what we were trying to get away from when we set out so long ago.

We pulled into the docks of Breves at about noon, and Dana took a handful of cruzeiros and went and bought six little loaves of bread and a couple of sweet soft drinks which came in plastic bags. Before he got back, I was surrounded by perhaps 300 curious townspeople who had poured out of their houses, having heard we were here. Some of them stood knee-deep in water to get a better look at us.

One gentleman approached and said politely in Portuguese, "Who are you?"

"One moment," I said, and I pulled out the letter that explains our trip in Portuguese and passed it to him. In no time, the crowd was abuzz.

Streethawkers sold us four popsicles, then someone bought us four more and stood gawking at us while we ate.

Having hung around for half an hour, all we could think of was protection from the sun and from the inevitable rains to come. We set off east and, about 3 miles beyond Breves, hailed three men who directed us a mile further to a shoreline factory where they said we'd find good shelter.

We were soon on the roofed dock of a small "palm heart" plant. One *casco* after another would pull up to the docks and unload tightly-furled palm-leaf stalks, each a couple of feet long and about an inch and a half in diameter. These were collected and counted by a dock worker, who set aside one of every ten as a counter and stacked the rest like cordwood.

Soon after we arrived, the manager of the plant came down to the docks to visit us, bringing three 18 oz. cans of "Ibel Palm Hearts". We opened a can and found it neatly packed with 4-inch peeled lengths of palm stalk in brine. According to the manager, the hearts are a gourmet delicacy, and the factory ships them all over the world.

All afternoon and evening, the *cascos* kept coming, carrying anywhere from 150 to 200 stalks each. I asked one of the Indian paddlers how much he was paid for a stalk. Four cruzeiros, he told me. At this rate, 200 stalks would bring the equivalent of five dollars. These cutters have to paddle miles to get to an unworked area, then tramp through the swamp to find decent palm stands. Having climbed to the tops of the palms to get the new shoots, they back-pack them out and paddle up to 20 miles to the plant, then home for a night's rest. All for five dollars a day.

This evening, a few Indians brought a little portable television down to the dock and plugged it into the factory's power supply. There they sat in the darkness, riveted to their set, which cast a jumpy blue light onto their faces. Dana and I joined them for a few minutes, but found the picture so jittery we couldn't watch it.

At the moment, we're situated on the Breves canal, which ends about 15 miles from here. We travelled a few miles this morning on the larger Rio do Pará and will be back on it tomorrow. We expect the waters to be 8 or 9 miles wide and aren't looking forward to the winds.

APRIL 25: *near Ilha Coroca, on the Amazon Delta, Brazil*
I suppose Richie Gage will be leaving Winnipeg in a day or so for our
rendezvous on the 1st. He'll want to be in Belém a few days in advance,
so he can get settled and possibly come out to meet us on the Rio do
Pará. He told me when I talked to him from Manaus that we should contact the British consulate in Belém a few days before we get there, so
that he'll be able to get the latest on us when he arrives. The problem is
that we never see a telephone or two-way radio out here on the delta and
may not be able to make contact till we get to Icoraci, about 10 miles this
side of Belém.

All day, we've paddled the north shore of the Pará, and are holed up
tonight at an isolated river school on the tiny Ilha Coroca, just off Ilha de
Marajó. Like all other buildings around here, the 50-desk school is built
on stilts – at the moment the tide is just beneath its floorboards. It has
several outbuildings, including a woodworking shop and a little home for
the teacher, Venencio da Silva, whom we met when we arrived. Naturally,
the kids come by boat, but, as today is Sunday, there's nobody around.

We had a chat with Venencio about an hour ago and were surprised
when he told us he'd never heard of Canada. We hear the same thing
from almost everyone around here. "Ca-na-da," they say with puzzled
looks when we try to tell them our story. "*Dos años* – Ca-na-da." Some of
them pretend to understand, but we know they're confused when they
tell us, as several have, that it's much too far to paddle 80 or 90 miles to
Belém. Have I mentioned, incidentally, that Belém is the Portuguese word
for Bethlehem? It seems fitting somehow that we should be ending our
journey at Bethlehem.

About an hour after we went to bed in the woodworking shop, we heard
a slow-chugging river launch approaching the docks. Before we were properly awake, five Brazilian soldiers clomped into our quarters, holding spotlights on us. "Are you hippies?" one of them demanded in Portuguese.

"No hippies!" I said.

"Hippies!"

"No hippies!"

"*Armas?*"

"*No armas!*"

Our documents had a stunning effect on them – they were suddenly
very respectful and apologetic. Was there anything they could do for us?
Would we come with them as guests to their town? Never one to turn
down an opportunity, I requested that they contact the British consulate
in Belém and inform them of our impending arrival. Of course, no problem, yes, yes.

In the meantime, a number of locals arrived to see what was going on. Our interrogators didn't hang around, but the new visitors stayed for two hours while we answered their dozens of questions about who we were, where we'd come from, how we'd come across the sea. "You are big," one of them said to me in Portuguese. "Big and tired," I replied in Spanish.

APRIL 27: *near Ilha do Capim, on the Amazon Delta, Brazil*
The trip has brought Dana and me close in so many ways, but even now at the end we haven't fully resolved our differences. This morning before dawn as we prepared to paddle, I issued one instruction too many, and Dana got upset. For an hour or more, he paddled in his own little world, and I in mine. By 8 a.m., we were at the mouth of the Rio Atua, the spot at which we'd agreed we'd make the 6-mile crossing to the Rio do Pará's south shore. In spite of perfect conditions – tide in our favour, no wind – we couldn't agree on how to make the jump. Dana wanted to go straight across; I wanted to angle across to save miles. We made something of a compromise but, on reaching the far side, were still on pretty grim terms.

About 2 p.m., we pulled up at a big shaky river house, where a warm-hearted man named Jibuzcio came striding down an elevated walkway to meet us. His wife and six children soon joined him. They invited us to stay, and I sent one of the young sons off in his *casco* to buy nine soft drinks, one for each of us. He returned with five, explaining that he'd bought out the store. He also brought back my 1000-cruzeiro note, worth about $6 U.S. The drinks were 175 cruzeiros, and the store hadn't had enough cash to make change. Jibuzcio couldn't make change and told us it was unlikely his neighbours could either. No one around here has wage-paying work, and most things are bought and sold on the barter system, so currency is rarely needed.

We eventually gave the 1000-cruzeiro note to Jibuzcio, and in return he gave us 10 kilos of manioca, which, by conservative reckoning, was worth 400 cruzeiros. Later, he located 200 cruzeiros of his own and gave it to me, so that everything came out about even. He would pay the storekeeper.

When Dana and I had bathed and shampooed, I asked Jibuzcio if he had a razor. "*Sim*," he said, and he produced a rusty old razor blade fastened with thread to a popsicle stick. Our trip has taken us many thousands of miles, and I've yet to laugh at anyone's misfortune or poverty. But when I saw that old razor blade on the popsicle stick, I couldn't help bursting out laughing. There was no way I could shave with the thing.

"Will you shave me?" I said to Jibuzcio. "*Sim*," he said, and in no time I was seated in the main room of the house with my head back.

For fifteen minutes, Jibuzcio scratched away at my beard, throwing the scratchings out the window into the river. At one point I asked him if he'd built his own house and when. He'd built it, he said, but he couldn't remember quite when. "Maybe 25 years ago."

A few minutes later–still with my head back–I happened to glance at a rafter which was deeply inscribed with the numbers "27 4 55". It had to be a date, and, after a few seconds, it dawned on me that it was today's date, but 27 years ago. I waited a minute and said cryptically, "Your house is 27 years old, not 25," and I pointed at the inscription. He peered up at it for a few seconds and excitedly called to his family. All of them rushed in and stood gazing into the rafters at the numbers. The house was 27 years old today, and the whole place instantly took on a birthday atmosphere – and I didn't get so much as a nick from my shave.

Our location here is so beautiful with its jungle and calm waters that I hated to see the darkness coming on. Nonetheless, by 7 o'clock we were nestled inside with the lamps glowing. As in many Brazilian dwellings, the interior of the house is liberally hung with religious pictures: Christ, Mary, the Pope, Joan of Arc. Surprisingly, there's even an old picture of St. George, the patron saint of England, slaying the dragon.

As I lie here in my comfortable hammock, I'm thinking about how well we've adapted to our nomadic way of life; it's going to be very difficult to go back to civilization. Of course, it's much easier to write such things now than it would have been on the coasts of Honduras or Colombia, where the advantages of civilization were more apparent. I do know that when we get home I'm going to need several weeks of isolation before returning to the more predictable way of life.

In the meantime, I'm enjoying a tremendous sense of personal achievement, which I'm fully content to indulge while it lasts. I'm unashamedly proud to have come all this way by canoe. By avoiding jets and motorboats, and other convenient means of travel and accommodation, we've seen and learned things we never could have otherwise. We have come in the back door and have lived with the real people of the rivers, lagoons and coasts. And now here we are, and, in spite of what you might call the length and breadth of it all, I'm still preoccupied with the fidgety little concerns of getting where we're going. At the moment, I'm wondering whether Richie Gage will be there to meet us in Belém. It'll be a help to us if he is. If not, of course, we'll do what we've learned to do best – depend on ourselves.

For the time being, all we can do is stay cool and try to keep the lid on. So far, Dana's doing a much better job of it than I am. I'm surprised, in fact, at how little emotion he's shown about the ending of the trip. Maybe he's not sure what emotion to show. Maybe I'm not either.

APRIL 30: *at Ilha Jararaca, northwest of Belém, Brazil*
We paddled most of the morning in a thick rainy fog, which, at times, limited our view to about a hundred yards. But just after 11 a.m., the fog lifted briefly. "There it is, Dad," said Dana quietly. Across the Baía de Guajara, maybe a dozen miles away, was the ghost-like skyline of our golden city – we had reached our Bethlehem. Appropriately enough, the height of the buildings seemed exaggerated by the low profile of the land and water around them. What a thrill to see this city, which, over the past dozen years, has become a magical place for us. Curiously enough, I didn't have much to say about my feelings. What I really wanted to know were Dana's feelings; but he, too, was pretty guarded.

Right now it's dark, and I'm looking about 10 miles across the water to the city lights, which sparkle like a long string of jewels. We've seen nothing like it since Caracas and Port of Spain. The water catches the lights, and I feel as if I could reach out and touch them. I'm tired at the moment, but can't seem to bring myself to go to bed. After so many months, it's all come down to a matter of hours. I want to savour them.

Journey's End

We were up briskly at dawn, but spent the next three hours in slow motion, getting ready for our triumphal entry into Belém. It was as if we didn't want to go. We bathed and shampooed and dressed up smartly in our Canadian-flag T-shirts.

By noon, we had crossed the Baía de Guajara and were coming in along the dirty shores of the city's outskirts. At one point, in an odd pantomime, some Indians pretended to shoot rifles at us. "*Malvinas!*" they shouted. "*Malvinas! Inglaterra! Boom! Boom!*" It was if they were trying to communicate something, but we were clueless as to what it was. We laughed and carried on.

Dozens of ocean freighters were docked along the big piers of the harbour, and as we paddled towards them we kept a sharp eye out for Richie, who surely had to be somewhere on the waterfront. We cruised slowly along beside the boats, asking anybody we could see if they'd spotted a Canadian on the docks during the past day or so. Nobody had, and by 2 o'clock the truth had begun to dawn on us. We were on our own. We'd come 12,192 miles, and there wasn't a soul here to greet us. We continued along the waterfront, and then, for a few minutes, we just sat in the canoe, in a kind of unbelieving numbness. Our trip was over.

We still had to get home, however. Beginning to think practically again, I said to Dana, "Let's paddle over to that Dutch freighter and see if anybody speaks English." The ship, the *Saba*, was from Rotterdam, and, as we approached it, I said whimsically, "Look out for a tall blond Dutchman – he's bound to speak English." No sooner were the words out of my mouth than a strapping blond Dutchman emerged from the ship onto the concrete pier. We called to him in English, and, sure enough, he answered us in our own language. His name was Willem; he was the *Saba's* second officer. In no time, we were aboard the freighter enjoying a soft drink.

We relaxed for 20 minutes, and then had to be on our way, as we wanted to get to the British consulate to see if there were any messages for us. We also wanted to contact the Canadian embassy in Brasília to let them know we'd arrived.

We left the *Saba* and had paddled about 200 yards when we heard a sharp whistle behind us. We looked back, and Willem was at the rail, frantically beckoning to us.

We were soon back on deck, where Willem introduced us to the *Saba's* shipping agent, who had come aboard just after we left. The man's name was St. Roas, and, by grand coincidence, he happened to be the acting British consul in Belém, the very man we were setting off to find. Willem had told him about us when he'd come aboard. "Yes," said St. Roas matter-of-factly, "I have a letter for you in my office and a message from a reporter in Winnipeg, advising you that he can't get here to meet you."

I guess deep down we'd still hoped to locate Richie, and the finality of the news hit us hard. We'd counted so much on the *Free Press* helping us get the canoe back to Canada, as Richie had said they might. What would we do with it now? We certainly couldn't take it by plane – and we couldn't just leave it, as we'd once thought we might; we were far too attached to it. The immediate problem was not to get it home, however, but to find storage for it while we figured out our next move. How were *we* going to get home?

Willem was sympathetic to our difficulties, and after a few minutes of discussion went off to talk to the ship's captain, returning shortly with positive and surprising news. The *Saba* would be sailing for Puerto Rico in nine or ten days, after a trip up the Amazon, and Captain Schaap would be happy to take us to Puerto Rico if he could get permission from the shipping agent, St. Roas. It was possible we'd be able to take the Amazon part of the journey, too.

While this was unfolding, poor *Orellana* was tied to the *Saba's* side, taking a pounding against the freighter's metal hull, since the waves coming in off the Baía de Guajara were a good 3 feet high. We expressed our concern, and, within seconds, Willem was in the water with a cargo net, gasping and sputtering as he fitted the thing carefully around *Orellana's* hull. In a matter of minutes, the canoe rose from the sea like a big orange goldfish and was plunked down on deck. *Orellana* had landed.

We ate our supper with the crew and officers and, in the early evening, Willem informed us that the shipping agent, St. Roas, had declined us

permission to travel up the Amazon aboard the *Saba*. There are insur-
ance regulations that apparently can't be breached. Seagoing vessels are
less restricted, however, and Captain Schaap has since told us that if we
aren't out of Belém by the time he returns, we can sail on the *Saba* to
Puerto Rico on the 8th or 9th.

This is wonderfully reassuring for us. We've been in port fewer than
eight hours, and our travel problems are well on their way to being solved.
All we have to do is find a place to stay until the 8th. It's even possible
we'll get out of here on the *Saba*'s sister ship, the *Brazil*, as early as the
6th. St. Roas suggested the *Brazil*, though we'd prefer to wait for the *Saba*,
now that we're getting to know and like its officers. Holland and Canada
are great friends, going back to World War II when Canadian troops helped
liberate Holland from the Nazis. Many Canadian soldiers married Dutch
girls, and many more lie, dearly remembered, beneath white crosses in
Holland. And Captain Schaap has his own relationship with Canada. Last
year he took the Gold Cane Award for piloting the first ship of the year,
the *Saba*, through the ice into the Port of Montreal on the St. Lawrence
Seaway.

I am lying here tonight in my berth thinking back over two incredible
years of travel. In many ways it all seems like a dream, from which I'm
quickly waking up. Our arrival here this morning was a pretty stark rev-
eille, and I won't deny that it would have been nice to have somebody
here to meet us. Then again, we've been on our own since Veracruz,
Mexico – why should it be any different at the end? We deserve our fate;
we've come too far.

MAY 4: *Belém, Brazil*
The day after our arrival, St. Roas moved our canoe and equipment by
truck to a fenced-in storage area on the docks. He then drove us into the
city, where we found a room in the Hotel Milano. From our window we
can see out over the thousands of red-tiled roofs of Belém. In the distance are the docks and harbour and, further off, the far shores of the
Rio do Pará. Everything seems unreal. We sit in our room here or go out
and walk the streets, trying to make ourselves at home. But, for the most
part, we feel lost.

This morning we bought copies of Belém's two newspapers, *Liberal*
and *Província*, and were staggered by the news of war in the Falkland
Islands, or the Malvinas Islands as they're called here. We now understand what the Indians were shouting about as we paddled into Belém.
They must have taken us for Englishmen, with our Canadian flag.

We visited the shipping agent's office this afternoon and found out that the *Saba* may connect with a ship in Puerto Rico, and that we'll be able to travel all the way to the u.s. While we were waiting to speak to St. Roas, we were handed an official-looking letter from the Canadian embassy in Brasília:

Dear Sirs:

It is with great pleasure that I learned of your safe arrival in Belém after such a long and hazardous trip from Canada.

It is good to know that the spirit of adventure which has always been a vital component of Canadian life is alive and well. Your feat, the first of its kind, is a landmark in the realms of anthropology, sport and human endurance. I regret that I am not able to be in Belém for your arrival but I join with the staff of the Canadian Embassy in congratulating you on the successful completion of this most important voyage. Your achievement has brought credit to Canada and the profound respect of the staff of this embassy.

Sincerely yours,
D.G. Ryan
Chargé d'Affaires

MAY 5: *Belém, Brazil*

This morning, we moved to another hotel, a little less expensive than the Milano. For most of the day we walked the streets and, in the late evening, went to an outdoor restaurant/bar where we sat for a couple of hours drinking soft drinks. The wild night life of Belém swirled around us.

When we got home we discovered that our passports were missing, and I remembered a shifty Colombian sailor who'd chatted us up in the bar and whom I'd very much distrusted. I think he somehow got his hands on our document case. We won't be able to board the *Saba* without passports.

MAY 6: *Belém, Brazil*

After a frustrating morning trying to get through to the Canadian consulate in Brasília, I reached a Mr. Freed, who said he'd phone Ottawa immediately to get clearance to issue us emergency documents. We're to phone him back at 8 a.m. tomorrow.

Tonight, as I was sitting on the steps of a downtown bank, a young streetwalker came up to me and struck up a conversation. We talked for a few minutes, and then, as we parted ways, she pressed a 20-cruzeiro note into my hand. All I can think is that I must look pretty bedraggled.

MAY 7: *Belém, Brazil*
Our emergency passports have been issued, and are supposed to reach us by mail within a day or two.

We ate at the Malouka Restaurant tonight, and heard some good Brazilian music. Dana sat in with the band for a while, then gave a half-hour solo performance – he got good applause.

MAY 8: *Belém, Brazil*
Today, as I was looking around the Belém tourist bureau, I felt a gentle tap on my shoulder and turned to see the Colombian sailor whom I suspected of stealing our passports. I glared at him, and he said to me in Spanish, "I have a problem. Could we go outside to talk?"

"Let's talk here," I said.

"Outside," he insisted.

I followed him out and down a lane, and he told me quietly that a friend of his had found our passports and needed money badly. Could I help out? Before the charade got any more complex, the friend appeared, and the two of them got right to the point. I could have the passports back for 3,600 cruzeiros, about $20 U.S.

It was a far lower demand than I'd expected and, as our new passports hadn't arrived from Brasília, I wasn't about to turn my back on the deal. But I wasn't about to let these guys off easy, and quickly told them that we had new passports and that the old ones were useless to us except as souvenirs. I also told them that we'd reported them to the police, who were on their tail.

"Two thousand cruzeiros," muttered the sailor.

"I don't want to waste my money," I told him.

They looked at one another with long faces, and the friend said "One thousand."

We haggled for a few minutes, and I gave them 200 cruzeiros, about $1.10, and walked away with our passports. I relayed the news at once to the Canadian Embassy in Brasília.

MAY 10: *Belém, Brazil*
The *Saba* came in yesterday with a cargo of Brazilian hardwood, and we boarded in the late afternoon with our equipment and canoe. We were informed that we were to be part of the working crew and would spend our days on board chipping paint from the steel decks and fixtures, and

repainting them. It's apparently a constant requirement aboard these old freighters and isn't a popular job among regular crew members.

Last night was party night, and by 10 p.m. there were as many women on board as there were crewmen. The guests arrived and left by water-taxi. They wouldn't have been aboard at all if it weren't for the leniency of Captain Schaap, who is well liked by his crew.

At about 11 tonight, the port pilot came aboard, and the big diesel engines sounded below. I stood at the bow rail as we slid out of the harbour towards the dark Atlantic. We're going home.

MAY 17: *aboard the* Saba

This morning, after two days of waiting offshore, we entered the harbour at La Guanta, Venezuela, near Puerto La Cruz. The *Saba*'s orders have changed to our advantage: after our stop in Puerto Rico, we sail to Haiti, then on to Gulfport, Mississippi, from which Dana and I can easily make our own way to Winnipeg.

These long days at sea are not nearly as easy as they might seem. The paint chipping is brutally hard work, and the evenings tend to be long and lonely. All the books in the ship's library are in Dutch, and, although I like chatting with the officers and crew, it tends to wear thin after so many conversations. For the most part, when the work day is over, I go up into the bow and watch the sea go by – sometimes for hours.

MAY 26: *aboard the* Saba

It is now 16 days since we boarded the *Saba*, and I've gained a pound for each day aboard. At this rate, I'll weigh 200 by the time we get home. The ship's meals are terrific and give us something to look forward to during our long hours of work. Pound, pound, pound, all day with our hammers. I eat with the captain; Dana eats with the working crew.

We made a brief stop on the 20th in San Juan, Puerto Rico, and another in Port-au-Prince, Haiti, on the 23rd. At the moment, we're about 70 miles off the north coast of Cuba. Somewhere out to the southwest is the U.S. naval base at Guantanamo Bay.

Tonight on television, we watched a Cuban baseball game from Havana. Afterwards, I went to my favourite spot on the bow deck and stared out into the darkness. I can barely look at the sea, barely *listen* to it, without being reminded of our noble, feeble effort by canoe.

MAY 30: *aboard the* Saba

It's 6:30 p.m., and we're at anchor off the Mississippi coast. Through the binoculars, I can see dozens of colourful sailboats and windsurfers on the waters off Gulfport. The *Saba*'s expected cargo, a load of dynamite, hasn't reached port yet, and we won't be given permission to dock until it does.

Just now, a tired swallow set down on deck and made friends with Dana, who I sometimes think is the reincarnation of St. Francis. Dana tried to feed the little thing, but all it wanted was to sit for a while on his shoulder, then his head. Eventually, it took off, its strength renewed.

JUNE 1: *aboard the* Saba

Two years ago today, we left Winnipeg. We are still waiting for orders to enter port.

JUNE 2: *Gulfport, Mississippi*

Finally landed after three days of waiting. Said our goodbyes to the ship's crew and immediately searched out a Mississippi Motor License bureau, where I managed to get a driver's licence, since my Manitoba licence is no longer valid.

Late this afternoon, we rented a good-sized station wagon and loaded *Orellana* on top. By early evening, we were on the road.

JUNE 5: *Grand Forks, North Dakota*

What's left to say? We pulled into Grand Forks this morning and dropped off our U-drive. We had contacted Jeff by phone, and, just as we left the car-rental agency, I spotted him coming down the road in my old red Datsun.

I have no idea how he felt as he got out of the car and came towards us. I have no idea how Dana felt. There were tears that needed crying, but, at that moment, none of us had a mind to cry them. We said hello, and I took Jeff in a powerful embrace, and then he embraced Dana. And that was about it. We loaded the car and headed north.

Epilogue

Six months after arriving home, Don Starkell returned to work at the Winnipeg YMCA. He retired permanently six months later. In 1984, he cycled from Winnipeg to Prince Edward Island, and in 1986 canoed with a friend from Vancouver, British Columbia, 800 miles up the Pacific coast to Ketchikan, Alaska. In the near future, he hopes to fulfil a last canoeing dream: to paddle from Churchill, Manitoba, on Hudson Bay, through the Northwest Passage to Tuktoyaktuk, Northwest Territories.

Since returning from South America, Don has given numerous slide lectures on his and Dana's travels. He said recently, "Our trip taught us an awful lot about how small we are in the broad scope of things – and about the importance of faith and determination in overcoming that smallness. . . . From facing death so many times, we gained a whole new understanding of the fragility and value of life."

Don lives alone in the Winnipeg suburb of East Kildonan.

Within weeks of returning to Winnipeg, Dana Starkell won top prize in the Senior Classical Guitar category of the Manitoba Music Festival. He has since released two classical-guitar records, and is at work on a third. He gives regular concerts, and plays frequently in Winnipeg restaurants and clubs. He participates in the Manitoba Arts Council's Artists in the Schools program. Although Dana's asthma still affects him, he has not taken medication for it since 1980. He owns a house in the north end of Winnipeg, and has no plans for future adventure.

Several months after his return from Veracruz, Mexico, Jeff Starkell began two years of electronics-technology studies at Red River Community College, Winnipeg. On graduation, he worked for two years as a technician for Manitoba Hydro, resigning in 1985 to enrol at Lakehead University in Thunder Bay, Ontario. He is currently in the final year of Lakehead's electrical-engineering program. He is a competitive soccer player, and, during summers, races his rebuilt Ford Mustang.

Gabby Delgado is a marine engineer in Veracruz, Mexico. He is married and has one child.

Acknowledgements

The author and editor wish to thank Betty Carpick, Hume Wilkins and Dan Diamond for their valuable contributions to this book. Sincere thanks are also due to the Canada Council for its generous financial support, and to Doug Gibson for his editorial wisdom and his unwavering faith in the project.

The Starkells would like to express their sincere gratitude to the following people, and unnamed others, for their varied kindnesses and contributions to the voyage of *Orellana*:

Ed Allman, Colston Harvey, Bill Brigden, Charlie Mitchell, Jim Thorsteinson, Lindsay Hall, Win Hammerstead, Don and Lois Matthews, and Naomi Jenson, Winnipeg; Richard and Elaine Sabourin, St.Jean Baptiste, Manitoba; Jim Mullen, Vermont; Gene Johnson, Fargo, N.D.; Gene and Betti Labs, Browns Valley, Minn.; Gayle and Colleen Hedge, Ortonville, Minn.; Gary Meier, Minneapolis; Joe Akers, Chester, Ill.; the hospitable people of the City of Vicksburg, Miss.; John and Ronnie Kenny, Galveston, Texas; Pat and Bob Smith, San Antonio, Texas; Dr. James McLendon and Dr. James Johnson, Houston, Texas; the u.s. Army Corps of Engineers; the staff of the u.s. Coast Guard bases at Galveston, Freeport, Port O'Connor and Port Isabel, Texas, and at Keokuk, Iowa; Israel the jeep owner, La Pesca, Mexico; Juan Osorio, Eloina Butt, Don Gerardo Sánchez, Alex Cazares Carrera, Enrique Menéndez, and Roberto, of Veracruz, Mex.; Werner Haas and family, Tampico, Mex.; Dr. Antonio García Canul and Francisco Romero Juanes, Mérida, Mex.; the Leachey family and the staff of Leachey's Boatworks, Belize City, Belize; the crew of the *Yankee Trader*, Belize City; John Ebanks and family, Ticua, Honduras; the villagers of Hua Hua, Nicaragua; Alwin, George, and Blanche Cuthbert, Pearl Lagoon, Nic.; anonymous portager and son, Boca Río Colo-

rado, Costa Rica; Ken Cameron, Río Colorado Lodge, C.R.; the fisher-
men of Lime Point and the villagers of Calovebora, Limón Donosa and
Salud, Panama; Commodore "Pretty" Webber, Colón Yacht Club, Pan.;
Susan Stabbler, Panama Canal Commission, Colón; the Cuna Indians
of Isla Porvenir, Playon Chico and Mansucun-Comarco de San Blas; Capt.
Giovanni Pollio, Naples, Italy; the Sarmiento family, Bogotá, Colombia;
Bronco the American, Rodadero, Col.; Gabriel Fernando Rojas and the
Maritime Police, Santa Marta, Col.; Jesualdo and family, Bahía Confusa,
Col.; Dr. Douglas Jatem, Coro, Venezuela; the villagers of Cocuy, Ven.;
Chimo the fisherman, Guasare, Ven.; the Betancourt family, Istmo de
Medanos, Ven.; Ali and Nelida, Punta Fijo, Ven.; Port Capt. Miguel
Quintero, Puerto de la Vela, Ven.; Dr. Mauro Scagliola and family, Valen-
cia, Ven.; Capt. Jan Schurman Van Putten and Lt. Oscar Izurieta, Puerto
Cabello, Ven.; the fishermen of Cabo San Andres, Ven.; Port Capt. Vicente
Larez, Caraballeda, Ven.; Martial and Edith Beau de Loménie and fam-
ily, Timo Nenonan, Dr. Jean de la Chesnais, Julio Comacho, Oswaldo
Castillo Fajardo, and Luis Delepiani and friends, all of Caracas; the staffs
of the Camuri Grande beach club, the Isla de Oro beach club, and the
Playa Pintada beach club; Carlos Flores Fabare and friends, Barcelona,
Ven.; Walter and Lila Low, Puerto La Cruz, Ven.; Capt. Ramon Antonio
Osorio and Capt. Mario Bodillo García, Carupano, Ven.; the villagers of
Unare, Puerto Viejo, Mejillones and Uquire, Ven.; Jean Blanchard, Paul
LaBerge, Roy Beatty and family, Raul Barrow and family, Phillip, Johanne
and Phyllis Keiller, John Fortune and wife, Steve Agard and Russell Ben-
jamin, all of Port of Spain, Trinidad; Chas Khan, Pointe-à-Pierre, Trin.;
Dave Bharat and family, Columbus Bay, Trin.; the staff of the Guardia
Nacional base, Pedernales, Ven.; Juan Suarez, Isla Tigre, Ven.; Ildemaro
Romero, Tucupita, Ven.; the Canas family, Ciudad Bolívar, Ven.; Christian Jaque and family, Port Capt. Victor Narvaez Serra, Dr. Alfred Forti
and family, and Marcos Antonio Ochoa, all of Puerto Ayacucho, Ven.;
the staff of the Guardia Nacional base, San Fernando de Atabapo, Ven.;
the Barkmans, Fyocks, Dawsons, Temples, Bodins, Dycks, Cochrans, *et al*,
Misión Nuevas Tribus, Tama Tama, Ven.; the lone Indian family on the
Casiquiare Canal, Ven.; Edison Modesto Pena, Cucuí, Brazil; the Katz
family, Barcelos, Br.; Laszlo Szabó, Manaus, Br.; Sr. Antonio Fernandes
dos Santos and the staff of the Estalaeiro Santo Antonio Boatworks,
Manaus; the Sutton and Emsheimer families, *et al*, Misión Nuevas Tribus,
Puraquequara, Br.; the people of the mission at Boa Morte, Br.; Capt.
Schaap, Willem, and the crew of the *Saba*, Belém, Br.; Capt. E.A. St.Roas,
Belém.

Appendix:
What Happened to the Chaika?

The mystery of the wrecked Canadian yacht, the *Chaika* (described on pages 135–6) left me determined to find out what had happened to her. My letter of enquiry to the Royal Vancouver Yacht Club in time produced a response from Dr. Bill Knight, which I quote here:

"The story of how *Chaika* came to be on the beach at Tusicocal is as follows: when I retired in 1980, I decided to sail down the coast of the U.S.A., Mexico, Guatamala, El Salvador, Nicaragua, Costa Rica and Panama on the Pacific, through the Panama Canal to the Caribbean – cruise the San Blas Islands and then on to Roatan and so on.

Until Panama and the San Blas Islands the crew of the *Chaika* were my wife, my youngest son, aged 18, and myself. My son left us in Porvenir, San Blas Islands and returned to Canada. My wife and myself were four days out from Panama, a rough 4 days I might add, we were very tired, and we found ourselves, just before dawn, in the outer layer of six layers of breakers *and that was that*. We walked ashore, as it is very shallow, the water only four or five feet deep. The sandflies that infest those beaches were too much for my wife, so that she was taken to the home of Frank Goff, the local Miskito Indian boss man, who put her on the weekly 45 year old DC 3 that flies from La Ceiba every Wednesday on a fairly good schedule. The local Indian village is across the big lagoon there, as the sand flies make living on the beach impossible.

I stayed on the beach for a month, stripped the boat of valuable equipment, and returned to Vancouver. The following year (1981) I went down, recovered my stuff, and spent a month with the Indians cruising up and down the coast in the Indian boat the *Margarita*.

. . . The pages of children's books scattered on the beach is another story. My son and I landed on a remote beach in our Zodiac on the Coast of Baja California Sur, Mexico, and found a solitary grave and some personal belongings scattered around including some children's books which I took aboard the *Chaika*."

One mystery is solved, another remains.

D.S.

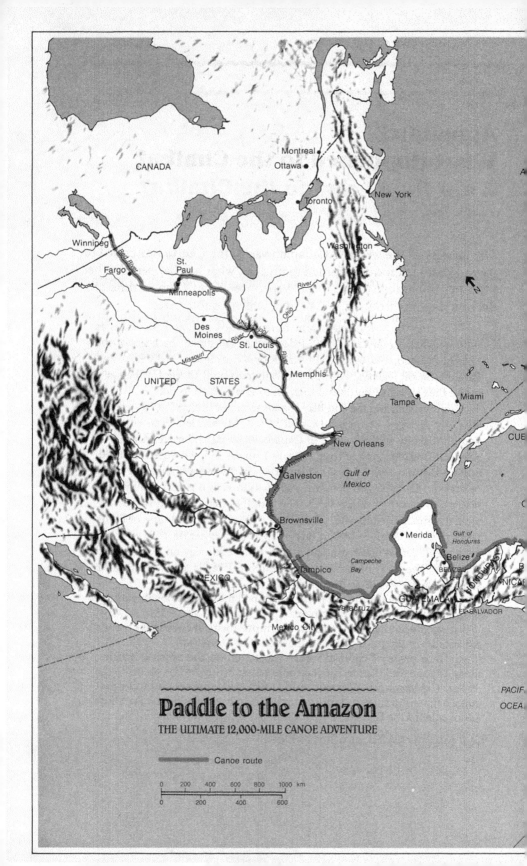

Paddle to the Amazon
THE ULTIMATE 12,000-MILE CANOE ADVENTURE

▬▬▬▬ Canoe route

0   200   400   600   800   1000   km
0   200   400   600

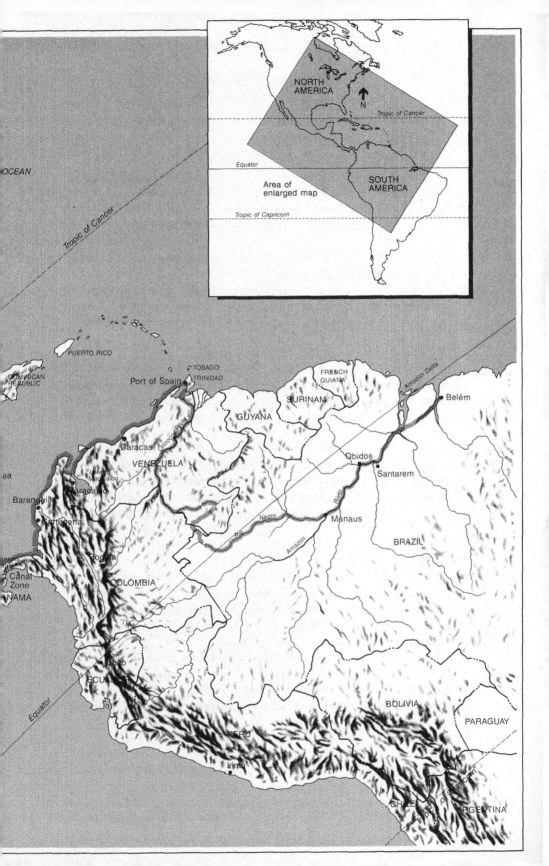

OCEAN

NORTH
AMERICA

N

Tropic of Cancer

Equator

Area of
enlarged map

SOUTH
AMERICA

Tropic of Capricorn

Tropic of Cancer

PUERTO RICO

DOMINICAN
REPUBLIC

TOBAGO

Port of Spain   TRINIDAD

FRENCH
GUIANA

SURINAM

Amazon Delta

Belém

GUYANA

Caracas

Orinoco River

VENEZUELA

Maracaibo

Barranquilla

Obidos

Santarem

Maracaibo

Cartagena

Negro

Manaus

BRAZIL

Rio

Amazon River

Bogota

COLOMBIA

Canal
Zone

PANAMA

Quito

ECUADOR

BOLIVIA

PERU

PARAGUAY

Equator

Lima

CHILE

Tropic of Capricorn

ARGENTINA

OTHER TITLES FROM
DOUGLAS GIBSON BOOKS

PUBLISHED BY MCCLELLAND & STEWART LTD.

PADDLE TO THE ARCTIC *by* Don Starkell
The author of *Paddle to the Amazon* "has produced another remarkable book." *Quill & Quire* His 5,000-kilometre trek across the Arctic by kayak or dragging a sled is a "fabulous adventure story." *Halifax Daily News*
Adventure, 6 × 9, 320 pages, maps, photos, trade paperback

AT THE COTTAGE: A Fearless Look at Canada's Summer Obsession *by* Charles Gordon *illustrated by* Graham Pilsworth
This perennial best-selling book of gentle humour is "a delightful reminder of why none of us addicted to cottage life will ever give it up." *Hamilton Spectator*   *Humour, 6 × 9, 224 pages, illustrations, trade paperback*

STILL AT THE COTTAGE *by* Charles Gordon
The follow-up to the classic *At the Cottage*, this is an affectionate and hilarious look at cottage living. "Funny, reflective, and always insightful, this is Charles Gordon at the top of his game." – Will Ferguson
Humour, 6 × 9, 176 pages, illustrations, trade paperback

CRAZY ABOUT LILI: A Novel *by* William Weintraub
The author of *City Unique* takes us back to wicked old Montreal in 1948 in this fine, funny novel, where an innocent young McGill student falls for a stripper. "Funny, farcical and thoroughly engaging." *Globe and Mail*
Fiction, 5½ × 8½, 272 pages, hardcover

ROLLERCOASTER: My Hectic Years as Jean Chretien's Diplomatic Adviser 1994–1998 *by* James Bartleman
"Frank and uncensored insider tales of the daily grind at the highest reaches of the Canadian government. . . . It gives the reader a front row seat of the performance of Jean Chrétien and his top officials while representing Canada abroad." Ottawa *Hill Times*
Autobiography, 6 × 9, 376 pages, hardcover

WHO HAS SEEN THE WIND *by* W.O. Mitchell
First published in 1947, this wise and funny novel of a boy growing up on the prairie has sold over 750,000 copies in Canada, and established itself as a timeless popular favourite. Complete text edition.
Fiction, 5½ × 8½, 392 pages, trade paperback